The Saloon and the Mission

The Saloon and the Mission

Addiction, Conversion, and the Politics
of Redemption in American Culture

Eoin F. Cannon

UNIVERSITY OF MASSACHUSETTS PRESS
Amherst and Boston

ISBN 978-1-55849-993-5 (paper); 992-8 (library cloth)

Designed by Sally Nichols
Set in Minion Pro
Printed and bound by Thomson Shore, Inc.

Library of Congress Cataloging-in-Publication Data

Cannon, Eoin F., 1973–
The saloon and the mission : addiction, conversion, and the politics of redemption
in American culture / Eoin F. Cannon.
pages cm
Includes bibliographical references and index.
ISBN 978-1-55849-993-5 (pbk. : alk. paper) — ISBN 978-1-55849-992-8 (hardcover : alk.
paper) 1. Alcoholism—Social aspects—United States—History. 2. Alcoholism
—Treatment—United States—History. 3. Alcoholics—Rehabilitation—
United States—History. 4. Temperance in literature. 5. Alcoholism in literature.
6. Rescue missions (Church work)—United States—History. 7. Recovery
movement—United States—History. I. Title.
HV5279.C37 2013
362.29′15750973—dc23
2013001343

British Library Cataloguing-in-Publication Data
A catalogue record for this book is available from the British Library.

To Michelle

The Drunkards in the street are calling one another,
Heeding not the night-wind, great of heart and gay, —
Publicans and wantons—
Calling, laughing, calling,
While the Spirit bloweth Space and Time away.

Why should I feel the sobbing, the secrecy, the glory,
This comforter, this fitful wind divine?
I the cautious Pharisee, the scribe, the whited sepulchre—
I have no right to God, he is not mine.

* * * * * *

Within their gutters, drunkards dream of Hell.
I say my prayers by my white bed to-night,
With the arms of God about me, with the angels singing, singing
Until the grayness of my soul grows white.

> —Vachel Lindsay, "The Drunkards in the Street" (1913)

I love to listen to them tell their stories of ruin; I'm a sucker for
a good resurrection story.

> —Anne Lamott, *Traveling Mercies* (1999)

Contents

Preface and Acknowledgments   xi

INTRODUCTION

Addiction Recovery and the World as It Should Be   1

Part I

Redemption and Ideology

1. The Drunkard's Conversion and the Salvation of the Social Order   23
2. "What a Radical Found in Water Street"   52
3. The Varieties of Conversion Polemic   83
4. New Deal Individualism and the Big Book of Alcoholics Anonymous   115

Part II

Literature and Recovery

5. Literary Realism and the Secularization of the Drunkard's Conversion   155
6. The Drinker's Epiphany in Modernist Literature   177
7. *The Iceman Cometh* and the Drama of Disillusion   200
8. Recovery Memoir and the Crack-Up of Liberalism   223

CONCLUSION

Addiction in a New Era of Recovery   248

Notes   263
Index   311

[ix]

Preface and Acknowledgments

THIS PROJECT HAD TWO ORIGINS, one professional and one personal. In the first, I was on the lookout for popular or vernacular counterparts to what Michael Szalay has termed New Deal Modernism in literature. I was interested in narrative, imagery, and social practices in the 1930s and 1940s that expressed neither radicalism nor reaction but that spoke, in one way or another, to the reinvention of liberalism as a social ethic rather than a market principle. Candidates for study included urban neighborhood life, sports, voluntary organizations, and World War II reportage. I was seeking to theorize an organic culture of New Deal–era liberalism against the common suppositions that models of mutuality in the 1930s came from the politically active left while postwar liberal culture mainly reflected repressive institutional forces.

The second impetus for this book was more accidental. During this time, I sought treatment for alcohol and drug abuse. Although I was an active member of Alcoholics Anonymous for only a couple of years, I was able to observe and experience recovery culture at work in the Boston area. I was struck by the community-building effects it had in struggling neighborhoods, and by the procedural principles and ethical traditions groups used to manage individual differences and sustain collective purpose. These practices were in no way overtly political, but neither were their organizational energies redirected away from wider community needs. I saw their positive effects reverberating far beyond the problems of addicts, through the influence of the many people who had learned how to listen, speak, and serve in recovery groups. As a student of culture, I was fascinated by the capacity that a simply structured recovery narrative had to order in convincing and empowering ways such a wide variety of human experiences.

These two interests converged when I began to research the creation of

A.A. in the 1930s. It seemed to matter that this high-stakes form of mutual-aid community was born during the Great Depression, and that the factors distinguishing it from earlier sobriety movements were not experiential sympathy or narrative testimony but rather its stylistic and ultimately procedural ways of structuring them. I was not the first to observe that the journey in A.A. narrative from delusional self-reliance to life-saving mutual aid was similar to liberal redefinitions of individualism in response to the Depression. But with my background in literary study, I approached this analogy as a question of form as well as context. I looked widely at patterns of decline, crisis, revelation, and redemption in representations of alcoholism in evangelical revivals, sobriety movements, literature, and popular culture dating to the mid-nineteenth century.

I found that across these historical and generic contexts, stories of recovery share a formal mechanism that inevitably produces meanings beyond addiction, meanings that partake of and enter into the social, political, and philosophical discourses of their times. In these stories, addiction breaks down illusions of autonomy and social power, exposing the limits of agency and even of individual difference. Recovery turns on the discovery of an alternative organizing principle of self, one that finds concrete expression through the social relations within a community of mutual support. The addict's reconstruction attests not just to the efficacy of a method of staying sober but also to a new vision of community. It is no surprise, then, that the most influential of these story forms have emerged during times of social upheaval, when large numbers of people found themselves alienated from, and even by, the very values surrounding private will and social custom, autonomous consumption and familiar habit, that they had been taught to revere. Sobriety movements and individual recovery stories don't just bring their adherents back into the mainstream fold, they renegotiate a society's most fundamental values.

Finding this structure of meaning in so many different places, connecting such a range of private and public concerns, and deployed on behalf of so many different ideals, I began to wonder whether addiction recovery has been one of the most important modern sources of the perennial trope of redemption in American culture. Redemption provides a narrative means of managing moral and material failure for individuals, communities, and the nation itself, especially when starting from within the confines of an unforgiving success mythology. Since the late nineteenth century, as physical stimulation and habitual consumption became central to labor, recreation, and the economy, addiction recovery may have been a more influential source of redemption storytelling than even the Christian conversion narrative that has so often been its generic parent. As a response to the physical crisis of addiction, recovery takes on a pragmatic flexibility that both loosens it from the constraints of prescriptive belief and bolsters its plausibility as narrative. From its earliest appearances, the recovery story has not remained bound to its religious ancestry, nor has it been isolated to any particular variant of sentimental culture or any particular theory of addiction. As a genre it has proved very amenable to formal imitation and metaphorical redeployment. Recovery has served as a concrete model of redemption far beyond the evangelical turn in American religion, moving into the heart of modern life writing, political rhetoric, and popular psychology. In this context, the A.A. era seemed to represent not so much the end of programmatic recovery narrative but the sublimation of its ideological function into a model of reconstructed selfhood that in its character as empirically discovered truth has been all the more powerful. I decided that the book should focus on how recovery narrative had acquired and reshaped the formal tools for conveying this kind of truth so effectively.

Working back through the traditional routes of A.A.'s religious, intellectual, and social influences, I noticed references to church missions that seemed to complicate the anti-temperance and post-religious rhetoric surrounding A.A., but which were neglected in its histories in favor of the more immediate role of the Oxford Groups. Rather than dismissing the missions as simply the musty religious holdovers that some A.A. pioneers happened to pass through, I wanted to learn more about where they came from, what happened in them, and how they linked the world of religious temperance to modern recovery cultures. The stories of Jerry and Maria McAuley and their friends in the Manhattan rescue missions of the Gilded Age were revelations, windows into the historical secularization of the evangelical Christian conversion narrative that opened wider every time I found another text that they influenced. But they were a challenge to interpret, seeming to invite the most suspicious hermeneutics and easy conclusions linking religious reform and elite social control. Finding myself, as students of addiction sometimes do, in something of a disciplinary no-man's-land, I looked for examples among studies of temperance, addiction treatment, alcohol history, and A.A. I was inspired by the small band of inventive and independent scholars I found there.

Scholars of recovery culture and its precursors have had to forge innovative methods for bringing to light connections that traverse the social, religious, cultural, and therapeutic contexts in which recovery appears.

Drawing on a dizzyingly interdisciplinary range of scholarship that runs from sociology to theology to critical theory to neuroscience, they have opened up new vistas of understanding, which have formed the foundations and shaped the methods of this book. Historians and social scientists dedicated to understanding addiction treatment and recovery, notably Ernest Kurtz, William L. White, Sarah W. Tracy, Ron Roizen, and Robin Room, in addition to A.A. historians such as William Pittman and Mel B., have laid essential empirical and conceptual foundations for this field. Literary scholars have been equally important models for my approach to recovery narrative. Tom Dardis, Thomas B. Gilmore, and Roger Forseth helped pioneer the field of alcoholism in and around modern literature, and Edmund O'Reilly and George Jensen have provided deep structural analyses of recovery narrative in literature and mutual-aid practice, respectively. Most important conceptually to my thinking has been a collection of seminal studies by John W. Crowley, describing a historical arc from the Washington Temperance Societies to A.A., and from sentimental culture to modernism, that has made it possible to think about recovery simultaneously as a narrative genre and a historical category. Works by social historians, including Catherine Gilbert Murdock and Lori Rotskoff, have been essential in illuminating the construction of modern alcohol narrative, via the determinative role of gender in modern drinking practices and problem definitions. And, most recently, Trysh Travis's exhaustive exploration of the print culture of recovery since the 1930s has laid a challenge at the feet of a larger humanities community that seems incapable of taking popular spiritual discourses seriously.

I have been heartened at key moments in this project to find myself a part of this dispersed community of interest, in exchanges with some of these scholars. So my first debt is to them, and to the many more cited in this book. In my pursuit of the various iterations of the "drunkard's conversion," I hope I've made a contribution to this field worthy of their examples. I also hope that, like many of them, I've aided in the project of bringing these phenomena to the attention of a wider scholarly community. Recovery and its antecedents are incredibly rich resources for understanding American religion and secularization, grassroots social movements, and the politics of the self in relation to intermediary institutions and ultimately the state.

Likewise, I am extremely grateful to everyone at University of Massachusetts Press, notably Brian Halley and Mary Bellino, kind and patient editors. I could not have asked for a better press when it comes to the subject matter at hand, as was evidenced by the extraordinarily helpful comments of the anonymous readers.

In the earliest stages of this project several people gave their time and energy to nurturing it. Susan Mizruchi and Carlo Rotella exercised great patience in helping to guide me through what must have seemed a perplexing and at times incoherent set of interests. I am profoundly grateful for their ongoing support. I'm also grateful to Werner Sollors and the other teachers and students at the Summer School of the Clinton Institute for American Studies at University College Dublin, who gave me invaluable feedback on an early iteration of this project. Similarly, scholars at Northeast Modern Language Association and American Studies Association panels offered responses that helped to shape subsequent drafts. I want to thank Trysh Travis for inviting me into the online conversation at Points, the blog of the Alcohol and Drugs History Society, in the last couple of years. As I've driven this project to a conclusion, it's been extremely helpful to follow the real-time thinking of a group of vivid thinkers, and to try out spinoff ideas for this ideally knowledgeable audience.

I offer special thanks to colleagues and students at Harvard University, particularly Jeanne Follansbee and everyone in History and Literature, for their support and inspiration. My teaching in the History and Literature concentration and the Freshman Seminar program played an essential role in the development of this project. A seminar on addiction allowed me to present some of the materials in this book in fresh ways, and the students' thoughtful responses to these texts often opened up new lines of thought. At the same time, regular conversations with History and Literature upperclassmen about research and argumentation have been more helpful to me than they ever knew. I am truly lucky to have worked in such a dynamic environment.

I thank Donald Seckler for his wise guidance. I thank my friends David Courage, Liam Seward, Burns Stanfield, and everyone at Fourth Presbyterian Church in South Boston for their untiring support and their helpfully honest feedback on some of the ideas I shared with them from this book.

I thank my parents, Frank and Maura Cannon, for their love and support.

And most of all I want to thank my wife, Michelle, for her enduring belief, and our two boys, John and Michael, for their transformative energy.

Addiction Recovery and the World as It Should Be

> "I'm quitting drinking," I told her. . . . Actually, the seeds of my deci-
> sion had been planted the year before, by the Reverend Billy Graham.
>
> —George W. Bush, *A Charge to Keep* (2001)

> Junkie. Pothead. That's where I'd been headed: the final, fatal role of
> the young would-be black man.
>
> —Barack Obama, *Dreams from My Father* (1995)

NEITHER GEORGE BUSH NOR BARACK Obama claims to be an alcoholic or a drug addict. Nevertheless, in these turning points in their
autobiographies, the forty-third and forty-fourth presidents invoke conventions of addiction recovery narrative to convey their passages from early-life
drift to sober purpose. Bush's late turnaround fits the template of the classic drinker's salvation, in which an experiential low point (a bad hangover)
prompts acceptance of the God-given regeneration modeled by an evangelist. Obama, by contrast, casts his turn from the path to addiction as part
of a process of racially inflected identity formation, in which a young black
man must confront a set of historically determined social roles as he undertakes the task of self-definition. He does so using themes common to artists'
recovery stories, recalling a philosophical excuse for escapist self-destruction that, after the discovery of a sense of purpose, is revealed to have been a
pose masking deep self-doubt.[1]

These tropes of redemption did more than provide safe havens for potentially risky admissions, made just prior to decisive election campaigns
(Obama's for his first office, Bush's for the presidency). They also authenti-
cated public identities and governing ideals, by grounding them in transformative private experiences. These narrative turns helped articulate the deep

foundations, social and conceptual, of Bush's and Obama's broadest political visions.

Bible study introduced Bush to new networks of men and new models of manhood that led to his first run for office. His mastery of the emotional language of evangelical Christianity not only helped him communicate with Texan voters, but also was the rhetorical vehicle for his campaign philosophy of "compassionate conservatism," the moderate appeal on which he based his run at the presidency. Finally, the very story of his drinker's conversion became political currency, circulated among evangelicals nationwide to secure their sympathies and motivate them to vote.

For Obama, his path away from the lure of drug abuse led to social justice work that ultimately also was fitted to a religious redemption narrative. The campus activism that helped solve the identity crisis behind his drug use deepened into a career commitment, eventually leading him to Chicago and Trinity United Church of Christ. There he found a religious tradition with active recovery ministries and a broad vision of communal, post-traumatic healing, one that engaged both his personal and professional identities.[2] His subsequent ascent as a progressive politician owed significantly to his incorporation, in both oratory and idea, of the redemptive and transformational themes he found in it.

While their use by aspiring presidents may be new, the conventions Bush and Obama drew on, both to make these confessions and, more essentially, to use them to authenticate broad visions of societal reform, have much longer histories on the American cultural scene. In the chapters that follow I explore that history, finding in the development of addiction recovery narrative a discourse about the nature of self and society that reaches far beyond the immediate problem of the individual's habit. Recovery and its antecedents have played several significant roles in American culture since the early nineteenth century. They have been influential locations of exchange among religious and secular languages for expressing how life ought to be lived and what society ought to look like. They have been vanguards of popular psychology and its revision of American values surrounding agency, morality, and the management of emotions. And, most surprisingly, they have been a cultural battleground on which different political ideologies have contended for ownership of powerfully appealing stories of rebirth, tales that communicate foundational beliefs about social relations in a democratic society. Bush's and Obama's life stories are political documents, and many of their critics have found their conversion narratives to be insincere. But ultimately, the reason they could so naturally put conventions for describing recovery from addiction to public political purposes is because that is what they were designed for.

Making Meaning in Recovery

The sobriety movements that have shaped American alcoholism narrative emerged during times of deep economic stress: working-class Baltimore men founded the Washington Temperance Society in the midst of the six-year depression that followed the Panic of 1837; underclass ex-drunkards and their religious patrons opened the "gospel rescue missions" that proliferated during the Long Depression of 1873–1879; and disgraced men of the middle class developed Alcoholics Anonymous during the Great Depression of the 1930s. In addition to methods for staying sober, these movements provided ameliorative services for many of their hard-up members, finding them food, shelter, and intensely sympathetic social networks. But the stories they told claimed much more than that, and affected many more people than the excessive drinkers who were candidates for membership. In each case, their respective redemption, conversion, and recovery narratives described models of transcendent deliverance from woe in communities of intimate mutual support. Each movement ultimately captured a wider public's imagination, not only by providing culturally resonant images of what inebriety or alcoholism looked like, but also by supplying a model of transformative social sympathy during the period of reorganization that followed these depressions. Each helped to articulate a foundational ideal for a new social order.

In this book I examine the relationship between alcoholism narrative and sociopolitical ideals in and between the latter two movements, arguing that the passage from rescue mission conversion to A.A. recovery negotiated foundational values in modern American culture, not just of the self, but of society. I look at the formation of these movements and the narratives they produced, the strands of continuity between them, and the secondary discourses that responded to them in political reform, popular culture, and literature. What I find is that modern recovery narrative, which still shapes the cultural role of alcoholism and addiction today, was the product of an ideological contest over the meaning of religious conversions told by drunkards between the 1870s and the 1930s. Across this period, stories of returning from chronic, incapacitating drunkenness appeared in evangelical biographies, treatises on economic reform, philosophical lectures, advice manuals, memoirs, and literary fictions. Patterns of social and political meaning run through these stories, meanings that have been obscured by binary distinctions such as religious versus secular, moralistic versus therapeutic, dry versus wet. More specifically, I focus on a key element of formal continuity, in the way that the turning point from alcoholic decline to sober regeneration expresses a vision of an ideal world. The power of this formal structure to assert a foundational ideal in a dramatic, realistic narrative made it subject to a variety of ideological claims on its true meaning: progressive, conservative, radical, and philosophical. These various interpretations supplied many of the conventions of the recovery narrative that emerged after World War II as an apolitical, psychospiritual language of the self.

Literary writers helped shape this discourse, by telling stories of alcoholic decline and redemption that drew special attention to the form's construction of sociopolitical meaning. Ironic realists of the late nineteenth century often satirized the drunkard's conversion as a manipulative and self-serving affair for its elite religious patrons. Socialist writers, by contrast, appropriated the form, telling of long-exploited workers who were drinking themselves deeper into misery and alienation until they found their way to a political meeting that played much the same role as the religious mission. Some of the modernist writers of the 1920s and 1930s who are most closely associated with the cultural backlash against temperance also, in fact, adopted the redemptive alcoholism narrative, but adapted it to their more reticent styles and inward-looking philosophies. Recognizing this structural and even, at times, temperamental affinity between modernist drinking stories and early recovery narrative bridges a cultural rift that has obscured the central role addiction as a narrative pattern has played in modern culture.

This framework thus revises the conventional historical story, which focuses on a sharp reaction against temperance politics and morality in the aftermath of Prohibition, and the resurgence of the disease concept of alcoholism after a decades-long dormancy. This view is reflected in cultural history, when we think of programmatic alcohol narrative as a phenomenon of the long nineteenth century. Indeed, the assumption of political and cultural significance has guided the study of the temperance movement, inebriates' reform, and Prohibition. Drunkards' redemption narratives played featured roles in the era's reform and religious discourses, illustrating the temperance case for total abstinence and the fruits of evangelical rebirth since the Second Great Awakening. In stories of sensational degradation, ecstatic transformation, and sentimental social reintegration, it is easy to recognize cultural resonance far beyond questions of alcohol and religion. Scholars agree that performed and published variations on the drunkard's redemption, from the 1840s to the end of the century, "aimed at a total reformation of American society and nationality," addressing everything from race, class, and gender norms, to public and private spatial division, to "the nature and strength of individual volition" in an industrializing society.[3] Whatever the underlying experiences of abstinent ex-drinkers were, their stories of sin and salvation constituted popular genres that imagined solutions to "an entire set of issues relating to almost all aspects of social life." Although the sorrows and joys of reformed drunkards were presumably no less real than those of twentieth-century alcoholics, we are nevertheless willing to bracket their private experience so as to read their stories as evidence of a "market for suffering," an emblematic rather than a documentary status. Their influence on literature and politics, as well as social movements, is well established.[4]

In contrast, the accepted cultural role of recovery from alcoholism, the variously medical, therapeutic, and spiritual phenomenon that supplanted temperance discourse in public health debates and drinking narratives in the twentieth century, is much more circumscribed.[5] Because it remains a vehicle of realism in popular memoirs and biographies, as well as in support groups and treatment centers, recovery is known less as a narrative genre than as a profound experience that many Americans share, one of coping with a dangerous affliction. Methods of describing this experience do not occupy a prominent place in cultural history, but instead are traced to a middlebrow self-help trend that arose in the 1930s in tandem with a newly institutionalized, and depoliticized, science of addiction. Recovery's emotional affect, political neutrality, and embrace of total abstinence left it on the wrong end of a newly hierarchical and hard-edged cultural order, and disconnected from the great public debates of the post-Repeal era.[6]

Recovery fuels an immensely popular print culture, in forms often tried out by literary writers, and it influences a range of media from television drama to spiritual autobiography. But in the cultural marketplace, its narratives appear as transparent windows on intensely real experience, rather than as an expressive genre with its own formal history. Scholarly critics may acknowledge it as a cultural phenomenon, but very few have considered it worthy of investigation. Those who have taken it up have often had to struggle against seemingly intractable biases, both temperamental and disciplinary, against vernacular spiritual and psychological discourses. From high-cultural perspectives, and for much of the community of humanities scholars, the "purely clinical" problem of the alcoholic remains largely uninterpreted and culturally insignificant, in stark contrast to the penitent drunkards who were dear to the hearts of Abraham Lincoln, Walt Whitman, and leading reformers and intellectuals of the nineteenth century.[7]

In this book I seek to challenge the sharp distinction between an expansive understanding of temperance narrative and a narrowly defined subculture of recovery, by asking new questions about how the former gave way to the latter. Chronologically, I bridge these eras by examining some of the key routes, between the Civil War and World War II, by which the drunkard's redemption became the alcoholic's recovery. Critically, I draw from this history a more consistent approach to understanding the social implications of sentimental redemption, religious conversion, and addiction recovery stories. By identifying their formal continuities and piecing together the conversation that connects them, I am able to recognize more subject-centered meanings in the earlier period and advance a historical case for the wider sociopolitical significance of recovery in the latter. The ultimate purpose of this comparative and connective method is to shed new light on the roles that alcoholism and addiction have played in constructing modern conceptions of self and society.

A recurring spatial theme helps to illustrate this synthetic approach. At key moments and in key texts I find superimposed the historical roles of the saloon and the mission, two major sites of folk, elite, and literary cultural production in American history. Instead of assuming a hostile opposition between the barstool and the mourner's bench, I see an ongoing dialectic in American culture between the languages of alcoholic and religious intoxication. Both reform movements and recovery narrators sought not to flee from the social bonding and performative culture of the saloon, but to transfigure these qualities for higher purposes. As sinners became saints, in mission halls that had once been barrooms, they brought with them their desires for mutual understanding and their willingness to form a sympathetic audience for dramatic performances of self.

Beyond addiction discourse, this history of narrative exchange reveals recovery's role as a cultural form that has helped shape the modern American imagination, by defining a site where the deepest self-knowledge speaks to the broadest structures of society. Reformers have long described the addict as a quintessential victim of modernity—its fast pace and high pressures, its alienating social forces, its economy of desire and pleasure, its pharmacological quick fixes. By extension, the addict's redemption symbolically redeems the flaws of modern society itself. And the ideal scenes of social sympathy that lead alcoholics out into the light are inevitably in conversation with contending visions for reforming society and its governance. They are formative sites of the modern American cultural, political, and religious obsession with redemption.

In almost every drunkard's conversion and alcoholic's recovery, the definitive moment of hope arrives not in the unmediated touch of God's grace, but in a vision of renewed social sympathy, a glimpse of what philosophers, theologians, reformers, and radicals have called "the world as it should be."[8] This vision structures—and is proved true by—the drinker's subsequent regeneration. Sobriety is the unifying goal, but the sympathetic relational ethic is the foundational virtue that gives rise to a redeemed, sober community. This community resituates the isolated, addicted self in a social world, in a manner that will not only vouchsafe sobriety within a corrupting wider environment, but will do so by creating a model within that society for its own transformation.

Recovery's history as an emergent genre in times of social reorganization is analogous to that of the jeremiad, the Puritan sermonic form that constructed and contested visions of an ideal early American society.[9] As a confessional testimony rather than a hectoring sermon, conversion-recovery has been especially suited to this role in the period since evangelical deliverance displaced congregational order at the heart of Protestant culture in the nineteenth century. In this relentlessly first-person mode, the narrative of an individual's relationship to God could convey all manner of social and political commentary. Arising as an instance of this genre, recovery narrative developed as a cultural technology for resituating the addict's relationship not first to his or her own desires, but to transcendent truth and its expression among fellow human beings.

The Rise of the Drunkard's Conversion

The concept of addiction did not emerge in the United States until the late eighteenth century, and then mainly as a theory of learned medical men, with limited circulation in the general population. Prior to that, intemperate drinking habits were laughable, or regrettable, or even vicious, but they were rarely described as compulsive. Observers described people who were regularly incapacitated by drinking as inebriates or drunkards, but reductive applications of the label were largely reserved for those on the margins—the village drunkard, the broken-down city prostitute, the drunken Indian. Respected members of the social order, by contrast, possessed the colorful or unfortunate character trait of intemperance. But this attribute was not widely perceived as a tragically involuntary condition or evidence of certain damnation, until the era of the temperance and revival movements.[10]

The apparent inability to stop drinking did not take on the character of an affliction until it began to seem irrational, a threat to Enlightenment self-mastery and, ultimately, a respectable social identity. A precursor to addiction is apparent in the work of the arch-rationalist (and arch social commentator) Benjamin Franklin. Franklin described habitual drunkenness as a quintessential failure of reason, knowledge, and self-direction. Twice in his *Autobiography* Franklin describes close associates who squandered opportunities, and became generally unreliable and unsuccessful, because of drinking habits. Early in his life story he uses a critique of drinking to display his own youthful command of reason. He recalls trying to educate his fellow printer's men in London, who overestimated the nutritional advantages of beer and underestimated its depressive effects and its cost.[11] Habits of consumption were to be analyzed and planned, in order to produce as "errata"-free a life story as possible, in Franklin's printing analogy.

Franklin's method of preempting inebriety in his own life is a rationalistic precursor to recovery narrative, one that invoked a rudimentary concept of addiction. He listed temperance as the first in his roster of thirteen virtues, but he defined it as the avoidance of eating "to dullness" and drinking "to elevation." Intoxication, and not necessarily compulsion, was the primary danger to be avoided, as an unwise rather than immoral or sinful threat to self-mastery. If virtues are habits, Franklin believed, they are easiest to maintain if they are practiced, starting slowly and building up a repertoire. Temperance was the key first step, because it protected a level-headedness that was necessary to guard against "the unremitting attraction of ancient habits, and the force of perpetual temptations."[12] Franklin recognized the tendency of habit to deepen into a compulsion that could overmaster the will.

An explicit disease concept of addiction arose first in medical theory and then in moral discourse. While the early disease theories did not gain significant public influence, nevertheless the popular language surrounding problematic drinking began to convey the notion of involuntary compulsion. The leading early proponent of the medical theory of addiction was Benjamin Rush, a physician, polymath, and signer of the Declaration of Independence. In a widely reprinted 1804 tract, Rush delineated the physical and mental effects of habitual drinking of "ardent spirits," expressly distinguishing the behavioral phenomenon that initiates the problem from the "disease" it becomes.[13] But beyond the influence of Rush and other medical men, it was not until church leaders and moral reformers took up the cause of temperance that daily drinkers and occasional bingers went from being considered ordinary men in a rough-and-tumble world to men in the grips of a fatal illness or a spiritual crisis.

While the extent of early American drinking is uncertain, it seems clear that the citizens of the young republic were, culturally, unapologetic tipplers. Alcohol had long played a prominent role in both folk and professional medicine, as well as in work and in social life. Daily drinking and sporadic bingeing were norms, and social and even civic events were marked by widespread public intoxication. Drinking is thought to have spiked between 1780 and 1830 as a result of the economic and political upheavals of the era and the weakness of social institutions for structuring people's passages through them. Regular drinking was a way of managing energy, pain, stress, and social interactions, while public bingeing provided a rudimentary ritual of communal bonding and pressure release. This surge was followed by an equally remarkable drop-off in consumption rates, attributed to a new emphasis on social control and, more specifically, a new culture of morality surrounding alcohol. Starting in the 1820s, religious elites held up complete abstinence as a physical and moral ideal, and the idea spread that drinking was both physically and spiritually dangerous. Two decades later, Lincoln recalled this shift with some amazement, as having abruptly changed "the abuse of a very good thing" into "the use of a bad thing."[14] Temperance organizations, in concert with the churches, were the institutional patrons of this change in values.

Temperance ideals alone were not sufficient to produce the classic shape of the drinker's redemption story. The particular power of its narrative turning point was instead a product of the rise of sentimental culture, especially through the model of the religious testimonial. Affective evidence of divine contact had become a necessary sign of authenticity in evangelical Christian conversion narrative, especially through the reformed Protestant traditions of Methodism and Baptism. As early as the first Great Awakening of the 1740s, Jonathan Edwards wrote about the problem of distinguishing imitative emotional affect from the true presence of grace.[15] But when we look for precursors to the nineteenth-century redemption story in *drinking* narrative, the emotions we find are those of straightforward condemnation, or of the carnivalesque elements of humor, violence, and ribaldry (paradoxically, another aspect of Benjamin Franklin's interest in drinking).[16] Images of drinking's destructive potential abounded, but they were not organized into tales of tragic decline, nor certainly into the exemplary transformations that characterized the mature nineteenth-century genre. It was not until the rise of sentimental culture in the United States that stories of the drinker's redemption became prominent.[17]

The first major grassroots sobriety movement, the Washington Temperance Society, captivated public attention on the strength of its dramatic narratives of degradation and redemption. Begun in 1840 by a handful of Baltimore artisans intent on helping each other stay sober in a time of severe economic stress, the Washingtonians grew explosively in both membership and cultural impact. Speakers such as John B. Gough became national celebrities, producing a corpus of popular redemption narratives that writers imitated in novels and plays. As John W. Crowley observes in *The Drunkard's Progress,* the Washingtonians pioneered and popularized much of what we recognize as confessional addiction recovery narrative, in their mutual-aid practices as well as in their public performances. The movement's public stages were politically suggestive, too, featuring working-class men using the cultural power of sentimental storytelling to make their voices heard in a republic undergoing economic and political turmoil. Lincoln said they showed the nation "a more enlarged philanthropy." They inspired the young Walt Whitman to write a temperance novel that envisioned a Washingtonian rally as the self-purification of the American demos.[18]

But the prominence of Washingtonian narrative on the public stage was brief. The Washingtonians' isolation from both temperance and religious institutions left them vulnerable to criticism from on high as well as the whims of public interest. Though they adopted a revivalist style in line with their Second Great Awakening context, Washingtonian leadership remained resolutely secular from its foundation through its brief heyday in 1841–42. Their commitment to sentimental storytelling above all other modes of advocacy left them without the support of theological authorities or the political allegiances that temperance institutions cultivated. After well publicized relapses by leading speakers, these fraught relations with both church and temperance powers allowed for quick fragmentation. Its leadership and its energies dispersed into less public and less testimony-driven fraternal temperance orders and into Christian denominational activity that did not maintain a strict focus on drinking.[19] The Washingtonians collapsed, but their dramatic history shows that a sentimental, affective style of redemption narrative was a compelling response to the new concept of inebriety. This style—in some cases through the influence of former Washingtonians—eventually found a powerful ally in evangelical Christianity.[20]

Like its twentieth-century descendent in recovery narrative, the drunkard's redemption did not answer to the problem of bad choices, but to that of involuntary compulsion. This seemingly paradoxical relationship between an emotive story and the often-materialistic concept of addiction is evident as early as in Rush's disease theory. While describing habitual drunkenness as a chronic, hereditary, mental and physical illness, Rush began his list of the condition's cures with the following three items: "a practical belief in the doctrines of the Christian religion" or "divine efficacy"; "a sudden sense of guilt contracted by drunkenness, and of its punishment in a future world"; and "a sudden sense of shame."[21] Rush ended his tract by quoting the various Bible verses that inveigh against drunkenness. From their earliest formulations, the disease concept of addiction and the spiritual route to sobriety went hand in hand.

The "gospel rescue missions" that flourished in American cities from the Civil War into the first decades of the twentieth century embodied this relationship. Often founded and operated by reformed drunkards from impoverished backgrounds, they provided food, shelter, and a nightly testimony service and prayer meeting. These nondenominational performances produced a repertoire of succinct storytelling techniques, a roster of colorful, exemplary characters, and a copious literature of conversion. Drunkards reformed in the rescue missions described them not just as places to spread salvation, but also as sites that enacted a truer and more practical form of religion, and modeled a more humane and just social order. This symbolic function inspired the reform discourse that is the subject of the first section of this book.

This attention to rescue mission culture, rather than to the testimony meetings and sentimental narratives of the antebellum Washington Socety, is a distinguishing aspect of my approach to the nineteenth-century precursors of modern addiction recovery narrative. Because of the Washingtonians' uncanny similarities to A.A. and their brief but extraordinary cultural prominence, most studies of temperance and sobriety movements identify them as the key nineteenth-century antecedent to twentieth-century recovery culture. I scrutinize the postbellum drunkards' conversions instead because, although they may have had smaller audiences both in person and in print, their influence on the sources of twentieth-century recovery narrative was far greater. While Washingtonian narrative was a distant cultural memory by the Civil War, the chapters that follow reveal that Gilded Age rescue mission conversions were the immediate templates for many addiction narratives of the modern era, including some that helped birth the recovery culture that still predominates today. Performed on a nightly basis for decades in hundreds of missions across the country and published widely in pamphlets and books, these testimonies inspired the political reformers, religious revivalists, novelists, and intellectuals who forged the modern American language of redemption.

A Chain of Influential Conversions

The drunkard's conversion formulated at the rescue missions was the linch-pin narrative through which a century of religious revivalism and temper-ance activism in the United States produced widely held assumptions about the progress of addiction and the possibility of recovery. It was transmit-ted via evangelical activity that started in the Second Great Awakening, was debated by reformers and intellectuals well into the twentieth century, and was the first mode of recovery offered to the founders of A.A. Through-out this century of performance, printed record, and imitation, the conven-tions used to describe the conversion experience remained remarkably con-stant, while the particular social, political, and cultural pressures around it changed.

Law student Charles Grandison Finney's conversion, on October 21, 1821, occurred after a day of solitary prayer in the woods of upstate New York, culminating in a crushing "conviction of sin" that "broke [him] down before the Lord" and allowed in a "mighty baptism of the Holy Ghost." Weeping uncontrollably, he experienced "waves of liquid love" and a "breath of God" that "seemed to fan me, like immense wings."[22] In the decade that followed, Finney became the leading revivalist of the Second Great Awakening, a nationwide movement that swept interdenominational evangelical Chris-tianity to a permanent place in the center of American religious practice. Unlike frontier revivalism, the movement Finney pioneered was city-based and drew heavily on urban theatrical culture and sensational media dis-course. In New York City in 1836, he renovated a former theater and chris-tened it the Broadway Tabernacle.

There, in 1842, a merchant named Jeremiah Lanphier was born again, leading him to become active in the church life of the city and eventually to quit business for full-time lay evangelism. In 1857 his noontime "business-men's" prayer meetings at the North Dutch Church on Fulton Street stimu-lated a citywide revival, the newspaper coverage of which helped instigate a nationwide "awakening." That year Lanphier led a door-to-door evangelical sweep of the city, in which the response among the poor was so promis-ing that it spurred the creation of a new ministry. One of the most public successes of this outreach in the waterfront wards was the conversion of Orville "Awful" Gardner, a notorious prizefighter, criminal, and drunkard. Gardner's conversion became a press sensation, and myths about its details proliferated. One had him spending a day on a river island doing battle with a jug of whiskey, which he eventually buried for fear that smashing it would release irresistible fumes. Gardner too was moved to carry the message of salvation. He chose as his field the ranks of the hopeless poor and convicted criminals from which he had sprung.[23]

During one such visit to Sing Sing prison in Ossining, New York, in 1862, the young convict Jerry McAuley was in the audience. McAuley had crossed paths with Gardner in the criminal underworld of New York and was shocked to see him in the prison chapel standing beside respectable ministers. Gardner soon stepped down onto the floor to be among the prisoners, and as he spoke of trading a life of crime for one of service to God, "tears fairly rained down out of his eyes," McAuley recalled. Gardner knelt down and prayed, sobbing until the whole room of hardened convicts joined in. Back in his cell, McAuley began reading the Bible, and after a few weeks became convinced of both his sinfulness and the possibility of salvation. One Sunday, after a young woman missionary had knelt and wept with him, he determined to spend all that night struggling in prayer for relief from his sins. It was not long before his halting prayers were answered in a "hand laid upon my head," a voice offering him forgiveness, and a "heavenly light" and "a perfume like the fragrance of sweetest flowers" filling his cell. His soul "all taken up with great joy," he had experienced God's touch.

Though McAuley became a model prisoner and was released early, without any way of earning a living he soon returned to robbery and drunkenness. But he continued to interact with missionaries, and finally he was saved again, in the parlor of a well-to-do family, where all who were present wept as Jerry recited the "Publican's prayer" of Luke 18: "God be merciful to me, a sinner." In 1872, McAuley, now sober and backed by moneyed supporters, took over a saloon-turned-mission at 316 Water Street, in his old neighborhood, and opened what is hailed as the first gospel rescue mission—a homeless shelter with a nightly revival meeting—for destitute alcoholic men. McAuley spent his remaining twelve years of life feeding, sheltering, evangelizing, and mentoring drunkards, earning a national reputation as a devil-turned-saint and a pioneer of urban evangelical missionary work.[24]

McAuley's second mission on West 32nd Street was where Samuel Hopkins Hadley, after twenty years of gambling, theft, fraud, and habitual drunkenness, surrendered to Jesus. Hadley had trained with a physician in his Ohio youth, and under the patronage of his brother, a successful life insurance salesman, he had been sporadically employed in business. But most of his adult life had been spent perpetually conniving to raise enough money to get drunk and stay drunk. Sitting in Kirker's Saloon at 125th Street and Third Avenue in Harlem on Tuesday, April 18, 1882, broke, starving, and trying to manage an extended bout of delirium, Hadley felt "some great and mighty presence," which he afterward determined was Jesus prompting him into a conscious conviction of his burden of sin. Everywhere he looked, his sins "appeared to creep along the wall in letters of fire." His response was to have himself locked in jail for the night to avoid drinking. In his cell, a battle commenced for his soul that did not end until he offered the Publican's Prayer.

The following Sunday, after drying out at his brother's house, Hadley went to a prayer meeting at McAuley's new mission. McAuley himself uttered his few sentences of testimony, followed by dozens of other "redeemed drunkards" who spoke after him, "every one of whom told my story." When McAuley asked him to pray for himself, Hadley hesitated; then "with a breaking heart," he said, "Dear Jesus, can You help me?" Christ's response brought Hadley to a height of ecstasy as unutterable as had been his depth of misery: "From that moment until now I have never wanted a drink of whiskey, and have never seen money enough to make me take one. The precious touch of Jesus' cleansing blood in my soul took from my stomach, my brain, my blood and my imagination, the hell-born desire for whiskey. Hallelujah! What a Saviour! . . . I promised God that if He would take me from the bondage of strong drink, I would work for Him the rest of my life. He has done His part, and I am trying to do mine."[25]

Before the year was out, Hadley was superintendent of McAuley's original mission on Water Street. Taking over the work of McAuley, who died two years later in 1884, Hadley would become a leader in the Holiness Movement, and its leading expert in converting the down-and-out. His conversion narrative—published in missionary pamphlets and in his book *Down in Water Street* (1902)—would become a foundational piece of data in the emerging field of the psychology of religion (fig. 1). As we will see in chapter 3, William James premised his argument for taking religious experience seriously on the evidence of Hadley and other drunkards.

Before his death in 1906, Hadley converted his "roustabout" son Harry, who eventually took up the family trade as superintendent of the rescue mission founded in 1926 by Calvary Episcopal Church on 23rd Street.[26] (By this time the mainline churches had begun to emulate the nondenominational born-agains in their methods of slum and skid-row outreach.) Shortly after the second Hadley's death in 1933, an unemployed alcoholic stock tout named Bill Wilson staggered into the evening service at Calvary Mission, to make a histrionic and dubious "decision for Christ." Though he barely remembered this conversion, after a group of evangelists headquartered at the mission visited him during his next hospitalization, he did finally experience a

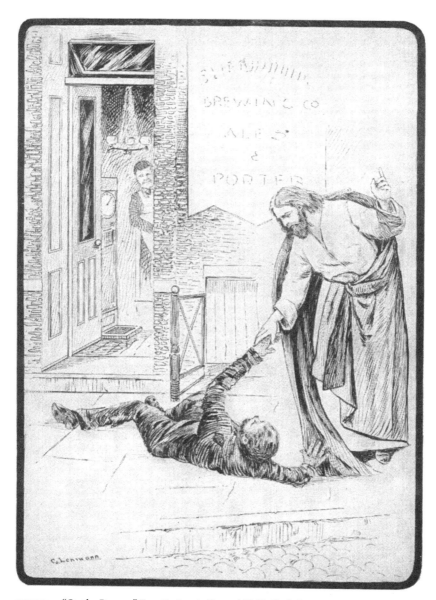

FIGURE 1. "On the Bowery." Frontispiece to Samuel H. Hadley's *Down in Water Street* (1902).

"blaze [of] indescribably white light," a "wind, not of air, but of spirit" that "blew right through me," and "a sea of living spirit"—in short, a conversion remarkably similar to the one Finney had a century earlier, to what Wilson called "the God of the preachers."[27] Wilson never drank again, and upon his conversion he built Alcoholics Anonymous and its spiritual program of recovery, the mutual-aid institution that would inform a large part of popular therapeutic culture in the second half of the twentieth century. The drunkard's conversion made famous at McAuley's Water Street mission was not just a precursor to the recovery narrative that still structures much popular memoir, but was a direct ancestor of it.

Part I of this book, "Redemption and Ideology," retells the preceding story by examining more closely the ways narratives by and about alcoholics changed in response to new social, economic, and political contexts. These chapters focus on the role of social and political reform discourse in the passage from the drunkard's conversion to spiritual recovery. In chapter 1, "The Drunkard's Conversion and the Salvation of the Social Order," I argue that the rescue mission conversion narratives constructed a pathway to social visibility for a variety of once untouchable people, at a time of massive demographic change and economic upheaval.

These stories, effectively secular in their pragmatic reorientation of salvation narrative toward material needs and social problems, not only were precursors to progressive social work, but directly influenced some of its leading theorists and practitioners. In chapter 2, "What a Radical Found in Water Street," I look at this influence on progressive voices in religion and reform, focusing on the largely neglected writings of Helen Stuart Campbell. Campbell used lessons learned at the rescue missions to relocate the spiritual crisis of consumption in herself and the middle class, illustrating how the drunkard's conversion helped construct the progressive imagination around visions of redemption.

Chapter 3, "The Varieties of Conversion Polemic," reveals the roles that the drunkard's conversion, and the rescue mission stories in particular, played in William James's life, thought, and legacy. Instead of jumping forward three decades to his well-documented influence on A.A., I compare contemporary responses to James's handling of the conversions, focusing on socialist and conservative interpretations by Jack London and Harold Begbie, respectively. Their polemical tales of alcoholism produced storytelling styles that shaped subsequent drinking and recovery discourse—including, ultimately, A.A.'s narrative form—at least as much as James's own ideas did.

When I turn to A.A. in chapter 4, "New Deal Individualism and the Big Book of Alcoholics Anonymous," I draw on the preceding history both as a realm of influence and as a critical model for rethinking recovery narrative's relationship to religious and political ideals. I argue that the social vision expressed in early A.A. narrative is closely analogous to liberal ideals for reforming individualism as the deep groundwork necessary to reorganize society in response to the Great Depression. Starting from a common underlying crisis of labor and consumption, the A.A. story shared a form, a style, and a philosophy with the national recovery narrative articulated by Franklin Delano Roosevelt to explain the New Deal. A.A.'s mutual-aid ethos is a model for social relations in a state that sees individual and collective welfare as inextricable. Recovery narrative was an outcome of modern cultural politics, assimilating and supplanting progressive, socialist, and reactionary alternatives in a way analogous to and informed by liberalism's rise at the level of the state.

In Part II, "Literature and Recovery" I examine the role of alcoholism in literature across this period, finding in it both an influential component of this conversion-recovery discourse and a source of deeper insights into its workings. From the beginning, the literary contemporaries of the drunkard's conversion not only took notice of it, but also assimilated it to the point that the form should be considered a convention of the era's fiction. Sentimental and religious writers embraced it, to be sure, but the most skeptical and ironic voices of literary realism recognized it, too, as a cultural force to be reckoned with. In chapter 5, "Literary Realism and the Secularization of the Drunkard's Conversion," I look at the various ways that pioneers in various modes of realist-era fiction, from Mark Twain to Upton Sinclair, variously parodied and appropriated the drunkard's conversion. I argue that these assaults did not signal the form's demise, but rather that their diversity represented its cultural dispersal, as drinkers' redemptions spread not only through religious and therapeutic cultures, but across the emergent hierarchy of high and low imaginative culture as well.

In chapter 6, "The Drinker's Epiphany in Modern Literature," I argue that depictions of compulsive drinking in modernist literature have much more in common with the burgeoning culture of recovery than critics have recognized. I show that the drinker's decline remained a standard plot structure through the 1920s and 1930s, and that in canonical novels, especially, it produced redemptive insight and sociopolitical meaning using the same mechanism as the drunkard's conversion. Comparative scrutiny of John Dos Passos's *Manhattan Transfer* and Djuna Barnes's *Nightwood* reveals how even the most experimental fictions made use of this form to connect deeply interior crises to sociopolitical questions. The novels also expose the problem of social inequality that would trouble the subsequent paths of both recovery narrative and liberal politics. As structures of change, decisive epiphanies, like recovery testimonials and equal-opportunity policies, are only available to subjects who are eligible for public social rehabilitation.

Chapter 7, "*The Iceman Cometh* and the Drama of Disillusion," is the only one to focus on a single work, and it does so because Eugene O'Neill's 1939 play imagines and interprets the same cultural history that this book is devoted to understanding. Its constellation of aborted alcoholic epiphanies dramatizes the ideological contest at the heart of the construction of alcoholism in the long modern period, including its missionary origins, its political uses, and its apparent conclusion in the rise of recovery narrative. While not overtly political, the play recognizes the public meaning of private self-knowledge. Announcing a coda for the cultural dialectic of the saloon and the mission, O'Neill warns against the potential for an internalized subjugation in the soothing, reductive spiritual language emerging in both alcoholism and politics.

In chapter 8, "Recovery Memoir and the Crack-Up of Liberalism," I trace the progress of the literary home of alcoholism and addiction narrative since the rise of A.A., finding a life-writing paradigm that has remained as troubled as the liberal political order under which it emerged. While twelve-step practices have remained relatively protected in their grassroots milieus, the commercial genres of recovery more directly reflect the fates of liberal ideals. Here I survey varieties of recovery memoir that reflect the legacy and the critiques of postwar reorganization. From individualistic triumphs that articulate the interests of powerful public-private institutions, to minority stories that make variously tenuous claims on the promises of full citizenship, to the rise of right-wing religious therapy, to left-liberal visions of redemptive multicultural intimacy, the increasingly popular recovery memoir remains much less monolithic and much less apolitical than its detractors have suggested.

The survival of this narrative's essential structure, from its origins in revival meetings and slum missions, through conflicted uses by progressives and reactionaries, to a contemporary home in treatment clinics and published stories, is the strange cultural journey this book investigates. It almost seems too obvious to say, given its place on the long-running *Oprah Winfrey Show* and its arrival in the White House, that the drunkard's conversion did not lose its role as an influential vehicle of ideology after it became the alcoholic's recovery. In the conclusion, "Addiction in a New Era of Recovery," I examine this contemporary role in light of the economic recession that began in 2008 and the political realignments proposed as responses to it. As during the Great Depression, addiction-redemption rhetoric was called on to imagine and legitimize these programs. The state of addiction theory, meanwhile, suggests that these new programmatic uses of the tradition might play a role in the formative stage of a future paradigm.

Recovery stories convey meaning at both depth and surface levels, from the deep-structural worldviews of their sympathetic visions to their sometimes explicit justifications for particular social and political programs. George Bush's and Barack Obama's redemption narratives helped create coherence in their life stories, making cultural sense of their public identities for different constituencies. For both, these logics extended into explanations for their world-historical roles. What these presidents' public stories have in common, and what they draw from the cultural history traced through this book, is the use of 150-year-old storytelling conventions to establish ideals, and purposes, higher than the individual's sobriety. That these conventions turn the personal experience of failed agency toward purposes that reach as high as totalizing visions for the nation's, and indeed the world's, salvation, stems from the original, transcendent stakes of the drunkard's conversion. This tradition took shape in a particularly influential way, I argue in the opening chapter, in evangelical Christian missions in the slums of American cities after the Civil War.

PART

I

❖

Redemption and Ideology

1

The Drunkard's Conversion and the Salvation of the Social Order

"You are damned," said the preacher. And the reader of sounds might have seen the reply go forth from the ragged people: "Where's our soup?"

—Stephen Crane, *Maggie, a Girl of the Streets* (1893)

I wonder, is it better to go to church to seek social connections, or business relationships, or to exhibit a new bonnet, than it is to go to church for a corned-beef sandwich?

—Ray Stannard Baker, *The Spiritual Unrest* (1910)

JEREMIAH MCAULEY, BY EVERY NINETEENTH-CENTURY indicator, was doomed to a wicked life and an early death. Heredity, upbringing, environment, religion, habits—each was as bad as could be, and the sum predicted irreversible degeneracy. His father was a counterfeiter in Ireland who abandoned his family. He was raised by a foul-mouthed Papist grandmother, then sent to New York City at thirteen to live with a sister. There he commenced a life of drinking, brawling, and stealing, in the notorious Fourth Ward on the East River waterfront. As an adolescent he became an accomplished river thief, and in 1857, at the age of nineteen, he began a fifteen-year sentence for robbery in Sing Sing. There he ran afoul of the guards and was treated to the "shower-bath" punishment, a version of what is now called waterboarding. Offered salvation by a visiting missionary, he exhibited the ignorant and impassioned prejudices of the Romanist, throwing down his Bible in disgust when he came to what he perceived as anti-Catholic bias in Paul's warning against priestly asceticism. Even after a subsequent conversion experience and an early release in 1864 for good behavior, he soon backslid, resuming a life of crime and dissolution in his old haunts. By then it was the demon rum, more than anything else, that put him beyond reclamation. He was a far-gone drunkard, given to begging drinks at the doors of saloons, and so by the ironclad logic of the temperance era, his fate was sealed. And if any doubt was left as to his potential for reform, his physiognomy told all too clear a tale. "He was born to be bad," the reformer Helen Stuart Campbell whispered to a companion on her first sight of McAuley. "How can he help it, with that type of head?"[1]

By the time he died, in 1884, Jerry McAuley had not only changed his ways but had become one of the most admired figures in American Christendom. At his funeral in the Broadway Tabernacle, "uncounted thousands" joined the leading clergymen of New York City to pay him tribute. The longest and most personal eulogy was given by A. S. Hatch, the president of the New York Stock Exchange and McAuley's mentor. The Rev. Charles Deems called the presence of "men of means" and "women of culture" before the casket of "a hunted river-thief" a "romance of grace and providence" that defied the very laws of nature. "It was not his ancestry, his beauty, his brains, or his services to science that brought out these thousands of people," Deems marveled. "It was all because one day in prison Jerry accepted God's offer of salvation, and took Christ as his present, personal, and sufficient Saviour then and there."[2] McAuley was not only an exemplar of born-again faith, but powerful evidence of God's continuing intervention in the world. The very elites who saw their own status through the lens of determinism in ancestry, beauty, and brains gloried in McAuley's triumph over moral science.

McAuley's transformation was the focus of his life story, but he had become a cause célèbre for reproducing it in others. After his conversion took hold permanently, McAuley founded mission shelters on Water Street in the rough-and-tumble Fourth Ward in 1872, and on West 32nd Street in the Tenderloin vice district in 1882. Career missionaries credited him with efficacy unprecedented in the slum field, attributing it to both the special height of sanctification afforded such a deep sinner and to his insider's knowledge of life in the tenements, alleys, and saloons. His "gospel rescue missions" were imitated all over the city and eventually all over the country, producing some of the leading evangelists of the era. At the center of it all, at every nightly mission service on Water Street, in each fundraising request, and every piece of publicity, was his own life story, often told as simply as this: "I used to be one of the worst drunkards in the Fourth Ward, but Jesus came into my heart and took the whole thing out of me, and I don't want it any more."[3] McAuley's story was the most famous example of the "drunkard's conversion," in which the most disreputable of men told of defeating inebriety, and all manner of attendant social afflictions, by accepting God's grace.

In this chapter I examine the drunkard's conversion narrative of McAuley's era, showing how in public performance and printed record it crystallized the practical theology and the redemptive social logic that would turn sobriety stories into sites of intense ideological contest as the nineteenth century gave way to the twentieth. The story of personal rebirth that had become the dominant religious narrative in American culture found in inebriety a material habit that ran to a spiritual depth, and one that, through the temperance movement, came with a readymade equation of personal crisis with public concern. Habitual drunkenness was so certain to produce irreversible physical, moral, and mental degradation that its defeat gave spiritual resonance to all the social and material improvements that flowed from sobriety. This pragmatic religious dynamic produced what was essentially, and often explicitly, a social commentary. By conflating spiritual redemption and social rehabilitation, when the drunkard's conversion template brought a subject into the body of the respectable public it gave divine sanction to its vision of that social order. The drunkard's conversion simultaneously performed two redeeming functions, one for its subject and another for the society that welcomed him into the fold. McAuley's well-to-do mourners radiated deep self-satisfaction in the act of admiring him.

The narrative's affirmation of a moral social order makes it the type of genre that is often read suspiciously from contemporary critical perspectives. It raises the question of whether the essential purpose of the drunkard's conversion was disciplinary. After all, it offered outcasts the reward of social acceptance in exchange for submitting to, and thus symbolically affirming, the system that had denied agency to them and their kind to begin with. Gerald Peters describes the fundamental "authorizing power" of all conversion narrative as being that of "a social operation designed to induct the individual into a prevailing sociopolitical power structure." Critics have attributed such reactionary purposes to every major sobriety movement, from the Washington Societies of the 1840s to Alcoholics Anonymous.[4] Neither has this debunking spirit spared the late nineteenth-century documentary styles of writing that secular reformers used to report on the rescue missions' activities. Skeptical readers long have perceived the reformers' brand of realism as voyeuristic "slumming" aimed at surveillance and, ultimately, control.[5] The drunkard's conversion seems tailor-made for these kinds of analyses. Reformers and evangelists asked converts to submit to and endorse a hierarchical social order, along the way documenting carefully their passages from unruly to pleasing behavior.

But the reduction of conversion's meaning to this top-down, disciplinary effect cannot account for the social dynamics of the rescue missions that produced this new cultural form, nor can it offer insight into why the converts felt themselves to be facing down oppressive social conventions when they voiced their own stories. Reformed drunkards founded and managed the missions, exerting considerable influence over the reproduction of their narratives, both in print and in adoption by fellow outcasts. Often men and women from the immigrant underclass, they paradoxically seized agency in their acts of submission to God and commanded public recognition through the enunciation and circulation of their stories.[6] Their conversions responded directly to material deprivation and ethnic difference, the kind of "profound social disturbances" that Amy Kaplan cites as factors which cannot be accommodated by the simple equation of voyeuristic realism with an exploitative middle-class consumer culture.[7] In their accounts of finding God and getting sober, the converts did not disown their poverty, class, or ethnicity but redeemed them, by claiming equality, exercising agency, calling for tolerance, and building countercultural social relationships.

These liberating aspects of conversion narrative have been explored before, in other contexts. There are precedents for recognizing how converts, especially those in socially marginal positions, can turn an ostensibly regulatory genre to their own uses. In Virginia Brereton's account of the "submerged plot" of women's conversions in this era, for example, converts "had to act anything but submissive and retiring; they had to . . . exhort relatives, enter strange homes, address groups of strangers, inspire and organize other women, and, of course, publish their stories."[8] Feminist scholars have made similar arguments about temperance activism and sentimental fiction, describing their languages of moral regulation and redemptive change as platforms on which women claimed intellectual and political influence.[9] These recognitions of the liberating effects of moral discourse tend to be grounded in historical examination of the social institutions that produced the forms, as opposed to the isolated textual analyses from which the skeptical readings flow.

Looking at the rescue missions as such institutions, I find that the purpose around which the postbellum drunkards' conversions formed was not merely one of changing behavior to fit established norms, but one of revising the rules of a social order that had become too rigid to accommodate new realities. At rescue missions like McAuley's, the idea of world-transforming change at the heart of Christian conversion was adapted to the industrial-era social conditions embodied in the crowded tenement neighborhoods of lower Manhattan. In its equation of social and material suffering with spiritual crisis, the drunkard's conversion modeled a solution to the problem of the increasingly numerous masses who did not meet the existing (and at times narrowing) standards for membership in a national public.[10] Joining a rescue mission community and performing this genre publicly offered converts a social lifeline and a public identity. At the same time, their stories neutralized the threat they implied to this public, by acting as a mechanism to turn feared outsiders into cherished insiders. This reconciliation, in turn, re-sanctified American society as a vehicle of God's expansive grace.

The postbellum drunkards' conversions may not have called for the overthrow of a hierarchical social order, but they did demand, and perform, its lasting revision. This call to change began when the disreputable targets of missionary activity themselves leveled at their evangelists a form of skepticism similar to that which today's critics express. In the first half of this chapter I examine this street-level evangelical discourse in the development of the rescue mission movement and its main cultural output, the drunkard's conversion. The missions and their conversion literature emerged from a process of negotiation, sometimes as tense as it was mutually beneficial, between reformers and reformed. As the resolution of such tension, the conversion genre's sentimental heart was the sympathetic encounter across class difference, typified by McAuley's uptown funeral, at which several people were reported to have spontaneously converted. In the second half of the chapter I investigate more closely these social dynamics in the conversion narratives themselves, finding that they were aimed at changing the social perceptions of the reader as much as they were seeking to win his or her soul to God.

The drunkard's conversion narrative gained wide cultural influence by dramatizing contagious individual healing as both a real and symbolic solution to problems of social fragmentation. In the process it became a template for the way recovery narrative would, in various forms, allow people to describe the experience of addiction in ways that modeled foundational reform in the ethics of social relations. This function remained quite malleable, though, giving rise to reactionary, reformist, and radical adaptations. The story's ability to premise the reconstruction of social relations on a personal journey to the foundations of the self is what made the drunkard's conversion a compelling template for the variety of political, literary, and therapeutic narratives of alcoholism examined in this book. Eventually, through lines of influence traced in the following chapters, this narrative structure played a key role in establishing a foundational principle of popular therapeutic culture in the twentieth century: the universal availability of moral redemption and psychological healing.

Drunkards and Religious Social Reform

The chain of religious conversions and evangelical ministries recounted in the introduction to this book is a historical thread that binds two major social and cultural phenomena of the nineteenth century: the evangelical revivals that transformed American religious practice, and the temperance movement that, though briefly sharing the spotlight with abolitionism, was the center of gravity for moral reform between the 1820s and the 1920s.[11] Though the conversion of drinkers had long been a feature of revivals and confessional testimony was central to the temperance societies of the 1840s, historians reserve the term "gospel temperance" for the definitive union of reform and revival that arose in American cities after the Civil War.[12] This movement took institutional shape in the rescue missions that spread rapidly after the success of McAuley's shelters in Manhattan. They created a grassroots, revivalist wing of the temperance movement, and they revitalized the missionary component of both evangelical and denominational Christianity. The nightly testimonies at these missions adapted the conversion narrative that had been popularized in the Second Great Awakening—one of intensely emotional moments of transformation recounted in a manner designed to bring others to the same experience—to the problem now known as alcoholism. The "gospel cure" was, in fact, evangelical Christianity applied as a method of treating addiction that in its practices, if not its degree of religiosity, prevails to this day. In their nightly meetings, narrative performances, and missionary activity, the saved drunkards were doing practically everything that recovering alcoholics and researchers agree makes Alcoholics Anonymous effective for many people.[13] The rescue missions enthusiastically blended mutual aid, charitable support, and temperance activism under the umbrella of a leading religious trend of its era.

This successful union of grassroots temperance with evangelical Protestantism is what distinguished the Gilded Age rescue missions from their now better-remembered precursor, the secular Washington Temperance Society movement of the 1840s. Whereas the Washingtonians lacked support from established church authorities, the rescue missions enjoyed the patronage of nondenominational networks of powerful individual Christians. In this the rescue missions were beneficiaries of the wide social reach of the urban revivals of the late 1850s, epitomized by the businessmen who attended the Fulton Street Noontime Prayer Meeting. Major denominational establishments by the time the rescue missions arose had accepted the benefits, and very often the theology, of evangelical revival. The Holiness Movement, which spread from Methodism through both mainline denominations and the wider evangelical world, was characterized by both revivalistic fervor and a commitment to social work that embraced drunkards as archetypal success stories. While the Washingtonians had strong cultural appeal in the heyday of the sentimental novel and thrived on the resulting public popularity, the rescue mission movement boasted powerful patrons in the worlds of religion and temperance and was able to grow quietly and steadily for many years with appreciative, but not sensational, public attention. Leading rescue mission speakers avoided large public stages and disavowed both sensational material and lengthy oratory. Their more persistent, sustained presence is what allowed their stories to exert direct influence on alcohol discourse well into the twentieth century. Prominent voices in reform, religion, psychology, and social commentary cited their active example as early as 1882 and as late as 1909.[14]

The pragmatic confluence of the languages of personal religious rebirth and moral reform is evident in the ways evangelical narrative and temperance analysis fuse in the genre of the drunkard's conversion. The temperance model of inebriety was established culturally in a decline narrative, in which the drinker who begins with an innocent social drink descends through well-defined steps into alcoholic degradation and ultimately suicide or an otherwise ignominious death.[15] In the face of this terrifying power attributed to alcohol, God's direct intervention was, in the words of longtime WCTU president Frances Willard, the only "true deliverance" for the habitual drunkard.[16] Conversion narrative presents the alcoholic's decline to social isolation and physical misery as an incapacitating spiritual crisis; but it forestalls the drunkard's death by the miracle of grace, giving way to a triumphal regeneration of character and fortunes. The reformist message in the drunkard's conversion emerged in this traffic between the personal and the universal. In revival theology, the subjective experience of personal breakdown plumbed to a depth beneath the unique self, to a place where human sinfulness and divine grace are the only facts. The credibility of this religious dynamic was boosted by the concept, established in temperance culture, that the inebriate's compulsion did indeed constitute a disintegration of the self. The drunkard's "bondage" was defined by the absence of the human quality of free will, resulting in an animalistic or "brute" existence. The prevalence of such temperance rhetoric helps account for the intensity of the conversion's dramatic turn: with the fatal logic of decline so well established as to seem formally unavoidable, its evasion could only be supernatural.[17]

The adaptations of the Christian conversion narrative to the temperance question occurred in a series of institutions: Methodist urban missions in the middle decades of the century and their application of the Holiness doctrine to social outreach; the daily prayer meetings and vice-district evangelism of the 1857–58 revival in New York City; and the series of revivals in the 1870s, many of them with a temperance focus, in which public prayer and conversion testimony became even more prominent a part of evangelical Christianity than they had been before. Facilitating these developments was an experiential, conversion-driven theology, an ongoing project in nonconformist Protestantism since the spread of the Wesleys' Methodism, and in American revivalism since the teachings of Jonathan Edwards, but which rose to a position of dominance in American culture in the rhetorical styles, reform works, and political ideas covering a wide ideological spectrum in the late nineteenth century. The few historians who have discussed the rescue missions movement have attributed it to the spread of the Holiness Movement from Methodism to nondenominational evangelical social work, and have used the umbrella term "Practical Christianity" to cover the movement's ties to both theologically conservative church authorities and Social Gospel innovators. Ultimately, though, it was drunkards themselves who not only developed the mature form of their narrative but also founded and managed the institutions at which it was reproduced. They did so not under the direction of temperance organizations or church authorities, but in the rescue missions they founded with the help of street-level religious reformers.[18]

This grassroots dynamic—more so than any sensationalism attached to its "wicked men redeemed" stories—was a key reason why, despite a series of closely related precursors, the rescue mission movement was recognized as a new and unique phenomenon in the decades following the Civil War. Churches had long practiced both charity and evangelism in the cities, and both slum missions and street prophets were well known phenomena. But the rescue missions' embrace of even the most "vicious" of the unworthy poor, their management by reformed criminals and drunkards, and their popular testimonial practices, marked a new phase in Christian social work. At a time when doctrinal division in response to cultural modernism had not yet rent Protestantism as openly it would by the 1920s, the rescue mission movement became briefly the most widely hailed fruit of Protestant social activism, a visible embodiment of the holiness teachings of revivalistic

Christianity.[19] McAuley became renowned throughout the evangelical world for his example and his success, while Hadley led the creation of missions in cities across America, affiliating in 1906 in a national federation. Among the missions founded in imitation of Water Street, often with Hadley's guidance, Chicago's Pacific Garden Mission produced Melvin Trotter, who led the movement for three decades after Hadley's death, and Billy Sunday, the most popular revival preacher of the era. The movement was renowned, in fact, for the number of its leaders who were themselves products of the missions.[20]

The prominent role of ex-drunkards in leading the missions helps explain why, as a movement, it left a relatively light imprint on historical memory, despite its deep and broad influence.[21] This focus on the paradigmatic experiences of certain individuals, especially those who had recently been destitute and criminal, made its leaders more like symbolic figures on the public stage than actual activists. The rescue mission movement was more institutionally coherent than is often thought, through its lines of spreading influence and the aforementioned associations. And it did indeed enjoy powerful, elite patronage. But it is better placed in the tradition of loosely organized mutual-aid associations, like its precursor the Washington Temperance Society and its heir Alcoholics Anonymous. Rescue missions predated, and remained distinct from, the much better known phenomena of the Salvation Army and the Social Gospel movement. They lacked the pomp and central organization of the Salvation Army, and made no outright claims on intellectual or political theory as did the Social Gospelers. The latter emphasized systemic reform rather than individual salvation, as is implied in the title of Walter Rauschenbusch's 1912 *Christianizing the Social Order*. The rescue missions, by contrast, admitted no explicit shift away from the intensely individualistic focus of evangelical faith. Indeed, conservative ideology today pits the rescue missions against the Social Gospel, as private versus collectivist models of Christian charity. Marvin Olasky, in a book that served as the intellectual source for the "compassionate conservatism" that George W. Bush invoked in his 2000 presidential campaign, holds up McAuley and his Water Street mission as exemplary nineteenth-century "holistic," individualized charity, an anti-progressive ideal that Olasky argues was undermined by the rise of technocratic social work and the welfare state.[22] Closer scrutiny reveals that the rescue missions' vision extended beyond the individual, to encompass and address problems with the social order.

Theology on the Streets

The ex-drinkers themselves turned the drunkard's conversion into a religious narrative with a reformist purpose. The story form developed in a process of contestation and collaboration among revivalists and their disenfranchised targets, starting from street-level evangelical confrontations over the benefits of salvation, and leading to a nationwide network of institutions run by reformed drunkards. Missionaries reported an array of skeptical responses to their preaching in the slums, in mini-dramas that not only advertised the obstinacy of the sinner and the power of the evangelist to overcome it but also revealed the ways the poor demanded that salvation answer tangible needs in their lives. A resulting emphasis on the more pragmatic advantages of conversion appeared in both the direction this missionary work took and the conversions that were published to advertise it. Together the rehabilitation of the saved drunkard—in health, respectability, even employment, housing, and food—constituted a kind of social salvation. Rescue mission conversion in this manner reflected, more than did other evangelical narratives, its dialogue with skeptical counterclaims based in earthly social problems. This dynamic continued to inform and invigorate the rescue missions throughout their heyday as the heart of evangelical slum proselytization. "Down here people have learned deep things out of life itself," the progressive journalist Ray Stannard Baker observed of the Water Street clientele in 1909. "They have been shaken down and tried out. What they want is not books or doctrines or advice or churches; all these superficial things they have spent out with their money and got beyond. Any religion that touches them has got to live, and show visible works; there is no other way around it, or about it."[23] From the beginning, a skepticism born of being "shaken down and tried out" pervaded the streetscape in which the missionaries plied their wares, and it pushed the resulting narratives in a pragmatic direction.

In public perception and in reform circles, too, in the immediate postbellum era slum proselytization operated under a cloud of suspicion and even open ridicule, as the folly of softhearted idealists and the con-game of waterfront grifters.[24] The early rescue missions were burdened by quite recent scandals that had made slum reform an object of derision. Working-class temperance narrative had been through at least two cycles of prominence and discredit, beginning with the highly publicized Washington Society's loss of standing, brought about by increasingly salacious confessions and well publicized lapses by leading figures.[25] Missionary anti-vice work was under a similar cloud. In 1868, a group of New York City's religious elite were humiliated by their participation in the publicity-driven, short-lived conversion of Water Street itself. In this episode, missionaries descended on the Fourth Ward and transformed spaces given over to vice into spaces of worship. Two notorious proprietors of saloon-brothel-bloodsport emporiums, John Allen and Kit Burns, rented their dance floors and rat-pits for prayer, hymn-singing, and testimony meetings. The apparent personal commitment of Allen was sensationalized in the press as the conversion of "the wickedest man in New York." But Burns refused personal conversion, mocked Allen as a fraud, took the reformers' money, and when he tired of hearing his regular business practices abused, he "rat-ified" the proceedings by flinging live vermin into the worship-space while his disgruntled gamblers sang mock hymns in glee. This insult to the ministers and ladies was a step too far, though, and within weeks the police had closed him down permanently.[26] After such scandals, the very genre of the "wicked man reformed" was in a disrepute analogous to that attributed to its pre-conversion narrators, requiring a redemption that only a street-bred figure like McAuley could provide.

As discredited as the earlier reformers were—the *New York Times* report suggested the missionaries had paid for false conversions to try to spark a real revival—these waterfront episodes left a lasting legacy in the urban landscape. Unlike the earlier city revivals that had been church-centered, in Water Street saloon and mission sat side by side, and even shared and traded space. This spatial context is important to the evangelical/skeptical dialectic that shaped the conversion narrative. When McAuley was released from Sing Sing, returned to his old neighborhood, and eventually began his missionary work there, scenes of mutual invasion between the mission and the saloon had become a staple of the streetscape. McAuley's first contact with a missionary after his prison term came in the aftermath of what he called the "John Allen excitement," when missionaries were still trolling the saloons and tenements. When he undertook his own rescue work in 1872, it was by buying one of the notorious Water Street saloons and converting it into the "Helping Hand for Men," the first mission targeting drunken and disreputable men. McAuley's "rescuing" of 316 Water Street fulfilled the symbolic ideal of saloon-transformation established in the Allen episode.

These evangelical efforts at slum-conversion produced not only a missionary presence on Water Street, but also a set of performative and narrative conventions based on this sharing of space. These tropes included the bold appeal to the most hardboiled sinners, and, importantly, engagement with their skepticism. "But, see here, did you ever see Christ?" the street preacher Henry Gibbud reported a shell-game operator asking of him. "No, but I expect to see Him; I have His word that I shall," Gibbud responds. His faith is mocked as an obvious con: "Come here, fellows, and see a chump who's got a promise of seein' Christ." A crowd gathers, raising the stakes in what has become a public contest of wits. Gibbud recalls the "typical Bowery crowd— Jew and Gentile, a number of sporting-men and thieves, two or three fallen women, several drunken men, and others attracted by the noise, eager to see what was going on." In other words, it was that body of urban outcasts and spectators that in both its apparent apathy and in its merely voyeuristic interest in moral drama posed such a challenge to the reformer's worldview. Gibbud, of course, stitches up the scoffer with puns from scripture, to the delight of the crowd, and sets on the path to conversion a drunken man whose ear has just been bludgeoned off in a fight.[27] In sum, he wins a match on the home turf of the enemy and at the same time illustrates how the evangelist's pitch can be adapted to even the lowest and most cynical audience.

Drunkards' conversion literature pointedly incorporated responses to the critics who mocked it from its first appearance, and it identified the origins of these criticisms in the mouths of its targets for conversion, as obstacles to their faith. Such arguments were set inside the missions, where evangelists and converts described a constant stream of intrusions by drunken and otherwise disrespectful street figures, some of whom were triumphantly converted, others who had to be dealt with by wit or brute force. One such scene served to contrast the transformed McAuley and his friends with the unconverted ethnic drunkards around them. Helen Campbell described her first meeting on Water Street being interrupted by a drunken woman who, leaning out of her tenement window, turns her wrath on the mission in a melodramatic immigrant voice:

> "Cursèd heretics. Bunch o' liars. I sphit on ye all. Ah, but wouldn't I like to get at the eyes of yees, ye ivery one! An' me fine lady there at the organ! Oh, ye sit there an' fan at yer ease ye ——, do ye? Think ye could earn yer own livin', —— ye! Comin' down an' sittin' there an' niver carin' a —— if all of us has our hids knocked off! What do ye know about throuble, —— ye? Ah, let me get ye once, an' I'll tear ye to slithers."[28]

The woman is inflamed with the satanic Irish wrath that, in temperance discourse, only alcohol can produce, but she gives voice to the real charges that the missionaries' critics (then and now) leveled at them: that they were only there for their own purposes, that they made no real effort to understand the challenges of poverty, that they cared more for abstract souls than they did for the hides or heads of real poor people. In Campbell's account, the woman's rage does not dissipate until a lone child begins singing a hymn in an angelic pitch, providing yet another model of spiritual victory at the mission. More importantly, the woman's critique is answered blow-by-blow in Campbell's subsequent conversations with McAuley.

In addition to buying buildings, missionaries continued to enter dives in force to sing hymns and save souls. In these scenes, dating to the first foray into John Allen's, it was typically reported that the prostitutes, especially, were moved to tears by the old-time songs, and often joined in.[29] When the prostitutes didn't break down en masse, the crusaders could count on at least one pair of eyes to register sorrowfully a pious childhood and a long-lost hope of redemption. In one case published in 1892, Gibbud, shepherded by a fearless boxer who is undergoing a moral awakening, trolls a series of saloons and underground dives looking to save a young alcoholic prostitute, whose story closely resembles that of the title character in *Maggie, a Girl of the Streets*, Stephen Crane's novella of the following year. Gibbud's nonfiction account of "Jennie" has precisely the opposite ending to Crane's, when Jennie, moved by news that her mother wants to forgive her, is coaxed out of a "stale beer dive," cleaned, dressed, and converted, and restored whole to her pious home.[30] Crane's irony targets the sentimentality of this type of story, savaging the figures of the good mother and the charitable cleric. But in the reformers' accounts, it is skeptical realism that represents conventional thought, while their belief in the prostitute's potential for reform constitutes new thinking. They based their own "realism" on the experience of having visited the saloons and brothels themselves and engaged the spiritual and material hopes of the women they found there.

This series of mutual invasions between saloon and mission featured reformers and converts alike intervening in the established purposes of public spaces and ultimately changing the nature of the social landscape. The conversion discourse about individuals tells of crossing from the public qualities of open drunkenness, dirty clothes, and criminal records into those of visible piety, bodily cleanliness, and saintly reputation. In order to initiate such passages, though, social boundaries had to be broached and, further, one side of the evangelical dialogue had to be ceded to the unconverted. The result was that the dualism of what can seem in isolation a religiously reductive narrative was not just that of bad and good, immoral and moral, or unsaved and saved, but also that of empowerment versus manipulation. In the literature, targets of evangelism constantly ask for evidence of the material rewards of conversion, and, suspicious of elite legalism, they want, and are ultimately given, concrete answers.

The narratives that result attempt to dispatch suspicions of manipulation by literalizing the benefits of salvation. In an exchange that sentimentalizes as well as materializes rescue mission conversion at one of its founding moments, the missionary who finally wins McAuley back to the path of salvation does so by offering to pawn his own coat for a meal, if it will stop Jerry from going out on the river to steal. An aphorism often attributed to McAuley held that "there's lots of religion in a beefsteak, if you give it to the right man at the right time." The line has its origins in the days after the missionary's offer, when a fellow drunken thief mocked his conversion, asking, "Will the Lord come down from heaven to give you a beefsteak?" As Hadley relates it, when McAuley first told him the story, they were sitting down to a steak dinner, and McAuley added, "He has sent us down a beefsteak, hasn't he, Brother Hadley?"[31] This jest was not a precursor to prosperity-gospel materialism—in fact it derided such an attitude as that of the unconverted scoffer. Instead the effect was to sacralize the outcomes, material and otherwise, of the sustained service work and relationship-building that produced such transformation, as being in the very nature of salvation.

Responses like that of the con-man who mocked Gibbud's "promise of seeing God" forced missionaries to adapt their pitch and make more material promises. While the conversions culminate in acts of submission, the converts already have intervened, to a degree, in the regime they are submitting to. This agency may be limited, but it is more substantial than that which occurs within more established religious settings, and certainly more real than skeptical interpretations of revival culture can account for. The struggle to sustain a credible missionary presence among the saloons of Water Street, among men and women who knew a con-game when they saw one, was an important factor in producing the genuinely reformist purposes in the genre. Socially powerless converts did not simply submit to the religious regime and in doing so empower themselves through elite approval. They reworked, toward their own needs, the institution they joined and the narrative template they fit their experiences to. The missionaries, having come down to the slum streets, found themselves confronted not just by sin but by substantial challenges of practical theology. They openly theorized pragmatic responses, they welcomed to their own ranks some of those who converted, and they popularized the results in sentimental printed appeals that urged both a social and conceptual broadening of the transformative power of God's grace.

This process is evident in the rescue mission literature, and it was why, despite having antecedents in prior decades in temperance narrative and revival literature, these drunkards' conversions could present themselves, and exert influence accordingly, as a new and transformational development in both temperance and Christian reform.[32] After cycles of high fervor followed by damaging discredit enervated both the Washingtonian movement of the 1840s and the revival of the late 1850s, the rescue missions' grassroots ethos, insistence on humble service rather than heroic sobriety, and minimization of rank essentially performed the service of redeeming redemption. Its scenes provided concrete examples of the development of practical Christianity from the union of holiness doctrine, revival culture, and grassroots self-advocacy by the marginalized in the era immediately preceding the more recognizable developments in the Social Gospel. Rather than being imposed from above, by the intellectual influence of theologians, or the homiletic directives of high-ranking ministers, this phenomenon arose directly from the realm of real social and material need that religious idealists discovered in the industrializing city.

The purpose of emphasizing this collaborative dynamic is not to mystify the reformers' essentially regulatory aims, but rather to argue that it was the mutual-aid practices of the reformed men and women that made possible conversion's role as the basis for later forms of recovery narrative, and ultimately for a major premise of popular therapeutic culture in the twentieth century. The form of salvation that emerged from these confrontations shifted its balance of earthly and eternal reward in the direction of the social, material, and psychological crises that recovery sets out to solve. The cultural influence of the rescue missions began in the landscape of rapid urbanization, in the exchange of space among the saloons and missions that shared the crowded buildings, streets, and neighborhoods of nineteenth-century New York. Evangelists conducted their assaults on saloons not by smashing them with axes or padlocking them, but by competing within their doors for the hearts—and narrative subject-positions—of drinkers. They transformed saloons into missions by taking advantage of their roles as performance spaces, substituting infectious piety for the addictive and the carnivalesque qualities of intoxication. But they could only sustain the appeal of the Godly way by proving its material and psychological benefits. This dialogic, performative, and spatial competition shaped the reform culture of the missions, in practices and texts that helped give rise to the concept of recovery.

A Print Culture of Salvation

The earliest rescue missions were funded by collections taken at middle-class revival meetings, and with the help of wealthy sponsors. Once established, they began to produce literature as a vehicle of both evangelism and fundraising. McAuley published his own biography, with the help of patrons, in the 1875 Water Street mission pamphlet, "Transformed." After his death in 1884, McAuley's wife published a book-length biography titled *Life and Work of Jerry McAuley*. This book contained "Transformed," plus incidents in the life of the mission dictated by McAuley to friends, recollections by various supporters, and narratives of men converted at Water Street who went on to open their own rescue missions. It went through several editions and remained popular enough in 1907 to be republished by the American Tract Society as *Jerry McAuley: An Apostle to the Lost*. Hadley's life story, too, was first published as a mission pamphlet, and later incorporated into a book by a leading Christian publisher, the Fleming H. Revell Company. Hadley's book, *Down in Water Street: A Story of Sixteen Years Life and Work in Water Street Mission*, was subtitled "A Sequel to the Life of Jerry McAuley." It recounts McAuley's life, followed by Hadley's autobiography, episodes in the life of the mission, and nine mini-biographies about men who were converted there. Hadley's book concludes with the lengthy certificate of incorporation for the Water Street mission, and a form for leaving bequests to it. On Hadley's death in 1906, Revell published a biography by J. Wilbur Chapman titled *S. H. Hadley of Water Street, a Miracle of Grace*. Other books about rescue mission conversions included Emma Whittemore's *Delia, formerly the Bluebird of Mulberry Bend* (1893), and Hadley's brother Henry's *The Blue Badge of Courage* (1902).

This literature had a lasting influence on Protestant reform culture and ultimately, as we will see in subsequent chapters, on storytelling about alcoholism and recovery. Its immediate impact was to popularize and invigorate gospel temperance narrative. Henry H. Hadley's *Blue Badge of Courage*, for example, chronicled and cemented his rise from the rescue missions to a public role as the "leading spirit" of the National Christian Abstainers Union and the Blue Button Army.[33] These Abstainers and soldiers, many of whom were, like Hadley, Civil War veterans, used military rhetoric to promote Christian faith as the key to sobriety, in a model of conversion that emphasized abstinence more than it did Christ. Hadley's autobiography, and the movement he called "the new school of temperance," though still nominally Christian, were among those secularizing and politically active steps by which conversion narrative moved closer to what we would now call recovery narrative. Reviews described *The Blue Badge of Courage* as more colorful and broadly focused than his brother Samuel's *Down in Water Street*.[34] It turned the rescue mission conversion model toward wider cultural appeal and clearer social and political purpose.

At first glance, this literature seems organized exclusively by the goal of winning souls for Heaven. With McAuley and the two Hadleys' lives as models, every aspect of the rescue mission books was dedicated to reproducing the conversion narrative. The reasons, both stated and implied, for publishing the narratives were to encourage readers to seek the conversions of themselves and others and to support the missions' work. The texts open with introductions by prominent ministers testifying to the evangelical power of the authors' lives and works, and both are stocked with before-and-after drawings and photographs, material proofs of spiritual transformations. The life stories themselves are presented as engines of evangelical transmission, inviting identification and imitation. The publications cited their own earlier editions and source material as the evangelical spur to readers' conversions.[35] Texts by the reformers who worked in and around the missions would follow similar formats, almost always citing McAuley's life as the first exemplar.

These stories define a social order, preoccupied as they are with descent and ascent through ranks of class and status. McAuley, who did not have far to fall from his humble immigrant beginnings, emphasized the social redemption that came to him after his conversion in the form of legitimate jobs, the confidence of wealthy and powerful men, and the compassion of refined women. Hadley's tale is of a man falling from middle-class status and potential wealth through addictions to gambling and drinking. Recounting the night he hit bottom, he foregrounds the location as "a saloon in Harlem," making clear that he has not grown up in such dives but has descended to them.[36] The drunkard's conversion as a genre could understand the immigrant, criminal, convict and menial laborer McAuley by the same logic with which it handled the Midwestern, middle-class, sometime businessman Hadley. Joining them at their shared low points, what one contemporary analyst called "the last equality of degradation," it remade them from social pariahs into esteemed guests of polite society, men given divine sanction to address any kind of audience.[37] This leveling function failed to obliterate social distinction, though, because the terms of their respective rehabilitations, the processes by which salvation was made visible, were those of their differing social needs.

For McAuley, in the context of Protestant reform writing, conversion solves the problem of his status as a poor Irish Catholic immigrant.

Importantly, evidence of his origins is not erased from his identity, as it is also evidence of the scope of the Protestant God's grace. This identity is primarily rendered through his voice. Robert M. Offord, the editor and some-time narrator of McAuley's life story, hints at the way alien speech stands in for the inaccessibility of interior experience, in the following thanksgiving for the availability of Jerry's example: "Saved from a life of sin, let us thank God that Jerry McAuley was TRANSFORMED; saved forever from suffering and sorrow, let us thank God that he has been TRANSLATED."[38]

McAuley's speech was "translated" in two different voices, depending on the occasion. In long-form autobiographical narrative, it was rendered in correct, even sophisticated English; in direct accounts of his testimony at mission services, it was given in a thick Irish accent. The long form typically opened with a scene illustrating the early sources of his irreligion and criminality. "I was placed at a very early age in the family of my grandmother, who was a devout Romanist [who cursed and swore.] I can distinctly remember thinking, though I could not have formed the thought into words, 'What sort of religion is this that requires such foolish worship, and allows such sinful ways?' I can trace my infidelity to Rome to just these incidents."[39] This version of McAuley's voice, transcribed or wholly "translated" by an editor, is literate, and it tells a Protestant readership what it wants to hear about Catholicism.

When reformers wanted to conjure the sentiments of interclass sympathy, they quoted McAuley in an uneducated, immigrant voice. Hadley recalled the moment McAuley's testimony drew him in: "he had been a 'tief, an out-cast, yes, a regular bum; but,' he would add, 'I gave my heart to God, and He saved me from whiskey and tobacco and everything that's wicked and bad.'"[40] McAuley's enunciation of his low-status immigrant origins—the absence of the "h" from "tief" does much of this work—heightens the sentimental dynamic by which a former insurance man from the Midwest could identify in such a figure his own degradation and potential salvation. The dramatic appeal of this evangelical moment drew on this self-consciously countercultural expression of equality.

This emphasis on the linguistic aspect of social identity was repeated in the stories of other ethnic, working-class converts, whose identities were advertised in their names and epithets, such as Ira Snyder ("Bowery Ike"), "Billy Kelly, the Ex-Barkeeper," and "John Jaeger, the Anarchist." Jaeger was a German immigrant converted at McAuley's Water Street mission in 1881. He had been a "drunken bum," "anarchist," and "thoroughly bad man all round," but by 1901 he was the superintendent of the Mission of the Living Waters on Christie Street, adored by "men and women of distinction in Christian life." Jaeger's conversion was a cooperative project among the respectable and the redeemed to widen further the evangelical net. In the story of his redemption, a missionary shepherds a distraught Jaeger to Water Street, where McAuley prompts him with typical gruff compassion to "Pray, German man." Jaeger's supplication gives the monoglot immigrant access to the English language, through the divine power of the name of Jesus, and the miracle is extended, when Hadley claims that after his conversion, despite still having no English and being illiterate even in German, Jaeger prays for and is granted the ability to read the Bible.[41] In these ways the rescue mission literature seized on language difference, the most prominent medium of social division, as the site of God's healing work.

By reading the Christian notion of signs in the everyday urban landscape of class difference, the rescue mission literature illustrated the miraculous bridging of social chasms. It was not just a record of souls saved, but very explicitly an account of how social fissures caused by immigration, economic depression, and class stratification were mended—while at the same time taking care to eliminate affiliations such as anarchism and Catholicism. With industrial efficiency—most published accounts were the length of a short book chapter, and rescue mission testimonials were typically limited to one minute—the conversion story remade subjects by recasting their experiences and their identities using the simple binary of unsaved and saved. With the great social and spiritual sin of inebriety as an entry point, the narrative could recycle sin of almost any degree (even, sometimes, women's sexual license) into not only useful but exemplary spiritual energy, as the deeper into sin the subject fell, the greater the miracle of the conversion, and the greater the sentimental power of the convert's social rehabilitation.

Visual Narrative and Social Theory

Drunkards' conversions in print featured a visual rhetoric of transformation, both in persistent physical description in the texts and in photographs and sketches that accompanied them. This before-and-after imagery epitomized the simplicity of the narrative's religious logic, by turning the physical signs of dissolution (in hygiene, posture, and facial expression) into their redeemed opposites. These images responded to an established visual culture of temperance. The logic of the drinker's inevitable, step-by-step downfall across every phase of life, so central to temperance belief by the mid-nineteenth century, had been promoted in a popular mode of visual allegory, epitomized by the oft-cited Nathaniel Currier lithograph of 1846,

"The Drunkard's Progress." The rescue mission imagery implicitly, like the textual conversion narratives, built on but then interrupted this temperance story. But, also like the drunkard's conversion, this visual sequel to a near-fatal decline was not an innovation. Currier also visualized the basic terms of the drunkard's conversion in that earlier period, in a series called "The Bible and Temperance."[42] What was new in the rescue mission imagery was its invocation of a changed kind of viewer, a dynamic that helps to clarify the more nuanced way in which the discourse in general summoned change in the social order. At the visual level, especially, it responded to the prevalence of pseudo-objective determinism in social economics, criminology, temperance culture, and Christian theology. It did so by fusing a traditional, allegorical mode of narrative, favored by temperance advocates and religious revivalists, with the new epistemology of realism. Its testimonies were what one writerly observer called "pages out of the book of common life . . . true stories, like that of the blind man."[43] The conversion cure for alcoholism could be true in both the empirical and allegorical senses.

The realistic imagery of photography provided apparently objective evidence of the reversal of dissolution in each of the physical, moral, and mental processes where it was held to occur. But while this rhetoric invoked the power of objective proof, it was also bound up with the discourse's insistence on changing viewers' perception of the poor and the inebriated. The viewer could take from these transformations not just evidence of real change, but a new way of looking at the as-yet unchanged. From today's perspective, this conflation of perception and reality would seem to demystify the before-and-after change, making of it nothing more than a combination of the viewer's sympathies and the simple beneficial effects of food, shelter, and hygiene for a destitute person. But for the missionaries and their supporters, in the context of deterministic social theories and hardened attitudes toward social identity, these two types of change—of the viewer as well as of the viewed—were each, and especially together, miraculous. It was a literature that took the powerful new cultural emphasis on the consumption of real information, and put it into the service of a traditional, allegorical mode of reading religious narrative.[44]

Revisiting the problem of McAuley's physiognomy helps make sense of this fusion. Helen Stuart Campbell, a leading reformer and pioneer in home economics, opens the volume that established her reputation as a social analyst, *The Problem of the Poor*, with an account of her first foray into the slums, when she was confronted by the sight of Jerry's "repellant" features (fig. 2). "Nature had not lied," she remembers thinking, but in a tone that suggests

JERRY McAULEY

Founder of the Old McAuley Water Street Mission, 1872
Cremorne McAuley Mission, 1882

FIGURE 2. Jerry McAuley and the face reclaimed from physiognomic doom. This photograph was published in biographies of McAuley beginning in 1885. This version is taken from *Jerry McAuley: An Apostle to the Lost* (1907).

she still believes that his face and body are evidence of the inevitability of his first, and more "natural," fate: "This retreating forehead, small and deep-set eyes, heavy, projecting nose and wide mouth, indicated, and could indicate nothing but the bully and the ruffian. The tall, firmly-knit frame, long arms and great hands showed immense brute strength, and the keen and quiet observation appeared that of some powerful animal speculating on possible danger and ready to annihilate an enemy. The strongest face in the room was this—a man who, as a Fourth Ward rough, must have been incredibly reckless, fierce, brutal." Campbell, a close friend and mentor to both Jane Addams and Charlotte Perkins Gilman, had been taught that this cruel face and animalistic body were essential facts behind the "problem of the poor."[45]

In her account of coming to know the mission world, Campbell's understanding of that problem is transformed by further scrutiny of McAuley's face. Not only assumptions about his character, but her very perception of his face, changes when she sees McAuley coaxing confessions and conversions out of penitent inebriates. Despite the detail of the previous description, she soon claims only to have seen his "full face" for the first time as he addressed would-be converts who had just confessed their sins. "No tenderer soul ever looked upon human pain than that which now shone in his eyes and glorified the coarse features," she concludes, seeing "a look more convincing of the power at work there than years of argument could have been."[46] If God could make a man with a bad face good, he could also turn a bad face into a good one. "The Lord wipes out the lines," Maria McAuley told a new visitor who wondered why, if the converts had been so bad, their wicked pasts were not inscribed on their faces. "I watch them going out week by week," she reported. "You'd think they never could. Deep seams in their faces, and yet they all go."[47] Both McAuley's surface/depth appearance and this action of grace as a miraculous skin treatment defy the conventional logic of visible moral character.

This visual spectacle in mission culture both materially and spiritually reproduced the conversion it was based on, in scenes whose effect on the senses transcended reason and proved that God was using the coarsest material of humanity for the highest good. This formula took the logic by which conversion apotheosizes subjective experience, as figured in the supernatural effects of the narratives, and applied it to the position of the witness, and by extension, to the reader. Ultimately, this discourse rendered any location, from mission hall to printed page, a vehicle for the kind of power the revivalist Charles Grandison Finney called "faith as a present experience."[48] By narrating her witness to McAuley's transformation and the changes it made

THE OLD COLONEL.

THE NEW COLONEL.

FIGURE 3: The Old Colonel and the New Colonel, a before-and-after combination published in Samuel H. Hadley's *Down in Water Street* (1902).

in her, Campbell puts herself in the position of the reader as she negotiates the passage from theories of fixed character and natural social hierarchy to universally available narratives of transformation.

For readers who could not visit the missions in person to see such miraculous changes, before-and-after pictures offered the plainest evidence, and they encouraged readers to experience similar transformations in their sympathies. This form could account for both the ascension of the underclass brute, and the return of the man fallen from the middle class. A man nicknamed "the Colonel" embodies the latter. A drawing titled "The Old Colonel," of a tattered and emaciated skid-row bum holding out his hat for alms, is juxtaposed with a photograph titled "The New Colonel," showing a neatly coiffed, beefy man of middle age in a smart suit (fig. 3).[49] The difference indicates a complete restoration of respectability. The social effect is emphasized by the contrast between drawing and photograph, as if the Colonel had passed from caricature into humanity, and religion itself had passed from the pre-modern, exclusionary theology to a new evangelical technology available to all. The fact that the "before" images were drawn in retrospect (by necessity, there having been no reason to photograph an unredeemed drunkard) makes concrete the way conversion narrates inebriety from the "after" or saved perspective.

This disjunction in the media calls attention to the way that patrons and

DELIA

One of the Converts of the " Door of Hope," founded by
Mrs. Whittemore

FIGURE 4. Delia Loughlin, "the bluebird of Mulberrry Bend," presented in before-and-after fashion in *Jerry McAuley: An Apostle to the Lost* (1907).

publishers controlled the rendering of the narrative, a phenomenon more visible in regard to women converts who, unlike their male counterparts, rarely rose to positions of leadership. One telling before and after sequence is that of Delia Loughlin, a convert at a women's mission who achieved some renown as "the former bluebird of Mulberry Bend."[50] In her photograph, Delia (the Water Street books supply no surname) is a fair-skinned woman of immaculate appearance and posture (fig. 4). She holds an open Bible and wears small crucifixes at her neck and waist, as well as a modest hat, a small purse, and a bracelet. Her face is serene, and is tilted slightly sideways and upward, as she looks into the distance as if to God. Inset, at the upper left, is a drawing of Delia before her conversion. Her hair is unkempt and uncovered, her face is tanned or dirty, and she looks directly at the viewer with bold, beady eyes and a saucy grin. What is most obvious in her rendering as an inebriate and a prostitute is that she simply failed to meet the criteria of Victorian-era womanhood. The photograph, by contrast, describes a woman of purity, sweetness, and some material comfort.[51] In Loughlin's conversion narrative, the illustration is captioned, "The work of grace upon a human face within a year."[52]

Loughlin's "after" portrait reflects the different demands placed on women converts than on men. Unlike men, in whom sin could be understood to go all the way down, and grace come entirely from without, it was typical to find in female converts evidence of a deep-seated goodness that lay beneath the faults and external influences that had led to sin. Maria McAuley, for example, referred to a life of sin that included drunkenness, unsanctified common-law marriage, and, it is suggested, prostitution. But none dared render a "before" image of so revered a figure, and little trace of her old life is ever said to linger in her appearance. In contrast to Helen Campbell's first impression of Jerry, the reformer describes Maria as a "sweet, motherly looking woman" with a "face and figure . . . full of strength and helpfulness," and "deep gray eyes . . . wide with feeling." After Jerry's death, Bradford Gilbert, a prominent architect and the missionary who brought John Jaeger to his conversion at Water Street, married Maria.[53]

But women's sexuality remained a thornier type of sin than any other, and most of the time, as with Maria, it was only alluded to indirectly under the cover-all state of inebriety. Unlike the men's missions, at the women's "homes" that sprang up soon afterward, distinctions were maintained between women who were given over to sin and those who were only beginning to stray from the righteous path, with a strong suggestion that virginity was the distinguishing factor. Despite this double standard, the reformers embraced the possibility of redemption for sexually degraded women, and held it up as the highest example of God's grace. Nellie Conroy was famous in such circles for epitomizing both the possibility and the rarity of women returning from the lowest depths. Henry Gibbud published an anti-prostitution tract around his discovery of Conroy, drunk and in the clutches of her "burly Negro" pimp, exhibiting all the signs of the deepest state of sin: "a dirty calico dress was all the clothing she had on, and that was not in condition to cover her nakedness." Not only did Conroy convert, but she became a sought-after evangelical speaker until her death two years later, at the age of twenty-nine, after bearing with Christlike resignation a painful illness that was the "harvest" of her life of sin.[54] The same fate befell (and apotheosized) Delia Loughlin. That God would transform these "despised Magdalenes" was evidence of the unlimited reach of His grace, but the language called on to illustrate such sin's depth, along with the implied rarity of such conversions, underscores the way gender distorted the spiritual logic of the discourse.

The Politics of Full Personhood

In each of these ways that the drunkard's conversion described and accomplished social rehabilitation, it not only remade a subject but also transformed that subject's relationship to the social order. Unacceptable origins and even traits became acceptable by changing from versions that threatened the public body to versions that reaffirmed it. McAuley did not cease to be Irish, but he ceased to be drunk, Catholic, and untrustworthy. Jaeger remained a long-bearded, heavily accented German, but he ceased to be a beer-swilling, hot-tempered, monoglot anarchist. Nellie Conroy remained an ex-prostitute who would die young for her sins, but she defeated Hell's Gate and the life it represented in a way no reformer could, even as her beatification came through the Florence Night Mission and the reformist lecture circuit. Drunkards' conversions brought outcasts into the body of the knowable public in ways that broadened it and, in doing so, sentimentally legitimized it, by making it the vehicle of the grace of God. We can see the obvious limitations of this social saving grace, in a lack of concern for the soul and the drinking habits of Conroy's "negro pimp." But within the bounds of its social vision, missionary conversion in this manner did cultural work that charity could not, by having the poor and the disreputable not only assent to the legitimacy of social authority in their self-narratives, but also revise its rules while doing so.[55]

Submission to authority is indeed a central trope of the drunkard's conversion narrative. With the infusion of the holy spirit into their bodies, subjects of these stories also internalize a public discipline that causes them to have themselves put in jail, to become model prisoners, and to glory in achieving acceptance by polite society after lives of vice and crime. Prominent gestures include kneeling, falling down, and lying prostrate, and keywords include "conviction," "submission," and "resignation." These factors suggest an exceptionally regulatory genre.

But despite these signs of obeisance, what the drunkard's conversion authorizes is not just entry into an established order but an intervention in it. The convert does not simply adopt a ready-made social identity, but helps to construct a new template. He does not speak himself into the good graces of a monolithic authority, but proposes, authorized by his new or renewed sanctification, a more graceful one. The main cultural work of the drunkard's conversion, in both the narratives themselves and in their framing by reformers, is to negotiate this change. Skeptical interpretations of conversion assume that it affirms a fixed authority at any given time.[56] The first-person subjects of drunkard's conversion are not only speaking their new selves into being but speaking a reformed social order into being. This reform, as a joint project of the converts and their patrons, was a formative and essential feature of the narratives, and is what gave the genre its more lasting role as a template for narrating transformational change.

As institutions, the rescue missions implemented their universalist theology in a way that explicitly did battle against the notion of the undeserving or vicious poor, just as McAuley himself was held up as proof against physiognomic science. Samuel Hadley, at an 1894 conference called "The Ministry of the Holy Spirit," inveighed against the division of the poor into good and bad, challenging his audience of churchmen and women, "If you have worthy poor, keep them to yourselves." Though the vast majority of visitors to his mission want nothing more than "to beat me out of a night's lodging or a ten-cent piece," he confessed, it is only by accepting them on these terms that any can be saved from their earthly suffering and their eternal perdition.[57] Fifteen years later, the journalist Ray Stannard Baker adjudged that most of those who stood to make public prayers at a nightly meeting on Water Street were "impostors, who come merely on the chance of getting a bed-ticket, or a dime, or a sandwich." But it was from among these same men, he continued, that the deepest conversions were won, on the strength of the limitless tolerance and even love shown to them. "Someone exercised great patience with me twenty years ago when I came in here a hopeless drunkard," explained the superintendent who had succeeded Hadley, "or I should not be here to-night."[58]

In their narratives, the subjects of the drunkard's conversion strategically and explicitly resisted the aspects of a social hierarchy that would disrespect either them or their former selves, whom they identified with still-suffering sinners. Drunkards' conversions remained closely bound to the mission movement: it was paramount that converts remain in the settings of their low points and understand everyone there to be capable of goodness and admiration through God's grace. The converts who rose to positions of real leadership in not only the missions but also the broader evangelical movement resisted patronizing control, and took care in their own narratives to head off rhetoric of charitable condescension or natural inferiority.

The effect of these narratives was not primarily to preserve class relations, but to alter them to allow for social recognition, and to qualify their significance in assertions of spiritual equality. This egalitarianism was not just a promise of the afterlife, but was brought to life on earth, especially by the converts who rose to leadership positions in the rescue mission movement. John Allen, "the wickedest man in New York," had attributed the failure of the 1868 evangelical experiment on Water Street to the missionaries' lack of respect for the fallen women of the saloons, who had been prayed over using humiliating monikers such as "scarlet whores of babylon." He told a newspaper that his "girls . . . have feelings which those missionaries should have respected but did not."[59] However disingenuous Allen was (he was essentially their pimp), in the literature of the subsequent rescue mission era very little of such callous rhetoric is seen. McAuley's wife, Maria, a leading mission superintendent after his death, was a former prostitute herself, a fact alluded to unambiguously but with delicacy, and always couched with admiration. Missionaries in rescue mission circles made it a point, as far as they could from within the bounds of their worldview, to respect the dignity and personal feelings of their targets. McAuley actively promoted this change by aggressively policing the attitudes and language of visiting reformers, clergy, and upper-class spectators.

McAuley's demand for respect was both a statement of evangelical theology and a convention that illustrates how the site of transformation in rescue mission discourse expanded to include the middle-class observer. McAuley made his own distinction among members of the upper classes, between those who demonstrated a commitment to the doctrine of spiritual equality (both in their own sense of sin as well as their acceptance of others' salvation) and those who paid it lip-service but failed to acknowledge their own sinfulness. Beset by a constant stream of well-intended reformers and curious observers, McAuley was famous for retaining one kernel of intolerance: he despised pious hypocrites and mocked the "kid-gloved sinners" and "dainty professors" who allowed degrees of sin to mark social distance.[60] The only thing he asked of upper-class visitors to his services was that they pray for God to save them from their own depths of sin, rather than praying out of pity for the poor wretches they saw around them. In this way the reactionary quality of evangelical religion—it personalizes sin and minimizes environmental pressures or systemic failings—also performed a leveling function. McAuley embraced interclass sympathy as the fuel of evangelism, but he would not suffer condescension. Everyone had to be self-aware and ready to be changed.

This dynamic of transformation that swept up both convert and observer, narrator and reader, poor and middle-class, played out in the rescue missions' influence. The newly universal evangelicalism and practical salvation of rescue mission culture negotiated the transition from theories of fixed character and natural social hierarchy to widely available narratives of transformation, a key process in the popular emergence of therapeutic culture. When set in historical perspective against the more explicit propositions of the Social Gospel, missionary evangelism was theologically conservative. But in the views of many reformers, the reality of conversion discourse seemed a radical alternative to the theories of fixed identity that justified an increasingly stratified social order. In one elite response to this demand for change, Helen Campbell premised her progressive social theory on the defeat of conventional wisdom and the redemption of class difference that she experienced at Water Street. Campbell and others applied this logic of subjectively experienced transformation that they witnessed in Water Street to their own middle-class self-concepts and based their commitments to particular visions of social reform on their resulting conversion experiences. The following chapters explore such cases, in which the drunkard's conversion was taken out of the slums and used as a vehicle of cultural politics in the early twentieth century.

2

"What a Radical Found in Water Street"

The saloon furnishes material to be saved faster than the settlement
or residence or Rescue Mission work can save it.

　—Charles Sheldon, *In His Steps: "What Would Jesus Do?"* (1897)

The individualistic gospel has . . . not given us an adequate understanding of the sinfulness of the social order and its share in the
sins of all individuals within it.

　—Walter Rauschenbusch, *Christianity and the Social Crisis* (1907)

T
HE CONVERSION NARRATIVES TOLD BY drunkards in the rescue
missions of Lower Manhattan were popular stories in the Protestant
America of the late nineteenth and early twentieth centuries. In addition to
appealing to religious sentiments, they showed middle-class society how it
could affirm its own righteousness by redeeming the outcast and even the
degenerate, and in doing so safely open its ranks to a broader social spectrum
in a time of economic and demographic transformation. In this manner, the
sanctification of formerly drunken men and women did some needed cultural work in Gilded Age America, helping imaginatively to make sense of
how once-untouchable people (whether drunkards or merely immigrants)
could now be members of the working and middle classes.

But this was not the whole story of the drunkard's conversion in this era,
nor even perhaps its most historically significant role. Its more lasting influence did not come in terms of how the middle class viewed the poor and the
addicted, whether with these new sympathies or, as some have suspected,
with voyeuristic fascination. The drunkard's conversion had a second life in
the ways that social reformers and intellectuals in the Progressive Era used it
as a model, both for overcoming their own spiritual crises and for imagining

solutions to the problems afflicting society as a whole. The stories that non-alcoholic writers told about the influence of drunkards' conversions on their lives and ideas played an important role in reform culture and eventually helped make the tropes of addiction and conversion central to both popular psychology and political rhetoric. In personal, political, and scholarly interpretations of the drunkard's conversion, post-religious recovery narrative was taking shape as a method of communicating simultaneously Americans' deepest private experiences and their most pressing public concerns.

In an evangelical culture not yet associated with reactionary fundamentalism, one of the most revealing examples of this influence can be found in the writings of a pioneer of feminist economics. Helen Stuart Campbell, the domestic reformer who documented the work of the McAuleys in New York, understood and publicized her experience there as a secular conversion, one that both launched her professional reform career and also formed the foundation of her progressive ideas about personal and societal transformation. This chapter examines closely the role of the drunkard's conversion in Campbell's thought, situating it among contemporaries in both Social Gospel Christianity and secular progressive activism. Among the former, Charles M. Sheldon and Ray Stannard Baker followed Campbell's lead in looking to the rescue missions for the spiritual passion and new social relationships necessary to imagining Christianity playing a leadership role in the era of progressive reform. Among the latter group, Jane Addams and Charlotte Perkins Gilman, Campbell's own friends and protégées, adopted the dynamics of personal-political transformation Campbell had established in her work at the rescue missions and beyond. Examining Campbell's evolving theory of "conversion" sheds light on the deep structures by which both religious and secular progressives came to believe in, and practice, forms of activism at once more radical and more practical than they had been taught to believe were possible.

The drunkard's conversion narrative was the source of an essential trope in progressive thinking, illustrating (and proving possible) the inner, moral revolution needed to uproot and displace the deeply ingrained habits of mind and body sown by the seemingly intractable forces of the modern world. The material changes brought on by industrialization, urbanization, and immigration, under the pressure of the long-lasting economic stagnation that commenced in 1873, created the conditions under which drunkards like McAuley and Hadley had enacted the language of eternal salvation in newly physical and social ways. These same conditions brought Campbell and her ilk to the slums, where they experienced the secular revelation that they could not hope to alleviate these crises without changing the foundations of their own existing social assumptions. Effective material change would require a dramatic decentering of their own self-concepts, in a degree made manifest by the successful conversions of compulsive drinkers. Campbell's reform career was predicated on the evidence of gospel temperance culture that anyone, even the most far-gone in involuntary behavior, could successfully resuscitate his or her will and imagine a new fate in the face of the great forces shaping individuals and societies alike.

Campbell was not alone among progressives and radicals in taking both inspiration and ideation from the rescue missions, although she may have been the most explicit about it. But Campbell is barely remembered, cited far down and without elaboration on lists of social reformers, slum documentarians, and proto-feminists. Further, the dynamic her work makes visible in other, better known Christian and progressive activists has been obscured by a couple of critical and historical conceits: first, that immersive slum writing was largely a reactionary effort to regulate the behaviors and the voices of the poor; and second, that, partly for that very reason, the systemic Social Gospel dislodged the soul-focused slum mission as the state of the art in liberal Christian social thought. Against the skeptical interpretation of slum reportage, I will argue that Campbell's interest in drunkards' conversions was more focused on uprooting the mental and material habits of the middle class than it was with pacifying the poor. Against the historical assumption that rescue missions faded from the minds of liberal religious thinkers, I show that Campbell, with others, presented her systemic vision of Christian reform as a *product* of the rescue missions' innovations in democratic leadership and interclass relationships. Campbell and her ilk reveal a dynamic between revival and reform that is more nuanced than a succession narrative. Sheldon the popular novelist, Baker the muckraking reporter, Addams the settlement house innovator, and Gilman the unrelenting analyst all built their progressive visions of foundational transformation on some version of the ethic of personal conversion.

In these progressive interpretations of drunkards' conversions, addiction recovery was beginning to take on its modern role conceptualizing escape from the grip that all manner of material dependencies and environmental triggers hold on people's mental and social habits. As a little-recognized aspect of progressive thought, but a major component of progressive culture, conversion stories were adapted to secular forms as ways to describe liberating oneself from these habits, and re-grounding oneself in higher ideals, ideals that would in turn redirect those material forces to make a better society.

Independently of the temperance movement and its specific political goals, the language of personal moral and spiritual reform was playing a newly secular role as a way of talking about ideology and social change. Examining this progressive discourse is essential to understanding the formative period of addiction-conversion narrative, before recovery became its own arena of discourse, ostensibly isolated from ideological controversy.

"Literal Regeneration"

If it was the poor drunkards' material and social needs that shaped the conversion narratives told at the rescue missions, it was the emotional longings of their sober, middle-class admirers that helped make addiction recovery a lasting model for deeply personalized ideological transformation. The earliest hints of this role come in the attentions that the missionaries, reformers, journalists, and other observers paid to drunkards' conversions. Their presence at the missions and in the stories was necessary to the testimonies' novel presentations of interclass sympathy, which provided much of the social proof and sentimental effect of the conversions on display. Leaders among the converted drunkards themselves understood the significance of their guests' responses, because they counted on them to produce moral and financial support. The converted drunkards only came to wide public attention after these emissaries from polite society entered the slums, to change themselves as much as to change the poor.

Rescue mission culture demanded that observers' responses be self-referential, rather than charitable or sympathetic. This injunction drew on the theology of Original Sin and the evangelical logic of revival, the purpose of which was to make observers into participants. McAuley and Hadley described two kinds of effects mission services had on well-to-do visitors. "Hypocrites," as McAuley called them, exhibited a condescending preoccupation with the social division across which they gazed, offering high-toned prayers for the souls of everyone there but themselves.[1] Those who were properly attuned to what it meant to witness God's grace, on the other hand, often were "broken down" themselves by it, instantly identifying their own sins (including that very class condescension) as being just as grave as the vices of the "vulgar and vicious" people around them.[2] Some of these observers became participants, experiencing conversions of their own, or feeling their salvation reconsecrated.[3] Socialite Emma Whittemore reported that "God got such possession" of her and her husband during their first time at Water Street "that we were both held in painful silence as we were convicted of our useless lives. We no longer felt superior to the 'poor creatures' . . . but actually hung our heads in shame."[4] As much as they could, the Whittemores gave up the philanthropic attitude and took up full-time missionary work themselves. Their "convictions" show how concern with one's own spiritual state was considered more noble—not only more pious but more honest and egalitarian—than concern for others, compassion for the poor, or the desire to solve social problems. But this spiritual self-interest could only be fulfilled in the selfless pursuit of those latter goals. In the cases that would have the widest impact, this imperative gave rise to careers in secular reform.

Progressive reformers who wrote directly about the rescue missions not only embraced this ethos as spiritually righteous, they also saw in it the subjective deep structure of their own burgeoning ideas about social transformation. The career of Helen Stuart Campbell provides the most explicit example of this pattern of thought and experience, in which the revelatory class dynamics of missionary reform work offered intimations of a wider societal redemption. Born in 1839, Campbell was a prolific author of children's fiction, novels, biographies, domestic science manuals, slum exposés, newspaper and magazine articles, and scholarly monographs. She was a close associate of leading Social Gospel thinkers, progressive economists, feminists, and socialists. She was a pioneer of political economics, in her efforts to document and theorize women's working lives.

Campbell's life was punctuated by several major upheavals. After publishing children's fiction as a young woman, she married an army surgeon who spent time away first during the Civil War and then as a federal Indian agent in the West. Campbell was divorced in her early thirties, after which followed two highly productive decades of study, writing, and travel. In 1893, after she read a paper at a world labor congress in Chicago, Richard T. Ely, an economist at the University of Wisconsin, recruited her to lecture on "household economics." The following year, a newly Populist-dominated board of regents at Kansas State Agricultural College hired her as a full professor of domestic science, a post in which she lasted only a year. A 1909 history of the college attributed her brief tenure there to a teaching schedule that crowded out her writing time, and also to "distasteful political conditions" and "serious objections made by her students and their mothers about some of her teachings."[5] She spent her final two decades continuing to mentor women's activists, but in relative personal obscurity. In her own writing, among all of these often abrupt transitions, Campbell focused on a single personal and professional transformation that took her from earnest but directionless idealist to systemic progressive thinker. It occurred at the McAuley mission on Water Street.[6]

Campbell's personal awakening at the rescue mission is the key to understanding the broad arc of her densely productive career. Her early fiction and biography often focused on women undergoing various states of duress. After her divorce in the early 1870s she became active in the home economics movement, cofounding a teaching kitchen in Washington, DC. Her book *The Easiest Way in Housekeeping and Cooking* (1881) is still in print. In the meantime, her adult fiction began to receive some notice. These efforts culminated in a position as both literary and "household" editor for Albion Tourgée's *Our Continent* magazine in the early 1880s. During this middle phase of her life, her attention was increasingly drawn to the more dire challenges facing working-class women in the industrial city. She began to extend her expertise in writing about domestic matters into the realm of social science, in detailed reportage and analysis of the economics of women's lives and the role these lives played in the wider economies. The first major work that resulted from this turn, and that launched her reputation as a social analyst, was *The Problem of the Poor* (1882), a narrative account of missionary social work in lower Manhattan that centered around the McAuleys. She built from this baseline of urban investigation a series of increasingly analytical studies, including *Prisoners of Poverty: Women Wage Workers, Their Trades, and Their Lives* (1887), and *Women Wage-Earners* (1891), which was recognized with a prize from the American Economic Association. Her 1895 lectures at Wisconsin were published two years later as *Household Economics,* a topic she described as "the connecting link between the physical economics of the individual and the social economics of the state."[7] This structure—the tracery of forces binding the individual's subjective experience to the most powerful institutions—was central to all of Campbell's analytical thinking, and it first took shape in her discovery of the rescue missions.

It was in these widely read reports on the slums that she established her reputation as a serious social critic, thus launching the second phase of her career, as a pioneer of women's economics. For Campbell, bearing witness to conversions on Water Street constituted her own arrival at a coherent belief in social progress and the personal sense of purpose to pursue it. In her writings she does not make this comparison lightly, but carefully develops it through the relationship she describes building up with the McAuleys and the access to insider knowledge they afford her. It was not an intellectual matter of finding new data and coming to hold new beliefs, though that was important, but

"ALL MY DRINKS 3 CENTS." AN EVERY-
DAY SCENE NEAR THE WATER STREET

FIGURE 5. A "problem of the poor" and the prelude to the drunkard's conversion. "All
my drinks three cents" appears in Helen Stuart Campbell, *Darkness and Daylight; or,
Lights and Shadows of New York Life: A Woman's Story of Gospel, Temperance, Mission,
and Rescue Work "In His Name"* (1892). The text surrounding the image tells the story of
Jerry McAuley's conversion.

firstly of *experiencing* one's place in society in a completely new way, something Jane Addams called a "subjective necessity" for middle-class youth. It was a secular conversion experience, one that would become an essential autobiographical convention for social activists in the twentieth century.

Drunkards' conversions thus served two main purposes in this key period of Campbell's work, which together illuminate anew the relationship between the rescue missions, the Social Gospel, progressive reform, and even radical activism. First, the scenes she witnessed at the rescue missions inspired her own transformation from edifying novelist and small-bore domestic science expert to big-picture economics scholar and social activist. Second, the drunkards' transformations supplied a concrete model on which she based her theory of the necessary condition for any broad-scale change: not just the standard progressive policies of cleaning up systemic corruption and educating the poor, but a subjective transformation in the way the middle class looked at its own habits of consumption and its economic role in the social order.

Campbell's first serious work of reform, *The Problem of the Poor,* offers deep insight into the intertwined personal, institutional, and ideological factors drawing women, especially, to social work early in the Progressive Era. In its first-person narrative of exploration and discovery, the book illuminates the way these dynamics took shape in relationships between reformers and reformed, as the subjects of drunkards' conversions provided models of change for the subjects of progressive political awakening. In it, Campbell predicates her very ability to witness the human truth of poverty on her discovery of Jerry and Maria McAuley and their missions (fig. 5).

Campbell frames the "problem of the poor" not just as one of poverty, but also as this very lack of vision in the middle class, one she elevates to the status of being the spiritual-intellectual crisis of the modern world. She opens the book by telling of the unhappiness that an unapplied and ultimately ungrounded "radicalism" had brought her to, in which she had no answers to the assaults of either Christian conservatives or secular radicals, and worse, no clear sense of purpose in her life. It is worth quoting at length from Campbell's introductory chapter, in which she traces the frustrations of reformers with the apparent obstinacy of social problems to the loss of metaphysical foundations in the modern world. As a preface to her discovery of the rescue missions, it illustrates a central finding of this book: that influential reformers and intellectuals embraced the drunkard's conversion because it modeled an ideal answer to their perception of modernity as a state of crisis running from the biggest social structures down to the deepest subjective feelings:

From one point of view life had broadened and deepened with each added year. Fresh possibilities of work, of knowledge, of happiness were discerned, yet through all, mastering the strongest hope, came the sense of limitation, the weariness of struggle; the doubt and question and sadness, underlying all the growth of this strange and wonderful Nineteenth Century. One by one, old landmarks had vanished. Speculation came, with no answer to its questions. One *ism* after another presented itself, seeming at first to meet the demand for truth; then paling and fading away under the light of investigation. Church people were stupidly intolerant; Radicals equally so. Where I belonged had been a mystery to myself. With the former, I was counted radical and destructive; with the latter, conservative and willfully blind to progress. Thus in spite of most active efforts to get down and stay somewhere, I was constantly ordered back to the fence dividing these two parties, neither of which allowed that I had any rights which either was bound to respect.

There are many in precisely this position: a few who admit it; a larger number who keep silence, but wonder painfully why life must be one long question, the asking of which brings down only a storm of indignation from one side, a half-contemptuous reception on the other. Radicalism takes in untold numbers, whose strong devotional natures are never satisfied with the amount and character of the worship permitted them, and who work with feverish energy in all schemes for regenerating humanity. Yet to bind themselves in old formulas, in dead doctrines, is impossible. The Christ shown them in the average church is not what they want; and when 'honest doubt' is met with horror, they fling off all old beliefs, cease to search for the soul of truth in the ancient forms, and persuade themselves that the only solution lies in utter rejection.

To this army I belonged; but the species of Brahminism I had tried to adopt neither soothed nor satisfied me. The sad condition of large classes in this country, who are literally 'conceived in sin and shapen in iniquity,' and whom the gospel of development scarcely promises to reach, made my own personal pleasure and progress seem almost a wicked thing, if they could not somehow share in it.

"I give it up," I said one day to a friend, who was always too actively at work to have time for speculation. "'Ethical Culture' may reach the middle class, in fact has reached many, but over the masses I despair. There is no regenerating power in them to draw upon. Badly born, badly fed and clothed and housed; vileness is their beginning and ending. There is no salvation for these poor wretches. The world is out of joint."[8]

Her interlocutor, with the bemused patience of one who has known this crisis but has been vouchsafed its solution, insists Campbell come to Water Street to watch a service.

And at the McAuleys' mission, she does indeed find the answer to her dilemma, personal and intellectual. The evidence on display in its conversion testimonies that the poor, even the dissolute, really can change, "changes" Campbell, philosophically by blasting away her pessimism, and psychologically by opening up for her an outlet for idealistic labors. Through them she comes to believe in "a literal regeneration" that would soon be a matter of "personal application" (23). In this framing narrative, the larger structure as well as the explicit content of Campbell's book tells the story of what secular reformers learned from the drunkard's conversion. It was the logic of mutual transformation: facilitating and documenting lasting conversions constitutes the reformer's own transformation from ineffectual idealist to purpose-driven activist.

The drunkard's conversion modeled for Campbell a dislodging of the self-referential perspective, a decentering she came to believe would be necessary for any reform movement led by the upper and middle classes. From this point of view, as in the stories of the converts, the narratives' relevant service to the existing social structure was not confirmation but intervention. Campbell saw the changes she witnessed in the missions as directly undermining the assumptions of mainstream liberal Protestantism. Throughout *The Problem of the Poor,* she highlights moments that challenge the kind of philanthropic liberalism in which the deficiencies of the poor are permanent and susceptible only to amelioration, not reformation. She concludes one account of moving conversion testimony by illiterate, alcoholic immigrants by urging, "Whatever the liberal thinker might feel as to the limitations of [the converts'] faith, however disappointed that certain theories . . . were beyond their grasp of comprehension, the fact remained that absolute reformation in bodily and mental habits had taken place, and was working powerfully toward a change in all about them" (23–24). Campbell used the physical, mental, and social scope of the word "habit" to present this discourse as culturally transformational. If a reader, doubtful of the mental and moral capacities of the poor, could perceive that escape from the mind-body-spirit bondage of alcoholic compulsion was possible, then this concession could be expanded to the larger realm of "mental habits" and conscious interiority, thus transforming "all about them," from slum neighbor to middle-class reader.

This mutuality was not merely structural, but was expressed in meaningful affect and interaction. Having had a change of heart on her first night at the mission, it was the subsequent relationships Campbell developed with the McAuleys that made possible the slum reportage that fills the body of the book, and which completed the arc of its framing identity crisis. She grounds these relationships in her respect for her new friends' own personal revolutions and for the effectiveness of their work among notoriously unreachable populations. Intimacy across class and gender lines was the sentimental currency of the drunkard's conversion, depicting the miracle of spiritual equality on the canvas of social difference. But such closeness was also the fuel for the middle- and upper-class reformers who found themselves changed by the overwhelming sentiments they felt at Water Street. The McAuleys do not appear as props in the drama of Campbell's self-discovery, but rather as exemplary reform workers, practical theorists of social change, and, in a limited sense, social equals, people Campbell treats with deference in their own milieu.

Campbell attests to an affection for McAuley that complements McAuley's experience of sympathetic concern by women missionaries. She suggests something beyond awe at God's work when she pays homage to this "tall man, whose face had become beautiful to me in the months I had known it" (67–68). When she realizes that McAuley grew up in the same unspeakable dens she was witnessing in her first tour of tenement interiors, her esteem grows so far as to outstrip language, "for written words can never hold the pathos, the tenderness, the strength, the quick-glancing Irish humor, which have made him the power that he is [and] render him the most wonderful of apostles to the roughs" (24). (She anticipates the benefactor at McAuley's funeral who said he "was strong as a lion for courage, yet had a heart gentle as a woman's.")[9] McAuley is not an "apostle," strictly speaking, to Campbell, who does not claim to need religious salvation. But he becomes, through his own redemption and its fruits, an agent of her life's transformation.

Though Campbell launched her work from the evangelical missions and presented religious conviction as capable of moving people more deeply than the humanistic "ethical culture" movement, her own story of transformation was not a Christian conversion. Despite her respect for the conversions of the poor and her claim to have learned both a purer and more real form of religion from them, she did not adopt the rhetoric of literal salvation she witnessed at the missions. Though Campbell expressed no doubt as to the conversions' divine source, her own transformation story, like those of many other progressives, was not one of eternal salvation but of philosophical revelation and psychological integration. Her introduction to the social work based in the rescue missions of Manhattan solved an identity crisis in her life by giving her a confident sense of purpose and possibility while simultaneously leading her to a new, integrated analysis of social issues. (The final chapters of *The Problem of the Poor* describe projects of teaching domestic science to tenement women with drinking husbands, embodying a career-long interest in uniting the fields of home and academic economics.) If Campbell's transformation was inspired by drunkards' conversions, it was itself a model for secular redemption through immersive social work.

Campbell structured her socioeconomic analysis by this same logic, arguing that progress could only come for the poor when her middle-class readers were transformed at a depth comparable to that of religious conversion. She first tried to change mainstream views of vice among the poor using her long-established talent for fiction. In 1885–86 her novel *Mrs. Herndon's Income* was published serially in Lyman Abbott's Social Gospel journal, *Christian Union*. The novel narrativized "the impossibility of living decently on the poor wages being paid women workers," and it presented a range of responses, from institutional charity to socialist revolution to Jerry McAuley and his mission, which appear in the fiction as themselves. While she leaves it for the reader to decide what conclusions to draw, the unambiguous problem of the novel is well-to-do women's "sheer ignorance of how their money is brought in." Its reception was lukewarm, both critically and politically, with at least one liberal writer expressing relief that "the key to the situation is in rousing the rich, not exciting the poor."[10] Campbell wanted better conditions for women workers, but in this period, her strategy increasingly sought to turn the target of reform writing—the beliefs of the middle class—into the primary site of conversion itself.

This direction in her thinking came to analytical fruition in *Prisoners of Poverty* (1887). Begun as a series of columns commissioned by the *New York Tribune* in 1886, *Prisoners of Poverty* marked Campbell's transition from first-person reporter into an analyst of labor and consumption on a par with the academic economists of the day. In it, she distanced herself from religious solutions to the material problems facing women working in the needle trades and department stores. Admitting that the missions and their conversions were not practical answers to poverty, she offered new prescriptions for reform: vocational education and cooperatively owned workplaces. But in the text it is clear that gaining her readers' moral assent to supporting such programs would not be enough. The problem ran deeper than that.

Middle-class families' spending habits, indeed their household economies, were dependent on the existing system. To achieve real change, she called on the post-Christian concept of "natural spiritual truth" as a necessary guiding force for reform.[11]

The way she put this point to her readers came straight from rescue mission culture: they had to reform their own "souls." In working among the poor, she wrote, "I discover not alone their ignorance and stupidity and grossness and wilfull blindness, but behind it an ignorance and stupidity no less dense upon which theirs is founded, —our own." The original sin, she explained, is the consumer mindset of the middle class, in which material possessions represent the highest ideals, but their manual production is despised. Salvation from this sin is society's only hope at redemption: "No church, no mission, no improved home, no guild or any other form of mitigation means anything till the whole system of thought is reconstructed, and we come to some sense of what the eternal verities really are." She was urging a conversion experience, and if her readers did not seek out such a redemption, she warned, it would come to them, as conversion comes to some drunkards, at the end of a very dark journey, "with whips of scorpions," and the "judgment [that] waits him who has chosen blindness."[12]

This was darkly prophetic language to aim at women for buying their hats thoughtlessly. It suggests religious punishment but also hints at social revolution. Campbell's advice for achieving salvation before such a calamity could occur returns again to the ethos of the rescue mission, urging middle-class observers to think of their own sins and not those of the more obvious sufferers they might be tempted to condescend to: "Ask first, then, not what shall we do for these women, but what shall we do for ourselves? How shall we learn to know what are the real things?"[13] In *Prisoners of Poverty*, the field reportage is structured so as to achieve such transformations, alternating narratives of working women's lives with accounts of well-to-do women shopping for the items the poor women are killing themselves to make. The intended effect was to bring about epiphanies in which women would connect their charitable sympathies with the conditions underlying their own consumerism. She aimed to start a progressive revival movement (fig. 6).

The wide reach of this new social interpretation of conversion is more legible in the context of progressivism's blend of religious, secular, and hybrid systems of thought. Campbell's career reveals the extent to which these realms overlapped, and the speed with which individual institutions, like the liberal church and the programmatic novel, were adapting to new ideas. Campbell's professional networks spanned them. She was published

A STALE-BEER DIVE ON MULBERRY STREET BY DAY.

FIGURE 6. Changing women's spaces. "A stale beer dive on Mulberry Street by day" and "Midnight lunch for street girls after evening service at the Florence Street mission." Engravings taken from photographs, in Helen Stuart Campbell's *Darkness and Daylight* (1892).

frequently by leading lights of the Social Gospel movement, in Lyman Abbott's *Christian Union* and Benjamin Flower's *Arena*. She was mentored into progressive academia at the University of Wisconsin by the economist Richard T. Ely. She was hired by midwestern populists at Kansas State Agricultural College to teach about the connections between home economics and societal economics. She herself mentored, and twice lived with, the secular feminist economist Charlotte Perkins Gilman. She managed a Chicago settlement house under the guidance of Jane Addams. And she was active in the Nationalist clubs inspired by the work of the socialist utopian writer Edward Bellamy. The trajectory of her personal religiosity took her from establishment to liberal Christianity, and then to some form of agnosticism or secular humanism, ultimately ending in the syncretic progressivism of the Baha'i faith.[14]

Rescue Missions and the Social Gospel

With Campbell's writings as a guide, we can more readily identify the ways rescue mission literature influenced both religious and secular reformers. More specifically, it was instrumental in creating a space where religious and secular languages of reform overlapped and even fused into a single rhetoric of personal commitment and transformational change. In its pragmatic focus on the material changes brought about by religious conversion, it forced secular thinkers who were concerned with solving social problems, or with understanding the mind-body connection, to take notice of what evangelists were doing. Through these attentions, its impact went beyond the popularity of its widely reproduced redemption stories. As the locations, character types, and affective appeal of the rescue missions became established in reform culture, drunkards' conversions supplied a narrative template for combining the symbolic resonance of religious allegory with the empirical force of urban realism.

Prior to its influence on secular reform, missionary narrative helped to activate a practical, progressive orientation in Protestant homiletics. Projects of spiritual edification, from church sermon to Sunday School lesson to weekly magazine and monthly book review, displaced doctrinal dispute as the center of Christian discourse in the second half of the nineteenth century.[15] This popular religious culture responded especially to new social and economic conditions, becoming an arena where middle-class morality worked out various ways of understanding industrial-era material inequality. The rescue missions' simultaneous answer to the questions of both temperance and social division made it a compelling source of narrative evidence for these projects of understanding and application.

The rescue mission, in all its material reality and social uncertainty, is at the heart of the most widely published and longest-lasting work of homiletic fiction. *In His Steps: "What Would Jesus Do?"* grew out of a sermon series Charles M. Sheldon gave at his Central Church in Topeka, Kansas, in 1889. The sermons told of ordinary people confronted by ethical dilemmas, learning to ask the still-famous question of the subtitle, and seeing their own lives and the lives of those they touched changed accordingly. They were published serially soon after Sheldon delivered them, consumed eagerly by readers, and widely borrowed and imitated by other pastors. The novel *In His Steps* was born when Sheldon put a number of them together under a framing narrative that fictionalized the real-life growth of the "applied Christianity" movement in American churches. Published in Chicago in 1897, *In His Steps* became an instant and perennial Christian favorite and one of the best selling novels in American history.[16]

In the novel, as in the lives of Campbell and others, rescue mission work overcomes the powerlessness that individual Christian reformers feel in the face of systemic corruption and injustice. A speech by a down-and-out visitor prompts pastor Henry Maxwell and members of his upper-middle-class flock at the First Church in the small midwestern city of Raymond to revivify their dull faith by asking how Jesus would respond to their own ethical dilemmas and moral obligations and committing to act accordingly. Ultimately stymied in these efforts by political and economic realities, they then consider how the question could be applied more systematically through social reform. The most ambitious project that emerges is the reclamation of their city's slum and vice district from control by saloon owners and their political protectors. The socially transformative energies of this process arise in the mutually beneficial redemptions of the elite reformers and the drunkards and prostitutes they seek to save. Rescue mission work is not merely individualistic evangelism, but instead acts as the vehicle that takes Christocentric ethics from the interpersonal to the systemic realms.

Both the structure and content of rescue mission revival, as delineated in the previous chapter, are thus necessary for this Social Gospel movement to occur in Sheldon's novel. These borrowings begin in the exemplary testimony of a poor, homeless man and the presence of an evangelical revival in the city's slum district. As items that come from beyond their own imagination and agency, for the members of the First Church they represent something akin to the movements of the Holy Spirit. First, the shabby stranger appears, and he "changes" Maxwell and members of his church in a class dynamic very similar to that of the rescue missions. Before any real commitment to Social Gospel ideas occurs, the spark of the whole movement is the transformative voice of a socially fallen man. The potentially radical implication is qualified somewhat, in Sheldon's story, by the fact that the tramp is an honest workingman, driven by a relatively recent unemployment to his homeless and penniless condition. But while his own life does not challenge the category of the undeserving poor, in the speech that launches the great change, he denies its significance and implies that it is a rationalization for poverty: "I don't know of any teaching of Jesus that makes one kind of a tramp less worth saving than another," he offers, pointedly, asking the congregation, "Do you?"[17] The stranger introduces the idea of rejecting the social order's moral hierarchy, an innovation at the heart of rescue mission discourse. In Sheldon's novel it becomes practical Christianity's fundamental challenge to the middle class.

The personally transformative experience of slum evangelization is what answers the "What would Jesus do?" question and takes it from the personal to the systemic realm. The circumstance necessary for the First Church members to act on the stranger's jeremiad is the existence of an active revival tent in the Rectangle, the city's neighborhood of tenements and saloons. Church members who give up other personal ambitions to go there and sing, preach, and shelter the undeserving poor are "changed" by the experience in ways that empower them to confront larger political and economic obstacles. The movement expands to Chicago, where a powerful churchman is moved to bear witness, and ultimately provide a job, to an alcoholic man who tries to rob him. The upshot of this last narrative thread is a great battle for this redeemed man's body and soul between the saloon and the mission where he has been embraced and employed. This ongoing contest furnishes further evidence that the political system that protects the saloon is what needs reforming before permanent change can take hold.

So even in this shift toward a more systemic vision of change, the voices of the lowly and the alcoholic, heard in the missions where they seek shelter, remain not just the precursors but the preconditions for a middle-class movement of Social Christianity. The novel presents slum revival as an existing model, with the implication that it does not constitute reform but rather a traditional, soul-by-soul salvation that is inadequate to the new economic and political conditions. The mission provides, nevertheless, a necessary spiritual engine and a social site on which the new Social Gospel activism can take shape. In the church members' first arrival at the Rectangle they find the "energetic" and courageous slum evangelist working side by side with "one of the converts, a heavy-faced man," arranging the chairs for the evening service.[18] There is a suggestion of genuine egalitarianism in the revival tent that is, in fact, not fulfilled in the subsequent First Church movement.

In His Steps dwells primarily and often sentimentally on middle-class service, which is among the reasons the novel and Sheldon earned reputations for lukewarm progressivism, if not downright reactionary individualism, among historians of the Social Gospel. Henry Maxwell's final vision in the novel is of a society transformed in a soul-by-soul revival, a conclusion from which critics concluded that Sheldon "repudiated Christian socialism" in favor of "social redemption through individual sacrifice."[19] This description of the novel's vision as limited to the social services respectable church people can offer in missionary contexts does not do justice to the novel's further case for concrete reform in business and politics. But it is true that in generating the spiritual energy meant to drive this reform, the First Church members' social work conflates, somewhat, the institutions of the rescue mission and the settlement. The First Church do-gooders refer to their reclaimed saloon in the Rectangle as a settlement, but they are more Christ-centered and conversion-seeking than even many church-based settlements were. In a sense, the term "settlement" represents their appropriation of the rescue mission as the stage for their own dramas of middle-class redemption. The sanctification implied by a young prostitute's death in the novel confirms as much.

Closer attention has shown that, despite the limitations of this model as a real-world strategy of activism, Sheldon was allied closely with a wide range of Social Gospel thinkers, and his novel was deeply supportive of the progressive causes of its time.[20] As a specimen of the rescue missions' influence on Protestant culture, it is evidence of the central role that conversion narratives had in reformulating the relationship between individual salvation and Christian social obligation in this era, an influence that cut across political differences. In fact, if *In His Steps* offered an unthreatening Social Gospel, it was not because it remained too close to the rescue missions, but because it did not follow very far their lead in moving the social imaginary of reform from the self-regarding *obligations* of the privileged into the idea of recognizing and rebuilding *relationships* between the middle class and the poor. Nevertheless, the novel pointed in that direction.[21]

Even as other Social Gospel thinkers more decisively asserted the insufficiency of the rescue mission as a model of change, progressives in the first decade of the twentieth century still looked to the slums for this kind of reorientation. Social Gospelers routinely presented their theories of social salvation as displacing the model of the slum mission that was bound to the role of individual salvation as the heart of Christian life. But when they sought to fire up their message of social salvation with the emotional energies of revival, it was often to the rescue missions that they turned. Not only did the rescue missions supply appealing stories of alleviating the suffering of the poor, but, as we saw in the previous chapter, they did so by using a missionary social dynamic that was already imagining reform. The American experience of religion, even if reoriented toward social meaning, still required subjective signs of the spiritual passion needed to provoke deep ideological reconstruction.

The journalist Ray Stannard Baker epitomized this dynamic in his book *The Spiritual Unrest* (1910). Baker was among the cadre of muckraking journalists hired by Samuel McClure at the turn of the century to write on social and economic issues, especially focusing on exposing corruption and prompting reform. After leaving *McClure's* in 1906 to cofound *The American Magazine* with Lincoln Steffens and Ida Tarbell, Baker wrote two books, first published serially in the magazine, that cemented his reputation as a leading progressive social critic. The first, *Following the Color Line* (1908), was a pioneering effort by a white journalist to explore the racial divide. The next, *The Spiritual Unrest,* examined the widely agreed upon crisis of vitality in American religion.[22] The cause, Baker concluded, was the church's near-total inability to offer a spiritual response to the widespread deprivation of an "overworked and underfed" nation. "They have no vision of social justice," he concluded of both the church's leaders and social workers. "They have no message for the common people." The structure of Baker's book presents the Social Gospel, properly framed and evangelized, as the solution to this problem. Further, he looks to this reinvigorated religion as a source of moral leadership and organized personal passion that could drive progressive reform.[23]

In *The Spiritual Unrest* Baker takes a hand in establishing the creation narrative of the Social Gospel at the expense of both the rescue missions and the mainline establishments. The book passes through three stages of social religion, from the rescue mission to the church settlement to the Social Gospel conception of all meaningful social reform as essentially religion by another name. Unlike Sheldon a decade earlier, in delineating the first two phases Baker unambiguously divided Christian social work into two institutions, the rescue mission and the church-based settlement. With New York City as his focus, he begins at 316 Water Street, the perceived birthplace of the rescue mission. Places "like the Jerry McAuley Mission," he writes, "emphasize individual regeneration," while "others, like Christ Church of New York City, emphasize social reconstruction." Baker explores the potential for church-led progressive reform by comparing these specific sites, "the one [which] lifts men individually out of the gutter, the other [which] also seeks to remove the gutter," and he asks, "Which is more necessary?" (142–43). Both, it turns out, inspire with their tireless workers and their minor miracles of social salvation; but both, also, are utterly inadequate to the scope of the task at hand. Rather than denigrate or displace these first two phases, though, Baker's Social Gospel narrative builds on them, and along the way finds in them the vitality, if not the theory or the power, necessary for religion to reclaim its place at the heart of American public life.

In mining the McAuley mission for these socially transformative energies, Baker rediscovers what Campbell and others had related about it two decades earlier. Baker's tour of the mission is given in the classic first-person sociological style that Riis, Campbell and others had pioneered.

> Walk into the small, narrow, stuffy hall of the McAuley Mission any night of the year, and you will find the seats filled with the last and lowest dregs of humanity—men who are thieves, ex-convicts and drunkards. Every sort of humanity indeed, from the university man downward, may here be found; they have all reached the last equality of degradation. . . . Nor are the sights and sounds pleasant to fastidious senses. But wait, we are at the very bottom of the ladder, and there are significant things here too, things well for all of us to know. (147–48)

The style, and the pedagogy, are familiar. The scene is recognizable, he suggests, but the real social implications require guided interpretation. While Baker's approach was not new, his rhetoric implies he is addressing a new audience of secular progressives who need to relearn this wisdom of the streets.

In rediscovering Campbell's substantive findings, Baker reinterprets them as evidence of the spiritual fuel and democratic ethos required of a truly social religion. As he sits in on testimony meetings, dines with converts, and interviews the superintendent who succeeded Jerry McAuley and Samuel H. Hadley, he begins to frame his conclusions about the rescue mission as defenses against its perceived limitations. The materialistic expectations of the supplicants do not corrupt the spiritual phenomenon, he urges, but only make it more real, and thus more spiritual than the equally materialistic social function of established churches. The brief, plainspoken testimonies of the converts are free of performed cant and full of literal, compelling descriptions of physical breakdown and social invisibility. Like every learned visitor before him, he debunks the skeptic's vision of pious scolds or self-righteous converts giving high-handed treatment to the unwashed.

For Baker, egalitarianism is the essential difference between the slum mission and the uptown or middle-class church, the substance that only it can provide to progressive religion. Unlike in those respectable institutions, "here no one preaches to anyone else. No one argues any dogmas or creeds; there is almost no sort of ceremony practiced." Instead, visiting sinners receive the invitation to conversion simply by being able to identify their own experiences with the descriptions of degradation they hear. Even the most blatant frauds and frequent backsliders are offered, time after time, unconditional acceptance, based on the drunkards' own recollections of their long years of sin and their debt to the evangelists who did not give up on them. The missions practice a religion that is deeper, more committed, and more true to social reality, a religion born of shared suffering and "visible works" of material and social redemption (148–53). These qualities of pragmatism and honesty are the keys to reinvigorating religion in a socially transformative direction, Baker argues.

Despite these inspiring people, stories, and values, ultimately, Baker finds, the material impact of rescue mission conversion is "feeble" compared to the scale of the social problems they seek to ameliorate. In those who are changed, the change is real and miraculous. But most who visit do not "go forward" at the altar call, and "for every five men rehabilitated, . . . thousands upon thousands of miserable creatures" never find the missions in the first place (160–61). Further, he observes, most of those who are saved remain physically and mentally damaged by their years of dissipation and want. He concludes in exasperation: "How futile the church seems under such circumstances! Is it any wonder that the clergy should be discouraged? Is it any wonder that the people should be crowding the church aside and looking to new ways of producing better results in our civilization?" (161). He turns to church-based settlement house work as the more systemic and progressive alternative to slum evangelical revival. But even there, all the educational, vocational, medical, and domestic improvement he finds being fostered at Christ Church Presbyterian add up to very little material change in its midtown neighborhood or, importantly, its middle-class membership's self-regard (178–79). Here, even more than in the rescue missions, it is evident that the well-to-do are not willing to allow their religion to affect their own economic habits or the structures of power in their own institutions.

Ultimately, Baker joined Sheldon and Campbell in concluding that neither church nor mission service was creating substantial change, nor could they be expanded so as to do so. Like them, he drew on Water Street for spiritual energy and proof of personal, progressive faith, but he turned elsewhere for both theories and strategies of reform. In his book, Baker looks to the Emmanuel Movement, a therapeutic treatment process developed by two Boston Episcopal priests, Elmwood Worcester and Samuel McComb, in 1906, for a model of transformative spiritual healing that showed promise for middle-class people (210–12). The Emmanuel Movement developed a specialty in treating alcoholics, and some of its graduates became the lay therapists counted among the leading public experts in alcoholism right through to the early years of A.A.[24] But finally, it is the leading intellectual of the Social Gospel, Walter Rauschenbusch, to whom Baker turns for a theory of how all these religious energies can be joined to the secular reform movements in a mutually transformative way. In his major works, Rauschenbusch made similar gestures toward harnessing the passions of evangelical personal religion under a social theology that could convict and thus convert the system.[25]

In the extended interview that concludes the book, Baker and Rauschenbusch discuss the latter's argument in *Christianity and the Social Crisis*, focusing on ways that it might be implemented. Baker claims that this book was the one most widely cited as an influence by Christian leaders doing reform work. But, in a telling exchange, twenty years after Campbell wrote *Prisoners of Poverty*, Rauschenbusch offered his own version of the hat-buying woman's epiphany, when asked by Baker what a "conviction of social sin" would look like. Rauschenbusch indicted an imaginary "idle woman living in wasteful luxury" for the death of a child of one of her husband's workmen (276). His gendered angle is less sympathetic to ordinary women and their consumption habits than is Campbell's direct address to women readers, and so his resulting "conviction" is both less wide-reaching and less radical. It effectively invites middle-class men to feel morally superior to wealthy women—not to mention to resent their own wives' financial expenditures—in a decidedly individualized conviction of the woman herself, an utterly conventional gesture then as now.

We might attribute this lazy rhetoric not only to Rauschenbusch's gender but also to his academic distance from the scene of the rescue mission. There, just as the middle-class observer is confronted by the equal humanity of the poor drunkard, the recently redeemed drunkard is called to look upon the middle-class and even the wealthy sinner as suffering equally under his

or her burden of sin, and thus equally in need of compassionate evangelization. As we can see in each of Sheldon, Baker, and Rauschenbusch's texts,
the Social Gospel often asked much less of the middle-class churchgoer than
did the rescue mission. These more famous Christian progressives were
clearly influenced by the rescue missions' model of spiritual change, but only
Campbell was willing to place her own awakening there at the center of her
secular, progressive theory.[26]

Together these thinkers' conclusions about the inadequacy of the rescue
mission movement help explain why historians (as well as liberal religionists) have reproduced a succession narrative in which the missionary model
was eclipsed by a more radical theology of systemic reform, its energies left to
the soon-to-be fundamentalist evangelicals. This idea originated in the more
intellectual precincts of the Social Gospel, with figures such as Rauschenbusch, who is one of the few of its thinkers still read by academics other than
church historians. Rauschenbusch wrote that the "individualistic gospel has
taught us to see the sinfulness of every human heart and has inspired us with
faith in the willingness and power of God to save every soul that comes to
him. But it has not given us an adequate understanding of the sinfulness of
the social order and its share in the sins of all individuals within it."[27] The clear
turn represented by this view remains prevalent in American intellectual and
political history, as the birth of "the newer, systematic approach that suggested
reversing the order of personal reformation followed by social rejuvenation."[28]

But in Campbell's work, and in Sheldon's and Baker's books, conversion
stories were necessary to unlocking such systemic visions. Baker spends
much time at the missions and expresses great affection for them, urging
on his reader the moving reality of the successful conversions he witnesses
at Water Street. Even *In His Steps* opens with a sequence that comes straight
from the heart of the rescue missions' social dynamic, when the pastor is
confronted by the needs of an honest poor man and is led to meditate on
the difference between their material situations in light of their fundamental spiritual equality. But it was Campbell who saw that the limitations of
converting the afflicted pointed directly to the necessity of converting the
comfortable. Her better known associates in progressive reform adopted
this lesson in their own work.

"A joy hitherto unknown"

Campbell structured both her popular and scholarly writings on poverty
similarly to the rescue mission publications: as narratives of conversion that

invited similar experiences among readers. The extent to which they had this precise effect is hard to know. But certainly Campbell's books anticipated both the arguments and the experiences of leading progressive commentators on religion. Turning now to more firmly secular reformers, a more direct influence seems apparent in the relationships between Campbell, Jane Addams, and Charlotte Perkins Gilman. Addams and Gilman predicated their progressive social theories on their own personal life-changing experiences, and on the very idea of personal transformation. Both used post-religious conversion experiences as methods for enacting the failure of one ideology and the construction of another from its ashes. Campbell's physical journey into the world of religious good works and back out into reform circles elucidates the broad historical movement of many progressives, especially women, from one realm to the other. Addams identified the roots of transformational social work in the early Christian vision, and suggested that the new movement was a historical fulfillment of that spiritual innovation. Gilman was a more wholly secular thinker, but she used conversion stories to dramatize the possibilities for liberating change within the intellectual framework of evolutionary human science. Together they illustrate the process of exchange between the literal and metaphoric uses through which addiction-conversion language developed in the early twentieth century.

Among the clearest articulations of the post-Christian, progressive conversion experience is in Addams's essay "The Subjective Necessity for Social Settlements." Originally given as a lecture at an Ethical Culture conference in 1892, it was printed with the other conference papers by Henry C. Adams in *Philanthropy and Social Progress* (1893), was included in Addams's landmark retrospective *Twenty Years at Hull House* (1910), and continues to be anthologized as an important theorization of the settlement house movement and Progressive Era social work.[29] Reading Addams's ideas about the deep transformational effects of social work in light of Campbell's predication of a reform career on experiences at rescue missions illuminates the way evangelical religious conversion served as the framework for a secular language of psychological salvation in the twentieth century. The opening chapter of Campbell's *Problem of the Poor*, "What a Radical Found in Water Street," anticipates in this regard Addams's much more widely read essay. "Subjective Necessity" echoes Campbell's approach by framing social work as the solution to a young, well-to-do, liberal Protestant woman's feeling of paralysis in the face of both society's ills and the limits of her own sphere of influence. Each of these ideas about how transformation would come about in the slums was also the author's life story as a nonreligious conversion narrative.

Addams's essay is more theory than narrative, but it takes on the same issue: the relationship between reforming society, working directly with the poor, and unlocking one's deepest personal potential in social work. For Addams the problem that social work answered was that of young people "being cultivated into unnourished, oversensitive lives" that have no practical outlet for the intensity of feeling with which they confront the difference between their ideals and the world's reality. The fleeting feelings they have of the unity of all humankind are overwhelmed by the suffering they perceive to be the portion of its largest segment, and they are frustrated by the social barriers that prevent direct communication with these masses. Though Addams describes these impulses to unity in ways that closely echo the melting feeling of the conversion moment, their fulfillment in social work is a salvation of the human spirit, not the divine soul. The poor remain to be redeemed from social dislocations that are spiritual in their depth, but the middle-class reformer needs saving from a psychological, not a soteriological, crisis. Addams's essay builds from the description of this experience into an argument for settlement work as its solution, both in its easing of the young reformers' anxieties and lessening the material injustices that are their source.

Whereas Campbell grounds her argument for the necessity of personal transformation in her experiences at the rescue missions, Addams concludes her similar analysis by reinterpreting Christianity based on the experience of the settlement house. She concludes with a discussion of the role of the humanitarian "renaissance" in Christianity, providing eloquent formulations of both the Social Gospel and the anticlerical interpretation of what revivalists called "primitive Christianity." Addams describes Jesus and his early followers as social revolutionaries who threw themselves, body and soul, into the lives of others, most especially the lives of society's most despised members. This was experiential revelation, a life of constant social conversion, "a new treasure which the early Christians added to the sum of all treasures, a joy hitherto unknown in the world—the joy of finding the Christ which lieth in each man, but which no man can unfold save in fellowship."[30] This joy is another instance of the trope of subjective "melting," used to great emotional effect by Finney and other revivalists of the Second Great Awakening, but applied by pragmatic Christian reformers as a model of social reconciliation. Addams simply reversed the cause-and-effect dynamics, in a manner already suggested by the rescue missions. The social exchange epitomized by the settlement house, rather than the action of God on the isolated soul, became the source of the conversion experience.

While Campbell and Addams were occasional colleagues, Campbell's role as a mentor to Charlotte Perkins Gilman was more decisive. Gilman has long been associated with her male influences, such as William Dean Howells and Lester Ward, while the role of Campbell, with whom Gilman lived and worked extensively, has been largely ignored. Before her marriage Gilman lived with Campbell in the San Francisco area in 1894–95, when they co-edited *The Impress,* the publication in which Gilman honed her early writing.[31] Campbell, unlike Gilman, was an established author on women's issues by then, and announcements of the journal's founding described her résumé and expected contributions, rather than Gilman's.[32] In 1896 they worked together in Chicago to establish a North Side satellite of Addams's Hull House.[33] In this period Gilman referred to Campbell as her "mother," someone "far nearer to me than my own dear mother," and often went to her for physical and emotional restoration, returning east to be with her during the winter of 1897, for example. Gilman "was formed, ideologically and politically, in the burgeoning reform activities of the 1880s and 1890s," her biographer Ann Lane writes. "She took what she needed and went off on her own, but it was the world in which she grew. It was, as she said, the kind of home in which she was at home, not a domestic setting but a social one. It gave her a place."[34] Campbell was an intimate friend and mentor of Gilman's during this time.

Gilman's subsequent writing, while even further removed from Christian institutions than Addams's, featured a similar pattern of secular conversion. In economic analysis and fiction alike she urged liberation, often at the end of hard trials, from destructive ideologies of narrow, deluded self-interest. The lectures and essays she produced during the time of her closest association with Campbell dwelled on the ways embedded ideologies falsely presented themselves as natural orders, and on strategies not only for exposing them but for building from this enlightenment alternative, liberating epistemologies. Further, she suggested that reorienting one's social behaviors toward the truth could produce not just sounder judgment but a new source of precognitive selfhood. "*Instinct,* mind you, is the result of habit—not habit of instinct," she told the Pasadena Nationalist Club in 1890. "It is the transmitted effect of repeated actions and can be changed like every other form of life."[35] If instinct was but deep knowledge of self and world, arrived at via habit, then old habits would have to be shaken off before new ones could be adopted. In much of Gilman's nonfiction this shedding is a simple matter of intellectual rigor; but in her imaginative writings, the experience of the old, habitual self's dissolution looks more like the habitual drunkard's conviction of sin and plea for mercy.

Gilman's best known work of fiction, the short story "The Yellow Wallpaper" (1891), imagines this kind of experience by using mind-body illness as a vehicle of ideological deconstruction. In this autobiographical tale, the narrator describes her experience undergoing the misogynistic "rest cure" for neurasthenia. Confined to her bedroom, she comes to believe that a woman, eventually one she identifies as herself, is trying to escape imprisonment in the pattern of the wallpaper, and the story ends with her bodily performing this figure's struggle for liberation. Though this behavior still leaves her insane from a societal perspective, critics have dwelled on the way in which it nevertheless enacts a kind of triumph. The epistemological framework of medical confinement breaks down along with her socially functioning self, clearing the way, if she can survive, for a potential reconstruction based on a new concept of self and world. The dramatic arcs of Gilman's novels often led male and female characters alike to conversions that illustrated her social theories. "The Yellow Wallpaper," in contrast, describes a wrenching interior prelude to her positive evangelism for transformational change in public matters.

Gilman's conceptualization of societal change is more commonly associated with her views on evolution, but these theoretical arguments bear close structural parallels to Campbell's post-evangelical mode of prophetic change. Gilman believed, with Lester Frank Ward and others, that social relations progressed according to natural laws, but that a society of enlightened minds could either influence the direction of that progress or adjust the culture more harmoniously to it. She argued in particular that patriarchal culture was badly undermining the universally liberating direction in which civilization was by nature advancing—and that middle-class anxiety about changing labor markets and domestic arrangements was a symptom of those unnatural constraints. This concept of evolution was as a redemptive power that Gilman urged societies and individuals to orient themselves by, or else know deep unhappiness. As such, it played a role in Gilman's thought comparable to the unfolding will of God in the religious reform tradition.

Campbell shared Gilman's interest in evolution. She taught in her 1896 *Household Economics* lectures, for example, not only that character was susceptible to "improvement," but that this change was heritable, and that thus society's greatest benefits would come from instilling good habits in youth, prior to the age of reproduction. But in Campbell's assertion that "our business here is to be better human beings—to be better and to leave behind us those better than ourselves," one perceives the optimism about "literal regeneration" that she discovered at the rescue missions, more than any close engagement with theories of social evolution.[36] A similar genealogy is recognizable, if not explicit, in Gilman's language, too. In *Women and Economics,* Gilman everywhere invokes the dangers of acting and thinking contrary to the "laws of social evolution," which "do not wait for our recognition or acceptance" but "go straight on." The "change in circumstances and change in feeling" evident in the culture of the day was heralding "radical change in the economic position of women," a change "coming upon us overpoweringly in spite of our foolish fears."[37] This prophetic tone—confident that the power moving the universe would have its way, but cautionary lest society put itself on the wrong side—echoes Campbell's still-Christian language in *Prisoners of Poverty.* Reformers such as Gilman drew on the authority of scientific social theory, but, as Campbell's work reveals, the structure of their thought owed much to the rhetoric of religious social reform.

Escaping the Mental Slums

Conversion was a key trope in progressive thought and culture, and it had many sources. Indeed, evangelical Christianity was by far the most prominent American language available to describe the kind of moral and social transformation that progressives sought. It would be trivial to dwell too long on the centrality of secular "conversion" to reform thinking, and inaccurate to attribute too much influence to the particular fusion of religious, social, and personal reform popularized at the rescue missions. But Campbell, coming before and exerting personal influence on Addams and Gilman, made a unique contribution through her personal witness of drunkards' conversions as treating simultaneously the identity crises of middle-class reformers and the social problems of the poor. In her reportage she helped establish the drunkard's conversion as a material and social fact, and in her commentary she urged it as a spiritual ideal necessary for lasting reform. Campbell's similarities to, and influence on, Gilman and Addams seem especially to flow from the what she learned in this experience. And this lesson was more than simply a dramatic illustration of moral transformation. The drunkard's conversion provided for Campbell an empirically robust and emotionally inspiring relationship between personal conversion and social transformation.

Considering Campbell's role as an activist and scholar of women's issues and a mentor to feminist pioneers, it is tempting to approach her use of conversion narrative as an instance of genre-appropriation, in which an oppressed group seizes an established form and adapts it to its own needs and purposes. Kabi Hartman, for example, argues that suffragettes in this era "manifestly rewrote the form" of conversion, transforming it from a "literature of inner conflict" to a "literature of political struggle . . . against a sinful, unjust government."[38] This model could describe the public, progressive uses of conversion narrative by Addams and Gilman in their social theories. More generally, their writings fall within a broader trend in the secularization of religious patterns of language and idea.

But Campbell's and even Addams's writings suggest that the relationships between religious and political conversion, and between their relative degrees of inner and outer meaning, are more nuanced than the appropriation model allows. Conversion narrative has always been public and, at least implicitly, reformist, and never more so than in the great revivals that gave birth to the rescue missions. In a figure such as Campbell, this political meaning simply rose to the surface because the genre served a particular social role: it mediated a class divide between reformer and the subjects of reform.

In this function, Campbell's use of the drunkard's conversion reveals often overlooked nuances in the class dynamics of urban reform, and by extension in progressive thought. Gilman's concern with the working class did not outlive her close association with Campbell. She, more than Campbell, is susceptible to the charge of a classist progressivism.[39] But this judgment has been leveled more decisively against urban reformers such as Campbell. Historians have long interpreted slum missions as efforts to regulate the behavior of the poor and to pacify them by channeling their potentially rebellious energies into religious passion. Further, critics of realist-era moral reform writing have identified the genre with the reactionary modes of surveillance and discipline.[40] Campbell's reporting on the rescue missions makes her a candidate for both charges: she used first-person, virtual tour narratives with visual accompaniments (sometimes in the form of Jacob Riis's photography), and for moral impact she drew on the sentimental religious tropes of redemption and sanctification. It is no surprise then that her work has been called a form of "slumming as social regulation," a mode that relieves class tension by having an outsider to the tenements pacify, through a moral discourse, previously mysterious and threatening insider voices.[41]

Not only do such accounts minimize the roles of McAuley and the other working-class converts, but also and equally importantly, they miss the self-correction that reformers such as Campbell documented side by side with their slum reportage. Just as the blanket claim that temperance advocacy was a form of class "bullying" fails to account for the experience and advocacy of the rescue mission converts, the term "slumming" reduces all documentary projects to the status of voyeurism, implying that there is no meaningful difference between the perspective from the tour bus and that from inside the saloon and the mission.[42]

Campbell's most popular (and most ostensibly voyeuristic) works open with the same long sequence of self-transformation facilitated by Jerry and Maria McAuley, an egalitarian act of sympathetic self-exposure before speaking about the lives of her subjects. Campbell takes control of slum voices in order to render them fit for edifying consumption, true, but she interweaves them with her own voice in a narrative of middle-class confession. Despite obviously regulatory aims by the reformers, and their voyeuristic aesthetics, the progressive embrace of the drunkard's conversion was not a project of panoptical social control but a site of middle-class self-revision in a time of shifting values. Reformers understood slum conversion as transformative for the poor, for society, and especially for themselves, in its provision of a more forgiving moral and psychological self.

In its ultimate progression, Campbell's reform writing became less about regulating the behavior of the poor and more about confronting the mental habits of the middle class. With Riis, an admirer of Campbell's work who provided photographs for *Darkness and Daylight,* her work was at least as concerned with revising middle-class attitudes as it was with altering the slum environment.[43] Campbell's humbling herself to learn from the McAuleys and their fellow reformed drunkards performed social reconciliation using confessional self-healing, a strain of middle-class psychology that rapidly expanded in the twentieth century, reaching its fruition in the A.A. era. The class dynamics of the rescue mission culture supplied the imaginative foundations of this therapeutic self that could be alternately consumerist and activist.

In their sentimental reception and endorsement of the conversions of the lowly, patrons and readers of missionary literature could be reassured that their participation in a desire-driven economy need not alienate them from God or the good. If the drunkard and the prostitute were redeemable, then so was the middle-class consumer—of material goods, of alcohol, of sexual adventure, and of whatever else was on sale that might destabilize the individual's relationship to public morality and secure self-identity. As

Emma Whittemore, superintendent of the women's Door of Hope Mission, told one audience in regard to a well-to-do lady drinker she helped convert, "You do not have to *go* into the slums to *get* into the slums."[44] The "slums" in this formula became a vice-ridden state of mind, a tendency to become fixated on the mental dark alleyways of fear and insecurity that seem always to lead to the stale-beer dives of escapist self-indulgence. This industrial-era spatialization of anxiety survived the adaptation into addiction-recovery's mutual-aid culture, in a saying used by the writer Anne Lamott in 1997, as well as many others: "My mind is a bad neighborhood I try not to go into alone."[45] The nineteenth-century missionary effort to convert "bad neighborhoods" and their denizens greatly shaped the recovery narrative which many Americans still use to feel safe in their own heads. But before they internalized this social pedagogy of the drunkard's conversion, leading professional psychologists took them up also, in ways that made them available for more diverse secular appropriations. This process is the subject of the next chapter.

3

The Varieties of Conversion Polemic

If the State, burdened and shackled by its horde of outcasts and sinners, would march freely and efficiently to its goal, it must be at the hands of religion that relief is sought.

—Harold Begbie, *Twice-Born Men . . .*
A Footnote in Narrative to Professor William James's
"The Varieties of Religious Experience" (1909)

James teaches to cease reasoning and to have faith that all is well and will be well . . . in order to escape the pessimism consequent upon the grim and honest exercise of reason. . . . Come. Your glass is empty. Fill and forget.

—Jack London, *John Barleycorn* (1913)

THE DRUNKARDS REFORMED AT EVANGELICAL rescue missions in the late nineteenth century anchored their conversion stories to pragmatic needs and oriented them toward egalitarian ends, and in doing so created a flexible form for applying addiction-redemption language to all manner of social purposes. But this reformist structure notwithstanding, in both performance and print, the original stories remained products of the sentimental culture of the nineteenth century; their sensational low-life scenes, dramatic plot reversals, and triumphant piety exhibit as much. The genre's popular appeal and plausibility as nonfiction depended on the contemporary prevalence of these devices. How, then, did the drunkard's conversion fare in the early twentieth century, an era in which cultural tastes became more skeptical, medical science made strong claims on behavioral health, and professional expertise became the currency of moral reform?

The broad answer is a central argument of this book: that the drunkard's conversion was adapted to serve various new uses, in the process becoming a master narrative of addiction discourse in twentieth-century culture. This legacy was not just a broad structural outline. Rather, the new genres conserved specific conventions for asserting the relationship between personal experiences and larger religious, philosophical, and political truths, redeploying them on behalf of new ideas and in response to new social circumstances. But how did these meaning-making elements themselves survive dramatic contextual change? How could a self-described skeptic like Bill Wilson credibly claim to have been "saved" from alcoholic compulsion in 1934 by roughly the same kind of conversion experienced by Bible-thumper Billy Sunday in 1887?[1]

One important reason for the form's endurance was that psychologists, owners of the modern, scientific discipline claiming epistemological authority over the nature of subjective experience, gave a nearly unqualified endorsement to the efficacy of spiritual conversion as a cure for alcoholism. At the turn of the century, when most commercial inebriety treatments still involved peddling various chemical elixirs, William James cited a "medical man" to the effect that "the only radical remedy I know for dipsomania is religiomania."[2] Following the lead of some of his peers in academic psychology as well as Christian and New Thought therapy, James devoted considerable attention to showing how religious awakening answered the problem of compulsive habit.

In *The Varieties of Religious Experience,* James used "the Jerry McAuley Water Street Mission" as a byword and, indirectly, a source-base, to delineate what seemed the unique practical benefits of religious transformation. Converted drunkards, their religious advisers, and even their doctors subsequently drew on James's intellectual respect to justify what risked appearing as an atavistic response to what was increasingly defined as a medical condition. More than thirty years later, Wilson, for example, was not willing to admit that he had had a conversion experience without making reference to James's book.[3] James, his scholarly peers, and their legatees essentially vouched for the drunkard's conversion in the modern world. George Santayana was prescient, as well as contemptuous, when shortly after the publication of *Varieties* he greeted his Harvard colleague by exclaiming, "You have done the religious slumming for all time!"[4]

James and his fellow scholars' stated interest was in religious fervor more than in alcoholic madness, but they saw in the latter a concrete problem of mind and body that the spiritual frame not only fit but seemed genuinely to solve. Psychologists at the turn of the century thus put great stock in religion's effectiveness in curing inebriety, and they did so in a manner that endowed the conversion phenomenon with an aura of empirical facticity.[5] As seekers after the limit-cases of interior experience, they did not privilege quiet, intellectual forms of conversion but cast their nets for the disruptive, emotional born-again experiences that were in discredit among traditional church authorities and free-thinkers alike. They gave drunkards' conversions, in particular, a kind of special permit to pass freely into the age of medical science. By midcentury, James's endorsement of spiritual transformation, and a similar avowal by Carl Jung, were key intellectual props in the recovery narrative's founding mythology.[6]

As important as this intellectual attention was to the *plausibility* of conversion as a response to alcoholism, it also helped ground claims of *ideological neutrality* in new conceptions of recovery.[7] How does this appeal to empiricism square with the way midcentury recovery narratives used conventions that had developed in the service of religious, social, and political goals? In order to take the ideological genealogy of recovery narrative more seriously, it is necessary to begin filling in the three-decade gap between James's endorsement of the drunkard's conversion and his drafting into the A.A. creation story.

The appeal to James as the godfather of recovery culture's empirical legitimacy has obscured the more programmatic reception his treatment of drinking and conversion received in his own era. This chapter focuses on the role of the drunkard's conversion in James's thought, and on two polemical writers whose responses to *The Varieties of Religious Experience* helped create key tropes of alcoholism narrative in the twentieth century. The first is Harold Begbie, whose collections of conversion stories, *Twice-Born Men* (1909) and *Life-Changers* (1929), exerted significant influence on the founding members of A.A. In the first book Begbie, claiming only to be presenting further proof of James's conclusions in *Varieties*, framed drunkards' conversions as evidence in an argument against government relief and secular reform. He called his stories of slum drunkards redeemed by the Salvation Army to lives of honest entrepreneurial toil "footnotes in narrative" to James's scholarship. In them he aimed to "bring home to the minds of politicians and sociologists really acquainted with the appalling condition of modern London, that here in religion is the one great hope of regeneration, the one certain guarantee" of progress against social breakdown. His later book offered the religious conversions of elite university students as the antidote to the dangerous intellectual and political modernisms threatening to destabilize the West's next generation of leaders.[8]

The opposite, but no less influential, response to James came from Jack London, who attacked the conversion paradigm in depictions and defenses of drinking spanning his entire career. Early in his writing life, London examined heavy drinking among the poor and the evangelical efforts to relieve it, concluding that the missions "cannot but be failures," because "until the evils that cause people to drink are abolished, drink and its evils will remain." London did not pioneer this systemic argument (indeed it was not uncommon among temperance activists), but he did break new ground when he appended it to a gendered, psychological theory of drinking. London urged that for men, constant intoxication was not only more pleasurable, but also more rational, behavior than the misery of an impoverished domestic life. He saw the sentimental response to habitual drunkenness, whether it came from a high-toned lady reformer, a nagging wife, or William James, as politically reactionary and personally emasculating. When he came, toward the end of his career, to apply a similar logic to defend his own self-destructive habit, London defined anti-domestic drinking as a morally regrettable practice but one that was a socially inevitable and, ultimately, intellectually purifying outcome of modern masculinity. In returning to this pattern of thought throughout his prolific career, London helped to create a romantic and philosophical image of male alcohol abuse that became a staple of modern literature, a language of drinking that the early A.A. narrators spoke even as they told their conversion stories. London defined this role for drinking by depicting first the rescue missions, and finally William James himself, as the chief sentimental antagonists to his hyper-rational worldview.

In this contentious discourse around James's work, Begbie and London began to articulate key tropes of gender, class, and affect that attached to alcoholism in modern culture, from the wry sentimentalism of recovery meeting and confessional memoir to the hardboiled sociability valued in modern fiction and barroom masculinity. These styles were first given definition in print as cultural expressions of the polemical positions taken in an ideological contest over the meaning and value of the drunkard's conversion. Recovery narrative then repurposed these ideologically charged gestures to prepare the ostensibly neutral ground on which the recovery movement's claims to truth were built. In other words, the legitimacy James conferred on conversion entered into recovery narrative not just intellectually, as a theory about the nature of spirituality, but also culturally, in his role as catalyst for politically purposive storytelling strategies for negotiating the tensions between masculinity and sentimentalism.

It would be a mistake to assume that Begbie and London simply made category errors by mixing up science and politics and distorting James's objectively neutral ideas to serve their own, biased ends. It is evident in their engagements with James, and in James's work itself, that his interpretation of the Water Street conversions was actually quite compatible with, and even facilitated, the genre's role as a site of ideological controversy. James's analytical method in *Varieties* itself was a model for adapting religious structures of thought to secular, public purposes. By reducing the welter of social and cultural exchange that went into transmitting conversion narrative into claims about the universal architecture of the human mind, James transformed particular types of successful cultural performance into objective scientific data. New producers of the narrative could then wield this objectivity as currency, whether to support a political argument, or to develop a method of addiction recovery, or both. James did indeed play a key role bridging the melodramatic drunkards' conversions of the nineteenth century and the modern culture of addiction recovery. But what he provided was not a scientific end to conversion ideology, so much as a method of rationalizing and authenticating the conventions with which the genre produced social meaning.[9]

Discussion of James's influence on the development of modern recovery narrative has long focused on the role *The Varieties of Religious Experience* played in Bill Wilson's and other early A.A. members' understanding of spiritual change as a flexible and undogmatic phenomenon. From this perspective, James supplied the innovation of pragmatic spirituality, and Wilson, with his talent for synthesis, incorporated it into the recovery narrative.[10] This approach takes James's contribution as intellectually *sui generis,* forgetting that his own thinking was a product of the world of the drunkard's conversion. The discussion that follows resituates James in the passage from nineteenth-century drunkards' conversions to twentieth century addiction recovery narratives. In producing the Gifford Lectures that became *Varieties,* James drew on his own various personal and cultural resources, from frequent instances of alcoholism, mind-body illness, and spiritual awakening in his own family, to the printed drunkards' conversions of the Water Street mission. His findings were then taken up in new kinds of narratives, such as those of Begbie and London, whose influences on the cultural meanings and linguistic styles of alcoholism and recovery stories were much more deeply embedded than Wilson's dramatic memory of being handed James's book the morning after his conversion experience. James's response to his own influences, and the ways he was read in his own time, constitute the actual sites of his mediating role in this history.

William James's Drunkards

Long before he brought them together for intellectual purposes in the Gifford Lectures, alcoholism and spiritual conversion were touchstones in William James's life. James's public role in drinking discourse began in the scientific wing of the temperance movement and concluded with support for spiritual recovery therapies. Speaking in his official capacity as professor of physiology and citing the latest research, in 1881 he recommended total abstinence, rather than moderate drinking, to Harvard undergraduates. In the last years of his life, he became a supporter of the Emmanuel Movement, which— in line with the examples he had examined in *Varieties*—applied religious techniques to psychological dilemmas in pragmatic and scientifically legible ways.[11] But beyond these widely spaced public statements, James wrote throughout his career of the snares of habitual drinking and the challenge of rehabilitating drunkards, drawing on sources that were more personal than membership in any reform organization.

Alcoholism ran through James's family and his close social circle, as Howard M. Feinstein's biography, *Becoming William James,* reveals. His father, Henry James Sr., claimed to have been addicted to alcohol from childhood well into young adulthood, with enough associated prodigal behavior to permanently alienate him from his own father and thus shape how he treated his four sons, one of whom became a lifelong alcoholic. Henry Sr. had a younger brother and a nephew who were also apparent alcoholics. William James's wife, Alice Gibbens James, lost her alcoholic father to suicide at the age of sixteen. Chauncey Wright, one of William's early intellectual mentors and the stern, empiricist "boxing-master" of the Metaphysical Club in the 1860s, fell into depression and alcoholism in the last decade of his life, just as James's career was taking off.[12] Most significantly, William was a lifelong confidant of his brother Robertson, whose alcoholism made him a constant burden and concern to the whole family. In the years leading up to the 1898 Gifford Lectures, William several times helped to arrange in-patient treatment for "Bob" at sanatoriums.[13] James's most intimate relations can fairly be said to have been blighted by alcoholism, such that he was not taking rhetorical liberties with his readers' imagined social circles when he instructed them to "ask half the common drunkards you know why it is that they fall so often a prey to temptation."[14]

The experience of living with alcoholics must have shaped James's ideas about psychology. Consider the following scene from the James household in Cambridge in 1881. The year before she and her husband both died, a seventy-one-year-old Mary Walsh James wrote to her son Robertson's wife to update her on Bob's recent institutionalization at an asylum. Bob, in his mid-thirties and separated from his wife after just a few years of marriage, was living back at the family home with his parents, William, and their sister, Alice. His mother thought he had been doing very well, staying sober and taking exercise, when he had a sudden impulse to be reunited with his wife and an accompanying strong resentment toward his family for seeming to stand between them. He rushed to the train station to travel to her, but was confronted by a five-hour wait, and so began to pace the streets. The night wearing on, he began to weaken, which "led him to take a glass of ale, indeed he took three while waiting for the car," his mother reported. "This he said maddened him and in that state he got home. He expended his violence upon us in angry words, and we told him to leave the house until he was sober and sane, and then he might come back. He went off to William's rooms, and after a couple of hours returned completely subdued, and said he wanted to be taken to the Asylum, where he might rest and be taken care of. William and we all expostulated with him, but he persisted and we took him. He has been very much depressed since, but still calm and content."[15] At thirty-nine years of age, nearly a decade into his Harvard professorship, William James was still intimately involved in scenes of domestic turmoil surrounding a beloved brother's drinking problem.

In his work of this period, James frequently used inebriety to illustrate his most pressing psychological concerns. The innocent regular drinker who wakes up one day to find himself a drunkard was one of his favorite examples of the unwilled impact of habit, while the confirmed drunkard's endless rationalization of temptation was a decisive case of the disordered versus the healthy will. When he drew on this imagery, his language was colored by emotion that went beyond his usual rhetorical dramatics. Compare the distressing experience recounted above to two points that James makes about the will, in the monumental text that culminated his work in the 1880s, *Principles of Psychology*. In his account of disorders caused by dissociation of the will from other mental objects, he insists that drunkards are not morally insensible but, on the contrary, are tortured by exceptionally refined moral imaginations. "No one eats of the fruit of the tree of knowledge as they do," he urges. "So far as moral insight goes, in comparison with them, the orderly and prosperous philistines whom they scandalize are sucking babes." But, tragically, this sensibility is "an inert accompaniment" to their will, and "the consciousness of the inward hollowness that accrues from habitually seeing the better only to do the worse, is one of the saddest feelings one can bear with him through this vale of tears." Later in the same chapter, he betrays not only sympathy but also anger, in his account of the drunkard's process of rationalization for taking the first drink. "How many excuses does the drunkard find when each new temptation comes!" he exclaims, proceeding to elaborate with nine laughable examples, including instances that recall Bob's bad night in 1881, such as "it isn't drinking, it is because he feels so cold," and "it is a means of stimulating him to make a more powerful resolution in favor of abstinence." This suddenly vivid and bitter specificity serves James's case that in a properly functioning will, the key "effort of attention" is addressed not to acting but to correctly framing the case for action. Only when the drinker "holds to it that this [temptation] is *being a drunkard* and is nothing else, he is not likely to remain one long," he laments. "The effort by which he succeeds in keeping the right name unwaveringly present to his mind proves to be his saving moral act."[16] James's slide from the drinker's hypothetical self-realization to the accomplished case of sobriety resounds with wish fulfillment.

The pattern of James's own mind-body trouble was quite similar to that of the struggling addict, especially in the desperate hopes and increasingly bitter disappointments produced by willed, moralistic self-correction. From adolescence until his early thirties, James struggled with mental and physical ailments diagnosed as neurasthenia, the "nervous exhaustion" that Victorians associated with the unprecedented sensory and spiritual stresses of modern life. Like his brother Bob and his sister, Alice, he frequently found himself overcome by anxiety and debilitated by pain. When rest cures, health kicks, and intellectual exertions in his twenties seemed to offer no permanent relief, James began to practice the science of habit reformation, a precursor to the concept of pathway reinforcement in neuroscience, and in its applied, moral dimensions, also to the positive-thinking systems of the twentieth century. While James later developed his own, more nuanced theory of habit, his self-treatment at this earlier stage involved punishing efforts to reign in his speculative, exploratory tendencies, through disciplined academic work. These periods of resolve produced temporary constitutional improvements and new intellectual insights, but often they ended in even deeper troughs of despondency.[17]

Characteristic of his family, he was unable to separate his sense of personal well-being from his metaphysical system and his expectation of a high calling. Between his early, idealistic ambitions of being an artist, his proven potential in science, and his deep engagement with philosophy, the young James was unable to commit to a career, despite completing medical school in 1869. His conceptual orientation toward medical science compounded his nervous troubles by suggesting that they were not only physical in origin but also potential genetic life-sentences. The focus of his worst anxiety was the terror of an impending degeneracy to total madness. This fear finally took on a completely paralyzing intensity—the low point of what he would spiritualize in *Varieties* as "soul-sickness"—in a breakdown in 1872. It came upon him during one of Bob's troubling visits to Cambridge.[18]

James's long emotional and professional ascent from this low point combined revelation, reason, and social support in a model of nonreligious spiritual conversion that itself presaged recovery culture. Biographers do not report evidence of any single experience alleviating the crippling fear James felt during his breakdown. His ultimate recovery from neurasthenia seems to have commenced with his first experience of steady, paid work, in his appointment as a professor of physiology at Harvard the following year in 1873. But the two-steps-forward, three-steps-back frustration produced by his self-propelled efforts at habit reformation led to seize-ups that seem to have required the kind of revelatory "surrenders" that both the drunkard's conversion and addiction recovery are built around. Robert D. Richardson describes James's narrative of one nadir in 1868 as (ironically enough) a "headlong, AA-like" confession, which "may well have been the hour at which religion finally struck for him, just when the clock had pointed to despair."[19] Or, as James wrote in the version of his final break that he inserted into *Varieties*, "I have always thought that this experience of melancholia of mine had a religious bearing."[20]

James's crisis was the kind, in other words, on which a conversion narrative turns. He described one moment of recovery as "an experience of life which woke up the spiritual monad within me as has not happened more than once or twice before in my life." In defiance of the materialism that as a scientist-in-training he found inescapable, but as a self-examiner he found intolerable, he concluded that "there is an inextinguishable spark which will, when we least expect it, flash out, and reveal the existence, at least, of something real—of reason at the bottom of things. . . . [A]ll is nature and all is reason too. We shall see, damn it, we shall see!"[21] Despite his high intellectual seriousness and his free-thinking patrimony, James's patterns of thought were never very far from popular Protestant culture. His exclamation at the end of that letter suggests the young would-be hard-headed realist's version of the contemporaneous hymn's chorus, "We'll understand it better by and by." In these moments, unwilled revelations in the materialist darkness vindicated the meaningful self (if not the soul), but knowing these visions' ultimate import would require long years of devotion.[22] By the turn of the century, in the Gifford Lectures, James concluded that "probably every religious person has the recollection of particular crisis in which a directer vision of the truth, a direct perception, perhaps, of a living God's existence, swept in and overwhelmed the languor of the more ordinary belief."[23] In this manner, while James did not have an unambiguously spiritual conversion, his recovery from chronic anxiety and intellectual paralysis did coincide with his simultaneously emotional and intellectual acceptance of religious structures of change.

If the long rhythms of James's inner life alternated between habit-reform and crisis-conversion, throughout his psychological writings one finds efforts to resolve the tension between cumulative habit formation and sudden transformative revelation. In explaining his theory of habit in *Talks to Teachers* (1899), he addressed this apparent contradiction explicitly, as an anti-religious implication that he had been charged with. In a passage shot through with references to drunkards as the paradigmatic victims of bad habit, he argues that sudden conversions "unquestionably do occur," but that they are simply extreme examples of the "new stimuli and new excitements" that can redirect habit. Such "critical and revolutionary experiences" can indeed "change a man's whole scale of values and system of ideas," he writes. "In such cases, the old order of his habits will be ruptured; and if the new motives are lasting, new habits will be formed, and build up in him a new or regenerate 'nature.'"[24] The dialectic of reason and revelation that increasingly shaped James's thinking on both psychology and religion matches his personal experience of willed habit reformation punctuated by the occasional flash of conversion.

I emphasize—perhaps exaggerate—the implicit conversation between drunkards' conversions and therapeutic self-culture in James's life and psychology writings for the purposes of the present analysis. But it is a very real structuring element in the background of *The Varieties of Religious Experience*. *Varieties* is influenced by drunkards' conversions to a degree that has gone unrecognized. Despite its reputation as a comparative study of mysticism, *Varieties* is in fact centrally concerned with examining the psychological reality and moral efficacy of the Christian conversion experience.[25] And for evidence, James relies considerably on drunkards' reformations as proof that conversion constitutes a total upheaval in mental structure and behavioral habit. For James, alcoholism and conversion were phenomena that tied together the scientific and spiritual responses to modernity, and through which his favored patterns of thought flowed among his personal burdens, his philosophical explorations, and major social questions of his era. What-ever other intellectual purposes the Gifford Lectures served, *The Varieties of Religious Experience* is the culmination of these efforts at resolving the tension that ran through James's life between hard facts and high reason, and between morally sound habit and ecstatic inspiration. For the evidence with which to forge a final synthesis, he looked, among other places, to Water Street.[26]

James did not pioneer this interest in the drunkard's conversion as a key that might unlock the relationship between mind and body, or between spiritual ideal and material process. In fact, drunkards' conversions were the basis of an emerging scholarly conversation around this question.[27] James's main secondary source in *Varieties* on conversion in general was James Leu-ba's lengthy 1896 study of fourteen contemporary conversions and several historical ones. Nine of the fourteen original narratives Leuba collected were by reformed drunkards—not surprising, given that he located them with the help of the leader of the Fulton Street Noonday Prayer Meeting in New York. This was the daily prayer service founded in the late 1850s by Jeremiah Lanphier, the evangelist whose slum revival laid the groundwork for the rescue mission movement. Among the previously published conversions that Leuba also drew on were those of Lanphier's mentor, Charles G. Finney, the famous eighteenth-century "rake reformed" Col. James Gardiner, and John B. Gough, the foremost speaker of the Washington Temperance Society, the largely nonreligious 1840s precursor to gospel temperance and A.A.[28] In sum, both the immediate and the deep evidentiary roots of *The Varieties of Religious Experience* are swarming with drunkards' conversions.

The centrality of conversion itself in the lectures emerges through James's effort to understand the role religious experience has played, across western history, in defining and responding to the psychological condition of "morbid melancholy." Three of the instances of "soul sickness" that James quotes from and discusses at greatest length describe a telling trajectory: *Pilgrim's Progress* author John Bunyan's; his own, disguised as that of an anonymous correspondent; and Samuel H. Hadley's.[29] (Hadley, recall, was born again in Jerry McAuley's mission after a long binge, and became his successor as its superintendent.) Together these crisis narratives construct a dialectical sequence from the orthodox conviction of sin in reformed Christianity, to its counterpart in secular psychological breakdown, to an apparent synthesis of the two in the drunkard's spiritual collapse. Each features the same incapacitating horror of existential obliteration, but they are distinguished by the different contents of these fears. Bunyan's terror is wholly a sense of sin and judgment. James's is a fear of biological degeneracy, but with a "religious bearing" in which uttering reassuring scriptural phrases sustained him, mantra-like, through the worst. (A footnote directly compares the physical symptoms of his low point to Bunyan's, implying that they are the same psychological condition but with different surface expressions; while another note directs the reader to Henry James Sr.'s transcendental conversion narrative, suggesting a kind of historical continuity from the religious to the post-religious inner life.) Hadley's morbidity has its nadir in the scene of delirium in the Harlem saloon recounted in chapter 1. James distinguishes his interpretation of this scene from Leuba's take, by arguing that drunkards' conversions are not specific to the symptoms of alcoholism, but are instances of the broader category of morbid melancholy. Thus defended as having general significance, Hadley's narrative becomes the centerpiece of James's "Conversion" lecture and the turning-point of *Varieties* overall, insofar as the structure of conversion narrative itself is reproduced in the lecture sequence. "The Jerry McAuley Water Street Mission," he avers, "abounds in similar instances."[30] The proven case of the contemporary drunkard's conversion stands as the most convincing evidence that spiritual experience can effect radical mind-body change. This was the kind of attention that enabled James's widely read book to exert a deep and long-lasting influence on alcoholism discourse.

From "Footnotes" to Recovery Narrative

James may not have invented the psychological study of conversion in *Varieties,* but the book's success did inspire its growth as both an academic discipline and a subject of popular writing. Not surprisingly, it found a particularly eager audience among advocates of evangelical revival and gospel temperance, who interpreted James's findings as a boost to their public standing and intellectual legitimacy. General reviewers hailed *Varieties* as a "work of genius" and an "epoch-making classic" for its success putting science and religion into a single, modern conversation.[31] Religious reviews displayed more ambivalence, because they focused with greater specificity on how James defined religious experience, and on what impact the book was likely to have on the reputation of religion in the twentieth century. Establishment church readers lamented that James located religious experience in "abnormal" or "morbid" emotional states, while seeming to dismiss doctrine and institution.[32] Intellectually engaged evangelicals, on the other hand, while expressing some dismay at the freedom with which James set aside the historical reality of the Christian stories, recognized that his analysis was deeply reassuring to what was by then their most pressing concern: that conversion's direct experience of the divine would remain relevant or even plausible in the rationalistic modern world.

Those taken up with the challenges of evangelization in the era of industrial efficiency and documentary realism saw that James's potentially threatening scholarly approach only reinforced the positive message he seemed to be conveying about conversion-based religion. More than one referred to his "careful and cool" tone, and his "philosophical" and "scientific" methods, as indicators of the intellectual legitimacy his conclusions conferred on the born-again narratives he used as data.[33] "So far from Revivalism being opposed to the teaching of modern science, it is nothing more nor less but the practical application to the human heart of principles set forth by the latest psychological science," wrote W. T. Stead, an English reformer who advocated religious revival in the United Kingdom and United States alike. *Varieties,* he urged, "should be attentively studied by all who are anxious to understand the *rationale* of Revivalism, the psychological law which is seen in operation in conversion."[34] The idea that *Varieties* was a great boon to literal religious belief was well enough established by 1906 that one skeptic complained, "Nothing written on the subject has created a deeper impression, or been more cordially welcomed by the supernaturalist."[35]

James's close attention offered an especially profound validation of revivalism's role in the era of social reform. Both Social Gospel Progressives and Old Time Religionists believed conversion to be a morally and, by extension, socially, transformational good that was not just epistemologically relevant but desperately needed in an age of unrest. In James's work, reformers and polemicists found scientific legitimacy for their belief that religion was the only force for change that could bind together and act simultaneously on every level of human experience, from the deepest inner self to the most powerful institutional structures. Stead, for example, was the author of the widely read Social Gospel reform treatise *If Christ Came to Chicago!* (1894). The book originated in a series of lectures that the celebrated activist-journalist was invited to give to clergy and reformers in Chicago. The first half was a catalog of municipal sins that rivaled the subsequent work of the secular muckrakers in its detailed factual reportage. In the concluding chapters, Stead advocated a compassionate and politically engaged "universal" Christianity as the answer to the vice business and its corrupt political backing. A decade later, in the articles in which he promoted *Varieties,* Stead embraced the Welsh revival of 1904 as a model of societal transformation that arises in men's hearts rather than in policy prescriptions or moral dogmas. Protestants already understood good-government reform as a straightforward application of Christian morality. The phenomena James seemed to legitimize was the less easily rationalized movement of the spirit necessary to generate social forces in its favor.

This legitimacy did more than secure respect for religious reform; advocates wielded it as ammunition in the stronger argument that religion was the *only* way to solve social problems. Revivalists used the case from psychology less to urge salvation in its own right than to bolster their claims that conversion was the surest means to the social ends sought by reformers of all stripes, most notably progressives. In James's work and that of other psychologists of religion, they felt they had found empirical proof of their argument. "To make a bad man good, a cruel man merciful, a lazy man industrious, a drunkard sober, and to substitute selfless struggle to help others for a selfish scramble to seize everything for oneself—that is the aim-all, the be-all, and the end-all of all those who seek the improvement of society and the progress of the world," Stead wrote, invoking *Varieties*. "And when it comes to be looked at scientifically, there is none of the whole diversified multitude of social, religious and political reformers who can deny that a great religious Revival does succeed in achieving the results which they desire more rapidly, more decisively, and in a greater number of cases than any other agency known to mankind. We may discount it as we like. But the facts are there."[36] James had provided a scientific theory to make sense of these presumed "facts," a platform which by Stead's implication elevated the case for conversion above ideological dispute. But these facts remained, in form, narratives. And how they would be told, even with this implied scientific backing, remained firmly a matter of political purpose.

One of the most successful of these transatlantic appeals to James came in the form of a collection of Salvation Army conversion narratives called *Twice-Born Men,* by Harold Begbie, an English journalist. Originally published in England as *Broken Earthenware,* the edition renamed *Twice-Born Men* in 1909 gained attention on both sides of the Atlantic. It was subtitled, "A Footnote in Narrative to Professor William James's 'Varieties of Religious Experience,'" and was dedicated to James. Begbie's expository preface deploys the scholarly authority of *Varieties* as the foundation for his own framing argument: that evangelical revival is a necessary, and largely sufficient, means to alleviate the social ills of poverty and crime. In liberal quotations from *Varieties,* "Professor James" proves, for Begbie, that personal conversion experience is the source of all religion, and that this "primordial" religion is the only power in the world that can wholly "regenerate" a person, from the deepest sense of self to all outward behaviors.

For Begbie, the humdrum business of "Social Work," in which society places so much stock, is insignificant in comparison to the "terribly real" force of conversion, which can make a "dipsomaniac of a sudden lose all desire for alcohol." This "strange, individual, and elemental force," legible from the *Book of Job* to *Pilgrim's Progress* to, now, the slum mission, "reveals in the hearts of men whom science and law would condemn as hopeless of reformation . . . possibilities of purity and devotion" thought even by religious believers to be mythical. In the service of these claims, James provides not only a theory of religion, but "well-authenticated histories," "evidence for the reality" of which "is overwhelming." "The fact stands clear and unassailable" that conversion "does not alter, it creates a new personality," making the religious concept of "a new birth" a "fact of the physical kingdom." Pivoting on James's single reference to the Salvation Army in *Varieties*, Begbie concludes by claiming that its material results depend wholly on the "miracle of conversion."[37] From there he turns to a case against secular reform plans and direct government intervention. James's role is as the scientific authenticator of an evangelical revivalism that makes redundant the progressive vision of the state.

Begbie was not primarily a religious writer but a political commentator, and he presented the religious activity in *Twice-Born Men* as the policy solution to the most urgent problems facing western societies. In doing so he joined a long list of writers who had reported on London's "outcast poor" with intermingled moral and political, sober and sensational, and secular and religious purposes.[38] But if much of his scenery and his tone were familiar, the universe of social and political debate to which Begbie explicitly addressed his findings made his approach distinct to his own moment. While his attitudes do not neatly track a progressive-reactionary divide (he was a "liberal social reformer" in the British context), his book frames the success of Salvation Army–coaxed conversions as overwhelming evidence for the necessity of religious personal change, as opposed to material relief or systemic restructuring.

Begbie weaves an argument against secular government interference into his documentary claims about the effects of conversion among the poor, making it appear a natural consequence of them. His stated goal was to "bring home to practical men the immense value of personal religion in the work of social regeneration, that is to say, in the work of developing national character."[39] He was not against aggressive government action per se, but he thought it largely wasted effort unless it was facilitating religious awakening. Even in advocating for progressive goals such as humane prison reform and child protective services, he essentially urged the state to turn over both prisoners and poor children to organizations modeled on the Salvation Army. The central problem Begbie appealed to was the "burden" the poor place on society and the State; just as only conversion can turn bad men good, he insisted, only evangelical religion can "convert the burden into assistance." "There is nothing else; there can be nothing else. Science despairs of these people and pronounces them 'hopeless' and 'incurable.' Politicians find themselves at the end of their resources. Philanthropy begins to wonder whether its charity could not be turned into a more fertile channel. The law speaks of 'criminal classes.' It is only religion that is not in despair about this mass of profitless evil dragging at the heels of progress—the religion which still believes in miracle" (18–19). Begbie saw evangelical revival as the only institution capable of achieving the results that progressives were calling on good government to effect.

The drunkard's conversion was Begbie's model of individual salvation as social progress, established in his first story, "The Puncher." Begbie describes the life of a once-famous prize-fighter who descends into crime, penury, and alcoholism. Tortured by his degradation yet still spurning the indignity of reform, the man had decided to murder his wife and die "gamely on the scaffold," as his last chance at glory. Heading to a public house to gird himself for the deed, he was approached by a Salvationist, "himself a converted drunkard and wife-beater," whose parting words were, "God has got a better life for you, and you know it." At the bar, he had a vision of himself on the scaffold, while his son was subjected to public ridicule. "For the first time in all his life he was stunned by realization of his degradation and infamy," Begbie intones. "He knew himself" (51–54). This moment, in the established narrative of Christian conversion, is the man's "conviction of sin," a necessary precursor to God's bestowal of grace.

Begbie's description of what happened next matches countless versions of the narrative of sudden conversion. The man goes straight to a Salvation Army meeting and performs, "at the penitent's form," a direct request to God for deliverance, drawn from the Publican's Prayer of Luke 18:13: he "cried out that God would be merciful to him, a sinner." In a pervasive convention of the drunkard's conversion, God's response is rendered as the unrenderable: "He says that it is impossible to describe his sensations. The past dropped clear away from him. An immense weight lifted from his brain. He felt light as air. He felt clean. He felt happy. All the ancient words used to symbolize the spiritual experience of instant and complete regeneration may be employed to describe his feelings, but they all fail to convey with satisfaction to himself the immediate and delicious joy which ravished his consciousness" (55). Supernatural physical effects that produce an ecstasy said to be beyond language, aimed at in near-sexual terms, were conventions of evangelical conversion, as were what followed in Begbie's account: the alleviation of addiction and the imperative to evangelize others. The Puncher, despite a relapse, soon becomes a tireless salvationist among his neighbors, renowned even among longtime Army officials for his "love for souls" (56).

Begbie's vision of grassroots social transformation is contained within a familiar middle-class view of the slum. In *Twice-Born Men* he uses the conventions of conversion narrative as a mode of social regeneration for alcoholics and criminals. But he frames this phenomenon not as part of a broader reform coalition but rather as a rebuke to its secular interlopers. In his depiction, the release of the convert's burdens, leaving the lightness of an individual soul, out of time and in contact with God, is also a shedding of social, economic, and political causes of misfortune. Grace has the power to define and obliterate the past along with all its causative factors. In this solution, a "past" becomes an individual's burden of sin, which for the convert "drop[s] clear away." The stresses of poverty reappear for the Puncher and other such converts, but they are transformed into the trials that prove the strength of the redeemed soul, rather than opportunities for expanded reform work. Conversions that for progressives inspired social activism, for religious reactionaries promised to universalize personal religion.

The gender and class dynamics of Begbie's narratives illustrate further the social politics of this ideology. Unlike the rescue mission narratives, which place women and the poor in positions of responsible leadership, in the neighborhood Begbie depicts the lines of social division remain clearly drawn. The adjutant of the Salvation Army corps devoted to Begbie's "deplorable quarter" is "a beautiful and delicate girl" who, in addition to nursing the dying and teaching the young, "went into public-houses and persuaded the violent blackguards of the town to come away," "pleaded with the most desperate women at street corners," and "stood guard over the doors of men mad for drink and refused to let them out" (36–37).[40] The effect of such a woman's mere presence on poor men is encapsulated in one drunkard's vow that he would "never insults the likes of you, because you care for the likes of us" (37). The sentimental words underscore and endorse the distance of class, in order to make its bridging seem a supernatural phenomenon.[41] Gender provides transcendence, in the heavy-handed articulation of female purity—"so gracious, so modest, and so sweet. . . . She has left in these foul streets the fragrance of her personality, a fragrance of the lilies of a pure soul"—and its miraculous ability to neuter the implied sexual danger in affection shared with low men. The power of a respectable woman's compassion is a miracle of social condescension that moves poor drunkards to penitence and conversion. Though this version of slum revivalism also cast itself as a moral revolution, it cemented rather than challenged hierarchical gender and class relations in order to render its divine effects.

Begbie's interpretation of the drunkard's conversion was not recognized, in its day, as fundamentally opposed to its progressive counterparts. He shared their concern with urban poverty in the industrial age. But unlike the rescue mission converts and their progressive patrons, Begbie adhered to the traditional boundaries of moral reform, with the separation of observer and observed, good and bad, upper and lower, rigidly maintained. He too described the recognition of the humanity of the poor as a phenomenon that altered the experience of selfhood. But if for progressives, this recognition demanded self-reform, for Begbie and other religious conservatives, its effect was almost the opposite: "The apprehension that every unit in the multitude has his own individual silence of the soul, his own impenetrable chamber of thought, his own unbroken and incommunicable solitude, brings home to us the knowledge that one's own pressing sense of personal identity is the property of all mankind, that sameness is ultimately impossible, that variation is the law, that the swarm is composed of separate and individual *ones*" (12). In the phenomenon of the London masses, Begbie sees the sacralization of individualism. In *Twice-Born Men,* mission conversion elevates the individual into an exemplar for his existing social environment, rather than integrating him into a newly humane social order. Drunkards' conversions, now with James's scientific stamp of approval, proved the truth of this view.

Reviewers accepted the premise of the close relationship of *Twice-Born Men* with James's scholarship, sometimes even adding the book to lists of works in the field.[42] Some researchers cited Begbie's book as contributing to the body of data on conversion. One psychologist of religion in the prominent Clark University circle listed *Twice-Born Men,* along with the popular Bowery drunkard's conversion memoir *Mamie Rose,* with James's *Varieties* as the latest sources of evidence for the "psychology of Jesus" and its "meaning for the modern mind."[43] The book also found a lasting place in the early twentieth-century literature of Christian inspiration, a role through which it came to influence the founding members of A.A.

In the 1920s, Begbie's belief in the social benefits of religious revival became more decisively reactionary, a shift reflected in his turn from the Salvation Army to the Oxford Group movement. His 1923 book *Life-Changers* was another collection of conversion narratives, but this time lionizing the American pastor Frank Buchman for successful evangelization among young British elites. For Begbie, Buchman's strictly private, exclusionary approach avoided the perennial temptation of slum missionaries to ally with government reform efforts, a model of foolish compassion and ideological corruption. *Life-Changers* centered on intelligent and athletic young men troubled by the challenge of finding their place in a dramatically changing world and, under Buchman's influence, coming to conclusions like this: "He could not escape from the thought that all the social and political problems with which he had hitherto amused his intellect—problems convenient enough as topics of conversation—were so many molehills in comparison with this single mountainous fact of human sin."[44] In the 1930s this anti-politics in fact had a political orientation, inspired partly by fascism in continental Europe. Taking up the mission of "world-changing," Buchman observed that a spiritually enlightened dictatorship would make the best form of government, and it emerged that Group emissaries had gone to Germany to try to "change" Hitler. After considerable backlash, the Oxford Group quickly transformed into "Moral Rearmament," a religious coalition to rally public support for American intervention in World War II.[45]

Begbie's politically framed accounts of both East End and Oxbridge conversions were high on the reading lists of A.A.'s pioneers, and they prefigure elements of the early movement's recovery narratives. The book *Alcoholics Anonymous* (1939), still the foundational text of twelve-step addiction recovery, echoes key elements of *Twice-Born Men*, from its plain-man style to its allegorical titles ("Fired Again," "The Car Smasher," etc.) that invite the reader to expect inspiration in the life of a type of person they had assumed to be irredeemable.[46] The persuasive technique of framing a traditional conversion experience by emphasizing aspects of the person's life that predisposed them *against* having one is another continuity with Begbie's style. A.A.'s prototypical recovery narrative is that of Bill Wilson. Although Wilson was a professional man and a onetime paper millionaire, his story reads at the moment of conversion precisely like that of the down-and-out Puncher. And it was Frank Buchman's followers who evangelized the founders of A.A. in New York City and Akron, Ohio, in the early 1930s, in the methods Begbie's later book describes.[47] Begbie, Buchman, and A.A. shared the Jamesian notion of a core divine reality to conversion that did not need much, if anything, in the way of religious content. Begbie and Buchman anticipated the ways A.A. would deemphasize Christianity, referring almost exclusively to God rather than to Jesus and using churches as sympathetic meeting spaces rather than doctrinal authorities. The Twelve Steps themselves are an ecumenical, codified form of the revival practices that Wilson and the other early members learned in Oxford Group settings.

A.A. did not focus on Begbie's and Buchman's reactionary attitudes toward politics, though its founders did express versions of them privately. More important, the conventions of pure, self-focused spirituality that Begbie anchored to an anti-government ideology, using James's endorsement, survived into the early A.A. recovery stories. Built into these tropes was the argument that spiritual regeneration preceded and eclipsed the importance of political or economic reform in the lives of individuals and, by extension, as matters of public concern. Furthermore, Begbie's frequent illustrations of the happiness with which poverty could be borne by those who were saved anticipated A.A.'s political quietism and recovery narrative's commitment to continual humility over spiritual triumphalism or promises of prosperity. A.A. conducted its own modifications of conversion narrative, significantly shifting the focus of the individualism that Begbie and Buchman endorsed, as we will see in the following chapter. But their reactionary interpretations of an unbiased, pragmatically testable Jamesian view of spiritual change helped shape A.A. narrative and culture. Another very different but similarly politically fraught reading of James illuminates what drinking had meant in the lives of these same men.

Anti-Jamesian Drinking

Jack London's direct response to *The Varieties of Religious Experience* came in his 1913 memoir, *John Barleycorn*. In what turned out to be a late-in-life retrospective, London presented his drinking history as a cautionary tale that argued in favor of Prohibition. More salient in his prose, though, was London's defiant flaunting of the manly drinker's philosophy of disenchantment, arrayed against what he saw as James's feminized refuge in spiritual redemption. In tying this intellectual stance to his manly exploits, London offered a preview of the way heavy drinking would serve as a site of masculinity in much canonical modern literature.

John W. Crowley has provided a definitive reading of how *John Barleycorn* establishes major tropes of drinking that reappeared in the fiction of Hemingway, Fitzgerald, and other leading male modernists. In *The White Logic* (named after London's personification of alcohol in *John Barleycorn*),

Crowley shows that London's memoir goes beyond celebrating the rough-and-tumble of the barroom to a "gendering of alcoholism itself as exclusively and homosocially male."[48] Crowley's analysis brings into sharp focus the way the modern writer's refuge in hard-drinking masculinity expressed panic in the face of social change. My purpose is to trace these meanings back, through London's career, to engagements with rescue missions in the heyday of the drunkard's conversion.

Before confronting his own drinking in philosophical terms, London had developed a critical stance toward the drunkard's conversion narrative in his depictions of drinking men at the very moments when evangelists and elite reformers were making their offers of redemption. London's contempt for James has a prehistory in these earlier texts, in his take on the kinds of source material that James had used in *Varieties*. London initiated this trajectory at the turn of the century in *The People of the Abyss*, an account of poverty in the English capital. His withering socialist critique of slum evangelism was the mirror-image of Begbie's subsequent tribute to James and the Salvation Army. Later, at the midpoint of his writing career, London took on the interpersonal class dynamics of the drunkard's conversion. In the autobiographical novel *Martin Eden* (1908), he savaged the social condescension inherent in an angelic bourgeois woman's offer of redemption to a working-class drinker.

Reading these works as engagements with the same cultural source material James used in *Varieties* helps to ground the hallucinatory passage in *John Barleycorn* when alcohol itself, using the medium of London's mind, taunts William James and his defense of redemptive spiritual experience. Throughout his career, and even when discussing his own habits, London maintained that heavy drinking was unhealthy and morally destructive. But he saw the conversion narratives on offer by religious evangelists, reformers from polite society, and ultimately William James as dishonest and manipulative evasions of, first, the underlying socioeconomic causes of vice, and second, the darker truths of human existence. As his career and his drinking progressed, these arguments became increasingly personal. London clung to the conviction that it was *as* a heavy drinker, despite his physical disintegration, that a man could be more fundamentally honest about these matters. This rejection of the drunkard's conversion and its intellectual patron in James set the stage for much of the romantic drinking discourse in modernist literature and culture.

London was a working-class socialist, whose findings in *The People of the Abyss* read like a point-by-point, preemptive rebuttal of Begbie's response to poverty in the English capital a few years later. While Begbie wrote as a pious middle-class observer, London disguised himself as a stranded sailor to go undercover among the East End poor to try to experience as best he could their poverty and the mental states it produced. While Begbie described alcohol abuse as the habit of a soul given over to sin, London saw the compulsion to drink as an inevitable outcome of a system that actively prevented the poor from fulfilling middle-class ideals. Where Begbie depicted the Salvation Army's religion as a gratefully discovered lifeline, London treated its services as a hypocritical condition of charity that interfered with men's daily efforts to find work. While both Begbie and London depict women's drunkenness as an especially vile marker of degradation, Begbie located a redemptive social presence in angelic women, while London saw relief only in camaraderie among men. And, finally, while Begbie presented his book as an homage to William James, London's attitudes to drinking and religion established the terms on which, at the end of his career, he would confront James as the godfather of weak-minded sentimentalism.

London, like Begbie, claimed to be giving a comprehensive view of urban poverty, and, also like Begbie, he framed this world using scenes of excessive drinking, gender-role failure, and domestic instability, the knot of issues through which questions about what the poor "deserved" from society were typically discussed. *The People of the Abyss* opens and closes with meditations on self-destructive drinking among the poor, its causes and its meanings. After establishing his lodging and adopting his disguise, London's first close scrutiny of English poverty comes in a drinking session with a twenty-two-year-old sailor who "lived for . . . booze," and whose personal philosophy explicitly centers on having chosen alcohol over marriage. After quoting the man at length, London concludes that he is consciously and rationally choosing alcohol over the more respectable comforts of home and hearth, because he had observed growing up that economic pressures reduce such a life to "masculine misery." London adds that he was able to see the man naked, and that he had never seen a man "who stripped to better advantage," extenuating the tragedy of his imminent alcoholic decline.[49] London's argument is that this man, and the vast numbers in similar positions, are not acting irrationally when they spend what little money they can gather on drink instead of on a family. Where Begbie speaks of the "worst of men" becoming "saints," London says of the sailor that even in his drunkenness, "yet he was not a bad man."[50] Here and in his penultimate chapter ("Drink, Temperance, and Thrift"), London aims to show that when the poor shun middle-class values by escaping into drunkenness, they do so for rational reasons, not from stupidity. Society is arranged such that working toward such values only makes things worse for them, he argues.

Some of London's most animated polemics in *People of the Abyss* come in response to the idea of a compassionate religious solution to poverty and drinking. A chapter on the Salvation Army ("The Peg") depicts its officers as supercilious bullies and its religious imposition as a mockery of Christ's message of love (121–37). London's critique is characteristic of the skeptical treatment of missionaries in literature, similar to fictionalized scenes of evangelical ineptitude in Stephen Crane's *Maggie* and Upton Sinclair's *The Jungle*: "Weary and exhausted from the night's sleeplessness and hardship, suffering from the long wait upon their feet, and faint from hunger, they were yearning, not for salvation, but for grub. The 'soul-snatchers' (as these men call all religious propagandists) should study the physiological basis of psychology a little, if they wish to make their efforts more effective" (131). Elsewhere London satirizes Christian reformers by peppering his prose with biblical allusion (the poor "are the stones by the builder rejected") in the ironic manner that both points to the gospels' social message and mocks religious ignorance of it (40). At his most sympathetic, London joins the progressives of his era in calling rescue mission workers well-intentioned naïfs who "have worked faithfully" but "achieved nothing." Their inadequacy begins in the individualistic nature of their religion and culminates in the arrogance of thinking it could solve systemic social problems. "They do not understand the simple sociology of Christ, yet they come to the miserable and the despised with the pomp of social redeemers," London writes (306). In their misguided energies and false promises, they ultimately make things worse. In *The People of the Abyss*, London fundamentally rejects the idea that the Jamesian "regenerate character" could be a factor in the political economy.

As London's career as a writer and activist took off in his late twenties, he wrote more frequently and more intimately about himself, especially through the lenses of gender, class, and race. And as his career progressed, so too did his drinking, to a pitch that constituted alcoholism.[51] In his more self-referential work, London's treatment of drinking developed consistently from his observations about the British poor. He often deplored the kind of drinking he himself indulged in, but he understood it in terms of his identity and its role in his political thought.

In his 1908 novel *Martin Eden*, London critiqued more closely the social and subjective terms by which polite society proffers redemption to working-class men who drink. This autobiographical fiction tells of the formation of a working-class intellectual through the title character's passage from naïve, traumatized desires for beauty into deep self-awareness and sociopolitical understanding. This theme develops in Martin's temptation by, and ultimate rejection of, the love of Ruth, a beautiful and idealistic bourgeois woman. In a dynamic similar to that of the young lady missionaries and the hardened drunkards of the slums, Ruth's sympathetic attention triggers Martin's awakening and cures him of a drinking habit. Early in the novel, the possibility of a romantic relationship with Ruth causes the young Martin to undergo a "moral revolution." Feeling a "crying need to be clean" to make himself worthy of her "cleanness and purity," he quits drinking, despite having long thought it "the proper thing for men to do." As in many a convert before him, "the need for strong drink had vanished," because he was "drunken in new and more profound ways . . . with love and with a glimpse of higher and eternal life."[52]

In this novel, though, far from constituting the impetus to continual regeneration, Martin's infatuation represents a state of intellectual immaturity and undeveloped class consciousness. The political terms of this romance emerge when hard manual labor pushes Martin back to the bottle. Martin's work in a steam laundry allows London to make quite explicitly the argument that drinking is an inevitable consequence, a mental necessity even, of physical drudgery. Presaging the central conceit of *John Barleycorn,* it is the clarity of thought that drinking brings that allows Martin and a friend to see this fact plainly. "The whiskey was wise," London writes. "It told secrets on itself."[53] Martin's confession of this drinking to Ruth marks a turning-point in their relationship: a real epiphany for him, and a false one for her. He realizes that the bourgeois Ruth cannot imagine his experience sympathetically, and that he has grown beyond his infatuation with her. She, meanwhile, in her very horror at his confession, is inspired to the role of the redeemer, a role that London presents as fundamentally self-regarding and self-deceptive: "It pointed out to her how near she had drawn to him, and once accepted, it paved the way for greater intimacy. Pity, too, was aroused, and innocent, idealistic thoughts of reform. She would save this raw young man who had come so far. She would save him from the curse of his early environment, and she would save him from himself in spite of himself. And all this affected her as a very noble state of consciousness; nor did she dream that behind it and underlying it were the jealousy and desire of love" (161–62). This, then, is London's contemptuous take on the progressive goal of subjective awakening to social sympathy by the young members of the privileged classes. Instead of launching Ruth into a career of selfless reform, her vision of Martin's humanity constitutes greater self-regard than ever before.

Once Martin finally gains a full sense of his identity as a writer in a capitalist society, he is easily able to reject Ruth, even when she comes as a supplicant for his love. She insists she can love even his "smoking and swearing," but Martin is convinced more than ever that neither of them had ever really loved the other. He had loved only the ideal role she played in his mind, and "as much as she had liked him she had liked the bourgeois standard of valuation more" (377). He is confirmed in his conclusion when he finds out that she had not really risked anything to come to him, and, appropriately, he soon finds himself in the welcome company of an old workmate and drinking companion who is now a tramp.

Martin Eden does not turn to any socialist triumph. The leading socialist character, Russ Brissenden, is an elite, "cadaverous" alcoholic, a "chemical" dipsomaniac of the variety that London placed beneath the socially trained alcoholic. Martin holds revolutionary politics at arm's length, and he ends the novel drowning himself. But London does something decisive in the politics of drinking narrative when he routs the trope of the interclass romance. The novel rejects the notion that the bourgeois recognition of the humanity of the poor constitutes a redemptive historical moment, least of all one that could stand for a wider societal healing. And it rejects in particular the exploitation of destructive drinking among poor men as a grounds on which to foster such redemption.

London's sociopolitical analyses of drinking in *People of the Abyss* and *Martin Eden* return in subjective, philosophical forms in his nonfiction life-story in *John Barleycorn: Alcoholic Memoirs*. His defense of escapist drinking as a rational choice for the traumatized working-class of *People of the Abyss* and his rejection of redemptive class reconciliation as its solution in *Martin Eden* reappear in his memoir as ways of intellectualizing his own intemperate habits. This continuity is encapsulated in the earlier text's phrase, "masculine misery." The horror of an emasculating subjugation to a women's sphere links the young sailor to the writer-figure, the writer, and to a whole school of modernist fiction, in pitting alcoholic sociability against domestic duty. The gendered treatment of alcoholism that Crowley shows flowing through *John Barleycorn* and the canon of male modernist fiction can be seen, throughout London's career, emerging in engagements with the drunkard's conversion narratives that appeared in the slums of cities and the approving lectures of psychologists.

If *John Barleycorn* was not, as one present-day publisher has called it, "the earliest intelligent treatment of alcohol in American literature," it does seem to have marked a new phase in confessional writing about drinking. It is an eccentric kind of memoir, undertaken, London claims in the opening pages, to warn young men away from alcohol and even to convince society to elimi- nate it. Indeed, among its most important immediate impacts was as a suc- cessful propaganda tool in the Prohibition movement.[54] But the body of the text does more to defend drinking than to indict it, as it highlights the catalytic role drinking played in the extraordinary physical and intellectual adventures of London's life. As the narrative progresses, though, there emerges an effort to come to terms with why and how he lost control of his consumption in midlife. Adamantly denying he is an alcoholic, London claims that he first fell in love with the manly camaraderie of drinking and, later, became possessed by the stern, unsentimental acceptance of hard philosophical truth that he found alcohol enabled in him, a quality he called its "White Logic." Establish- ing, altering, or filling out many of the legends that attach to London's life, published at a time when social and scientific attitudes toward both alcohol and gender were rapidly changing, and airing a misanthropic pessimism that complicates London's career-long commitment to socialism, *John Barleycorn's* knot of motives and rhetorical strategies is hard to untangle. But, for the pur- poses at hand, it should be noted that the memoir was conceived as an intel- lectual response to *The Varieties of Religious Experience.*

London made out his notes for *John Barleycorn* on the flyleaves and in the margins of his copy of *Varieties,* during a five-month sailing trip in 1912 that biographers describe as his longest period of sobriety in several years. On this voyage, he appears to have been developing an anti-Jamesian philoso- phy of pessimism, using the aesthetic philosophers Violet Paget and Edgar Saltus as guides.[55] In the memoir, this pessimism takes shape in the intellectual and experiential journey of London's drinking life. In London's account, the destructive consequences of binge drinking are not what hasten this darken- ing mood; on the contrary, London describes alcohol purifying and strength- ening his intellectual faculties, if not his physical ability to act on them. In *John Barleycorn,* instead of providing an ersatz transcendence that can only be ful- filled by a truly religious transformation, alcohol's "White Logic" destroys all such ideals as illusory, revealing the ultimate meaninglessness of the conscious layer that sits atop man's essentially animal existence.

London recognized James as the intellectual patron of the drunkard's con- version, albeit from the perspective of one who was embracing its nearly literal opposite in his reading of Saltus's 1885 *Philosophy of Disenchantment.* Next to James's list of "saints" and their attributes in *Varieties,* London cited Saltus's work, and its list of "disenchanted thinkers," adding the name "John Barley- corn" as if to suggest alcohol personified the essence of anti-conversion.[56] Near the end of *John Barleycorn,* at something approximating the deep, dark heart of London's efforts to both confront and deny his compulsion to drink, the James of *Varieties,* and perhaps also of *The Will to Believe,* makes an appearance, offering hope. After London has described losing control over his drinking, the White Logic itself begins to speak as an interlocutor in the narrative, in a jeering voice not unlike literary evocations of Satan. In London and the Logic's philosophical joust, the Logic mocks James's attentions to faith as "rationality gelded to sentiment." Reason, in other words, is masculine—like London's drunken persona, it is "grim and honest"—until it is unmanned by James's sentimental wish fulfillment. Reason is thus both cause and justification for destructive drinking. Idealisms of all stripes are rendered sentimental, weak products of the feminine spheres of domesticity, reform, and revival. In this violent rejection of all that the conversion worldview holds dear, alcohol takes on its modernist role as a gendered medium of both pessimism and escape. Men drink and discover that the world is built on "vital lies"; then they drink more, in order to live with such disillusion.[57]

The journey through London's work that I've traced here suggests that this stylistic obsession with manly drinking responded to the role that missionary drunkard's conversions played in the public culture of progressive reform, a role for which James provided lasting intellectual authentication. Returning to the comparison of *People of the Abyss* and *John Barleycorn,* one can see the political anger in the former transformed, through the medium of a philosophical response to James (and perhaps, as importantly, through a decade of heavy drinking), into a set of personal gestures in the latter. Indeed, London claims in *John Barleycorn* that his memories of the East End in 1902 contain none of the political analysis of drinking that he recorded in *People,* but simply feature "the visions of shining pubs" and "calls for 'two of bitter' and 'three of Scotch'" among the men he drank with there.[58] The migration of his scrutiny of drinking, from the politics of working-class behavior to the cultural pose of the masculine writer, is a shared backstory to alcoholism narrative in modern literature. London's ultimate shift from critiquing the class politics of this discourse to a more abstract, philosophical contempt for sentimentalism was an instance of the phenomenon I'll look at more closely in chapter 6. The modernists' introspective turn, in this case from alcoholism as a sociopolitical phenomenon to alcoholism as a feature of writerly consciousness, was the counterpart in literature to the "depoliticization" of conversion narrative in recovery culture.

If Begbie helped create the narrative style that A.A.'s founders used to convey their therapeutic spirituality, London's literary approach to drinking is also legible in the background of recovery culture. As Crowley shows, London's late memoir inaugurated the purposes and methods by which male modernists invested intense social and philosophical meaning in self-destructive drinking. This vice ostensibly rebelled against Victorian repression and provided solace in an age of war trauma and lost meaning. But Crowley shows that the "modernist drunk narrative" that runs through the key texts of this mythology was, in its actual functioning, an attempt to shore up a dominant social identity that was threatened in a time of rapid cultural change.[59] This was a form of masculinity that helped to define the drinking lives of A.A.'s pioneers, and one that echoes through their recovery narratives in efforts to maintain distance from the feminine associations of religion and temperance.

The Hot Place: Narrative as Data

What was it about James and *The Varieties of Religious Experience* that made it a touchstone for this discourse? James's placement of drunkard's conversions at the center of a new "science of religion" had an obviously provocative, and ultimately legitimizing, effect. But more than that mere attention and respect, James's analytical method in *Varieties* was particularly effective at facilitating the genre's diffusion into ideological contexts and stylistic trends. In effect, James created an analytical mechanism for separating the genre's roles as cultural performance and as psychological data. This distilling effect allowed subsequent adaptations to recombine these functions such that the strengths of both could be put toward an overarching social argument.

James's broad project was to negotiate a productive détente between religion and science. To apply a scientific analysis to religion, while respecting religion's own claims to truth, James premised his argument in *Varieties* on the notion that religious narrative can be treated as unfiltered data about the human mind, and that patterns in such narrative are evidence, not of their social transmission, but of the universality of their underlying mental structures. This premise served both a model of religion and a theory of mind that were governed by the intense individualism James inherited from his religious and intellectual milieus.[60] In practice, to make the conventions of a religious tradition native to the human mind required James to distance the narrative form as far as he could from its role as a culturally reproduced genre. To accomplish this feat he and his fellow pioneers in the "science of religion" posited an ultimately arbitrary distinction between genuine conversion and "second-hand" religion or "cant."[61] This authenticating mechanism allowed them to read memorable conversions, including Samuel H. Hadley's, as "subjective realities" rather than "external practices," conferring the stamp of originality on narratives that drew heavily on conventions familiar not only from earlier famous conversions, but from sentimental literature.[62]

James acknowledged, for example, that Hadley's conversion was one of many similar ones that occurred on Water Street. He agreed with a peer who argued that Hadley and other drunkards represent the contemporary transformation of "religion" into "the conglomerate of desires and emotions springing from the sense of sin and its release." (This was another conclusion preordained by their evidentiary base, which centered in the evangelical turn in anglo-Protestant religion.) But instead of looking more closely at this cluster of conversions and the institution that facilitated it, James linked Hadley to an archetype, as evidence of a transhistorical pattern of mental experience. James concluded of Hadley's experience that it "corresponds to the subjectively centered form of morbid melancholy," established in his analysis of John Bunyan.[63] But, as we saw in chapter 1, Hadley did not learn to tell his own experience as a narrative, in the manner quoted by James, until after an evening service at McAuley's mission, where he heard dozens of ex-drinkers testify, "every one of whom told my story."[64] In other words, Hadley identified his own experience with those particular narrative conventions, and so, led by this identification to experience the rest of the story (conversion), he felt justified in retelling it himself.

Instead of seeing this process of identification and performance as a central aspect of religious experience or drunkard's rehabilitation, James saw it only as a way in which culture mimics genuine experience. After isolating conversion from the imitative and performative implications of its role as a genre, James is able to observe the kinship between religious ecstasy and sentimental literary sympathy without fear of contaminating religio-psychological phenomena with sociocultural ones. In an effort to convey the condition of "saintliness" produced by conversion, James offers the following comparison:

> The stone wall inside of him has fallen, the hardness in his heart has broken down. The rest of us can, I think, imagine this by recalling our state of feeling in those temporary 'melting moods' into which either the trials of real life, or the theatre, or a novel sometimes throws us. Especially if we weep! For it is then as if our tears broke through an inveterate inner dam, and let all sorts of ancient peccancies and moral stagnancies drain away, leaving us now washed and soft of heart and open to every nobler leading.[65]

James identifies precisely the moment of sentimental sympathy (when we weep) as the experience that mimics conversion, an equation familiar to students of nineteenth-century popular fiction. The power of Uncle Tom and Evangeline to effect conversions, for example, is expressed in the moments when they "melt" their companions' and readers' hearts and elicit their tears. Having insisted that conversion can be distinguished from the narrative performances that merely imitate its genuine reports, James turns to the mimicry of fictional narrative to convey that very experience.

James places alcoholic intoxication in the same category of ersatz religious transcendence by which he understands literature. Alcohol is "the great exciter of the Yes function in man" which "brings its votary from the chill periphery of things to the radiant core," making "him for the moment one with truth." This feeling of total union is nearly the same experience as literary "melting," and sits on the same level as literature in James's implied hierarchy of real versus illusory conversion. This familial relationship allows alcohol to substitute for literature, too: "Not through mere perversity do men run after it. To the poor and unlettered it stands in the place of symphony concerts and of literature; and it is part of the deeper mystery and tragedy of life that whiffs and gleams of something that we immediately recognize as excellent should be vouchsafed to so many of us only in the fleeting earlier phases of what in its totality is so degrading a poisoning."[66] A previous generation's preachers, including Lyman Beecher (father of Harriet Beecher Stowe) and Jonathan Townley Crane (father of Stephen) warned that literary imagination was as profane and dangerous an altered state as intoxication.[67] James's formula reflects the subsequent elevation of literature to the status of ethical culture, while still accepting the temperance logic of inevitable degradation for "so many of us" who drink.

By pitting alcoholic intoxication and literary elevation against one another as false, flash-in-the-pan suitors to the "radiant core" or "hot place" in a seeker's mental landscape, James acknowledged conversion's role as the master-genre of subjectively felt transcendence and its resulting character reformation. But his distinction between authentic interior conversion and mere linguistic behavior not only betrayed the "by their fruits ye shall know them" proto-pragmatism of *Varieties,* it also prevented him from recognizing in his literary example a guidepost—identification with the subject position in a narrative—to the mysterious process that effects spiritual transformation and habitual reform.[68]

It would be unfair to dismiss James's method as misprision, however. As Jeremy Carrette has written, the first psychologists of religion "set up the terms of the debate and wrestled with unresolved category errors in the attempt to determine different domains of knowledge," categories and domains, he adds, that contemporary scholars would be complacent in thinking are now unambiguous.[69] And to the extent that *Varieties* did compare different religious traditions, James recognized that his findings not only suggested universal religious tendencies but also revealed an essential arbitrariness in the beliefs attached to those feelings. In *Varieties,* James occasionally expresses a personal preference for the Protestant reformation's various practical and positivistic interpretations of conversion, and a distaste for the asceticism of Eastern holy men and Catholic virgin-saints. But James's ultimate conclusion regarding the contentless essence of mysticism applies also to the conversions (not least his own) he saw as the gateways to such experience.[70] While James's method of distinguishing the genuine from the authentic facilitated conversion's polemical redeployment, he, unlike many of those he inspired, recognized that no single ideology of conversion could claim special truth-status above the others.

In this manner James witnessed to and rationalized the efficacy of evangelical conversion, but at the same time detached its functionality from exclusionary religious tradition. His analysis of the drunkard's conversion confirmed the revivalists' belief that *only* spiritual regeneration could cure addiction, but psychologized it in such a way as to authorize and hasten its secularization. This movement toward a practically applicable, universal spirituality helped to create twentieth-century popular therapeutic culture, most decisively in the realm of addiction recovery.

But James's focus on structures of mind rather than cultural dynamics had implications for how his own findings would be received, both in direct ways, as in Begbie's and London's texts, and in this longer-term historical impact. The detachment of "genuine" conversion from its religious proprietors made it all the more available for ideological appropriation. As he vouched for its essential reality, he made it more portable. This transformation from exclusionary religious practice to universal psychological tendency made forms of conversion that downplayed doctrinal content all the more persuasive. Conversion was now a fact in the modern world, and this facticity would work, in concert with its modified but still very real sentimental appeal, on behalf of whatever new ideological clothing could be draped upon it.

And in fact, before A.A. and other popular therapeutic systems developed their notions of universal spirituality, James's polemical interpreters based their claims on precisely this accessibility. Conservatives like Begbie and progressives like Stead saw in drunkards' conversions a vision of the brotherhood of all humanity, and they presented their political implications as flowing directly from this innocent ideal. Begbie saw all social and political problems reduced to the "single mountainous fact of human sin," while Stead defined the "Church Universal" as "the union of all who love for the service of all who suffer."[71] In each case, if every individual tended to his or her own spiritual state and acted accordingly, the problems that arise at the levels of social and political relations would disappear. The drunkard's conversion, especially, in its materiality endowed the spiritual vision at its turning-point with the force of documentary reality. But to make this vision a social reality required particular political prescriptions.

James himself, in Talks to Students published the year after he gave the Gifford Lectures, made a similar gesture when he urged that universal human sympathy could play a transformative political role in palliating "the labor question" and "all sorts of anarchistic discontents and socialistic projects, and the conservative resistances which they provoke." He distanced himself from a tepid moderation by stipulating that such conflict is only "unhealthy and regrettable . . . to a limited extent." But that extent, he explained, was precisely the tribalism that prevented the rich and poor from recognizing that the same "nightingale of eternal meaning" sang in each other's hearts. If everyone could "really and truly believe it, how our convulsive insistencies, how our antipathies and dreads of each other, would soften down! If the poor and the rich could look at each other in this way, sub specie aeternitatis, how gentle would grow their disputes! What tolerance and good humor, what willingness to live and let live, would come into the world!"[72] As we have seen, the progenitors of twentieth-century addiction recovery did indeed see drunkard's conversions as symbolizing and even constituting the historical moment when the rich and poor recognized each other's humanity. It was, for these idealists, a moment in social history that had profoundly hopeful political implications, if only people would first recognize it, and then interpret it the way they ought to.

The apolitical, nondoctrinal spiritual conversion did not become established until A.A.'s growth in the decades following World War II. The influence of James's interpreters, such as Begbie, and also of his detractors, such as London, suggest that the relationship of recovery ethic to political contention was much closer to A.A.'s creation moment than its historical mythology has allowed. The next chapter explores these moments and myths.

4

New Deal Individualism and the
Big Book of Alcoholics Anonymous

These dark days will be worth all they cost us if they teach us that our true destiny is not to be ministered unto but to minister to ourselves and to our fellow men.

—Franklin Delano Roosevelt, first inaugural address (1933)

We are like the passengers of a great liner the moment after rescue from shipwreck when camaraderie, joyousness and democracy pervade the vessel from steerage to Captain's table.

—*Alcoholics Anonymous* (1939)

T HE BIRTH OF ALCOHOLICS ANONYMOUS in the late 1930s was a turning point in the cultural history of alcoholism and addiction. A.A. grew rapidly, and by midcentury it had taken hold not only as a means of recovery, but also as a source of conventional wisdom about alcoholism, informing its depiction in film, fiction, and memoir. While the efficacy of A.A. for alcoholics remains the focus of debate, its cultural impact is unquestioned.[1] Historians have attributed this proliferation to a number of factors. A.A. helped fill the post-temperance, post-Repeal need for a conception of the dangers of alcohol that limited the risk to a small subset of drinkers. A.A. embraced the disease concept of alcoholism in an era of rising medical authority and popular psychology. It formulated a spirituality that used the language of traditional Christian piety but was personal and pragmatic enough to sit comfortably with postwar prosperity. Perhaps as important as any of these contextual dynamics were the evangelical energies and professional expertise of its early members, many of whom were experienced in marketing and public relations. Between the late 1930s and the mid-1950s they went on radio programs, placed magazine articles, founded research institutes and public education agencies, and held conventions. Internally, they developed a flexible, bottom-up organizational structure, inoculating the growing movement against factionalization, external obligation, and mission drift. A.A.'s role in creating the new alcoholism discourse was, in the end, overdetermined.[2]

Whatever the various contributions of its conceptual innovations, A.A.'s cultural influence flowed through, and ultimately resided in, its narrative of recovery. Both its oral and print practices center on the sharing of testimony, and it is through this function that its models of alcoholism and recovery entered the popular imagination. A.A.'s injunction against personal publicity may only have deepened this influence. To this day, memoirists and interviewees adhere to this custom not by hiding their alcoholism but by avoiding specific reference to A.A. or its derivative programs. Thus they have spread its ideas and its phraseology as a natural language of recovery, rather than as a framework with an institutional history and a cultural genealogy. At the same time, tellers of addiction stories across various media—in fiction and nonfiction, in text and on screen—draw heavily from the narrative conventions and therapeutic insights established and perpetuated in A.A. meetings. A.A.'s deep cultural penetration is most evident in the way the recovery story it fostered can convey intensely personal, experiential truth, largely free from the implications of persuasion or imitation that attached to its precursors. A.A.'s institutional success is the background to the modern addiction story.[3]

In this chapter I situate that cultural achievement in the history of sociopolitical roles played by prior recovery movements and the popular narratives they produced. A.A.'s narrative model thrived not because, in focusing more rigorously on private experience, it turned away from this legacy. Rather, this new recovery story made sense of addiction in the middle of the twentieth century because it conducted its politics of self at a deeper level than its predecessors did. Its founders recognized the distracting effect of controversy and sought to insulate themselves and their movement from it. But while they eschewed polemics, they were still engaged with key ideological transitions of their time. In their narratives they constructed new selves that were not only rescued from oblivion but fit for productive work and useful public service. A.A. narrative participated in a multivalent revision of American individualism that had been initiated by labor, progressives, and socialists in the first decades of the new century, was catalyzed by the Great Depression, given initial political shape by the Roosevelt administration's recovery policies, and took mature form in the postwar social order. A.A. narrative—as a cultural technology for reconstructing selfhood from its putative foundations—articulated this shift in values in a peculiarly explicit and epiphanic way. In doing so, it altered, but did not foreclose, the historical relationship of alcoholism to the politics of reform. It offered its own New Deal in the cultural expression of American individualism.

During the Depression, America's national narrative had become one of decline and crisis, and imagining modes of recovery animated both political and cultural life. The New Deal embodied this imperative at the level of the state. Connecting, and ultimately superseding, an often inconsistent policy program, New Dealers built a narrative that described the redemption of the national crisis by turning it into a necessary and even triumphant revision of fundamental values. In this story, a destructive self-interest had collapsed along with the economic bubble it had fueled, clearing the ground for a cooperative recovery that would tap the deeply held communitarian values of the citizenry in order to restructure public and private institutions. It was a narrative not first of economic recovery, but of moral regeneration through the redemption of suffering, achieved through sympathetic social bonds. A.A.'s narrative was among a variety of phenomena during the Depression that similarly ordered and responded to the experience of socioeconomic failure. (Indeed some commentators, such as Will Rogers, referred to the speculative mania of the 1920s as a "financial drunk" and the Depression as its hangover.)[4] A.A. described a reconstruction of selfhood that paralleled Franklin Delano Roosevelt's effort to reconceive national values and rebuild American society from its lowest depths.

A.A. narrative shared this structure with the reformers' case for national economic recovery, and more than that, its redeemed narrators expressed an ideal of citizenship in the emerging liberal state. As a method of describing the subjective experiences of individual alcoholics, A.A. recovery stories served a categorically different purpose than did national political rhetoric. But the way recovering narrators described their experiences of decline and crisis drew on the same kind of social material that, writ large, defined the national problem: the bewildering failure of self-reliant individualism, as evidenced in job loss, privation, and family trauma. A.A. narrative, just like FDR's New Deal story, interpreted this failure as a hard-earned lesson about the limits of self-interest. Recovery salvaged downwardly mobile, disintegrating men of the middle class, and explicitly redeemed their failure, by using it as an opportunity to rebuild their concept of self from its foundations. It described breaking the alcoholic's cycle of binge and bust by reconciling the self to its limits—those of its own resources, those imposed by the claims of others, and those inherent in the structure of social institutions. As the outcome of this honest accounting, it offered not reduced expectations, but rather a vision of unprecedented fulfillment, in the discovery of a higher self-interest through social sympathy and service. In its mutual-aid practices, its Twelve-Step ethics, and the principle of anonymity it developed, it did not call for self-abnegation but for resituating the self in an egalitarian social universe, where an ethic of service and moral sensitivity was required to liberate one's best self. In other words, A.A. made sobriety a project of social reciprocity that, imagined as a form of citizenship, would enable the kind of society that Roosevelt and other liberals were describing. Further, in its preference for pragmatic procedures over dogma, in its collectivization of wisdom but not power, and in the democratic structure it ultimately adopted, A.A. enacted an ideal relationship between social ethics and organizational principles in such a state.

This affinity between the recovering self and visions of a more egalitarian society originated in social conditions, but it played out at the level of culture, in the recovery movement's provision of a new form of self-narrative. As a product of efforts by its early members to describe their personal experiences, the raw cultural materials of the recovery narrative were the tropes of white, male, and middle-class identity. The formal challenges they faced as narrative subjects were those of representing middle-class socioeconomic trauma and redeeming failed male agency, phenomena that were not at home with confessions of fundamental inadequacy. The cultural keynote of redemption in the New Deal era was reflected on the left and the right in images of working-class suffering and resilience, whether as revolutionary or nostalgic, respectively. But middle-class trauma was more difficult to imagine, and the traditional bourgeois commitment to individualism provided a built-in moral explanation that redirected it toward the shame of failure rather than redemptive sympathy. Further compounding the challenge was the way that self-consciously modern masculinity, especially among the Prohibition-era urban middle classes from which A.A. sprang, had come to rely on heavy drinking as a key social signifier. Framed more broadly, the cultural task the A.A. pioneers undertook in their own recoveries was to interpret individual failure during the Depression with only limited recourse to either the middle class's traditional moralism or its contemporary worldliness.

Conversion narrative had been, for at least a century, the go-to genre for managing this kind of success-myth failure, especially where vices played a role. As we saw in earlier chapters, progressives, socialists, and reactionaries contested the meaning of the drunkard's conversion, recognizing it as a potent symbolic vehicle of ideological legitimacy. Indeed, some of A.A.'s pioneers first began to tell their stories in the gospel rescue missions where the drunkard's conversion was born, as well as in churches and revivals with world-changing ambitions. In A.A. they were negotiating that same politically freighted narrative turn, by which conversion brought the outcast inebriate back into the social order in a way that changed it, as well as him. But the particular identities and experiences of alcoholics in the 1930s demanded a new kind of social rehabilitation, and thus outlined a new kind of sober citizenship.

Consistent with their interwar senses of masculinity, A.A. narrators spurned the mantle of the sinner redeemed, characterizing it as a sentimental cop-out and identifying it socially with low-status evangelicals. This attitude flowed from a particular kind of hardboiled self-image common to male self-expression in the 1930s. Even if he attributed his losses entirely to drinking, in his downward mobility, sporadic employment, and itinerancy, the worn-out drunk, like the wounded Great War veteran of canonical modern fiction or the exploited worker of proletarian literature, appeared in A.A. narrative as a representative figure of modern dislocation and disillusion. He echoed FDR's invocation of the "forgotten man," but he felt his obscurity to be social and relative to his original life chances, rather than a fixed position at the bottom of the "economic pyramid."[5] If the late nineteenth-century drunkards made progressive statements by bringing their identities as immigrants and slumdwellers with them into their transformed public identities, the social politics of A.A. recovery narrative was located in the conservation of this worldly self-image along a journey of spiritual rehabilitation.

The early A.A. members thus not only got themselves sober, they also did lasting cultural work, by refitting the drunkard's conversion to respond to new social conditions in the interwar period and beyond. Confessional recovery narrative brought the disillusioned drunk to God by transfiguring social qualities associated with modern secular life into bonds of spiritual sympathy. In intimate conversations and boisterous house meetings, A.A.'s pioneers reworked the conversion narrative to simultaneously achieve and describe a new ethic of sober selfhood. Their revision of the born-again story focused on overcoming the special barriers to theism put up by the world-weary skepticism and delusional self-reliance of their alcoholic personalities. In effect, A.A. modified the drunkard's conversion to fit a self-consciously modern mode of individualism: the stoicism born of suffering and disillusion. In exchanging confessional narratives, its members recycled the shared experience of hard living that justified that identity, turning it into a spiritual bond that, to borrow Roosevelt's formula, reformed individualism in order to save it. This accommodation of modern male affect to evangelical piety was the cultural expression of a New Deal ethos. Exposing the fantasy of hardboiled masculinity to the sentimental relief of mutual confession figured the reconciliation of middle-class individualism, traumatized by Depression failure, to the reality of mutual dependence.

A.A. thus secularized and modernized the drunkard's conversion, not primarily by refocusing it around a disease concept of alcoholism, but by updating the terms of its subject's social rehabilitation. In doing so it took up conversion's perennial role in American self-fashioning in order to help make sense of life in the modern world. This cultural innovation implicitly responded to the more widespread experience of social and economic dislocation that informed the rise of midcentury liberalism.[6]

Recovery and the Subject of Liberalism

The Roosevelt Administration's first major reform in its program of "National Recovery" was to legalize and tax alcohol sales. The revenues from the re-regulation of alcohol were essential to the funding of the early relief projects under the National Industrial Recovery Act.[7] But while this economic benefit had joined loosened attitudes toward drinking and the obvious failures of Prohibition to help Repeal win the day, the social costs of alcohol remained uncertain, both materially and morally. A.A., even when it was just a handful of men with no wider influence, operated in a cultural space defined by the collapse of the temperance movement. They ultimately filled this gap with a recovery narrative positing that alcoholics needed each other, not legal or even moral controls, to get sober. This narrative, even though it ignored the state, was about the kinds of changes to social values that liberal theorists and policy architects believed were an essential condition of whatever new role the state was taking on.

While A.A.'s pioneers were discovering the limits of self-reliant individualism in their own lives, since the 1920s artists and intellectuals had been reconceiving the nature of the individual in relation to a newly integrated and mechanized "mass" society. In sociological community studies, Freudian talk therapies, Marxist theories, and modern literature, the self increasingly appeared as something created by social and economic forces, rather than as a discrete core of being defined in opposition to its external restraints.[8] Changing the nature of such individuality was not a matter of personal conversion alone but, necessarily, of large-scale societal reform. Not just revolutionaries, but reformist liberal thinkers in the 1930s, in particular, argued that America's struggles proved the need for a restructuring that would reach from the most powerful institutional elements all the way down to the level of citizen subjectivity.

The era's most explicit and sustained articulation of the relationship between state organization and the social self came in the works of John Dewey. Dewey was heir to William James in both philosophical pragmatism and its application in wide-ranging commentary on public matters. For this reason in the effort to historicize recovery it is useful to think about A.A.'s innovations in Deweyan terms, to complement the large body of commentary on the influence of James's ideas of a generation earlier. In a sense, James's focus on religion and the will had evolved, in response to socioeconomic as well as intellectual change, into Dewey's concern with state organization and individualism. The titles alone of Dewey's essay and lecture collections in the 1930s—including *Individualism Old and New* (1930), *Liberalism and Social Action* (1935), and *Freedom and Culture* (1939)—suggest a project of constructing a liberal social ethic, and their contents plowed the deep theoretical soil where society and the self are mutually constructive. Dewey argued that liberalism, as the historic tradition dedicated to liberating the individual from unjust constraints, still offered the best hope for "the recovery of composed, effective and creative individuality," in an era of apparently unavoidable systemic consolidation.[9] But the liberal struggle to assert a vision as clear as either leftist collectivism or reactionary power-hierarchy arose, he thought, from precisely the same confusion that was causing a general crisis in American culture: habituation to an outmoded, frontier individualism that was profoundly ill-suited to the socioeconomic realities of modern life. In order for liberalism to fulfill its promise of personal freedom and to emancipate American culture from a paralyzing ideological confusion, it would have to develop a concept of individualism that recognized, finally, its own social construction.

Dewey's prescription for a "fighting liberalism" thus involved a necessarily two-way process, in which grassroots social movements to begin constructing this new individualism consciously met with top-down, "scientific" institutional restructuring to produce the economic and social relations necessary to facilitate individual flourishing. The social action Dewey envisioned was the work of education, conceived broadly as "all the influences that go to form the attitudes and dispositions (of desire as well as belief), which

constitute dominant habits of mind and character."[10] The total mental structure these elements comprise recalls the kind of change progressives had in
mind when they embraced the conversion narrative a generation earlier. But
while Dewey envisioned a similar degree of subjective transformation, he
did not countenance its development in any sustained way from personal
experiences of the old order's failure. Dewey believed that a new conception
of the self could not rise organically from romantic individualism's ashes,
because the latter was structured specifically so as to be blind to social relations—indeed, to see all organization as the enemy of autonomy. Top-down
restructuring (such as in publicly coordinated industrial, financial, and
labor policy) would be the primary driver of change, by reorienting actual
social relations under cooperative principles. Some architects of the New
Deal, especially in its first phase between 1931 and 1935, evinced a similar
belief in the power of rational systemic overhaul to facilitate a latent consensus among the citizenry.[11] But in their advocacy—the rhetorical projects in
which a policy program might more properly be said to operate in the realm
of cultural narrative—New Dealers spoke more directly to the subjective (or
what some called spiritual) side of the relationship between self and system.

The New Deal produced a collection of policies and agencies, some temporary and some permanent, some that were overturned by courts and some
that withered away, and some, like Social Security, that survived to reshape
assumptions about the role of the national government. Taken together, these
programs famously failed to cohere around a single principle. It was not
until the 1940s that even its own creators began to recognize a theory of the
state in the way it had changed the federal government.[12] In retrospect these
policies seem less to have been informed by political philosophy than to
have grown up around a series of keywords: "recovery," "cooperation," "security," "freedom." But the New Deal's overarching goals were first, and most
consistently, elaborated in something more fully realized: a narrative. FDR's
most broadly public case for the New Deal—more so than in speeches given
to business groups or scholars, which addressed particular challenges—tells
a compelling story more than it makes a sophisticated argument.[13] In this
persuasive rhetoric, Roosevelt described the transformative relationship
between self-concept and state structure as a fait accompli. The experiential
failure of the old individualism under the Depression already legitimated
the rise of a new kind of state. To convey this inevitability, FDR presented
the necessity of reconstructing the institutional order governing American
life using the logic and even the conventions of *conversion narrative*. More
specifically, his is a *recovery* narrative, one that prefigures A.A.'s in each of its

main components: decline to crisis, admission of failure, conviction of the sin of self-interest, and the pragmatic arrival at newly mutual frameworks for ethical behavior, under the sign of a higher power—all occurring as a matter of survival rather than ideology.

The recovery narrative FDR articulated in his major speeches was built very much like a drunkard's conversion story. The president hailed the nation, like the guilty sinner or the despairing alcoholic, in the midst of its suffering, at a moment stipulated as the nadir of its decline, a moment bestowed by this form of address with the potential for (and inevitability of) redemptive transformation. Roosevelt describes a material collapse so profound and seemingly intractable as to have become, like alcoholism to the individual, an existential threat. But, like A.A. and its predecessor movements, he argued that the material crisis is the symptom of a more fundamental maladjustment of values, and that suffering and failure are useful as undeniable empirical data about the deeper dilemma. The nation, in effect, must hit bottom, coming to the conviction that its operating principles—the values that brought about the Depression—must be revised if it is to survive. The Depression is the product of "a generation of self-seekers," FDR said in his first inaugural address. Their conduct "has given to a sacred trust the likeness of callous and selfish wrongdoing." Similarly, the A.A. pioneers would conclude that "selfishness—self-centeredness!" was both the cause of the alcoholic's suffering and the primary obstacle to alleviating it.[14]

This conception of the New Deal as an ethical and even a spiritual narrative was not just a rhetorical strategy shaped by communications technology and the exigencies of popular persuasion. Some of the Administration's own policy architects and intellectual supporters saw this national redemption story as its deep meaning. Thurman Arnold, as counsel on agricultural policy in the early 1930s, and antitrust enforcer later in the decade, was among the New Deal's leading legal officers. He was also one of its theorists, focusing on the social and philosophical assumptions that legitimated different approaches to government and industry. Writing in *The Symbols of Government* in 1935, Arnold argued that government was "as dependent on cultural factors as political ones," and further that these spheres of influence could be conceived as the difference between "spiritual government" and "temporal government."[15] Looking back at the 1930s, too, many liberals thought that the social transition the New Deal facilitated was more important than its policy record. Arthur Schlesinger Jr. wrote in "The Broad Accomplishments of the New Deal" in 1948 that its therapeutic achievements ran deeper than its admittedly gradualist economic reforms: "The New Deal took a broken and despairing land and gave it new confidence in itself," he wrote.[16] If the theoretical coherence of the New Deal remains in question, during the 1930s and afterward its cultural role was as an at times tenuous, but nevertheless overarching, national redemption narrative.

New Deal individualism developed as (and remains) an interpretive discourse, rather than a political, philosophical, or social program. It emerged in a set of post-hoc efforts to narrate a liberal history of Depression conditions and systemic responses in terms of a dramatic shift in pre-political national identity, toward a new conception of society to which individuals might feel they belong. As such, it enters the historical relationship between progressive thought and conversion narrative, drawing on the familiar analogy between spiritual rebirth and structural change. It is through this relationship that I propose we can think about A.A. in terms of the politics of its era.

But can theories of state and stories of addiction recovery really be said to share a deep root? The distance between national policy and a tiny, voluntary sobriety club is vast, and it is one that outstrips any evidence from political beliefs, as is clear in the attitudes of A.A.'s founders. In May 1935, the first full month Bill Wilson and Bob Smith spent getting to know one another, the Supreme Court ruled that the National Industrial Recovery Act and the National Recovery Administration it had created were unconstitutional. (Its architect and administrator, Hugh Johnson, had succumbed to alcoholism a year earlier.) The ruling marked the end of the first New Deal, the exhaustion of the highest ambitions of Roosevelt's famous first one hundred days.[17] Wilson and Smith, if they had any attention left over from their discussions to give to national politics, almost certainly cheered this turn of events. Both of them despised Roosevelt and his New Deal, despite the fact that both of their homes were saved by FDR's moratorium on foreclosures.[18] In 1933 Wilson wrote angry letters to the president denouncing the New Deal, and later, in his sobriety, his sensibility remained essentially libertarian, if apolitical in practice.[19] Smith's children, meanwhile, recall the "howl of pain and outrage" that the mere mention of Roosevelt's name would bring, an attitude toward the "Raw Deal" typical of Akron's reactionary upper middle class.[20]

My case for A.A. as a vehicle of liberal individualism does not flow from explicit political ideation, but rather focuses on the ideologically oriented social perspectives implicit in cultural modes of expression. Conversion narratives belong to the "culture" of social movements in the sense that David Lloyd and Paul Thomas describe in *Culture and the State*: as primary constructions of subjective disposition, rather than as secondary objects of aesthetic or moral judgment. The political meaning of culture at this level arises in its production of an ethical perspective necessary to accept and legitimate the organizational principle of a society.[21] This is the kind of relationship that Dewey, Roosevelt, and other liberals were invoking in their expectation that deep social change would be concomitant with a new role for the state. Believing in liberalism as the guarantor of individual autonomy, they did not conceive of this change as a process of manipulation, but of liberation. Consider again Dewey's broad concept of education:

> When, then, I say that the first object of a renascent liberalism is education, I mean that its task is to aid in producing the habits of mind and character, the intellectual and moral patterns, that are somewhere near even with the actual movement of events. . . . The educational task cannot be accomplished merely by working upon men's minds, without action that effects actual change in institutions. The idea that dispositions and attitudes can be altered by merely 'moral' means conceived of as something that goes on wholly inside of persons is itself one of the old patterns that has to be changed. Thought, desire and purpose exist in a constant give and take of interaction with environing conditions. But resolute thought is the first step in that change of action that will itself carry further the needed change in patterns of mind and character.[22]

Cultural historians locate the rise of a post-religious spiritual wisdom in New Thought and self-help languages that had roots in late nineteenth-century movements and entered the mainstream in the middlebrow publishing markets in the 1920s and 1930s.[23] But Dewey's words here highlight the ongoing intellectual counterpart to these trends in the tradition of earlier pragmatists and their progressive Christian contemporaries. Indeed, Dewey was not averse to using the word "spiritual" to describe this deep, social root of the self.[24] His "resolute thought" is only a slightly more rational experience than recovery's revelatory "moment of clarity"; and his impatience with the concept of personal moral belief, in contrast to the thoroughly relational processes from which a self really flows, echoes conversion's longstanding commitment to the ethical reorientation of the self in communities of reform.

Beneath these points of rhetorical contact between liberal philosophy, political speech, and cultural forms dwelled deeper roots of social experience. The kind of perspectival shift that Dewey called for, and that Roosevelt claimed as a mandate, was occurring experientially for many Americans in

the 1930s as they confronted the limits of material self-reliance and experienced the benefits of mutual support. And for no one were the collapse of
agency and the refuge of mutual aid more decisive life changes than for a
particular group of alcoholics.

"Ambulance Cases": A.A. as a Social Formation

A.A. dates its inception on June 10, 1935, when Bob Smith, a proctologist in
Akron, Ohio, took his last drink, two months after meeting Bill Wilson, a
recently sober stockbroker from New York. Wilson had been meeting with
a group of struggling alcoholics under the auspices of the Oxford Group, a
Christian revival movement among the middle and upper classes in Britain
and America. In Akron that April on a business venture and feeling vulnerable to temptation, Wilson had called a local minister affiliated with the
Group and had asked to be put in touch with an alcoholic. The result was a
meeting with Smith, who had been active in Akron's Oxford Group chapter but had failed to stay sober despite countless efforts. Wilson and Smith
bonded quickly, as each found relief in frankly discussing his struggles with
a fellow sufferer. As their friendship developed, their talks were informed by
the quest for "God-consciousness" that, as members of the Oxford Group,
they believed necessary to sobriety. Wilson had already had what seemed
to him a supernatural conversion experience during his last detoxification,
shortly after being evangelized by the Group in New York. Smith had spent
years in and out of the Group, struggling to achieve what it called "absolute
purity." Together, they were still practicing Oxford Group Christianity, but
they were doing so through the medium of the social sympathy engendered
by mutual confession among alcoholics.[25]

What became A.A. began to emerge when Wilson and Smith found that
ministering to other alcoholics deepened the effect, on their own sobriety,
of their initial discussions. The groups that grew out of their subsequent
outreach, around Wilson in New York and Smith in Akron, they called
the "alcoholic squad" of the Oxford Group. But while the "Groupers" had
helped the alcoholics orient their struggles in a spiritual direction, their
world-changing mission, their demand for "absolutes" of commitment and
conduct, and their love of publicity all proved ill suited to the drunkards'
life-or-death struggles with the bottle. Some Group members treated the
alcoholics as spiritual invalids, or what Frank Buchman at one point called
"ambulance cases."[26] Alienated by these factors, the alcoholics not only met
separately but also began developing alternative values, leading to what A.A.

would come to call its "primary purpose" of sobriety before all else, and a more forgiving "progress, not perfection" as its mode of spiritual development. It emerged as a movement in its own right in 1937, when the New York group shook free from Oxford Group oversight, and Wilson and Smith began to talk of the "program" they had developed. By 1939, the alcoholics' meetings in Ohio, too, were largely independent of Oxford Group activity, and together they had created a corporation to publish a book whose title, *Alcoholics Anonymous,* would become their new identity.[27]

This basic outline of A.A.'s formation—as consisting first in Wilson and Smith's relationship, and then in the gradual separation of the New York and Akron meetings from their Oxford Group sponsors—has been frequently rehearsed. But the story takes on quite different meanings depending on who is telling it. In A.A. literature and lore, it is rendered as a series of uncanny coincidences that suggest a divine guiding hand, as well as a set of object lessons in the tenets of the program. For biographers, it has often been a story of two strikingly complementary personalities finding one another at just the right time and under just the right circumstances. For some historians, it is a narrative that reveals the way A.A.'s conceptual innovations emerged out of its early members' experiences with religion. For my purposes, I will call on a further subset of historians who have focused on the *social* processes involved in these events. My larger argument, again, is that recovery's influence occurred not through convincing tenets, but compelling narratives. And its narrative innovation, I contend, was not a new formal structure, nor even a new economy of feeling, both of which remained essentially unchanged from those of the rescue mission drunkards' conversions. Instead, Wilson, Smith, and company successfully adapted this narrative to their historically particular social identities.

Matthew J. Raphael provides the clearest rationale for this approach, in the 2000 book *Bill W. and Mr. Wilson.* Raphael points out the extent to which A.A.'s formation has been told as a just-so story through the lens of the principles it arrived at. Looking for a perspective that can evade this logic of inevitability, he takes up a thread of observation that runs quietly through the work of A.A. historians, on the role of shared social identification beyond the mutual recognition of alcoholic suffering. Pointing out that both the Oxford Group and the A.A. experiences were defined by social mobility, Raphael suggests that class ought in fact to be considered as a category of analysis. "Although both organizations implicitly promoted upward class mobility," he writes, "A.A. was demographically centered on the cusp of the lower and middle classes, while the Oxford Group was positioned on the threshold of the middle and upper classes."²⁸ Raphael concludes that a sense of class identification was a necessary element drawing the proselytized alcoholics together and distancing them from the Oxford Group.

The effort to distinguish A.A. narrative from its historical precursors leads to a similar conclusion. What made A.A. seem so radically new to its founders, and what broader historical shifts made this sense of newness possible? A.A. recoveries were structured precisely like drunkards' conversions: steady decline to an experience of total inadequacy; contact with an evangelist who tells of surrendering this failed will to God; an experience of spiritual redemption and social rehabilitation within a community of believers; and a charge to deepen this state by sharing testimony with those in need of the same. The Twelve Steps were simply an effort to describe, in simple, easy-to-follow increments, what Wilson and Smith had done to follow the Oxford Group's similarly stepwise conversion process. If the Steps define A.A.'s therapeutic program, they do not distinguish it from nondenominational revivalism and the generally psychological turn in Protestantism. The most obvious and important difference is that A.A. made sobriety, not salvation, the organizing purpose. But even this prioritization is only a particular resolution, similar to that of other Christian self-help systems in the era, of the perennial tension in evangelical discourse between salvation's eternal guarantee and its earthly evidences.²⁹ Every aspect of early A.A. practice can be found in the wider evangelical tradition, and every piece of A.A.'s spiritual language can be found in Oxford Group writings and other works of psychological religious advice in the 1930s.

The innovation that remains is not a spiritual concept, but a narrative subjectivity—a different way of responding to the conversion appeal—that implies a social identity. In examining this identity, I place less emphasis than some have done on native social differences between the Oxford Groupers and the alcoholics. The Vermont origins of Wilson and Smith, for example, do not read convincingly as class factors within the wider spectrum of American social difference. (Indeed they are more familiar as among those minor differences that middle-class white men often invoke as a means of disowning their privilege.) What more decisively distinguished the alcoholics from their middle-class co-revivalists was the social degradation they had experienced as alcoholics and, furthermore, the self-concepts they had developed in order to make sense of this failure. Their needs were predicated not only on a definitive class location, but on their downward *movement* in the social scale. This movement is another reason for *narrative's* primacy as recovery's epistemological mode. Even when the precise nature of the status loss is obscure, the sense of accumulating failure and social alienation drives the felt progress of the narrative.

This identity thus was not only socioeconomic, nor only alcoholic, but a combination of the two that was experienced as a failure of middle-class values. In this sense of disillusion during the Depression, the early members of A.A. were representative of a widening strain of insecurity in the middle class. In particular, their alcoholism seems to have intensified in them a familiar but not universal *cultural* stance within middle-class masculinity of the interwar period, in the articulation and indeed performance of deep disappointment and self-doubt. This outlook already was associated with heavy drinking and a hatred of moralism. The alcoholics meeting in New York and Akron were not only talking about different past experiences than their fellow revivalists were, they were recognizing this sensibility in one another and developing a distinct, shared identity based on it. Much of what follows is an effort to tease out the nuances of this identity, identify its cultural building blocks, and understand how, in particular, A.A. narratives reconstructed it using the logic of the drunkard's conversion. This process of social formation around particular cultural cues is the key to my historical reading of the recovery narrative A.A. disseminated.

One of the key ways A.A. turned this experience into a lasting narrative template was by formalizing it in print. In 1939, with approximately one hundred self-described alcoholics meeting in New York and Ohio, the fledgling movement published *Alcoholics Anonymous,* a book explaining the method of recovery they had developed and illustrating it in first-person narratives by thirty of the early members. Wilson was the driving force behind the book and its primary author. It opens with Wilson's own narrative ("Bill's Story"), followed by several explanatory chapters, and then the remainder of the personal stories. Despite skepticism about the project's commercialism among some early members, what became known as "the Big Book" quickly moved to the heart of a burgeoning print culture of recovery. Through three subsequent editions (1955, 1976, 2001) that kept key early narratives and all the explanatory material unchanged while adding contemporary stories, the Big Book has remained the central text of A.A.

The framing and weighting of the book with narratives, along with the constant invocations of personal testimony in the explanatory passages, was designed to foster the experience of sympathetic identification that the early A.A. members had found so essential to their sobriety. This purpose arose out of Wilson and his collaborators' progress on the project. They first conceived it as a commercial enterprise to support the movement's growth, and specifically as an alternative to a scheme of hospitals and treatment professionals. They turned down an advance from Harper's in favor of selling stock in a company, The One Hundred Men Corporation, formed to self-publish. Their prospectus for investors describes the book as a "simple" and "universal" guide to spiritual transformation and outlines the potential profits to investors. But as Wilson began to write and circulate chapters, the feedback he got from members and other advisers convinced him that the book would have to address suffering alcoholics, rather than a wider market. It would have to engage alcoholics themselves at the level of their personal experience, ahead of intellectual understanding. The form the Big Book thus took was an attempt to embody in print the meeting groups' social processes of identification through narrative performance.[30]

This identification was the first step in the construction of an outward-looking ethic of spiritual "surrender" to replace the controlled rational autonomy that had become nearly essential to the modern definition of selfhood. In order to understand this experience as an ideological transformation, it is necessary to investigate the specific social identity this change worked on, and how the process reinterpreted its perspective. The white, middle-class nature of early A.A. was a limiting factor that subsequent generations of recovering addicts worked to break down. But the particulars of this initial identity remain historically significant because they shaped the narrative's participation in the revision of individualism in the 1930s.

The Big Book narratives drew on the terms of middle-class masculinity during the Depression to create a colloquial version of literary-philosophical "modern man" discourse. Its alcoholic addressee was skeptical to the point of cynicism, and felt alienated from the traditional language of religion and morality—but he was these things in the context of his failing career and social humiliation. The narrators were not interested in appealing to a wider cultural critique that would ameliorate the personal shame of this failure. Nevertheless, the A.A. understanding of alcoholism through narrative still provided an alternative way of ordering that failure using cultural material. And it was this cultural material on which the redemption of values would be enacted. The failure to control drinking was not necessarily the reason for, but the key to understanding, both a material suffering and an intellectual pride that had wider cultural presences. A.A. reconciled the disillusioned individual to a society that was itself undergoing trauma.

Wised Up and Born Again

The Big Book's explanatory chapters synthesized habit and value in an appeal to an all-encompassing spirituality, but its narratives did their cultural work on the social identity that governed these "modern" qualities. This identity is more familiar from Depression-era fiction, drama, and film than from A.A.'s Jamesian and Jungian intellectual props. The alcoholic subject is one who has been "through the mill" of hard experience and been "wised up" by it, who feels he has earned his cynicism and even misanthropy, but yet is defiantly democratic in social and cultural attitudes. These qualities describe what Christopher Breu calls the "avatars in everyday life" of the hardboiled literary masculinity that reigned between 1920 and 1945.[31] For Breu the hardboiled man is a "cultural fantasy," a ligature between the real and the imagined, capable of shifting between the reified and the consciously play-acted modes. Early A.A. narrators were downwardly mobile middle-class men who called on one version or another of this identity to explain both their drinking and their failure. They were believers in the fantasy who found that, as constituted, it could not sustain them through the realities of alcoholism and Depression.

The screenwriter Michael Tolkin makes the affinity between Big Book recovery narratives and hardboiled fiction impressively clear in his entry on A.A. in the *New Literary History of America*, published in 2009. Tolkin's essay opens with a passage constructed entirely of excerpts from Big Book stories and noir novels of the 1930s, blending them into a plausible scene of hard-drinking, hardboiled fiction. Tolkin writes that the hardboiled voice "brought into writing the authentic . . . spoken English of the Depression, exhausted, cautious—and added the paradox of defiant acceptance." The Big Book "sounds like noir," he says, because both crime and alcoholism bring men to "the bottom of society at the bottom of an economy."[32] But tellingly, while the rest of the essay investigates A.A.'s spiritual solution to this state, this opening performance draws only from the decline portions of the recovery narratives.

The narrative styles in the Big Book do not merely invoke the suffering behind the grim, rueful attitude; they seek to heal it through the ministrations of its ostensibly feminine opposite, in redemptive social sympathy. They enact a reconciliation of the hardboiled and the sentimental narrative modes, beginning with the reframing of evangelical conversion's sentimental release as an act of intellectual rigor and brave (even hardboiled) humility for modern men.

For example, A.A. narrators reinterpret the perennial Christian trope of the unwilling convert as a vindication of common-sense empiricism. Though A.A. narratives are explicitly evangelical—urging not just sobriety but submission to "our Father in Heaven"—most take care to point out how unwelcome evangelism is to the alcoholic or indeed to anyone with a modern sensibility. The "Educated Agnostic" interrupts his story to make an address for this purpose, promising that "you can't take less stock in the references made to God in this book than I would have" and "you have now too much intelligence and honesty to allow of such delusions."[33] This rhetorical lapel-grab applies the purpose of the decline narrative—to induce identification—specifically to the problem of intellectual objections to religion. The irony in the Agnostic's wry compliment is the real site of A.A.'s Jamesian attempt to reconcile modern intelligence with religion. "Intelligence" and "honesty" read as real, and valuable, attributes, but ones that are alienated from their full scope by the drinker's refusal to consider spiritual experience. The narratives conserve the modernity of their subjects by making them explorers in a systematic empirical investigation whose trying out of conversion gains them access to an area of reality previously closed to them.[34]

The philosophical ancestry of this kind of claim ultimately is less important in recovery narrative than is its conservation of the social and stylistic signs of modern identity. The demise of skepticism is in any case inevitable, intellectual understanding having proven no defense against addictive compulsion. But when the resulting desperation comes, it gives way to conversion only when it is met with the example of recovering alcoholics who, crucially, evince no sign of stereotypically holy behavior. "They were human every-day sort of people," "the Artist" recalls. "They certainly were not pious. They had no 'holier than thou' attitude. They were not reformers, and their concepts of religion in some cases were almost inarticulate. But they had *something!*" (383). Similarly, for the Agnostic, his first meeting draws him in not by its overt message, but "more by an atmosphere created by friendliness, sincerity, honesty, confidence, and good cheer" (354). These social settings initiate gradual conversions that are felt as radical transformations, yet conserve the personal traits, keyed to transparency and knowingness, of a modern man.

Wilson's version of this experience epitomizes the way the argument comes in a stylistic package that bolsters a social identity. He flaunts the derision with which he initially received his Oxford Group friend: "Last summer an alcoholic crackpot; now, I suspected, a little cracked about religion." In later versions of his narrative Wilson would play up the intensity of both his skepticism and his supernatural conversion experience, telling a biographer late in life of his attitude toward God that, "miserable and terrified as he was, he would not humble himself," but "go out swinging" as a skeptic.[35] While Wilson would overcome his hostility to religious belief, he would incorporate the lesson of his first response into A.A. outreach, writing another boxing metaphor into his dictum for making amends that "it is seldom wise to approach an individual, who still smarts from our injustice to him, and announce that we have gone religious. In the prize ring, this would be called leading with the chin" (89). Wilson's cavalier language about religion not only disarms the skeptic, but also illustrates a pervasive stylistic dynamic by which recovery narrative protects elements of modern masculinity during the experience of spiritual surrender.[36]

Style in the Big Book flowed from its collaborative editing process, which, as Trysh Travis has helpfully made clear, drew on both mutual-aid practices for fostering identification and market-driven methods for pleasing readers. Wilson submitted the explanatory chapters for comment to his Brooklyn group, and sent them to Akron for perusal by Smith and others. A journalist who was a member edited the Akron narratives, while in New York, Wilson at first co-edited the New Yorkers' stories with another member, in order to emphasize a range of alcoholic experiences. Eventually, though, he hired a professional editor—an experienced, even at times cynical, purveyor of middlebrow emotional uplift—to polish the whole collection. The heavy editing of the individual narratives is evident in the choppy, pre-publication manuscript that was sent to religious and medical authorities for comment. The narratives that created the template for recovery were socially generated, but professionally groomed.[37]

Most critics have read this hybrid style as essentially bland, built from the voices of religious self-help, how-to-succeed-in-business pep, and popular psychology, making its effective appeal to generations of alcoholics all the more surprising. Raphael and Travis identify a gothic note arriving through the confessional mode, especially in those moments when narrators do admit to specific crimes against laws and loved ones. Rather than gainsay such helpful observations, I want to reinterpret them as part of a pervasive pattern in which Big Book narrators try to perform, conserve, and correct the hardboiled style associated with modern manhood. The narratives make use of both of the modes Breu identifies in hardboiled performance: the play-acted, in the narrators' satirization of their former drinking-man's bluster; and the reified, in the rock-steady humility of their sober voices. A.A. narrative ultimately works not to displace the hardboiled style of masculinity, but to transfigure it from a voice of cynical isolation to one of sympathetic connection.

The voices of the narratives fall in a range between two distinct poles, each speaking as the product of hard experience: the suggestive banter of the man who knows the saloon (and wants you to know he knows it) but is no longer vulnerable to its snares; and the elevated, often cloying serenity of self-help wisdom, in which humility is always transmuting into triumph. These tones of rough jocularity and of unflappable peace both lay claim to having passed through the ravages of sin, of having witnessed and participated in the worst life has to offer, and of conserving the knowledge of self and world gained in the process. Invoking stylistically this journey of experience guarantees the authenticity necessary for effective witness.

The two modes are best exemplified by the main antagonists in the dispute over the Big Book's religiosity.[38] The rough mode is taken to its extreme in "The Unbeliever," the story of Henry Parkhurst, whose objections led Wilson to mute the Big Book's Christianity. The Unbeliever's style is ostentatiously literary, a fragmented recreation of the narrator's mental state during his last hospitalization. It is in the tradition of aestheticizing the drug-addled mind that runs from Thomas de Quincey to James Frey. In Hank's version it appeals to his era's modernist experiments with limited narrators. The former Standard Oil salesman opens with an exhibition of decadence: "This morning I reminded Doc this was my tenth visit. I had spent a couple thousand dollars on these trips and those I had financed for the plastered play girls who also couldn't sober up. Jackie was a honey until she got plastered and then she was a hellion. Wonder what gutter she's in now. Where was I?" (194). Most of the narrative is taken up by glimpses of his increasingly perilous condition, visits by an A.A. member (Wilson), and his incredulity at the purported cure. His skepticism reaches a crescendo when he promises "NEVER [to] be such a cowardly low down dog as to acknowledge God," who belongs to "two faced, gossiping Babbitts . . . with their sanctimonious mouthings, their miserable worshipping, their Bible quotations, their holier-than-thou attitudes, [and] their nicey-nice, Sunday-worshipping, Monday-robbing actions" (204–5). "Babbitt" signals an allegiance to literature over religion as the realm of truth. As a watchword for the hypocrisy of religious speech, "Elmer Gantry" might have been the more appropriate Sinclair Lewis reference, but Babbitt was closer to Parkhurst's own identity as a married businessman—a shameful respectability for a would-be rebel and one from which he still seeks distance, in his allusions to showgirls and days-long binges. The literary reference and the flamboyant style assert a social perspective from which religion's hypocrisy is an obvious fact.

By contrast, "Our Southern Friend," an Episcopal minister's son from Maryland named John Henry Fitzhugh Mayo who advocated for an openly Christian A.A., typifies the serene recovery mode. He opens in a childhood idyll: "Two rosy-cheeked children stand at the top of a long hill as the glow of the winter sunset lights up the snow covered country-side. 'It's time to go home,' says my sister."[39] Instead of the angry hostility to religion evinced by the Unbeliever, this narrator conveys the wistful feeling that the ideals of an earlier era have died. This elegized pastoral innocence is restored by God in the narrative's conclusion, when sunset gives way to the "dawn" of spiritual insight. Mayo's style performs humility and serenity as the products of experience, both of salvation and of the degradation that brought him to it.

The styles of Hank and Fitz, as they were known, fall short of the truly hardboiled world-weariness the term "wised up" typically invokes. It is hard not to read in them instead the shallow, insecure cynicism that revivalists have long found an easy mark for emotional conversions. Considering the physical and mental frailty of the advanced alcoholic, these are moments when A.A. narrative fulfills Freud's diagnosis of religious ecstasy as the release of tension that occurs in submitting, finally, to the authority of the Father.[40]

And yet recovery narrators lay claim to modern, wised-up sensibilities, by insisting on a great distance between their experiences and the old-fashioned theatrics of, as one puts it, "the drunk who plunges to the sawdust at the appeal of a religious orator" (212). The editor of the Akron stories attests of his own transformation that "it was no momentary emotionalism born of self-pity in a maudlin condition" (262), while a onetime hobo insists the fellowship that attracted him to A.A. involved no "canting or ranting" (313). These narrators assume the clarity of their distinctions between the discredited, cultural caricature of evangelical revivalism versus what they present as their own unfiltered experiences of redemption. Theirs is a familiar strategy of realism, in which the writer discredits the genres associated with the material, in this case by disowning a cultural ancestry in order to reassert unambiguously a direct reference to reality.[41] The distinction remains an appeal to style (or more accurately to its denial), in the difference between the exhausted conventions of preaching and the viable ones of plain, sincere, witness to one's own experience.

Though it is a stance that broadcasts transparency and claims to conserve only the mental habits of modern intelligence, it is grounded in facts of gender and class. The 1939 Big Book, despite its claims of casting a wide social net, constructs a shared identity that exists independently of alcoholism, in the self-consciously democratic ordinary man. This figure takes in a broad middle class, defining itself primarily against the implied pretensions of the high-born, over-educated, or moralistic. In the Depression era, especially, the plain-man persona required an appeal to hard experience, one that justified both escapist drinking and self-consciously rough language, in a style that could sustain social visibility while repudiating gentility. For A.A. narrators this style is essential to their relationship with their audience. It asserts their experience as men who have "been through the mill," to help win the attention of active alcoholics; and it reassures the candidate for recovery that sobriety and spirituality do not entail the feminine naiveté or hypocritical pretensions associated with temperance and church affects. Recovery style, in this manner, conserves the democratic straight-talk of the saloon. As Jack London had written two decades earlier, "When I thought of alcohol, the connotation was fellowship. When I thought of fellowship, the connotation was alcohol. Fellowship and alcohol were like Siamese twins."[42] While A.A. narrators sometimes make much of their social differences, they are almost all, they suggest, men who could have drunk together.

The discovery of a sober but no less hale and hearty fellowship among such men was, after the sheer desperation of the hospitalized drinker, usually the first act in the drama of early recovery. The Big Book's final explanatory chapter, "A Vision for You," makes this aspect of recovery the very social history of A.A., when it invites the reader into that story as a new member. The experience it describes rewrites old-fashioned evangelical fellowship as a dry cocktail party. The "irresistible" quality to which the new man "succumb[s]," is not God, nor group prayer, but that quintessential interwar phenomenon, the "gay crowd," with its bright, conspiratorial faces, and its "electric atmosphere." Only in this "haven" does he find he has "capitulated entirely"—to what it is not clear, except in allusion to the party's "upper room," a key site of conversion and discipleship in the New Testament, and the title of a Methodist devotional the early A.A. groups read. The camaraderie of the group merges with the qualities that answer intellectual reservations the newcomer/reader may have, the "very practical approach to his problems" bound to the "informality, the genuine democracy" of the scene. If there is any doubt as to the deeper source of this atmosphere, though, it is ended in the conclusion to the passage: "They had seen miracles, and one was to come to them. They had visioned The Great Reality—their loving and All Powerful Creator" (174–75). A.A. witness reassures the alcoholic that though he will indeed "plunge to the sawdust," he will rise up a good fellow, and not a religious bore.

Much of the work this sociable tone does to preserve its subjects' baseline identity is bound to norms of masculinity. The gender implications of the Big Book chapters "To Wives" and "The Family Afterward" are too obvious to belabor, with questions such as how wives should surrender "the family trousers" now that husband is back on his feet (144). These tropes rehearse the traditionally gendered imagery of problem drinking and its victims, but A.A.'s social style helps construct a new one.[43] The good cheer, vitality, equanimity, and tolerance of a vibrant couples' party are the social graces that join the intellectual traits of independence and practicality, as the qualities a reader can expect to recover with his sobriety. But now it is the men's collective spiritual project, before their careers or class affinities, that brings these families together.

Even the spiritual language of the Big Book owes something to the career identities of its most active contributors. Wilson and the closest thing he had to a coauthor, Parkhurst, were both salesmen, and the Big Book itself is on one level a sophisticated pitch. The book's spiritual language is a business lexicon, calling for moral "inventory," a spiritual "basis" for growth, and the "capitalization" of suffering. Parkhurst wrote the chapter "To Employers," which advises companies to facilitate the rehabilitation of alcoholic workers as a form of waste-cutting that could save big companies millions.[44] He characterizes the typical alcoholic employee as a man supervised by, but on a social par with, a company's "junior executives." He recommends distributing the Big Book to these managers, and even imagines the kind of conversation one of them might have with an alcoholic friend who works under him: "Look here, Ed. Do you want to stop drinking or not? You put me on the spot. . . ." (162). The alcoholic in this scene is a man who has violated an unwritten social compact in corporate culture. Accordingly, the attributes of the recovered alcoholic, those that preserve his masculine identity, are clustered around the values of the business class, in sociability, pep, and practicality, and the self-consciously democratic tolerance of minor social differences.[45]

The Big Book narrators assert this unpretentious identity in their very confessions. Their histories of violating polite values in their drinking and its consequences, so scandalous as to require anonymity and apologies for the shocking nature of their revelations, yet work to attest to their democratic identities as men of the world (26, 39–40, 146). Recovery narrative both rehabilitates a perceived marginality, in the return of the narrator to respectable society, and conserves that outsider persona, in the very fact of its revelation. This dynamic responds especially to the literary style of skepticism embodied by Parkhurst's Unbeliever, whose boastful reference to showgirl hellions complicates therapeutic pieties about the courage required for confession. Though A.A. culture (like the rescue missions before it) always has included a customary disapproval of sensational testimony, ultimately it is impossible to police the boundary between confessional bravery and self-serving bravado. And both serve the same social purpose.

Recovery makes some space for the romantic flair of self-destructive drinking, but matches it with the exceptionality of total abstinence, both phenomena distinguishing its narrators from the ordinary run of comfortable folk. The early members of A.A. left the Oxford Group, but they doubled down on the joys of a countercultural community, raising it to something approaching the camaraderie of the radical cell. Not only abstaining in social situations where drinking was expected, but ministering to one another, admitting to one another their failures and fears, and asking one another for help—in effect, creating a loving community based on the very aspect of their mental lives that had been the most isolated and pain-filled—was experienced as revolutionary by these otherwise quite ordinary middle-class men.

The transparent gender insecurities that run through the Big Book are not best understood as signs of social narcissism, but rather as evidence of the formal challenge presented by the very project they were undertaking. The fact that they do not fully resolve them describes the limits of the personal transformation they were seeking, but it also points to the difficulty of representing middle-class failure on its own terms at all. Early A.A. narrative effectively revised middle-class masculinity from within, showing that its characteristic social traits could be turned toward collective, non-material ends. In this function early recovery stories responded to more widely shared Depression-era social experiences.

Middle-Class Labors

A.A. narrative takes its place in the broader culture of the "recovery" era as a response to middle-class trauma during the Depression, a realm of experience whose elusiveness in representation was both an artistic and a political conundrum. Characters in modernist novels often tried to repudiate middle-class identities, while realistic efforts to represent middle-class family life often risked rejection by critics on similar grounds. In Clifford Odets's Depression-era drama, for example, the material decline and quiet mental illness of the middle-class Gordon family in *Paradise Lost* failed to engage audiences the way the frustrations of poverty did in *Awake and Sing!* or the hope of working-class resistance did in *Waiting for Lefty*. Leading critics regretted the play's "frowsy characterization, its random form and its inchoate material"—attributes that describe not just a failure of craft but also a failure of subject matter.[46] Eugene O'Neill, a recovered but unconverted alcoholic, whose plays dwelled on the impossibility of escaping compulsive desire, lamented this lack of representation for a fragile middle class, attributing it to its location in the no-man's-land between the two great organized forces of big business and labor.[47] In *The Crisis of the Middle Class* (1935), the Marxist economist Lewis Corey saw this invisibility as a political danger. Corey described the betrayal of the middle class by its own brand of individualism as a self-compounding psycho-political crisis, exacerbating middle-class frustration and mystifying its response, creating the potential for unforeseen, violent political shifts toward fascism or communism.[48]

Even in the midst of the Depression, the new recovery language was developing as a response to exactly this brand of individualism's failure. Early A.A. narrative records the experiences of men born around the turn of the century who found their lives disintegrating in the 1930s. Its historical specificity appears not in the difference between intemperance as a sin and alcoholism as a disease (a distinction that is barely legible in it), but in descriptions of labor instability during the Depression. Unlike the immigrants and ne'er-do-wells of the rescue missions, the early A.A. narrators were mainly professionals, executives, and skilled tradesmen, who describe faltering work trajectories not uncommon in the 1930s. A.A. narratives read at times like middle-class oral histories of the Depression.

Yet even in the Big Book, where failure is given a concrete cause in alcoholism, the nature of middle-class trauma is often elusive, lacking the definitive imagery of the breadline, the Dust Bowl, the hobo, or the financier leaping to his death. Middle-class failure, like alcoholism, is shapeless, characterized by drift and decline, without clear causes or opportunities for ennobling resistance—precisely the effects of drinking in A.A. narrative when it starts to become self-destructive. Though several A.A. narrators descend to beggary, they refuse to embrace its imagery (as in the 1933 film comedy of downward mobility, *Hallelujah, I'm a Bum*), instead taking refuge in the embarrassed formalities of the "social rescue institution" and "intervals of . . . hitch-hiking" (259–60). They describe long strings of second chances, gradually sullied reputations, charitable interventions by friends and family, and sudden removals to new places, near or far. Even Bill Wilson, who claimed his drinking had expelled him abruptly from a Wall Street that had felt like the epicenter of the modern world, in reality had experienced the drift of the unsteadily employed through the early 1930s, keeping a hand in some racket or other throughout the period.

Downward social mobility is the scaffolding for the alcoholic-decline portions of 1930s A.A. narratives. Unlike their temperance precursors, the Big Book narrators give more attention to the destruction of career prospects than the disruption of families. Rather than cowering in terror or dying tragic deaths, A.A. spouses and children tended to appear as sad, resigned figures, adapting to whatever mayhem the drinker imposed. The more central, volatile relationship is usually with one or a series of employers. The narrator of "A Business Man's Recovery" describes a continual loss of jobs and a constant series of reprieves, until his sobriety in 1937. He alludes to his wife's loyal efforts to help him, but it is his employers to whom he applies the qualifier "long-suffering," and to whom he addresses emotional words of gratitude (247). The predominant social context is work, not home.

The narrator of "On His Way" provides a decline narrative that illustrates the way conversion gives order to an experience that had been fragmentary. Despite his already being an intense binge drinker, the age of thirty-five, he writes, had

> found me with the following: a beautiful little home presided over by a kind, understanding, and lovely wife; a partnership in a firm I had helped to found years before; more than a comfortable income; many luxuries and many friends; opportunity to follow my interests and hobbies; a love of my work; pride in my success; great health; optimism; and hope on the credit side. On the other hand, I had a growing, gnawing fear of my recurring trouble.
>
> I slipped by far too easy stages to the bottom in less than eight years. Not a pleasant place, the bottom. Sometimes I slept in a cheap hotel or rooming house, sometimes a flop house, sometimes the back room of a police station and once in a doorway; many times in the alcoholic ward at a hospital, and once in a subway toilet. Sometimes decently fed, clothed, and housed, I worked at my business on commission with a large firm; sometimes I dared not appear there cold, hungry, with torn clothes, shaking body and muddled brain advertising what I had become. Helpless, hopeless, bitter. (376)

By making his age the subject of the first sentence, the narrator downplays his agency even more than the usual "I found myself" formula, disowning even his success. Recalling life as a bewildering series of static states—even near the bottom images of well-dressed employment appear—rather than as a trajectory of goals won or lost, he conveys lack of agency as the central fact of alcoholic drinking. Conversion narrative gives a broad sequential order to such a life, as well as an animating spiritual meaning.

This recasting of career failure as spiritual crisis is encapsulated in "The Backslider," whose title merges the traditional Puritan term for spiritual relapse with a story of upward and downward movement on a class-labor scale. The narrator was trained as a machinist, but during the 1920s boom had become a traveling salesman, until "fateful and fatal came the month of October in the year 1929." When the market crashes, he is laid off and goes on a three-day drinking binge, then drinks his way out of another job before quitting sales and returning to his original trade: "This seemed to be the only thing which offered [itself] and once more I discarded the white collar for the overalls and canvas gloves." Before his arrival in A.A. and his subsequent relapse, he already is a "backslider" in the terms of the national success myth. His submission to "God's law . . . of Love," his "daily communication with God," and, especially after his relapse, the unconditional support of his A.A. fellowship, redeem him not only from alcohol but from all the implications of this failure and the attendant "resentful feelings" that drove his drinking (267–68).

If "The Backslider" changed uniforms as he lost status, even the drinkers who do not actually descend in the pay scale describe hiding in the lower precincts of the social hierarchy to cover their disreputable style of drinking. One former "salesman for a large corporation" and leader in the voluntary civic groups of middle American life reports that after a particularly harrowing binge, arrest, and institutionalization, he ceased to drink socially among his middle-class peers. Instead, he says, "I began to use my head, I continued to drink but kept under cover or hid in the 'jungles' with the bums" (300–301). The world of the itinerant unemployed appears as a haven for the middle-class binge drinker, sheltering him from judgment and even reassuring him that should he fall that low, he will know enough to survive.

These phenomena of public presentation, of being well dressed in one memory and disheveled in another, of exchanging white collar for overalls, of hiding out, and of moving on, together describe the flux in the class hierarchy during the Depression. Members of the middle class, in particular, could sojourn across a broad swath of it, from country-club comfort to back-alley destitution. Accompanying this class movement is a relentless geographical wandering. Whether narrators enter adult life as rovers ("Riding the Rods," "The Rolling Stone"), embark on adventurism that turns into rootlessness, or are forced to move by some combination of personal inadequacy, legal trouble, social embarrassment, and tightening job markets, labor-driven itinerancy is a major trope of early recovery narrative. Such movement was also a feature of stable employment for the many early A.A. members who were traveling salesmen, a factor that facilitated its early spread.

Writing itself appears as an itinerant profession in the Big Book. Jim Scott, author of "Traveler, Editor, Scholar," describes studying for the law, where among a loose student crowd, "Burns and Byron and other colorful profligates were the literary idols" (255). This taste for the fast life leads him into clerking for British bookies and eventually migrating to America. After some high times in New York that include a drinking session with Jack London, he undertakes an endless string of jobs on newspapers, in advertising and public relations, in sales, and for the Federal Theatre Project and the Federal Writers' Project in Texas, interspersed with sporadic factory work and stints in workhouses and prisons. He takes pains to distance his conversion from "emotional religion" (260) turning instead to scripture as literary precedent, in watchwords for profligacy ("the fleshpots of Egypt") and redemption ("to return to his Father") from the King James Bible (264). He concludes by emphasizing the meaningful *work* that A.A. has given him: "I have tasks to do and am glad to do them, to see others who are alcoholics and to help them in any way I can to become sober men" (264). Chief among those tasks at the time of writing was the editing of the other Akron-based narratives in the Big Book.[49]

These first recovery narrators were men, mainly from the business and professional classes, whose identities were built on self-mastery and social performance, but who found themselves undone by the very habits that expressed these traits. Their stories of decline and recovery, even if attributed exclusively to alcoholism, describe career fortunes that track the middle-class economic situation between the wars. Despite the countercultural thrill they felt in forgoing a weary self-reliance in favor of faith and fellowship, they were barometers of mainstream sensibility, in these very reversals as much as in their business-casual writing styles.

Their stories about redeeming career failure and returning to work reveal how recovery narrative worked to reconstruct middle-class senses of self that were traumatized by common experiences in the Depression. If alcoholic decline narrative tracks Depression labor dislocation, recovery sees men put to purposeful work, returning them to their own professions and charging them with saving other alcoholics as a condition of their own sobriety (fig. 7). Some speak of the restoration of their actual careers, others refer

FIGURE 7. *Came to Believe* (1955), by Robert M., an illustrator for A.A.'s *Grapevine* magazine, depicts A.A. members sharing their stories with a suffering alcoholic. It was later renamed *The Man on the Bed*.

more obliquely to the "monetary benefits" of sobriety alongside the recovery of family relations (280). They allude to the equation of labor vulnerability with a weakened role as head-of-household, the sense of emasculation that drove the rise of men's self-help literature in this era.[50]

My method has been to look at A.A. through the lens of its conversion form, asking what cultural materials its pioneers used to revivify this structure. Those same building blocks of life narrative were in wide circulation during the transition into a liberal era. The redemption of the alcoholic itself remained a staple of popular sentimental storytelling through the decade, in films such as *The Champ* (1931) and *Stablemates* (1938). Looking more widely for New Deal individualism in culture, one finds versions of it emerging in texts that seem apolitically concerned with things like isolation and self-deception, community and redemption.[51] The death of the old individualism under modern economic arrangements appeared in stories of individuals this ideology had failed. To focus on one kind of man who founded and spread A.A., this pattern includes Eudora Welty's first short story, "Death of a Traveling Salesman" (1936), and Arthur Miller's famous play *Death of a Salesman* (1949). Both are about the collapse of an aging professional man's sense of agency and his inability, due to deeply imprinted illusions of self-containment, even to imagine the kind of love that might have saved him. At the same time, a new vision of American community in film saw individuals saved by each other through institutions, but not collectivized.[52] The joyous scene of sharing in the Big Book's "A Vision for You" links A.A. to New Deal–funded community murals as well as to film institutions like the youth gang (*Angels with Dirty Faces*), the military unit (*Guadalcanal Diary*), and the football team (*Knute Rockne, All American*) as vehicles of redemptive suffering and necessary but uncoerced mutual dependence. These stories did not ask Americans to adopt any specific attitudes toward the state, but rather they reimagined the self in its relationship to others, to institutions and, ultimately, to society.

The Two Recoveries

Bill Wilson and Bob Smith's hostility toward the federal government—and more significantly their commitment to A.A.'s necessarily grassroots nature—did not stop their interpersonal and organizational work from entering into the emerging public-private institutional structures of American life. Their model of rehabilitation was not only adopted by many thousands of alcoholics, it was also incorporated into systems of employment, medical provision, legal punishment, and public health funding in the decades after World War II. The Yale Center of Alcohol Studies, the National Committee for Education on Alcoholism, the early corporate "employee assistance programs"—the institutions of what historians call the Alcoholism Movement—were all either co-founded by, directed by, or run in collaboration with, A.A. members.[53] This era culminated in the July 1969 sessions of the newly created Senate Subcommittee on Alcoholism and Narcotics, when A.A. pioneers Bill Wilson and Marty Mann testified before fellow recovering alcoholic Senator Harold Hughes on the nature and dangers of alcoholism. Although Wilson did not advocate government support for A.A. ideas, the subsequent "Hughes Act" of 1970 establishing federal funding for alcoholism treatment brought A.A.'s legacy into the history of the state.[54] These implicit alliances with postwar institutions facilitated and reflected the rapid acceptance of recovery narrative as a governing cultural genre of addiction. Recovery had deployed the symbolic social renewal built into the drunkard's conversion in terms that helped make sense of the liberal transformation of American society.

This lasting public role was possible because A.A., unlike some earlier

manifestations of the drunkard's conversion, repudiated political meaning. A.A.'s "primary purpose" distinguished it not only from the memory of
temperance politics, but more immediately from its Christian sponsor, the
controversial Oxford Group. Buchman's movement was patently reactionary
in its aims and methods, paternalistically believing that by converting the
elite, it could bring about a more perfect society. The Oxford Group did not
present itself as conservative or nostalgic but as radical, seeking to stoke the
desire among the young and ambitious to provide direction and, ultimately,
salvation to what was felt to be a foundering modernity. It offered its gentle
intellectualization of conversion narrative to elite university students in the
belief that it was the direct rival of Communism for the idealistic impulses
of the young and the influential.[55]

In the 1930s, Buchman and his lieutenants became notoriously busy in
politics and public controversies. For example, although Buchman took an
agnostic line on the New Deal as policy, he insisted that conditions would
not improve unless leaders and citizens, businessmen and laborers alike were
morally "changed," that is to say, converted to selflessness in the vaguely Christian theism he spent his life promoting.[56] In utter contradiction of Dewey's
systemic theory of individualism, Wilson and Smith's Oxford Group spiritual
educations were premised on the explicitly reactionary belief that systemic
changes were futile, even irrelevant, compared to individual ones. Buchman's
comments on the rise of Hitler that a godly dictator would make the best possible government earned him widespread abuse, including a blistering critique by Reinhold Niebuhr, the leading liberal Protestant thinker of the era.
Niebuhr argued that Buchman's comments were the inevitable expression of
the "Nazi social philosophy" undergirding the group's entire "leading men"
evangelical project. Additionally, its "simple and decadent individualism" was
alien to both biblical humility and a realistic social vision.[57]

In this climate, despite an apolitical message and a carefully limited purpose, early A.A. concepts cannot be separated from the ideological competition in the 1930s for the revolutionary and reformist energies of dissatis-
fied moderns. In this contest, Depression trauma appeared as a potentially
world- and theory-changing new reservoir of energy. But while A.A.'s conversion narrative emerged from a reactionary movement, it shared with
FDR's New Deal rhetoric the unifying, transformative power of such collective experience.

In his pragmatic case for ideological reform, Roosevelt situated the nation
at a turning point in its life narrative. The undeniable example of the Depression revealed self-interest to have become self-destructive, an insight that

then transformed selflessness into a necessary survival strategy.[58] He implied that individualism unchecked, or not subordinated to a larger framework of meaning, destroys itself. FDR developed this theme in his major speeches of the 1930s, describing in his second inaugural address the "collapse" of prosperity due to the failed "practicality" of self-interest, bringing a "conviction" that "morality" must become the foundational principle governing economic behavior. The economic confidence that both the nation and its citizens lack "cannot live" without "unselfish performance." A.A.'s recovery narrative set out similarly to save the self-concepts of a stockbroker, a doctor, and a lawyer from the "self-will run riot" of the alcoholic.[59]

In their narrative arguments from pragmatic necessity, Roosevelt and A.A. both attempted to collapse distinctions between the voluntary, the coerced, and the inevitable. The Twelve Steps describe a program of recovery that is "suggested," but that is averred, sometimes through considerable social pressure, to be the only alternative to an alcoholic death, and yet also to be beyond the power of the will to effect. Roosevelt, as much as he could, tried to frame the New Deal as both chosen by the people and as the only alternative presented by the Depression. This duality was built into the National Recovery Administration, for example, whose price and wage controls were voluntary yet at the same time imposed by a bureaucracy and a consumer movement designed by the government.

The stylistic patterns of conversion narrative animate New Deal and A.A. rhetoric. The president's speeches and the explanatory chapters of the Big Book make similar uses of the first-person plural, the sermonic "we" emphasizing collective experience and unity of purpose, drawing the reader or listener into the narrative action. Specific colloquial phrases appear in both: the need to get our "house in order," to put "first things first," to solve "our common problems," to fulfill a "vision" of wholeness. The breaking of tension that comes in collapsing the duality of self-interest and public interest, when the latter is found to guarantee the former, releases a utopian energy: "We are beginning to wipe out the line that divides the practical from the ideal," Roosevelt continued in 1936, "and in so doing, we are fashioning an instrument of unimagined power for the establishment of a morally better world."[60] Embodying conversion's evangelical argument—surrendering self-interest is not only morally ideal but makes possible a far greater reward than self-interest can produce—both New Deal and A.A. recovery open tonally in the descriptive humility of recollected error (crisis), build in intensity through the damning insights this memory brings (conviction), then climax in a crescendo of transformative fervor (conversion). In each case this movement describes the birth of a new era of harmony in the liberation of fundamental but long suppressed values.

Both kinds of recovery narrative describe the adoption of ethical habits that will see the isolated self with its cycles of binge and bust give way to a socially integrated self that is not only more stable but capable of a higher order of existence. Even as, after the demise of the N.R.A., the byword of the New Deal shifted from "recovery" to "security," Roosevelt's rhetoric no less personalized and psychologized the national narrative. Consider, for example, the passage in the Big Book known as "the promises," as an iteration of FDR's "freedom from fear" theme: "We are going to know a new freedom and happiness. . . . *Fear of people and of economic insecurity will leave us*" (96; emphasis added). Roosevelt's narrative made national economic security also a matter of individual serenity, or "a kind of feeling within our individual selves that we have lacked all through the course of history."[61] This deep, inner security flows from a material sobriety that is itself predicated on a new conception of the self as socially embedded. It is at this level that economic and addiction recovery narrative meet.

Although they summoned the same root experiences and expressed similarly redemptive ideals, A.A. and liberalism took different historical journeys through the rest of the twentieth century. A key relationship affecting both of their fates was with a consumerist alternative to the newly socialized individualism they posited. In the case of the New Deal, historians describe the cooperative ideals of the early 1930s giving way, under the pressure of new economic realities, to the growth imperative familiar in political economy today. What Dewey and some inside the Roosevelt administration had conceived of as movement toward the collaborative management of production and consumption for the greater good garnered uncertain results as well as political and judicial opposition. Then, during the recession of 1937–38, what had been a relatively minor component of New Deal thought—stimulating consumption with public spending so as to spur production—emerged as a more plausible theory and a more politically attainable policy.[62] Ultimately, wartime spending and postwar growth validated this approach and unleashed the culture of abundance that has been so widely documented and critiqued. By the time liberalism turned to the challenges of fairly distributing this wealth, the social reformation of individual values that liberals such as Dewey called for, and that seemed to find articulation in Roosevelt's early speeches, had been eclipsed by the reorientation of identity around consumption.[63]

Recovery from alcoholism has from its birth featured a tension between mutual social practices and the consumer ethos of self-help marketing.[64] From the professional editor of the Big Book, who believed in psychological manipulation as a strategy for selling books, to the incorporation of the Steps into reality television, recovery culture has supplied material and markets for self-help. But A.A. has retained its foundation of social practice, and it has proved more resilient than any model of liberal government. Its ability to survive this consumerist ideology owed to elements of the radically democratic in the path it ultimately took.

A.A.'s most decisive rejection of worldly ambition came in an organizational structure that matched an internal politics to its theory of self. In the 1940s Wilson realized that because of his own missteps and the hostile reactions they incurred, the Twelve Steps and recovery narrative, divinely inspired though he believed them to be, could not by themselves guarantee the movement's survival. After a series of controversies centering on Wilson's control, in 1946 A.A. published its "Twelve Traditions," the organizational counterpart to the steps of recovery. The Traditions called for a maximally decentralized structure, preserving the autonomy of face-to-face groups; banned leadership in favor of temporary "service" positions; prohibited the ownership of property or payment of salary at any level; and made the organizational imperative the "common welfare," as an end without which "personal recovery" was impossible. The only authority would be "a loving God as He may express Himself in our group conscience"—divine will appearing through democratic rules of order. Lastly, in the Traditions A.A. foreswore all active publicity and apotheosized the personal practice of "anonymity" into the "spiritual foundation" of the entire movement, summed up in the adage, "principles before personalities."[65] Essentially, at just the moment that its cultural influence coalesced, A.A. disowned *power* at both the organizational and personal levels.

The elevation of anonymity into a spiritual commandment confirmed that A.A.'s model of individualism would remain pre-political (setting the ethical terms by which equitable power relations are possible) rather than apolitical (avoiding controversy and implicitly accepting the status quo). Tellingly, the concept initially arose in an instance of wised-up style, when the early groups referred to themselves as "a nameless bunch of drunks."[66] A more formal stricture on publicity became useful as a way of limiting the potential for high-profile relapses, like that of Cleveland Indians catcher Rollie Hemsley, to discredit the program, and for reassuring prospective members that their privacy would be protected.[67] But in Wilson's formulation of the Traditions, especially because of the challenges of his own celebrity, anonymity became the philosophical core of the movement, its incorporation of the pious assumption of human limitation into the more exuberant spiritual tradition of individual liberation.[68]

As a feature of what I've argued is a New Deal formation, anonymity risks invoking the bugbear of technocratic misanthropy. But modes of codifying equality are bound to downplay individual difference. Consider Michael Szalay's equation of statistical abstraction—a condition of identity in the New Deal's insurance-based approach to social welfare—with the ultra-objective style of some modernist poets, in their efforts to construct subjectivities that might avoid the ideological corruptions of the inherited self.[69] A.A.'s anonymity represents a parallel approach to individualism-in-the-collective, in, surprisingly, the highly personalized evangelical tradition. The spiritualization of anonymity in recovery narrative was a way for this born-again tradition to become aware of its own generic nature, in ways that many of its historical narrators were not. This recognition of evangelical conversion's central paradox—that it apotheosizes the "personal" nature of salvation by making its subjects conform to a rigid template of self-transformation—allowed the recovery subject to understand himself as a member of society as well as a child of God. Anonymity was a form of abstraction that reconciled A.A.'s idea that every individual has a unique conception of God, to the injunction that each of them develop it by serving others who have different "higher powers." It was religion as procedural liberalism.

The method by which A.A. codified the practice and meaning of anonymity was more explicitly a statement of political theory, invoking, in fact, a radical vision of democracy. It adopted a formal structure of governance based on the Twelve Traditions at its 1955 General Service Conference, memorialized as the moment when the "old-timers" of the late 1930s bequeathed the movement to the entire fellowship—now officially opened, in the Traditions, to anyone who professed a "desire to stop drinking." Speaking at the concluding session of this gathering, Wilson offered a clue that the Traditions had not come to him straight from A.A. experience, but were mediated by a particular theoretical influence:

> When we first come into A.A. we find here . . . a greater personal freedom than any other society knows. We cannot be compelled to do anything. In that sense this society is a benign anarchy. The word "anarchy" has a bad meaning to most of us, probably because one of its excitable adherents long ago threw bombs around in Chicago. But I think that the gentle Russian prince who so strongly advocated the idea felt that if

men were granted absolute liberty and were compelled to obey no one in person, they would then voluntarily associate themselves in a common interest. Alcoholics Anonymous is an association of the benign sort the prince envisioned.[70]

The "Russian prince" Wilson mentions is Petr Kropotkin, who advocated anarchy in *Mutual Aid: A Factor of Evolution* (1902). The last sentence positively asserts that A.A. is anarchistic, even suggesting that it fulfills the predictive content of Kropotkin's theory.

Wilson conceived A.A.'s new structure as an ideal of social, and perhaps even political, organization. In 1943, two years before he began the series of articles (published in the A.A. magazine *Grapevine*) that would become the Twelve Traditions, Wilson met and became close friends with Aldous Huxley, the author of *Brave New World* (1932) and a pioneer in New Age spirituality at midcentury. Huxley exposed Wilson to the latest in experimental social thought, and in turn would call Wilson "the greatest social architect of the century," in words reprinted by *Time* magazine when it named Wilson to its list of one hundred most important people of the twentieth century.[71] Huxley was an admirer of Kropotkin's theory, writing in a foreword to a 1946 edition of *Brave New World* that he would like to have included in the novel a "decentralist," "Kropotkin-esque cooperative" as a positive alternative to its primary dystopia.[72] In sum, though it has never been documented, it is likely that Wilson was familiar with Kropotkin's theory when he wrote the Twelve Traditions, and in fact crafted A.A.'s organizational structure on the anarchistic model of radical democracy.[73]

The Traditions' guarantees of autonomy at the individual and small-group levels have facilitated A.A.'s survival and its ability to adapt to cultural change, including increasing social inclusion and eventually accepting the complications brought by drug addiction and depression. If they codify human relations in a way that is both more democratic and more intimate than that required by the liberal state, still A.A. can be said to have been born under the sign of the New Deal, given sanction, by the temporary suspension of the success myth acknowledged by this national regime, to crack open orthodox individualism and rebuild it for a select group of sufferers. Doing so by recycling Depression failure into a natural resource, and channeling it into forms that were both new and yet predicated on old traditions, it created a lasting model of a liberal social ethic.

The cultural establishment of recovery narrative in the decades after World War II, as it became a source of conventional wisdom and a template for narrative realism, began in the social experiences of a relatively narrow stratum of society. Its growth owed to this class's cultural influence, whether in the local professional circles that embraced all manner of voluntary association, or among the newspapermen and aspiring novelists who wrote recovery memoirs in the wised-up, sentimental vein. More generally, A.A. grew with the postwar expansion of the middle class and the increased equation of national culture with its "other-directed" but still individualistic sensibilities. Like some New Deal policies, recovery narrative's universal promises were at first experienced only by white, middle-class men. But the A.A. pioneers, in their commitment to the autonomy required for authentic inner change, had built a respect for difference into the recovery structure that made it not only available, but appealing, to a wider spectrum of people. In the second half of the twentieth century, women and minorities adapted recovery language to their own personal and political challenges, bringing its model of transformative social sympathy far beyond its original social milieu. One of the reasons they were able to do so was because the early A.A. members developed their narrative as a way out of a hegemonic ideology from within.[74] In A.A. the redemptive outcome of the drunkard's conversion took the form of a carefully nurtured egalitarian social ethic built on the shared experience of shattered agency. Its appropriation by wider groups of people was analogous to the politics of justice in the long New Deal era, as the civil rights movements of subsequent decades demanded fulfillment of the liberal promises of citizenship. As these movements transformed liberalism, A.A.'s language and social practices transformed popular self-culture through the rest of the century.

PART
II

❖

Literature and Recovery

5

Literary Realism and the
Secularization of the Drunkard's Conversion

The fact is that the mystical feeling of enlargement, union, and eman-
cipation has no specific intellectual content whatever of its own. It is
capable of forming matrimonial alliances with material furnished
by the most diverse philosophies and theologies, provided only they
can find a place in their framework for its peculiar emotional mood.
We have no right, therefore, to invoke its prestige as distinctively in
favor of any special belief.
—William James, *The Varieties of Religious Experience* (1902)

Every banner that the wide world flies
Bloomed with glory and transcendent dyes.
—Vachel Lindsay, "General William Booth
Enters into Heaven" (1913)

B Y THE SECOND HALF OF the nineteenth century, the sensational conversion of very bad men was a well-established phenomenon in American
religious revival, so much so that it was a subject of satirical humor. Despite
also being the target of such mockery, though, the drunkard's conversion
remained popular in the literature of religious and moral uplift, accepted as
both the ideal and the reality of missionary endeavor among the poor of the
industrial-era city. Gospel rescue missions proliferated, and reformers both
secular and religious began to give close scrutiny to drunkards' conversions,
in particular. This was especially true as religious discourse incorporated
new languages of scientific knowledge in temperance, and of documentary
realism in urban reform. Physiological theories of inebriety, for example,
raised the stakes of what conversion was claiming to defeat, adding the

material cure to the moral conquest. The rescue missions and their publications, meanwhile, had become part of the popular literature of the urban low life as well as grist for the Sunday sermon. The drunkard's conversion was a prominent public stage for combining a range of responses to new realities under the protective umbrella of pious religious narrative.[1]

This world of material facts in unglamorous locales was at the same time being represented in the less emotive styles, less absolutist metaphysics, and more documentary aesthetics developing under the banner of literary realism. For this reason, it seems inevitable that the drunkard's conversion came to the attention of realist writers in the late nineteenth century. Both savage parodies and affectionate rehearsals of the form became common enough in the literature of this period to rank among its recognizable conventions. As an archetype of sentimental writing, the drunkard's conversion was a touchstone in an emerging divide in literary writing between ironic and sentimental modes. It came under literary assault from writers waging war on naive or manipulative forms of public discourse. The embrace of the drunkard's conversion in religious and sentimental writing, on the other hand, was a defense of these ways of knowing, proof that they could encompass unpleasant new material facts. A kind of cultural turf war was taking place over the nature and meaning of the realities of everything from economic inequality to bodily experience. By not only critiquing orthodox morality but doing it in an assertive representation of the low life, the missions were planting the flag of pious, sentimental Christianity on turf cherished and aggressively claimed by several major strands of realism.

If the overweening claims of the drunkard's conversion to modern material and social truth brought it to the attention of realists, it was the slippage between these claims and its still essentially sentimental appeal that made it a truly ripe target. Authors working in several modes of realism zeroed in on the paradoxical social logic of the drunkard's conversion: that to convey its vaunted spiritual egalitarianism, it depended on a framework of status-hierarchy. The opening chapters of this book examined the ways that low-status drunkards tilted the genre toward their own needs, while elite reformers used it both to affirm their own goodness and to inspire transformative self-knowledge among their peers. Literary critiques were more concerned with the ways this two-sided dynamic could be manipulated for social advantages by both the powerful (to assert high motives in their personal aims and justify their power) and the lowly (to claim the material benefits of social sympathy). In the hands of a variety of realist writers, the drunkard's conversion appeared as a transparently manipulative performance by grasping converts and as hypocritical cover for social control by self-dealing religious reformers. To disguise low motives was its real social utility.

Some of these writers—Mark Twain and Stephen Crane among them—entered the American literary canon in the twentieth century, and their hostility to religious and sentimental morality became the keynote of a burgeoning cultural divide. But other literary writers in this era, especially those with more actively political purposes, embraced the sentimental energy and transformative message of the drunkard's conversion narrative, incorporating it into their visions of a new social reality. The poet Vachel Lindsay, for example, drew on its message and its milieu to create a spiritually expressive style that was both popular and critically acclaimed. And in *The Jungle*, the most popular work of socialist fiction ever published, Upton Sinclair seized the entirety of the drunkard's conversion tale for collectivist, not theistic, societal revival. In this chapter I examine these works, too, as among the several ways literary writers appropriated the drunkard's conversion to mark out the redemptive social meanings of their realist projects.

The concept of appropriation doesn't tell the whole story, though. Literary realists did not mock or modify the drunkard's conversion into a cultural grave. The drunkard's decline served as a transitional narrative medium between what David Reynolds called the literature of "dark reform" in the nineteenth century, and what Philip Fisher termed the "plot of exhaustion" in the realist era.[2] The same essential story could easily shed the language of melodrama and take on a more materialistic edge—although, in truth, the drunkard's story had long invoked material causes, and more often than not in the realist era it retained its moral meanings. Instead, the more distinct contest took place around the plausibility and meaning of the conversion ending. The variety of literary attentions to this supposed relic of the revival era illuminates the cultural trajectories by which the religious genre became fragmented and secularized, often losing its explicitly religious content but gaining an even deeper formal presence as the narrative truth and framework of meaning for addiction, recovery, and redemption more generally. Evangelical Christian conversion, like temperance morality, was indeed losing credibility in the literary, the intellectual, and ultimately the middle-class cultures of this era. But its structure of feeling, instead of fading away, spread and was taken up strategically to advance a variety of redemptive ideologies. Sinclair exhibits this trend most plainly, as he discredited the religious drunkard's conversion simply in order to claim the same process, even using the same language and affect, to convey the felt truth of socialism. The realist satires of the drunkard's conversion were more straightforwardly critical, attacking both its religious claims and its sentimental language of class reconciliation. But as chapter 4 showed, in the formation of recovery narrative a middle-class culture could disown the evangelical tradition even as it renewed conversion narrative as a powerful cultural resource. In this manner, the prehistory of addiction recovery narrative consisted of a continual exchange between the drunkard's conversion and its literary critiques, in ways that were in fact essential to the genre's secular and literary legacy.

The Opposition Line

Drunkards' conversions played central roles in prominent realist assaults on sentimental morality, in styles ranging from the festively satirical to the harshly critical. In Mark Twain's *Adventures of Huckleberry Finn*, drunkards' conversions appear as fraudulent collaborations by reformers and con-men, and threats to the truly transformational work done on the raft between Huck and Jim. In the ironic inhabitation of moral reform discourse of Stephen Crane's tenement novels, the drunkard's conversion is a ludicrously unreal language, one that either debases its users with hypocrisy or consigns them to a powerless subculture of religious consolation. In Harold Frederic's disenchantment or anti-conversion novel, *The Damnation of Theron Ware*, the rebirth of low-status sinners is a pitiful spectacle, summoned by churchmen only to sustain the dying ember of Protestant conviction. In each of these models of literary realism, drunkards' conversions are foils against which authors define and shape their new approaches to both fiction and society. The conversions are targets not just as conventions of sentimental writing but as real-world sociolinguistic performances that redirect the aspirations of the poor into craven, melodramatic gestures aimed at satisfying the demands and activating the powers of sanctioned public morality.

In *Adventures of Huckleberry Finn*, drunkards' conversions are microcosms of the novel's main target: the public languages of morality that disguise and justify profound systemic injustices. Unlike abolition, temperance was still a live issue in the 1880s and beyond, such that the novel's attention to drunkards links its setting to the era of its publication. Southern romanticism has often been named the primary literary target of Twain's satire, because of its role in justifying both slavery and the betrayal of Reconstruction progress. But the scenes of religious revival in *Huck Finn* identify the role of divinely inspired moral reform as a genre that, by not even acknowledging its theatrical and generic natures, makes a more aggressive claim on American reality, morality, and politics than did, say, the novels of Walter

Scott. Romantic fiction inspired a deceptive antebellum idealism, while the combination of addiction and conversion conveyed something closer to unfiltered reality in the Gilded Age. The effect of the novel's treatment of the drunkard's conversion is to draw attention to the role of the audience in producing this false reality.

Twain's precursors in "Southwestern humor" had been pioneers in the lampooning of revival culture and its transparent social and sexual dynamics. In Johnson Jones Hooper's *Adventures of Captain Simon Suggs* (1845), for example, the charlatan-hero swindles a community of pious hypocrites by performing the role of the wicked sinner humbled at their camp meeting. The scene of the Captain eyeing the campground before plunging in provides the standard analogy between the con-man and the preacher: "Amid all this confusion and excitement Suggs stood unmoved. He viewed the whole affair as a grand deception—a sort of 'opposition line' running against his own, and looked on with a sort of professional jealousy. Sometimes he would mutter running comments upon what passed before him."[3] Religious persuasion—and especially the emotional rhetoric of the hard-drinking man redeemed—had long been charged with manipulating public sentiments. Suggs's suspicion that such religion is, in fact, an "opposition line" to his own performative profession, goes somewhat further, with the hint that it is an outright swindle. Twain would pick up this thread in particular and refer it to his own project: in his presentation, gospel temperance appears as an "opposition line" to literature itself.

The larger critical effect of Twain's satirical style is to expose the corrupt relationship between the popular language of individual morality and the realities of systemic, not just localized, injustice. The two most theatrical villains of Twain's novel, its most audacious users of moral language for self-serving ends, are seasoned performers of the drunkard's conversion. But because Pap Finn and the con-man known as "the King" are so ludicrous to the reader (and never more so than in their conversions), their successful performances are almost admirable in their shamelessness. The reader's sense of contempt seems more fittingly directed at the gullibility of their audiences than at their own amorality. This gullibility, Twain suggests, is not innocent.

Pap's night as a temperance miracle sees the sentimental account of vice reform not only justifying a rigid social order, but in fact preparing the way for an even harsher one. When a new judge decides to reform Pap rather than jail him for yet another drunken spree, he takes him into his own home, dresses him, hosts him at table, and lectures him on temperance, until Pap breaks down in tears and promises to reform. Together he, the judge, and his family weep the tears of sentimental union, melting away the class division between them. At bedtime, Pap gives a speech, offering each of the "gentlemen and ladies" present his hand to touch, "a hand that was the hand of a hog," but is now "the hand of a man that's started in on a new life, and'll die before he'll go back." They each weepingly take his hand in turn, the judge's wife sanctifying the moment by kissing it, and the judge calls the event "the holiest time on record." In its sentimental class dynamics Pap's performance echoes the "river thief" Jerry McAuley's final, permanent conversion when he utters the Publican's Prayer in the parlor of a well-to-do family, to tears all around.[4] That night Pap pawns his new coat for a jug of whiskey, destroys his new bedroom, and breaks an arm falling drunk off the porch roof. Giving up his reform career after just this one failure, the new judge concludes that "a body could reform the old man with a shotgun, maybe, but he didn't know no other way."[5]

The judge's embarrassing lesson is not the moral of the story, but rather is another distortion produced by the original sentimental hypocrisy. The manipulation involved in conversion performances, typically attributed to a fraudulent convert like Pap, shifts to the judge, for whom the episode begins in moral self-flattery and ends as a justification to write off the question of rehabilitation. By making the social problem one that can be solved by coaxing Pap, through the grace of class condescension, to individual conversion, his failure to reform both keeps the problem in the individual realm and relieves the elite family of further obligation. Pap's obscure and violent death, occurring off-stage and treated with dignity by Jim for its potential impact on Huck, aligns Twain's farcical treatment of drunkenness with its grimmer cousins in urban social critique. Pap's "gashly" face recalls the discovery of the alcoholic heroine Gervaise's rotting corpse, for example, at the conclusion of Emile Zola's naturalist tale of a drunkard's decline, *L'Assommoir* (1877).

The more explicitly religious style of gospel temperance appears in *Huck Finn* in the guise of a money-making scheme, as it did in some of Twain's source material. But here, too, Twain's satire is aimed at the manipulative and ultimately self-serving sentimentality in the audience. The elder conman Huck knows as "the King" is a practitioner of the temperance lecture racket, the proceeds of which go to buying liquor.[6] He is also adept at performing the born-again conversion. At a rural camp meeting he pretends to be a pirate of the Indian Ocean, miraculously converted by the preacher's call into "a changed man now," and into an evangelist in need of immediate funds to return to the ocean to convert his former comrades. Outlandish as Twain's satire appears, it is not so far from McAuley's well-publicized story of an urban river pirate who dedicated his ministry to saving fellow drunken criminals, including his former partners in the boats. The King promises the preacher and his flock that whenever he "saves" a pirate, he will make sure they get the credit they deserve for lighting the evangelical spark in him.[7] This dynamic replicates the rescue missions' relationship to elite patronage, embodied in its printed appeals and the pledge cards those books included. The performative fraudulence of the drunkard's conversion, in this view, serves rather than deceives its patrons. The reformers' insistence on play-acting a compassionate social order hypocritically demands the demonstration of this order's inequality.

Stephen Crane's style of exposing the hypocritical performance of religious morality was less farcical than Twain's, based as it was in the earnest world of urban reform rather than the already discredited milieu of rural revival. But Crane's scenes of drunkards' conversions aimed even more savagely than Twain's did at the site of the reader's reception. Crane included failed and fraudulent drunkards' conversions in both of his novellas of lower Manhattan, as centerpieces in his assaults on the sentimental culture surrounding urban poverty. In *Maggie, a Girl of the Streets* the young drinker and brawler Jimmie Johnson stumbles "hilariously" upon a missionary service where "the sinners were impatient over the pictured depths of their degradation" because they "were waiting for soup tickets." When the scene of sentimental apotheosis does appear, at the novel's conclusion, it is a monstrous hypocrisy: the drunkard Mrs. Johnson tearfully "fergives," in "a vocabulary derived from mission churches," the daughter she herself consigned to a prostitute's death.[8] In this climax the whole thrust of the novella is to destroy the unreal sentimentality of social transcendence which characterized the "angel from the slums" genre as much as it did the drunkard's conversion.

Crane's lesser-known Manhattan novel, *George's Mother*, takes on gospel temperance more directly, exposing it less as hypocrisy than as the frightened, submissive refuge of the cowed and aged Victorian holdovers in the city. George Kelcey is a young man learning how to drink heavily on street-corners and in saloons, while his mother is a pious, unhappy widow who cannot understand her son's moral apathy. Suspecting him of drinking, she convinces him to attend a prayer service, where, as in the missions, "one by one people arose and told little tales of their religious faith," some "tearful and others calm, emotionless, and convincing." But the converts and the preacher "had no effect on Kelcey, excepting to prove to him again that he was damned." When Kelcey is "almost reformed," it is only by a particularly bad hangover, and when he recovers his mental balance he resolves only to be more cautious. In the meantime, his drinking friends are revealed to be utterly self-interested and his drinking life a tedious series of performances of blustering masculinity. At the conclusion, at the deathbed of his mother and with a preacher by his side, Kelcey fails to produce the conversion anticipated of such a scene, leaving him only with a sensation of "hideous crabs crawling upon his brain," evocative of the language used to describe delirium tremens in temperance prose.[9] Inebriety and its temperance counterpart both appear spiritually insignificant: neither romantically intoxicating nor susceptible to religious revelation, but merely habits, one way or the other, of hiding in tired social identities.[10]

This generation gap in the ethnic neighborhoods of New York suggests that alcohol was a cultural touchstone in the loosening of tight-collar Protestantism's grip on American middle-class religion, especially as immigrants with less teetotaling traditions began to claim a place in it. In Harold Frederic's 1896 novel, *The Damnation of Theron Ware*, beer drinking marks the most immediate and decisive difference, both socially and theologically, in the passage from a Methodist camp meeting to a Catholic picnic that enacts the title character's loss of orthodox Protestant faith.[11] Beer in this sequence symbolizes mainstream America's as well as Theron's anti-conversion. An embodiment of sin in the old dispensation, it is revealed to serve a role in the social dynamics of conversion, when the unchurched sinners on the periphery of the camp meeting undergo the most violent conversions at its dramatic nighttime services. These performances serve social as well as spiritual needs: church members snub the newcomers during the day and bar them from the tents on Sunday, but in exchange for their nighttime acceptance the penitents provide the electrically transformational atmosphere that the regular members crave. This reciprocal dynamic is another iteration of the collaboration behind the urban rescue missions: the marginalized are accepted into the social fold in exchange for redeeming it and making real its claims to divine inspiration. The sad pity with which Frederic's novel dissects revival culture is as devastating as the satirical undermining practiced by Twain and Crane. Further, it applies more directly to intellectual admirers of revival culture like William James and Helen Stuart Campbell, insofar as they too used drunkards' stories to reanimate the moribund spiritual cultures they inherited.

These literary critiques did not act simply to discredit the drunkard's conversion, but rather played a role in the cultural shift that would more deeply embed the structure of the genre as a twentieth-century model of selfhood. At a time when progressive reformers were using conversion narrative to imagine democratic routes to societal redemption, and psychologists were seeking to extract the genre's universal or "spiritual" mind-body truth, the mockery of the genre's revivalist origins and sentimental content did not present a grave threat to its survival. Indeed, this literary disfavor may have helped to hasten its transformation into an influential secular model of both addiction-recovery and reclaimed selfhood in general.

The drunkard's conversion already had developed as a pragmatic and flexible kind of religious genre by responding to very similar criticism. Especially after the Civil War, rescue mission conversion was shaped by its dialogue with newly skeptical counterdiscourses. Long before the sentimental mode fell out of literary favor, the phenomenon Jerry McAuley's eulogist called "the romance of grace" in the slums was a seasoned contender for the mantle of realism in reform writing that was renegotiating the difference between moral sensation and documentary fact.[12] As sentimentally unreal as its satirists made it, on its own terms and for its own audiences it was responding to hard material conditions and new social upheavals.

In these origins, the drunkard's conversion shared the same social source material as literary realism. Not only did conversion stories interpret industrial-era socioeconomic conditions, but they also displayed the wit and practical morality, as well the real needs and picturesque sufferings, of the lowly. They combined high ideals and authoritative forms with the colloquial language of experience in a formal interpenetration that began on the actual landscape of urban reform, in the exchange of space among the saloons and missions that shared buildings, streets, and neighborhoods in nineteenth-century cities. As progressive reformers and academic psychologists attested, the voices of reformed alcoholics had produced a much-needed realism in religion. Further, the material orientation of drinking narrative allowed the drunkard's conversion to survive outside of its religious context in practically unaltered form.

For a concrete sense of how this range of literary responses to the drunkard's conversion could facilitate the secular uptake of the proto-recovery form, consider Vachel Lindsay's poetic voice. Lindsay speaks in an intermediate register, where salvation is not literal but redemption remains the controlling structure, bringing forth social and even political meanings. One of the most popular and critically respected poets in the first decades of the twentieth century, Lindsay's reputation-making 1913 collection *General William Booth Enters into Heaven and Other Poems* is a testament to the subtle secularization of the rescue mission worldview. Throughout this collection the religious language reads as neither ironic nor literal; rather, it echoes the progressive Christian style of biblical social criticism. But it does so with an eclecticism and a poetic distance that make it more populist-progressive than Christian. Lindsay draws on the rhetorics of drunkards' conversions, temperance campaigns, bohemian urban romanticism, and both social gospel and rescue mission anti-vice tropes, to create a world of low-life saints and self-sacrificing reformers.

The creation of this moral vision culminates in "Why I Voted the Socialist Ticket," which combines the evolutionary and the biblical pessimisms regarding "human nature," but imagines the political effort to collectively mitigate these flaws as the moment of surrender to God:

> Come, let us vote against our human nature,
> Crying to God in all the polling places
> To heal our everlasting sinfulness
> And make us sages with transfigured faces.[13]

This poem is followed by "The Wizard in the Street," a tribute to Edgar Allan Poe, rendered as an unbalanced street character:

> He drank alone, for sorrow, and then slept,
> And few there were that watched him, few that wept.
> He found the gutter, lost to love and man.
> Too slowly came the good Samaritan.

Lindsay's master narrative of redemption can put stoic agnosticism into conversation with utopian Christianity, and spiritual quietism with political radicalism. His religious-reform style was, broadly speaking, Midwestern populist, a mode whose political range encompassed Populism, Social Gospel progressivism, and Christian Socialism.[14] In the broad themes that ran through his work and in his darkly knowing but still hopefully sentimental voice, Lindsay evoked the drunkard's first glimmers of hope in visions of a more loving community. His poetry embodied the quietly consistent appeal of the conversion genre as it moved out of the religious realm and into explicitly secular ones.

Born-again Socialism

In socialist fiction the drunkard's conversion did more than suggest the deep structure of public-private transformation, serving instead as a model of personal political awakening and movement evangelism. Upton Sinclair's blockbuster 1906 novel *The Jungle* is best known for its grisly depictions of the meatpacking industry in Chicago, which prompted unprecedented federal action to regulate food production. But its full plot arc is dedicated to an exploited worker's descent into alcoholic destitution and his ecstatic salvation in socialism. Sinclair delivers this trajectory using the precise conventions of the drunkard's conversion, taking its entire structure and much of its specific imagery to advance his highest purpose in the novel. Sinclair's role inaugurating the literary socialist conversion narrative is forgotten in the memory of the novel's impact on industrial reform, but *The Jungle* does indeed anticipate a key convention adopted by leftist novelists through the 1930s, and it does so through what is in many ways a standard-issue rescue-mission drunkard's conversion.

If Jack London was only using a vernacular rhetoric of persuasion when he anticipated *The Jungle* making "converts" to socialism, the author and the novel he was promoting in *The Chicago Socialist* in 1905 were more deeply invested in the religious meanings of the term. Sinclair described his own recent conversion to socialism as an overwhelming, emotional transformation at the end of a deep depression.[15] In *The Jungle* he used the drunkard's conversion narrative to figure this discovery of world-saving truth and to predict the inevitable growth of socialism. The descent of his hapless immigrant protagonist into beggary, alcoholism, and crime after the deaths of his wife and son as a result of industrial exploitation in Chicago's stockyards owes as much to the nineteenth-century moral reform genres as it does to the mode of grim naturalism more commonly used to categorize it.

The Jungle's ostensibly documentary analysis of labor and power in Chicago—Sinclair insisted his novel was akin to a "statistical compilation" or "a study by a sociologist"—is a sensational depiction of urban evils that relies on the interplay of predatory capitalism, violated domesticity, and political corruption that constituted the temperance movement's case for reform.[16] Jurgis's climactic conversion to socialism, meanwhile, is drawn straight from the template of urban revivalism among the pathologized poor. The novel's socialist use of the narrative that Harold Begbie and others deployed on behalf of reactionary individualism illustrates the political malleability of both the drunkard's tragedy and the miracle of redemption. Sinclair's political appropriation of conversion narrative helped conserve its form, proving it an essentially secular narrative mechanism that could be fitted with various ideological clothing.

Sinclair did not simply borrow the drunkards' narrative as a useful plot structure, but maintained a lifelong interest in the issue and its cultural representation. Having been profoundly affected by his father's and uncles' inebriety, he was a teetotaler and a temperance activist, but one whose 1931 anti-drinking novel, *The Wet Parade,* concluded by agreeing Prohibition was indeed a failure. Late in his career, he wrote *The Cup of Fury* (1956), a memoir recounting the ways that alcoholism had destroyed many of his writer and artist friends. Arguably the last temperance tract by a major American author, it offered a ringing endorsement of A.A., and it also helped create the "alcoholic geniuses" interpretation of modernism. But despite these literary and political engagements with alcoholism that spanned an entire half-century career, Sinclair is absent from studies of literature and alcohol, neglected as a sober exception to those drunk moderns, the "innocent" who combined puritanical personal values and utopian social visions in a Victorian style. In its temperance didactics and its ecstatic conclusion, though, *The Jungle* is not an anachronistic exception to modern literary drinking, but rather is unusually transparent in its whole-cloth importation of reform conventions. As such it is useful for identifying the entry points and the fault lines in the emergence of a literary contest over addiction narrative.

The Jungle's conversion ending was (and continues to be) deemed a literary failure, indicating a twentieth-century consensus that the sentimental conventions of popular religion no longer had a place in serious literature. Professional readers since the novel's first publication have especially disdained the evangelical tenor of this conclusion. An early hostile review calls it the novel's "crowning touch of unreality," in which Jurgis " 'gets Socialism' exactly as a backsliding brother in a Methodist camp meeting 'gets religion.' " A favorable review, from future British prime minister Winston Churchill, offers the same response but in gently mocking tones: "Consolation? . . . Regeneration? . . . Salvation? . . . Hurrah!"[17] This attitude became nearly unanimous during the twentieth century, surviving into late-century critical assessments in which the novel's conversion is held to betray its own socialist intentions by confirming a reactionary cultural mode. Michael Brewster Folsom sums up as critical consensus on this "embarrassing episode" the judgment that it is "psychologically unconvincing, and seems to serve only the demands of Sinclair's didactic purpose." What is arguably the best-selling novel of both democratic socialism (in its aims) and progressive reform (in its effects) is deemed a literary failure precisely because it employs a conversion narrative.[18]

In the context of the full novel, the conversion ending is ineffective, but not, as critics long have suggested, by its mere anachronistic presence. It fails because Sinclair, in his effort at a comprehensive journey through the labor system, interposes a long period of drift between the nadir of Jurgis's decline and his contact with evangelists, dissipating the energies of total reversal that fuel the form. When it comes, conversion does not arrive as a hastily chosen exit strategy for an aimless plot, as critics have described, but as the traditional, if delayed, sequel to the novel's opening decline movement. Not only was conversion the sole element of the plot to survive from first sketch to published book, it was a product of Sinclair's personal and professional absorption in popular socialism's revivalistic culture. The novel first saw print in a forum that was saturated with Christian ethics and expressive forms. The Kansas-based *Appeal to Reason,* the most widely circulated socialist periodical in American history, was intensely evangelical, featuring socialist adaptations of Christian hymns and biblical parables, and reports from massive camp meetings and itinerant preachers.[19] *The Jungle's* appropriations of alcoholic decline and evangelical conversion for socialism were typical in this context.

Conversion not only serves Sinclair's didactic purpose but is its apotheosis, the only solution available to a decline narrative that is ushered along using temperance conventions. An early chapter offers the standard temperance depiction of how saloons make workers dependent on alcohol and neglectful of their home lives. The debt to temperance narrative is extended in a picture of domesticity as the only bulwark against the saloon's threat to moral and material survival, as "from all of these things Jurgis was saved because of Ona." After Ona's death, saloons continue to direct Jurgis away from his own interests, cheating him of money, luring him to crime, and enmeshing him in political corruption. His daily drinking as a laborer, and his binge drinking as a political machine hand, are finally revealed to have produced dependence, exacerbating the final decline that precedes conversion: "He labored under another handicap now. . . . The craving for it was strong enough to master every other consideration—he would have it, though it were his last nickel and he had to starve the balance of the day in consequence." The novel is only sporadically concerned with this alcohol problem, but it draws on the temperance movement's critique of the urban economy for its socialist analysis, and it borrows liberally from temperance narrative in its portrait of a family man's downfall.[20]

Socialism cures Jurgis's inebriety with energies that are sustained by the evangelical duty to a higher purpose: "It was so evidently a wicked thing to spend one's pennies for drink, when the working-class was wandering in the darkness, and waiting to be delivered; the price of a glass of beer would buy fifty copies of a leaflet, and one could hand these out to the unregenerate, and then get drunk upon the thought of the good thing that was being accomplished" (307). Evoking James, and anticipating Freud and Jung's ideas about religious monomania and addiction, the spirit of Jurgis's newfound religion intoxicates him in a way that usurps the desire to drink.

Before rendering Jurgis's salvation, *The Jungle* recognizes and de-legitimizes the proprietor of the narrative it is seizing. In the period of destitution preceding his political adventures, Jurgis spends an evening at a gospel rescue mission, allowing Sinclair to level what was by then a conventional charge against missionary charity.[21]

> The evangelist was preaching "sin and redemption," the infinite grace of God and His pardon for human frailty. He was very much in earnest, and he meant well, but Jurgis, as he listened, found his soul filled with hatred. What did he know about sin and suffering—with his smooth, black coat and his neatly starched collar, his body warm, and his belly full, and money in his pocket—and lecturing men who were struggling for their lives, men at the death-grapple with the demon powers of hunger and cold! . . . They were trying to save their souls—and who but a fool could fail to see that all that was the matter with their souls was that they had not been able to get a decent existence for their bodies? (218)

The difference between Christianity and socialism here is less doctrinal than it is experiential. Christianity, as it emerges later, need not be a stumbling block: Jurgis is instructed by his first socialist mentor that socialism "implied but the literal application of all the teachings of Christ" (299), and the novel's post-conversion polemics include a lengthy case for Christian socialism, made by an itinerant evangelical preacher who had embraced "the new dispensation" (314). Nor does the mission episode's case for material survival before spiritual salvation hold up: Jurgis's socialist conversion turns out to be entirely a matter of his soul. It is not the validity of the metaphysics but the voice of experience that is on the side of the socialists rather than the Christians. The preacher is "in earnest" but he cannot convey personal knowledge of the state his audience finds itself in, and therefore he cannot lead them out of it.

It is evangelism's own experiential warrant by which the novel elevates socialist above Christian conversion, in terms of the authenticity required to witness effectively. Central to the socialist speech that brings Jurgis to his knees is the orator's appeal to shared experience, when, like a reformed drunkard at a rescue mission, he spends much of his rhetoric preempting skepticism and fostering personal identification: "I know how much it is to ask of you—I know, for I have been in your place, I have lived your life, and there is no man before me here to-night who knows it better" (287). This claim is followed by the relation of a series of experiences, articulating the *spiritual* degradation of poverty, introduced by the clauses "I know" and "I have known." Such rhetoric does more than supply credibility; it is central to the evangelical mechanisms of testimony and identification. Transmission of the narrative depends on a convincing performance of the experience of fallenness as the prerequisite to salvation. This unleashes the spiritual power of emotional identification and the guarantees given by its physical signs.

These signs come in the speaker's dramatic effects on his listeners, a phenomenon familiar from nineteenth-century paeans to great evangelists. The presence of the speaker, modeled on Eugene Debs (whose alcoholism Sinclair would lament in *The Cup of Fury*), is psychically disruptive: "It was like coming suddenly upon some wild sight of nature,—a mountain forest lashed by a tempest, a ship tossed about upon a stormy sea. Jurgis had an unpleasant sensation, a sense of confusion, of disorder, of wild and meaningless uproar" (285). Jurgis's impression establishes that the speaker—or the source of power he has access to—is capable of rearranging mental and emotional landscape, of uprooting preconceptions from their deepest recesses, in the evangelical art (and Jamesian science) of turning despair into ecstasy. His capacity to impose a new metaphysical order lies in qualities less concrete, and more powerful, than his doctrine: "It was his presence, it was his voice: a voice with strange intonations that rang through the chambers of the soul like the clanging of a bell—that gripped the listener like a mighty hand about his body, that shook him and startled him with sudden fright, with a sense of things not of earth, of mysteries never spoken before, of presences of awe and terror!" (291). In Sinclair's supposed "statistical compilation," socialism takes hold in the mystical realm of the soul, not the analytical precincts of the mind.

The conversion which this Debsian "master-wizard" induces in Jurgis incorporates each of the steps of the Christian template. The crisis has worn down the would-be convert to a state of passivity, in which he does not so much seize his salvation as surrender to it. Jurgis is transfixed in the moment of identification with authentic witness, "motionless and rigid, his eyes fixed upon the speaker . . . trembling, smitten with wonder" (287). What ensues is his conviction of sin: "Jurgis was a man whose soul had been murdered, who had ceased to hope and to struggle—who had made terms with degradation and despair; and now, suddenly, in one awful convulsion, the black and hideous fact was made plain to him! There was a falling in of all the pillars of his soul, the sky seemed to split above him—he stood there, with his clenched hands upraised, his eyes bloodshot, and the veins standing out purple in his face" (291). Although in theory socialism convicts capitalism, not the individual who is its victim, Jurgis's recognition of the "black and hideous" fact is of his own fallenness. The novel is dedicated to illustrating the conspiracy in the environment, but it marshals its greatest emotional energies to describe the insufficiency of the individual to defy such surroundings, in the breakup of Jurgis's home, his subsequent moral abandon, and his final despair. Only when this failure has been accepted—once the self-reliance of Jurgis's "I will work harder" mantra has been utterly discredited—can the grace of socialist salvation enter.

In the mystical qualities of the "vistas" the speaker paints for Jurgis, his salvation from this conviction is indeed a submission to a Higher Power, even if it is one that subsequent socialist characters endeavor to describe in material terms: "He knew that in the mighty upheaval that had taken place in his soul, a new man had been born. He had been torn out of the jaws of destruction, he had been delivered from the thraldom of despair; the whole world had been changed for him—he was free, he was free! Even if he were to suffer as he had before, even if he were to beg and starve, nothing would be the same to him; he would understand it, and bear it" (293). Before any notion of political organization or socialist theory lodges in Jurgis's mind, the fact of conversion is established by an ecstatic emotional reversal, or what James called, in Christian conversion, the violent displacement of one idea by another in his "habitual centre of personal energy."[22]

Jurgis's rebirth especially echoes those of low-status Christian converts, such as the drunkards of the rescue missions and the Salvation Army. Such conversions pay careful attention to signs of class and the way spiritual equality makes possible previously proscribed, and highly charged, relationships. Such a social miracle precipitates Jurgis's conversion. Nodding off at the socialist meeting, he is gently coaxed to attention by a "young and beautiful ... 'lady'" who whispers "gentle and sweet" in his ear: "If you would try to listen, comrade, perhaps you would be interested." The kind and egalitarian tone she takes with him shocks Jurgis, who is used to being ignored, disdained, or feared by the well-to-do. Before Jurgis has heard a word of the speech, his conversion begins when he becomes transfixed by this woman's response to the speaker. Like Begbie's "angel adjutant," she offers a model of submission while implicitly inviting the untouchable man to look on a body that is socially forbidden. In Jurgis's conversion, the implications of such an encounter are very near the surface:

What was the matter with her, what could be going on, to affect anyone like that? She sat as one turned to stone, her hands clenched tightly in her lap, so tightly that he could see the cords standing out in her wrists. There was a look of excitement upon her face, of tense effort, as of one struggling mightily, or witnessing a struggle. There was a faint quivering of her nostrils; and now and then she would moisten her lips with feverish haste. Her bosom rose and fell as she breathed, and her excitement seemed to mount higher and higher, and then to sink away again, like a boat tossing upon ocean surges. (284–85)

It is only after this voyeurism that Jurgis turns his attention to the socialist orator who will convert him, out of a desire to know what "sort of a man" could produce such a response in a refined young woman. As in the drunkards' stories, while physical intimacy remains impossible, grace purges the sexual threat from the workingman's contact with the upper-class woman. This gender dynamic is a potent mechanism by which Christian conversion rhetoric not only maintained social boundaries but depended on them to make spiritual equality visible. It is also a function of the conversion form's ability to assign eternal guarantees and earthly rewards in ways that suit the needs of the movement using it. In *The Jungle* and elsewhere Sinclair deployed this same convention as part of his justification for the role of intellectuals in the socialist revolution.

The extent to which *The Jungle*'s socialist conversion remains bound to such conventions in its Christian template helps explain elements of the ending that have informed latter-day readings of the novel's condescending class dynamics. Sinclair's critique of rescue missions is analogous to the charge critics have aimed at Sinclair: that he failed to convincingly inhabit his working-class character's point-of-view.[23] The novel's touristic style urges such a reading, but the terms of conversion narrative—describing an experience that explicitly gets beneath class identity—anticipate this objection and deny its significance. Sinclair found it necessary to report his own conversion to socialism in writing about the novel after its publication, calling it the product of a leveling crisis that licensed him to write for the "voiceless" working class. His conversion was precipitated by a mental decline which had proved "the individual will . . . impotent" and had vouchsafed to him, "with a knowledge that no man could impeach, the cause and the meaning of all the evils that are raging in modern society—of neurasthenia, melancholia, and hysteria; of drunkenness, insanity, and suicide; of prostitution, war, and crime." Though later in life he would endorse A.A.'s mutual-aid theism for alcoholics, Sinclair's mental, spiritual, and physical savior was socialism. The movement came with its own evangelical imperative, resulting in *The Jungle*'s conclusion and the Intercollegiate Socialist Society that he founded with Jack London.[24]

Sinclair's self-aggrandizing justification for maintaining the distinction between intellectual and worker is what proletarian novels of the 1930s aimed to eliminate, or at least revise, in their revival of the conversion narrative as a figure for transcending ideological entrapment and material despair. *The Jungle* embodied the long overlap between the temperance movement and reformist cultural politics that dated at least to Walt Whitman and remained evident in the Progressive Era. "The slave of alcohol is too often first the slave of capitalism," wrote Horace Traubel in a review of London's *John Barleycorn* in 1914.[25] But even after temperance was a dead letter, many on the left continued to see self-destructive habits as products of economic injustice, and conversion from them as a figure for revolution. Mike Gold's *Jews without Money* (1930) ends with the most clear-cut version: a Jewish boy, Mikey, his family's poverty exacerbated by his father's capitalist pipe-dreams, sinks into despair and vice; on the last page of the novel, coming across a radical speaker, he has the sudden, ecstatic revelation that the Messiah he has yearned for since childhood is the Revolution. Michael Denning defends Gold's novel and its genre against critical disdain for what was called a grotesque combination of naturalism and religious sentimentality. Denning characterizes the consensus among many midcentury critics in language that echoes the assessments of Sinclair's ending: "If one reads the novel as a work of psychological realism, a novel of education, the conversion of Mikey seems unlikely, a flaw of craft and aesthetic."[26] But it is a mistake to read this genre as a clumsy hybrid, Denning argues. Instead, he coins the term "ghetto pastoral" to describe an allegorical mode in which the grim city streets appear through the lens of childhood magic, a realm in which moments of salvation are felt as previews of revolution.

Though Sinclair claimed in his essay "What Life Means to Me" that *The Jungle* marked the beginning of proletarian literature, Denning's apology for the later working-class novel cannot be retroactively applied to it. There is nothing pastoral about Sinclair's Packingtown, his narrator's perspective being that of the horrified tourist rather than the native child. Denning's invocation of allegory does, though, call attention to *The Jungle*'s debt to one of the ur-narratives of Christian conversion, John Bunyan's *Pilgrim's Progress*.[27] Jurgis is a kind of immigrant Everyman whose experiences tell the story of capitalist sin and socialist salvation. It is true that cynicism toward this device among even contemporary readers of the novel was a sign that literary taste was decreasingly tolerant of the emotional logic of popular religion and its narrative conventions. But it is inconsistent bracketing—in an episodic prelude and a sermonizing aftermath—that deflates the impact of Jurgis's conversion, rather than the way the decisive moment itself is written.[28] The second half of the novel reads as failed realism rather than spiritual allegory because it distances the moment of salvation too far from its most powerful images of sin and suffering. Sinclair could have learned something about narrative pacing from Jerry McAuley's one-minute rule for mission testimony.

Still, *The Jungle*'s conversion was drawn directly from a cultural template that still had currency, evidenced in the continuing popularity of revival preachers, including temperance warriors like Billy Sunday, saved from both damnation and drink at a rescue mission; and in attention to the form by the emerging field of psychology. In its use of addictive decline and restorative conversion, *The Jungle* drew from urban revivalism an established mechanism by which the middle class expressed sympathy for the masses and sought to imagine through them society's moral renewal.

Religious Form and Literary Secularization

This literary assimilation of the drunkard's conversion was more multivalenced than simple distinctions between moralistic reform and subversive literature can account for. As we have seen, the drunkard's conversion already had internalized its responses to satirical criticism, while sentimental authors long depended on its essential narrative form to tell their stories of crisis and redemption. American literature and evangelical conversion narrative developed in conversation with one another.

A number of scholars have provided models for recognizing such complex kinds of exchange between religious reform discourse and literature. David Reynolds, in *Beneath the American Renaissance,* for example, shows that the originality of the canonical authors of the nineteenth century did not come in their willingness to depict morally ambiguous subject matter, as had long been claimed. Instead, they took up, in critical and aesthetic ways, the already ambiguous narrative conventions of reform writing. Reynolds applies this mode of analysis specifically to temperance writing and fiction in his essay "Black Cats and Delirium Tremens." Noting that temperance's "rich fund of images and character types" were "adopted by all of the major authors," he identifies four types of "temperance-related" literary discourse:

conventional anti-drinking polemic, dark enjoyment of the most salacious details, ironic mockery of its pious qualities, and the ecstatic discovery of a transcendental sobriety.[29] If Herman Melville often drew on the dark and ironic depictions of reform preachers, Walt Whitman reveled in the joys of newfound sobriety. Later in the century, the arch-ironist Crane and a sentimental polemicist like Sinclair both could draw on the narrative conventions of gospel temperance.

American literature entered the twentieth century in dialogue with a range of cultural assumptions established in religious reform writing. In a model that applies specifically to religious reform, Tracy Fessenden argues in *Culture and Redemption* that fictions from *Uncle Tom's Cabin* to *The Great Gatsby* used the narrative practices developed to articulate the ostensible secularization of the public sphere in the mid-nineteenth century. Mainstream white Protestantism's policing of the bounds of religious tolerance worked subtly, and sometimes openly, to establish the ethno-racial terms of acceptable public identity, a discourse that became, in Fessenden's readings, the template for American fictions to model democratic space. My long argument in this book is structured similarly. I identify the drunkard's conversion as a religious form that, from the outset, served a secular social purpose, a purpose that then became the basis of its adoption in literature. And it was through this appropriation of the drunkard's conversion as an essentially secular form that literature participated in the creation of the spiritual redemption narratives associated with modern addiction recovery.[30]

My analysis is not the first to see the foundations of the modern psychological worldview being laid at the intersection of realism and reform in this era. Keith Gandal attributes to both the ironist Crane and the reformist documentarian Jacob Riis valorizations of street bravado that articulated the transition in popular morality from an ethos of piety to one of self-confidence. In *The Virtues of the Vicious*, Gandal shows these realists in literature and reform working through the contradictions of their techniques toward an ethical critique of sentimental morality.[31] Performing a new, bohemian sense of writerly masculinity, they identified positively with street toughs, and in doing so helped document and create a psychological morality of self-esteem. In this chapter and in Part I of this book, I identify a complementary process. Where Gandal sees Crane and Riis developing prototypes of aggressive confidence, I see Samuel Hadley, Helen Campbell, and even Upton Sinclair formulating, in the model of McAuley and his cohorts, the terms of A.A.-era redemptive healing. This machinery of social rehabilitation through universally available spiritual redemption was a counterpart to the psychology of self-esteem, narrating a route to psychological optimism even for those who had suffered physical, social, and economic trauma.

This ongoing reciprocity between models of conversion in religious and literary representation is thus not limited to the temperance era. But while there is a significant body of scholarship about temperance and nineteenth-century literature, alcohol in modern fiction remains largely grounded in unexamined assumptions of "wet" Prohibition politics and personal "rebellion." I propose instead that the process of exchange described in this chapter laid the foundations for modernist drinking narrative, too, through the same analogies between personal and societal redemption. Reformer and literary writer alike exploited the social dynamic of the drunkard's conversion to work out secular, psychological models of crisis and healing in depictions of behavioral pathology and religious passion among the poor. Psychologists' treatment of the drunkard's conversion, led by William James, legitimized its soical efficacy, and encouraged the separation of the experiential truth of conversion from its institutional religious home. Modern literary writers, rather than rejecting the analogy between slum vice and middle-class alienation, coopted it in alternative visions of self-destruction and ecstatic renewal. The drunkard's conversion thus fostered its own secular diffusion, by combining the sentimental pleasure of redeeming the poor with the credibility of documentary strategies in urban writing, and ultimately by the vision of societal redemption contained in its proffer of transformative grace.

Because cultural representations of drunkenness were so tightly bound to this style of social criticism and reformist polemic, even some of the most experimental writers of the modern era would not stray far from the form when making meaning out of destructive patterns of drinking. Modernist writers consummated the process, begun in Begbie, London, and Sinclair's works, of adapting it to the problems, addictive and otherwise, of the writer. Vachel Lindsay, once again, offers a preview of this turn inward. His 1913 "General William Booth" collection moves from the title poem's exuberantly evangelical homage to the Salvation Army's social work into a meditation on the nature of the writer's own "soul," fitting his spiritual progress to the scale measured by the groaning miseries and divine ecstasies voiced by "The Drunkards in the Street."[32]

I argue in the following chapter that although modern fiction moved in a similarly interior direction, in representing alcoholic compulsion it did not gain much distance from these basic structures—in both narrative sequence and sociopolitical framing—that were established by the drunkard's conversion. This framework remained in place because modernists, too, constructed their meditations on drinking, compulsion, and revelation by internalizing the meaning of vice among the urban poor. Even after abandoning religious conversion as intolerably submissive and sentimental, writers continued to use drinking stories as vehicles of descent through the social order, toward redemptive moments that were both fraught with doubt and rich with potential political meanings.

6

The Drinker's Epiphany in Modernist Literature

Take the moral law and make a nave of it
And from the nave build haunted heaven. Thus,
The conscience is converted into palms,
Like windy citherns hankering for hymns.
We agree in principle. That's clear.

—Wallace Stevens, "A High-Toned Old
Christian Woman" (1923)

I *hate* spectacular conversions.

—T. S. Eliot, letter to W. Force Stead,
February 3, 1927

T. S. ELIOT, IN HIS 1937 INTRODUCTION to Djuna Barnes's novel *Nightwood,* urged its readers not to repeat the mistake of an unnamed reviewer, who recoiled from Barnes's "horrid sideshow of freaks." Instead, Eliot insisted, one must understand her queer, dissolute expatriates as exemplars of the human condition. To read them as mere deviants, the poet wrote, would be "not only to miss the point, but to confirm our wills and harden our hearts in an inveterate sin of pride." For Eliot, *Nightwood's* frantic, lovesick, and alcoholic misfits illustrated the futile and compulsive nature of all desire. "It seems to me that all of us," he reflected, "so far as we attach ourselves to created objects and surrender our wills to temporal ends, are eaten by the same worm."[1] Eliot's "so far as" qualifier leaves open the possibility of an alternative orientation, which his diction points in the direction of religious salvation. But, he makes clear, to recognize this dilemma at all requires reading the humiliating descents of Barnes's characters as trajectories that express our own inherent limitations.

Eliot's phrase "surrender our wills" is a common Christian formula for the inevitable choice every sinner must make, either to serve worldly forces or to seek access to grace. The same year Eliot's review was published, the founding members of Alcoholics Anonymous were using this phrase to describe their method of recovering from alcoholism. A.A.'s pioneers were members of a Christian revival movement who adapted the "surrender" of evangelical conversion to the specific problem of alcoholism, understanding alcoholic compulsion as a spiritual crisis, in the tradition of the drunkard's conversion. If for Eliot the tyranny of the temporal produces the "human misery and bondage which is universal," for A.A. the source of alcoholic self-destruction is the "bondage of self," the illusion of autonomy that the alcoholic suffers in the extreme.[2] The difference between Eliot and A.A. regarding the possibility of liberation from this prison is, in terms of cultural style, one of high-church/high-modernist reticence versus evangelical/self-help assurance. In practice—that is, in their instructions for how to read addiction narrative as revelation—they are roughly equivalent. Where Eliot warns against readerly "pride," A.A. tradition arrives at the injunction "identify, don't compare," with testimony of even the most degrading consequences of addiction.[3]

This affinity between a high modernist's apology for the literary low life and the recovery movement's psychospiritual interpretation of the "gospel cure" is a product of the genealogy of addiction narrative that this book has explored. In this chapter I argue that the modernists, too, made meaning out of destructive drinking by using narrative forms inherited from the drunkard's conversion of the late nineteenth century. Complicating the longstanding assumption that modern literature is wholly antagonistic to religious temperance and its moral vision, writers in the 1920s and 1930s drew on the conventions of the drunkard's conversion narrative in their depictions of alcoholic decline. Furthermore, modern fictions relied on that tradition's mechanism of producing ideological meaning: coding stern social critiques into journeys of compulsive desire and tracing visions of societal redemption in the insights discovered at the bottom.

The literary echo of gospel temperance is more than a structural irony in the secular appropriation of religious forms. It provides a new critical window into literary drinking stories, revealing sociopolitical concerns built into the same passages from subjective breakdown to objective truth that animate its evangelical precursors and therapeutic counterparts. Modernist novels famously probed the limits of subjectivity and agency, and alcoholic crisis is a prominent vehicle of these explorations. But their participation in the tradition of addiction-conversion narrative reveals that drinking's philosophical resonance in modernism was also rooted in a more concrete reform discourse. The differences in the ways various modern literary texts depict alcoholic decline negotiate not just the nature of individual agency but also the social and political implications of culturally conditioned self-destruction. The drinker's collapse, in literature as much as in religion and reform, was an observant descent through a particular social order, while the truth remaining in the rubble of such a life described the possibility of this society's renewal.

The modernist novels I examine closely here—John Dos Passos's *Manhattan Transfer* and Barnes's *Nightwood*—are seminal experiments in form, and they are also representative of distinct types of literary alcoholism narrative. *Manhattan Transfer* represents what I call the "gestural conversion," whose alcoholic decline narrative leads to insight, but offers only a tentative motion toward potential renewal as its reward. Dos Passos's redemptive gesture is a characteristic modernist epiphany, of the kind that remains a stock vehicle for morality tales seeking hopeful conclusions without the embarrassment of polemical or happy endings. *Nightwood,* by contrast, I term a "conviction" narrative (from the evangelical "conviction of sin") that uses alcoholic decline to assert its social critique, but invokes conversion only to depict its failure in an irredeemably fallen society. Barnes's critique of redemption joins other texts by women and minority authors of the period that pursued the social criticism inherent in the drinker's decline but found that its final redemptive insight (whether modernist-stoic or religious-ecstatic) was unavailable to subjects who were not eligible for social rehabilitation. Together these two novels describe a pattern in the emplotment of alcohol abuse and dependence in twentieth-century literature: variations on the drunkard's conversion form that contest both the values it discovers at the bottom and the model of renewal those values project.

These ways of making meaning in alcoholism narrative appropriate the religious template differently, but they also implicitly respond to one another's rival claims on it. *Manhattan Transfer,* the story of a proletarian's death and a writer's epiphany, problematizes socialist conversion stories such as Sinclair's *The Jungle,* probing more deeply the role of the writer and the experiential journey by which his advocacy can be authorized. Barnes's novel, a collection of failed conversions among social outcasts, illustrates how much Dos Passos's attempt at a self-legitimizing foundational truth, like other male-modernist epiphanies, depends on a social position that is already justified. The discourse thus returns to the exchange between the drunkard's conversion and its literary parodies in the nineteenth century, similarly dividing around what insufficiency is truly confessed and what power remains disguised by the sentiments of redemption.

Finally, modernist depictions of alcoholic compulsion and its consequences illuminate the way the behavioral dynamics of the slum conversion were internalized in the self-concepts of the middle class, whether by reformers, recovering alcoholics, or novelists. In these works, writer-substitute characters routinely identify their spiritual crises with the pathologies of poverty and exclusion, making self-referential meaning out of the same class divide that missionary reformers saw as a social problem. Instead of building policy programs in this space, literary writers use it to critique the artist's role in relation to societal crises and the politics of reform. Literary constructions of alcoholism and redemption reveal this cultural ancestry in the journeys they take through the landscapes of social descent and urban reform. Just as these texts locate the felt truth of society's moral condition in the addict's self-destruction, they look for the authentic reality from which to begin its renewal in the haunts of the poor and the disreputable: slums, stockyards, roadhouses, and outhouses. Alcoholism in modern fiction partook of a literary obsession with the low life that cut across writing styles and politics, and both drew on and contested the narrative traditions of reform. The problem confronted by self-conscious reformers like Helen Campbell remained a question animating the fiction of alcoholism: how, in Eliot's terms, the respectable should read the horrid.

The Canonical Moment of Clarity

As we've seen, through the first decade of the twentieth century a wide variety of writers engaged with the drunkard's reformation story as a site where fundamental American values could be contested. The genre's presence was similarly unmistakable in the era of confessional writing after World War II. In the interwar period, though, both religious conversion and secular recovery seem to have been much less prominent in American literature. Prohibition has long served as the essential historical context for the relationship of modern fiction to drinking, and, as everyone knows, American modernists defied the great temperance victory in their opinions, in their personal habits, and in their works. This picture of an idealistic but jaded generation also has a home in the expatriate Parisian milieu, where modernists went to escape the stifling effects of moralism and commercialism in their native land. Memoirs of the expatriate experience contributed to both a popular mythology and a critical assumption of the symbolic role of "unapologetic" drinking as a function of the modernist interpretation of history. It is what John W. Crowley wryly calls "the alibi of the modern temper."[4]

This way of historicizing modernism suggests that the drunkard's conversion fell from favor because it embodied the kind of moral certainty and mawkish sentimentality that literary writers, especially, found could no longer bear authentic meaning or linguistic creativity. As true as this account is at key stylistic levels, it has obscured important aspects of drinking narrative in modern fiction. My approach is not to argue against the importance of Prohibition, or moral rebellion, or generational temperament, as historical contexts. Instead my purpose is to conduct a kind of thought experiment, by setting aside the calcified equation of literary innovation with bohemian social style, so as to examine instead the formal construction of modernist drinking narrative in relation to its literary predecessors and its therapeutic counterparts. The otherwise unavailable meanings that emerge help to create a broader framework for understanding the importance of alcoholism to the culture of the period than strict aesthetic hierarchies have allowed.

Before applying this conversion-recovery lens, an alternative context suggests itself, in the psychotherapeutic discourse that had dislodged the rescue missions' evangelical interpretation of alcoholic decline, especially in more sophisticated circles. The kind of therapies available to urbanites by the 1920s comprised psychoanalysis itself, its popular American adaptations, and the spiritual theories and New Thought techniques developed by mainline churches and self-help innovators.[5] These were the new psychological languages of alcoholism that A.A.'s pioneers recognized and often adopted, but ultimately found insufficient for either effecting or narrating deep, lasting change. This language of expertise spoke to an individual's mental machinery but lacked both the egalitarian social sympathy and the wide symbolic import associated with religion. The sense of this absence lay behind the Oxford Group's and the early A.A.'s belief in intimate spiritual community, or "primitive Christianity" as a way of life. I want to suggest that psychological theories of alcoholic compulsion were ill suited to inform literary drinking narrative, for similar reasons. The literary traditions surrounding alcoholic excess ranged from vehicles of communal catharsis, dating to Greek drama, to the elevated state of self best known from Romantic poetry.[6] Even the popular American tradition of "city mystery" novels, with their stark moral crises and violent spiritual rebirths, retained a symbolic resonance that the new clinical language did not.

The drunkard's conversion continued to appear as a plot trajectory, and to provide this symbolic register, in much literary drinking narrative of the 1920s and 1930s. Insofar as leading novelists told stories of alcoholic decline, the form was a source of the epiphany convention still associated with modernism. In these gestures toward conversion, an alcoholic decline leads to a moment of clarity that contemplates, but does not fulfill, the redemption of self and society. This revelation at the end of a breakdown is analogous to the evangelical conviction of sin in its decisive exposure of the limitations of a subject's own resources. This vision of sin, in the modern literary context as much as in evangelical theology, is as a fundamental human condition rather than a problematic behavior or a character flaw. In the conversion gesture, a character begins to act on this knowledge, typically striking out from a corrupt, alcohol-saturated urban milieu toward some idealistic, wholesome realm, one that may or may not be a nostalgic figment of the imagination.

Jake Barnes's "Isn't it pretty to think so" and Nick Carraway's "And so we beat on, boats against the current"—famously stoic closing epigrams—are drawn from the experience or witness of collapses brought on by compulsive desire. They spurn religious certainty, but they provide an interpretive sense of closure and an epistemological resting-place, a narrative conclusion typical of alcoholic decline. These conclusions also tend to confirm the stoic courage of their young male narrators in facing such hard truths. In texts in which women who drink are generally eligible for neither redemption nor insight, such truths typically arrive through finely honed versions of white masculinity. In this type of modernist alcohol narrative, the foreshortening of conversion into epiphany is meaningful, in that it refuses religious metaphysics in favor of an empirical subjective conviction. But it leaves in place the deeper structure of alcoholic surrender, in the revelation of unconditional truth at the nadir of an addictive decline. And in doing so, it leaves untroubled the social hierarchy that has produced this subjective journey, and which the progressive religious workers had sought, however naively, to emend.

Dos Passos's 1925 *Manhattan Transfer* exemplifies the preservation of the traditional conversion structure within a modernist aesthetic, because it maximizes both of these ostensibly ill-matched elements. Though it combines photographic, mass media, and architecturally inspired aesthetics in a fragmented narrative, the novel inherits from its realist and didactic precursors the inevitability of decline in an addictively materialistic urban environment. Malcolm Cowley included it, for example, along with novels like *Sister Carrie* and *The Jungle,* in his catalog of American naturalism, presumably because of its effort to narrate the deterministic effects of the commercial world of World War I–era New York.[7] *Manhattan Transfer* has more in common with *The Jungle* than an urban environment that lures and corrupts, though. Like Helen Campbell and Upton Sinclair, Dos Passos saw a general societal crisis producing the many individual breakdowns, but he also, like them, presented the traditional solution of individual redemption as a precursor and symbol of collective social change.

Manhattan Transfer was the formal breakthrough that made possible, when combined with a commitment to left politics soon afterward, Dos Passos's *U.S.A.* trilogy.[8] It does not have the later works' epic scope or prophetic voice, but it does supply a kind of Old Testament antecedent for them, in narrating the conviction of society's sin—the acceptance, in the evangelical formula, of its absolute need of redemption—and indicating the possibility of this redemption in a gesture. The novel's attenuated conversion narrative contributes not to political discourse but to the kind of literature concerned with the pre-political establishment of a correct subjective stance toward society's ills. In doing so, it also typifies the implicit politics of social identity that so often underwrites this formalism. *Manhattan Transfer* essays a strident critique of a capitalist society, and is sympathetic to labor, but the novel is ultimately about an upper-middle-class writer's identity crisis and his decision to save his own soul. As such, it rehearses the professional identity politics that animate *The Jungle* and other Progressive Era fictions.[9] To do so, it invokes the classic temperance tropes of individual and societal alcoholic decline and, for the writer-protagonist at least, the resulting redemptive insight.

The New York City of *Manhattan Transfer* is manic with ambition and addicted to alcohol. The city's various worlds—artistic, commercial, and political; rich and poor; immigrant and native—interpenetrate, through the filter of advertising-driven media technology and in the swirl of saloon-based social exchange. The port city is a crucible of modernity, a circulator of goods—notably illegal shipments of liquor—and of people and identities. The novel's characters make a roster of urban stereotypes: exploiters and victims, strivers and failures, of representative classes and ethnicities, many of them meeting at the intersections of their ambitions. Hierarchies of power abound, and money predominates, but there is enough fluidity of role and mutuality of exploitation that the outer-borough roadhouse that is the scene of a central, determinative chapter seems to stand for a drinking world that is the only democratic realm left in its America.

But this egalitarian ideal of the saloon is a temporary apparition. Since alcohol is the social medium of a corrupt city, its role as the fuel for delusions and humiliations comes to the fore. The characters, even those who are married to one another, seem to meet only in passing: each is intoxicated with an upward flight or flailing against an out-of-control descent. Within this tangle of trajectories, the novel contains two traditional and symmetric decline narratives. In the first half of *Manhattan Transfer*, a beaten-down farm boy arrives in the city as a fugitive, struggles to find work, and ultimately dies. The second half develops what is effectively the novel's protagonist in Jimmy Herf, a journalist with literary aspirations and radical leanings, who becomes disillusioned with the unprincipled striving he sees as the city's only value. In one of several imagistic arrivals by water to the city, Herf lands as a small boy in the care of his neurasthenic, widowed mother. Surviving the working-class bullies on his block, the conventional advice of rich, corrupt relatives, and, later, a failed marriage to an ambitious actress, he becomes a successful journalist but one whose artistic and political ideals are frustrated. Like Fitzgerald's Nick Carraway, Herf is more an observer than a participant in the destructive drinking that surrounds him. But his response to it gives the novel's overall arc the shape of an alcoholic's conversion.

Herf feels as trapped by the compulsions of New York as he perceives his compatriots to be, and he develops a powerful urge to flee. Toward the end of the novel, drinking to carelessness, Herf names his problems to Armand Duval (Congo Jake), a former stowaway and bartender, now a millionaire bootlegger:

> "The difference between you and me is that you're going up in the social scale, Armand, and I'm going down. . . . When you were a messboy on a steamboat I was a horrid little chalkyfaced kid living at the Ritz. My mother and father did all this Vermont marble blackwalnut grand Babylonian stuff . . . there's nothing more for me to do about it. . . . Women are like rats, you know, they leave a sinking ship. [. . .] I swear I've got the energy to sit up and make a million dollars. But I get no organic sensation out of that stuff any more. I've got to have something new, different. . . . If I'd had a decent education and started soon enough I might have been a great scientist. If I'd been a little more highly sexed I might have been an artist or gone in for religion. . . . But here I am by Jesus Christ almost thirty years old and very anxious to live. . . . If I were sufficiently romantic I suppose I'd have killed myself long ago just to make people talk about me. I haven't even got the conviction to make a successful drunkard."[10]

This passage encapsulates much of what animates canonical drinking fiction: a young man is drawing troubling conclusions after his first experiences of failure; he feels class guilt and identifies an ethnic, proletarian other as his double; his hatred of polite convention and his resentment of women serve a London-esque manly affect; and he recognizes suicide and alcoholism as the romantic responses to his dilemma. Herf's reference to the last-chance role of the drunkard alludes to the fates of his older cousin Joe Harland, a disgraced former stock-trading wizard whose desperate efforts to remain employed prefigure early A.A. narrative, and his own best friend, Stan Emery, heir to a capitalist fortune who lives in a perpetual binge. Because these characters closest in identity to him are each dissolving into alcoholic oblivion, Herf identifies their self-destruction as at least a definitive response—one requiring "conviction"—to his type of problem.

Instead of living out this conviction, though, Herf can glean its ultimate meanings through Harland and Emery, the depths of their alcoholic demises providing the insight he needs to be transformed. Brief, intense scenes of Harland's advanced alcoholism and Emery's extended blackouts weave in and out of Herf's story, offering images of his potential fate. While Herf is regretting his choice of a career, a young I.W.W. organizer takes Harland into his tenement home for a meal. Harland's hands are "dirtgrained and trembling, his tongue was like a nutmeg grater from the cheap whiskey he had been drinking the last week, his whole body felt numb and sodden and sour" (201). But despite the workingman's kindness, Harland clings at his alcoholic bottom to his utter conviction that the highest ranking capitalists will always win. Soon afterward Herf finds him destitute and begging for food and thinks out loud, "Funny you never think of your relatives as being people like yourself, do you?" (209). Harland advises him to be ambitious and cagy, his "scarecrow" appearance an implicit warning against careless self-indulgence. But Herf applies this lesson differently in his own interactions with the working class, gravitating instead toward radical politics.

Herf takes more than a redemptive lesson from the alcoholic demise of his best friend, Stan Emery. During yet another epic binge, Stan stumbles drunk into a working-class Irish saloon and is beaten up because he "aint one o de boys." He comes out of his blackout on a ferryboat, struggling to remember his own identity, hallucinating and craving another drink. He makes it home, only to laugh drunkenly as a fire engulfs his house and kills him (212–14). Stan is erased at his low point, and Herf inhabits the redemption portion of his story, achieving the maturity his friend had been incapable of by taking responsibility for the baby Stan had fathered with Jimmy's own ex-wife, Ellen.

Labor-leftism and self-sacrifice are the values thus revealed to Herf in the alcoholic collapses of his two doubles. But before these ideals can structure his regeneration, he must descend to his own low point. Sure enough, just as Herf feels himself to be falling apart, he is saved by a conversion experience that is wholly his own. Toward the end of the novel, he has begun to give over to frequent intoxication. He has been promising to turn his back on New York and his journalism career for some romantic foreign adventure, but is aware that his problem is as much a feature of the world he has inherited as it is one of his own mind. The crisis from which Herf flees seems embodied in the relentless way that technologically accelerated commerce usurps natural signs and selves, colonizing the landscape with advertising and obscuring the sun with overhead arclights. In the deepening of this crisis, and in its crossing from the material environment into the realm of a troubled young man's desires and habits, the novel invokes a narrative tradition that carries with it the strong expectation of conversion.

Consistent with this tradition, Herf's moment of clarity emerges out of his drunken low point. In the closing scene, he walks straight from a late-night party in Greenwich Village to a ferry port in the early morning. On the water as he sails from Manhattan, the effects of the alcohol wearing off, his senses are momentarily transfixed by a man with a wagonload of flowers: "The little warped wagon is unexpectedly merry, stacked with pots of scarlet and pink geraniums, carnations, alyssum, forced roses, blue lobelia. A rich smell of maytime earth comes from it, of wet flowerpots and greenhouses." After disembarking, Herf walks up a hill and looks back, presumably toward the city, but "he can seen nothing but fog spaced with a file of blurred arclights." He walks on, through a wasteland of industrial refuse. Sunrise comes, and a "pearliness" is giving way to red sunshine. He stops at a crossroads lunchwagon for breakfast, spending all but his last three cents, and asks a truck driver for a lift. The novel ends with the driver's question, "How fur ye goin'?" and Jimmy's response, "I dunno . . . Pretty far" (342). It is a gesture toward transformational change.

Such negatively hopeful endings, in which a moral choice is made to turn from corruption but no clear alternative appears beyond the unformed stirrings of the protagonist's conscience, have a long history in urban migration narratives and bildungsromans. Bound to the tale of the innocent confronting experience, they are common in American literature. In Jay McInerney's 1984 novel *Bright Lights, Big City*, the pathology of Manhattan's cocaine-fueled nightlife is finally brought into focus for a would-be writer by the nostalgic smell of freshly baked bread, a counterpart to Dos Passos's "rich smell of maytime earth." Critics hailed *Bright Lights, Big City*, like *Manhattan*

Transfer before it, as formally groundbreaking. Where Dos Passos rendered in image and prose style the morally disruptive, desire-distorting influence of a commercial landscape, McInerney wrote an entire novel in a frenetic second-person voice, conveying the divided self of a character allowing his life to drift with the social environment.[11] But beneath these engaging techniques, *Manhattan Transfer* and *Bright Lights, Big City* are old-fashioned city mysteries novels, with their intelligent but inexperienced heroes snared in worlds of violent intoxication and loose women. They are thematically of a piece with the young Walt Whitman's 1842 temperance novel, *Franklin Evans,* only substituting the writer's humble epiphany for Whitman's climactic, nation-redeeming temperance rally.[12] More skeptical approaches to this urbanization plot have not been a function of period, but of temper. In Nathaniel Hawthorne's "My Kinsman, Major Molineux" (1833), the young protagonist, Robin, suffers through a series of intoxicating exposures to urban corruption that break down his sense of self. He aims to return to his simple rural home, but a worldly stranger encourages him to stay.[13] Hawthorne's wry tale exposes the narcissism that troubles this often panicky moralistic genre, in its twentieth-century versions as surely as in a temperance fable.

This generic parentage is invisible in a critical tradition that identifies modernism with the "ambiguity" of gestural endings, underestimating the structural energies by which such narrative closure bears the weight of restorative certainty.[14] The redemptive gesture reconciles the structural demands of the narrative arc to the skeptical temper expected of literary fiction. By cutting off the character's descent not at its low point, but just afterward, at the moment of recognition that makes conversion possible, and by adding the first stirrings of manifest renewal, the gestural ending gives ground to the pressure for resolution, while retaining claims to philosophical and temperamental reticence. The effect of this half-measure is less to draw attention to the uncertainty of redemption than to transfer the entire felt burden of it onto the epiphany. Such gestures can easily read as guarantees of recovery, providing relief from the ostensibly tragic outlook of the modernist drinking narrative by smuggling in the satisfying closure and sentimental optimism of evangelical conversion, while maintaining the intellectual pleasure of stern pessimism.[15] It is the appeal of this double-duty that has made the gestural conversion a fairly calcified convention, turning its formal working-out of a technical challenge into a moral resting-place. For Dos Passos, though, the hopeful gesture was a precursor to political engagement.

Written on the cusp of Dos Passos's turn to left literary-political evangelism,

Manhattan Transfer critiques American society but is uncertain of the belief that it might be bettered, the kind of belief necessary in order to commit to activism. The novel's preoccupation with its protagonist's position in society is an effort to understand the obligations of a writer to discover and act on such a belief. To drink compulsively, in the novel's America, is to be carried along passively by a social scene that serves a socioeconomic structure. (This critical treatment of alcohol reappeared as the cocktail party trope in Dos Passos's magnum opus, *U.S.A.*)[16] Only when Herf, the drinker-as-unrealized-writer, finds that he is sinking does he turn desperately to the redemptive alternative, and this realization is supplied by the conviction moment of the traditional drunkard's conversion. In this manner too, gestural conversion can stand in for full conversion, because it solves the problem of distinguishing one's fate and foundational beliefs from those that are socially predetermined. Dos Passos moved on from this position, completing the socialist conversion that would shape his personal and professional life for the next decade. But some modern writers, and especially the critics who canonized them, took this ethos of the gesture and elevated it into the ethical endpoint of a literature devoted to the formal hashing-out of fine points of subjectivity. By this route the modern drunkard's conversion in literature can be as much a refuge from reform as a preparation for it. These different consequences of gestural conversion are analogous to the debates about the inherent politics of religious conversion and addiction recovery, which from different perspectives appear as either retreats into self-interest or models of world-transforming social sympathy.

Through this participation in the conversion tradition, modernist uses of alcoholism are much closer in spirit than they might at first seem to the recovery narrative initiated by A.A. The tragic-ironic representations of heavy drinking in canonical modern fiction are, temperamentally, very far from the optimism and sincerity of the recovery narrative. From this point of view, the ensuing era of recovery memoir killed off high modernist masculinity by exposing hardboiled literary drinking as a form of romantic egotism. There is a biographical logic to this view of periodization, insofar as prominent modernists associated their own drinking with their historical moment, several died young from alcoholism, and Fitzgerald, for one, openly disdained recovery as a cowardly refuge in atavistic religion and group psychology.[17] But at the same time, self-destructive drinking in modern fiction not only has a formal ancestry in the drunkard's conversion, but also performs a gendered, pseudo-therapeutic function that confirms its kinship to A.A.

Re-examinations of gender in modernist fiction have suggested the extent to which the famously masculine affective styles of key canonical novels were sentimental constructions that served to assuage deep insecurities. For much of the twentieth century, critics accepted these masculinities on their own terms: as anti-bourgeois rebellion, brave philosophical honesty, and the submersion of a stoic self into a spare form. But critical efforts to recognize and understand male sentimentality have opened up new perspectives on the cultural work these affective stances undertake.[18] In *The White Logic*, John W. Crowley shows that ostensibly stoic, controlled steady drinking in the canonical modernist novels, in particular, was often a highly fraught, compulsive response to changing gender norms.

A.A. narrative itself depended on managing this kind of gender affect. The self-consciously modern masculinity at stake in A.A.'s otherwise traditional narrative form—what one might call its stoic sentimentalism—invoked the aforementioned literary register to make itself legible. In chapter 4 we saw how A.A. narrators reproduced its tropes, both to critique their own former drinking habits but also to conserve their masculine identities in recovery. These identity markers signaled their distance from feminine arenas such as religion and temperance, but also compensated for the loss of their masculinity's leading sign, the capacity to drink. In what are effectively short stories, recovery narrators tried out literary techniques such as present-tense and fragmented narration, and they drew on common modernist themes such as postwar disillusion and hatred of moral hypocrisy. While their circumstances were often more like those of Sinclair Lewis's smug striver George Babbitt, or John O'Hara's country-club lush Julian English, their struggles with the paradox of heroic self-effacement echoed the distanced, romantic postures of Fitzgerald's, Dos Passos's, and Hemingway's honorable but tortured young men. One way to view A.A. narrative is as an adaptation of the drunkard's conversion for subjects that had adopted the skeptical, ironic tempers as well as heavy drinking habits of literary modernists.

But this comparison works both ways. Just as A.A. narrators drew on gendered literary tropes, modernism's hard-drinking masculinity appears through the A.A. lens to be a highly self-soothing affair, shoring up manhood so as to account for its failure and to justify retaining in society what A.A.'s Big Book called "the family trousers."[19] Recovery blurs modern fiction's momentous distinctions between middle-class fools and tragic antiheroes, revealing a George Babbitt and a Jake Barnes to be close relations, despite the self-conscious distancing strategies deployed by the latter. The masculinity Jake and his drinking partner Bill Gorton share in *The Sun Also Rises* is constructed not only in their tenderly satirical exchanges and the rituals of their fishing and drinking excursion but also in a contrast with the middle-class American family they meet on a French train en route. The vast chasm implied between them and its paterfamilias—like the one between them and Cohn, the Jew who can fight but can't hold his liquor—calls to mind the tortured exceptionalism V. S. Naipaul diagnosed in a later counterculture as "the great uneducated vanity of the middle-class dropout."[20] Drinking as a sign of such gendered self-exile runs through modern literature, pitting the denizens of the urban saloon and the expat café against bourgeois conventionality from Crane and O'Neill to Kerouac and Bukowski.

Modernist masculinity, as well as drinking narrative, is not as far from its A.A. double as it might seem. The wry self-deprecation performed by Jimmy Herf and Jake Barnes lies somewhere between the self-justifying cynicism of the unrepentant drinker and the studied humility of the confessional alcoholic. When Barnes admits powerlessness over his romantic life (the war wound a sexual counterpart to the sin/disease of addiction), he is one step away from the great submission that conversion requires—and the fact that he cannot feel God's presence makes him more, not less, eligible for it, in A.A.'s world. It is a submission designed to transform that very hardboiled irony into spiritual wisdom and the democracy of drinkers into mutual-aid fellowship, while conserving a wised-up perspective. Like the canonical modernists, A.A. recruited male bonding to make manifest a counter-cultural identity from within a powerful social position and to redeem its inherent paradoxes. In both cases this ethical self-work also exempted its participants from responsibility for larger, or what might be called political, concerns. By contrast, stories of dangerous drinking by women and racial minorities could not build therapeutic mechanisms on foundations of social dominance, and, accordingly, they tended to be both shakier and more radical affairs.

Protest at the Site of Conversion

The canonical modernist stories that arrived at conclusive epiphanies and redemptive gestures were those that, like religious and spiritual conversions, tended to universalize the meaning of addictive crisis. Their "convictions of sin" gained access to the felt grace of conversion by discovering a malady that lay beneath and before the self—a revelation that is the release-valve in the drunkard's conversion, by which the ego deflates and God's grace is allowed entry. Recovery narrative similarly repurposed, in the disease model of addiction, the impersonal quality of Original Sin. But such fundamental states of sin can only be divined from their temporal manifestations if other causes, such as personal failure or social exclusion, can be ruled out. This is why, despite their self-confessed wounds, figures like Jimmy Herf and even Jake Barnes read as heroic specimens of young manhood: their native nobility distinguishes them from ordinary sufferers. By contrast, fictions in which addictive failure flows from a particular social problem tend to have a much harder time producing admirable characters and redemptive transformations. This is doubly a crisis if the subject of the story does not have access to a social identity by which redemption can be made visible. In the modern era this dilemma gave a different shape to stories of addiction in socially marginalized subjects.

The result was often a kind of dead-end conviction narrative with no satisfyingly redemptive turn. The nadir of this descent tended toward the degrading, cataclysmic binge, in which the narrative approach to conversion plays out, but fails to deliver any sign of transcendence. Jean Toomer's *Cane* (1923), for example, ends in the story "Kabnis" with a series of failed conversions by a young black teacher who is conflicted about his identity, during a prolonged drinking session among rural southerners. Amiri Baraka adopted a similar denouement in the 1960s for a young northerner in the poor South, in his nightmarish prose-poem novel on racial violence, *The System of Dante's Hell.* Wallace Thurman in *Infants of the Spring* (1932) tried out an orgiastic bohemian scene in Harlem as an experiment in transcending race, but temporary ecstasies among the hard-drinking artists give way to failure, bitterness, and suicide. In each case, an identity crisis, and its attendant heavy drinking, are bound up with relationships, real or imagined, to the black poor and the historical roots of the racial dilemma. Conversions fail because the social problem cannot be solved, there being no secure social identity for the protagonist that is unbound from these masses, their history, and their ongoing oppression.[21]

These novels borrow intermittently from the structure of decline, conviction, and conversion, in characters whose drinking is compulsive and, in the tradition of temperance narrative, performed through a particular relationship to the vices of the poor. Djuna Barnes's 1936 novel *Nightwood* inhabits more wholly this traditional structure, revealing explicitly the form's dependence on social perspectives that are not universal. *Nightwood* is perhaps the most self-aware of the modernist expatriate drinking novels, in regard to both the genre's oppressive and moralistic gender dynamics and the pressure toward conversion built into narratives of debauchery and decline. Its particular iteration of modernist pessimism comes in its very use of the drunkard's conversion, when it confronts the genre as the only formal solution available to addictive decline, but one that is infected by the same disease that necessitates it.

In *The White Logic,* his definitive account of the "drunk narrative" in modern fiction, John W. Crowley identifies a panic in the face of shifting gender norms lying behind the nearly civilizational importance the canonical novels of American modernism seem to place on rituals of male heavy drinking. Crowley shows that Barnes's model of "transcendence downward" in *Nightwood*'s drinking plot inverts and exposes these gender elements.[22] In the discussion that follows, I make use of Crowley's positioning of Barnes's novel in respect to the male moderns, but I also endeavor to show that this formal dialectic around alcohol depends on the historical structure of the drunkard's conversion—and that as such, it constitutes yet another site at which this form was used to contest sociopolitical values.

With its Parisian setting, gay characters, and experimental style, *Nightwood* has never been associated with the tradition of urban realism, nor with either religious or therapeutic accounts of alcoholism. But Barnes's training as a professional writer was classic literary journalism in this vein, and her drive to both document urban characters and identify as one of them informs the construction of drinking in *Nightwood.* First for the *Brooklyn Daily Eagle* and then other New York papers from 1913 to 1919, she wrote, usually in the first person in some combination of observer and participant, of suffragists, workers, immigrants, prizefighters, artists, and policemen. Her articles "Chinatown's Old Glories Crumbled to Dust" and "Greenwich Village as It Really is" are effectively sequels to Stephen Crane's Tenderloin reports of the 1890s.[23]

This literary journalism provides a background to alcoholic urbanism in *Nightwood,* especially in the way Barnes the journalist identified with her subjects. For example, in a 1913 search for the last squatters of Brooklyn's notorious "Pigtown," "there creeps into your heart a mad desire to place your foot on earth and claim it as yours"; and of a Village artist's alcoholic lady friend she writes, "Way down deep I knew she was keeping things that she feared lived."[24] In *Nightwood* this tendency is built into both the characters' obsessions with street life and the narrator's abstractions: "Those who love everything are despised by everything, as those who love a city, in its profoundest sense, become the shame of that city, the *détraques,* the paupers; their good is incommunicable, outwitted, being the rudiment of a life that has developed, as in man's body are found evidences of lost needs."[25]

Nightwood's depiction of alcoholism is as a condition not only shared by bohemians and the lowly street people to whom they devote attention, but one that might somehow be decoded through this relationship.[26]

Nightwood's characters suffer from deep structural flaws that produce repeating patterns of self-destruction and bewildering processes of decomposition. Their defects are not merely their own but reflect failures of coherence between the person, the world, and the models of selfhood it provides. Their experiences are repetitive, but it emerges that they are worsening toward crises. Robin Vote, the boyishly beautiful expat in Paris, and her lover, Nora Flood, each implode under the burden of Robin's maniacal nightlife. The other characters—Robin's husband, Felix, her suitor, Jenny, and their confessor, the quack gynecologist Dr. Matthew O'Connor—each end the novel in alcoholic dissolution.

On the addictive axes of repetition and decline, the narrative is weighted toward the former, so much so that it reimagines decline as a non-narrative, atemporal quality. Each character embodies, even in moments of stasis, some version of this inherent damnation. Despite her beauty and the obscurity of her inner life, Robin gives off an aura of "decay" and "deterioration" (34); her face is that of "an incurable yet to be stricken with its malady" (41), observers sensing in her "a catastrophe that had yet no beginning" (48). Nora is "eternally moving downward, but in one place, and perpetually before the eye" (51). O'Connor theorizes explicitly that "descent," like "night," is a phenomenon that exists as a subjective condition, independent of the passage of time. The actual downward plummet, which he enacts in his final moment by crashing drunkenly onto an ash-strewn café table, only pantomimes what is inherently "maladaptive," to borrow the key adjective from the current clinical diagnosis of alcohol dependence.[27]

O'Connor's familiar modernist themes—historical fallenness, failed ideals, psychological repression—coalesce into addiction, as the compulsive and self-destructive pursuit of both pleasure and redemption. He explicitly names the failure of received ideals, and the compulsion to repossess them, as an addictive decline: "When a long lie [a romantic delusion] comes up, sometimes it is a beauty; when it drops into dissolution, into drugs and drink, into disease and death, it has at once a singular and terrible attraction" (137). His lengthy description of the meaning of the night is a discourse on the addictive compulsion of misery, epitomized by "the young, the drug addict, the profligate, the drunken and that most miserable, the lover who watches all night long in fear and anguish" (94). O'Connor speaks from and to addiction as the condition of fundamental truth, in the manner of Jack

London's White Logic; the difference is between his poetic compassion for the fallen and what London rendered as alcohol's jeering condescension. The antithesis of the brooding, systematic drinkers who play lead roles in Hemingway's novels, O'Connor is a voluble, effusive, dramatic drunkard, a libidinous gay cross-dresser, whose sympathy for humanity is broad and passionate, not limited to an in-group or stunted by cynicism.[28] As the novel's effective co-narrator, he does not partially exempt himself from these hopeless states; instead he identifies himself more than anyone else with them, his frustration at being misembodied as a man sensitizing him to thwarted desires and existential tragedies.

If the tenor of addiction in *Nightwood* is particularly modernist, the novel's glimpses of the urban low life carries on a fascination central to alcoholic narrative since at least the temperance movement. O'Connor's "night" equates the unconscious with the nighttime city streets as realms that harbor the deep truths of daytime and the conscious mind. O'Connor imagines an earlier, more chaotic Paris as the exemplar, "when the streets were gall high with things you wouldn't have done for a dare's sake. . . . The criers telling the price of wine to such effect that the dawn saw good clerks full of piss and vinegar, and blood-letting in side streets where some wild princess in a night-shift of velvet howled under a leech" (81). The bodily and social anarchy of the early modern urban maelstrom in O'Connor's imagination is the deep inherited truth of the novel's characters, made manifest in Robin's nighttime pursuits of intoxication and sex.

O'Connor offers this formula to Nora to explain why Robin is so drawn to a debauched nightlife. Robin narrates this identification in one of the few direct depictions of her drunk, or in any sustained conversation. Nora recalls for O'Connor a late-night confrontation between the two women that was redirected toward a drunken old prostitute:

> "She stumbled and I held her, and she said, seeing a poor wretched beggar of a whore, 'Give her some money, all of it!' She threw the francs into the street and bent down over the filthy baggage and began stroking her hair, gray with the dust of years, saying, 'They are all God-forsaken, and you most of all, because they don't want you to have your happiness. They don't want you to drink. Well, here, drink! I give you money and permission! These women—they are all like her,' she said with fury. 'They are all good—they want to save us!' She sat down beside her." (144)

The displacement of the booze-corrupted romantic relationship onto an object of the gutter epitomizes the literary drinker's obsession with the low life, as somehow both the pure form of the addict's crisis and the key to her salvation. It echoes Upton Sinclair's projection of his own socialist conversion onto an illiterate immigrant, Jack London's identification with the drunken young sailor in the East End in *People of the Abyss*, and even, more distantly, the temperance movement's fear of the urban street life because of its allure for middle-class youth.

This shared narrative tradition produces surprising points of contact between the modernist avant garde and therapeutic culture. Nora's inability to possess Robin and her desires not only articulates the existential problem of other people's minds, but does so in a way that echoes the lament of the drunkard's wife: "She was mine only when she was drunk, Matthew, and had passed out. That's the terrible thing, that finally she was mine only when she was dead drunk. All the time I didn't believe her life was as it was, and yet the fact that I didn't proves something is wrong with me. . . . I tried to come between and save her, but I was like a shadow in her dream that could never reach her in time" (145). Nora's lament anticipates the principle of addiction recovery culture, which holds that an addict's family and friends cannot save her. The A.A. source for this notion is pietistic, originating in conversion narrative: the addict does not actually save herself, but allows God to do so by "letting go," submitting her will to a higher power. It is such a conversion that Robin pursues.

Nightwood fulfills its conception of self-destructive behavior as a spiritual crisis with the traditional movement toward conversion that this vision enjoins. Each of the characters obsessively seeks redemption from built-in flaws, Felix through his son, Nora and Jenny through Robin, O'Connor through compulsive vocal performance, and Robin through religious conversion itself. Robin intermittently seeks out grace after the birth of her son. She appears at her own Catholic baptism "as if some inscrutable wish for salvation . . . had thrown a shadow" (46). She haunts out-of-the-way Parisian churches, where nuns pity her as someone incapable of asking for or receiving mercy, and she feels this quality herself in her attempt at prayer: "She could not offer herself up; she only told of herself in a preoccupation that was its own predicament" (47). The recognizable modernist trope of prayer that fails to find an auditor takes the form, in this instance, of the addict's dilemma: how to cure the self from a malady of self-obsession.

The plot drives toward two conclusions, both dramatic moments of conviction and failed conversion. Toward the end of the long penultimate chapter, O'Connor delivers a desperate, drunken cri de coeur against the confessional impositions others make on him, against the cruelties of his gender dilemma, and against the modern condition generally, ending in his ignominious collapse onto a dirty café table.[29] Having lived and told his life "abominable among the filthy people," now, "drunk as a fiddler's bitch," he physically finds his low point, with nothing left *"but wrath and weeping"* (165–66). O'Connor's arc concludes decisively in conviction, but not conversion, drunkenness, not sobriety, and tears of grief, not of joy. As dramatic and conclusive a scene as it is, though, as the terminus of his descent it remains bound by the logic of repetition, insofar as there is no signal that his life will actually change.

By contrast, Robin and Nora's ending parodically and pathologically completes the addiction-conversion structure of the novel. In the final chapter, Robin leaves Jenny in New York and circles toward the chapel on Nora's property, where, as Nora arrives, she performs a bizarre quasi-religious ritual, a sort of demonic anti-conversion, to the accompaniment of Nora's terrified dog: "On a contrived altar, before a Madonna, two candles were burning. . . . Before the image lay flowers and toys. Standing before them in her boy's trousers was Robin. Her pose, startled and broken, was caught at the point where her hand had reached almost to the shoulder, and at the moment Nora's body struck the wood, Robin began going down. Sliding down she went; . . . until her head swung against [the dog's]; on all fours now, dragging her knees" (169). While O'Connor had flopped face-first and prone onto a table, Robin slowly collapses, first to her knees, then flat on her back. In this image of apparent submission, Robin seems finally moved, not so much by Nora's appeals, but by spiritual exhaustion, the "hitting bottom" that is recovery's update of conviction.

What follows evokes the moment of ecstatic conversion in the Christian tradition: the climax of a long crisis, the exhaustion of the will, postures of joyful submission, the failure of language, unbearable happiness, tears. Crawling after the dog, Robin is "barking in a fit of laughter," "grinning and crying with him," and finally, "her hands beside her, her face turned and weeping" (170). If gestural conversion endings build redemption and rebirth into the moment of conviction, *Nightwood*'s ending collapses conversion itself into a deathlike conviction, the nadir of decline like a black hole from which nothing can escape. If in *Manhattan Transfer,* conversion is ostensibly deferred, yet completely felt, in *Nightwood* a conversion is acted out, but no triumph is found, the performance instead turning into a ritualized degradation.

This failure registers more than a simple loss of religious faith. The social aspects of conversion—the class and gender rehabilitation that the drunkard's conversion markets as the benefits (and evidences) of spiritual transformation—are here insoluble, in imagistic reminders of the codes of behavior and identity of which all the novel's characters have fallen afoul. During the ritual before the Madonna (rather than Christ), Robin's hair is still "swinging" as it did in the first scenes of her drinking, evoking Milton's image of female wantonness as it existed in the Garden of Eden even before the Fall. Eve's inferiority is fixed by the transgression that seems foreordained in that image, for which she is tamed by Adam and by God, as Brett Ashley is punished for her similarly sexual destructiveness by its relentless exposure in Hemingway's drinking novel.[30] In the midst of her "conversion," Robin's relationship to this gender logic is essentially unchanged, perhaps even worsened, as she is not only flaunting her hair but "dragging her forelocks in the dust." With the regime that pathologizes her desires still in power, to recover, to be rehabilitated, would require being remade by the very source of her maladjustment. So conversion becomes not the apotheosis of suffering but its ultimate abasement.

Robin's epithet, "an incurable yet to be stricken with its malady," evokes A.A.'s notion of alcoholism as a disease without a cure, and one that many believe they contracted before ever taking a drink. While this view has more recently found a home in genetic theories of alcoholism, the conversion tradition understands it as a fundamentally spiritual condition.[31] T. S. Eliot's reading of *Nightwood* helps flesh out this analogy and reveals its limits, which turn out also to measure the novel's distance from the canonical strain of modernist alcoholism narrative. In assigning the misery of *Nightwood*'s characters to fundamental human insufficiency, Eliot recruited the novel to the philosophical foundationalism of the addiction narrative that reveals underlying truth. Eliot's empathy makes Barnes's characters the lowlifes who emblematize a universal condition, whereas in the novel, the drunken prostitutes who serve in this role for Robin and O'Connor cannot be purged of the specific problems of gender and sexuality.

Eliot's take on *Nightwood*'s addictive pathologies suggests that even high modernism, so aesthetically and socially removed from the middle-class business lingo and evangelical optimism of A.A., was invested in the same contest over the meaning of the addiction-conversion relationship. Eliot's poetry, like much modernist fiction, draws on the conversion pattern to invoke a universal addiction. Though the earthbound soul remains an inherently tragic object, Eliot explores methods of keeping the eternal in sight so as to minimize and order earthly obsessions. These visions of transcendence arise in versions of the transformational decline narrative. In "The Waste Land," cultural and psychological dissolution gives way to a passive state of exhaustion that is also a promise of insight and even renewal. The poem emerges from the "unreal city" of corrupt ethics, diseased working-class drinkers, and sexually degraded young women to the quietistic "Shanti shanti shanti" of the ending. This passage evokes both the social ground and the formal structure, if not the triumph, of the conversion narrative, in which the will to control is exhausted and forced to surrender, and in which both the misery of the bottom and the ecstasy of salvation push language to its limits and ultimately outstrip it. Though Eliot's poem may be far removed aesthetically and temperamentally from, say, *The Jungle*, one can trace through each the narrative logic of the drunkard's conversion.

Eliot's conception of a universal misery, like the Christian belief in a salvation that transcends social station, meets its match in *Nightwood*'s anti-conversion scene, in which the terms of compulsive desire and its spiritual nadir are particular.[32] *Nightwood* constructs its model of addiction from the very gender blindness that runs through the addiction-conversion tradition, from the reformed-but-doomed prostitutes in the rescue mission literature, to Begbie's virginal "angel adjutant," to Sinclair's horror of childbirth, to London's vile East End women, to Dos Passos, Fitzgerald, and Hemingway's man-eating lady drinkers. In its awareness of the politics of conversion itself, its confrontation with this tradition is more rigorous, and much less self-satisfied, than those of the more widely read modernist drinking novels.

Modern literary adaptations of the drunkard's conversion thus contested the meaning of the narrative, and of alcoholism itself, in a subtler, more form-oriented manner than socialists, progressives, and reactionaries had done a generation earlier. My own purpose has been to revise the historical relationship between alcoholism and modern literature and, by extension, to reconsider the established periodization of literary drinking narrative. I have tried to show that, however much the modernists scorned the morality of temperance, they did not fundamentally break with tradition when it came to structuring stories through the progress of addiction. Furthermore, the tensions they created by inhabiting these plot forms with their subtler styles and modern tempers predicted the issues around which writers would structure both fictional and confessional addiction stories in the postwar era. As Barnes's novel reveals, only those with access to a performable public social identity could narrate the passage from compulsion to liberation. Those who did not, especially nonconforming women and sexual minorities, would have to narrate their recoveries as projects of social politics, either within or outside the liberal expansion of rights. As I argued in chapter 4, the rise of liberalism was the significant context for the emergence of this new culture of recovery identity. In the chapter that follows, I examine a modernist literary text that imagined the potential dangers of this redemptive model of politics.

7

The Iceman Cometh and the Drama of Disillusion

New York and Brooklyn bubble over with temperance meetings,
and the prayer-meetings by the women at Harry Hill's Concert
Saloon, while liquor-selling goes on with great earnestness, the
sales apparently being rather stimulated than otherwise.

—*The Temperance Record*, April 11, 1874

"General, on behalf of the former sinners of the future I would like
to protest the closing of this mission."

—Sky Masterson, in Frank Loesser's *Guys and Dolls* (1950)

EUGENE O'NEILL'S LIFE AND WORK seem to fit the pattern of the alcoholic modern writers. Born in 1888, he was a ferocious binge drinker in his early adulthood, accruing the kinds of legends that make a hard-drinking writer's reputation. From 1907 to 1915, between trips at sea, he spent lengthy periods in some of Manhattan's rougher saloons and boardinghouses.[1] Biographers credit this time spent in the lower depths for helping to form his philosophical pessimism and his democratic social ethos. His plays often use heavy drinking to signal these values, in scenes that resonate with the canonical modern novels. *The Iceman Cometh,* especially, as the play that drew most directly on those experiences, presents a world of men who drink as both a desirable norm and a countercultural rebellion, flouting polite customs (and temperance values) as effeminate and domesticated. They exhibit instead a cynicism and world-weariness, leavened only by the humor and camaraderie of the saloon and the occasional euphoria of drunkenness. Like many modernist literary texts, *Iceman* uses alcohol as a medium of both hard-edged social content and skeptical philosophy. In it, compulsive drinking enacts the empty rites of a world that has lost faith, suggesting a death-drive that is timeless, but particularly resonant with modern cultural pathology and social insecurity.

Closer examination reveals that O'Neill's relationship to alcohol, in his life and in his most drink-sodden play, exhibits significant variations on the canonical pattern.[2] To begin with, there is O'Neill's own long-term abstinence after undergoing psychoanalysis in 1926, and his depiction of heavy drinking as, if often inevitable, rarely heroic. While for writers like Jack London and Ernest Hemingway drinking facilitated manly confrontations with tragic truths, in O'Neill's late plays, especially, drunkenness is an impotent, delusional state. In *The Iceman Cometh* alcohol preserves the comforting illusions the characters call "pipe dreams." O'Neill's depiction of alcoholism is closer to those of socialist writers like Upton Sinclair and Mike Gold, for whom compulsive drinking literalized the mystifying and self-thwarting effects of capitalist ideology. Unlike the radical writers, though, O'Neill does not coopt the drunkard's conversion as a way of imagining a route to political consciousness. Instead the play writes and endlessly rewrites the conversion story itself as the master-narrative of illusion. The decay that drinking wreaks in *Iceman* does not clear the ground for self-knowledge of any kind, much less the awakening, political or religious, such knowledge might make possible.

I take up *Iceman* in detail in this chapter because it brings into focus, and offers a commentary on, the broad narrative tradition this book has explored. The play is built from the bones of the drunkard's conversion, from its linguistic and performative conventions to its social and geographical origins to its various ideological valences. But far from reassembling this material into another secular alternative, O'Neill exposes, historicizes, and laments the entire meaning-making apparatus of the form. The play announces the genre's historic collapse upon the failure of the social, political, and religious programs that called it into being, into a single, supine therapeutic self-interest. This post-ideological redemption evokes the recovery rhetoric of both Alcoholics Anonymous and the nascent liberal state, such that its ultimate exposure in the play as a murderous deception articulates deep anxiety about what future turn these new therapeutic languages heralded.

Reading the play through the lens of the drunkard's conversion helps make sense of a style and a sheer repetitive density that have confounded and divided critics. Its stylized recreation of urban naturalism mourns not so much the artistic or political ideals of an earlier era, as it does the exhaustion of a century-old source of American vernacular, a site both real and imaginary that I term the culture of the saloon and the mission. This conceptual world includes historical places like Harry Hill's Concert Saloon, Jimmy the Priest's bar, and Jerry McAuley's Helping Hand mission, as well as imaginary ones, from T. S. Arthur's barrooms to drunkard routines on the Vaudeville stage to the Save-a-Soul Mission of *Guys and Dolls*. While culture-makers like Damon Runyan and Walter Winchell were busy mythologizing this world in print, O'Neill marked its passing as a genuine and even frightening loss for American culture, not only as source material for the theater but also as a site where ordinary people could dramatize their roles as citizens. As we have seen, radicals, reformers, and reactionaries claimed its spaces and used its narrative forms to tell of personal and collective responses to the crises of modernity. The performative world of the saloon and the mission was a site of the vernacular drama of democracy that O'Neill had made a career formalizing in print and on stage.

Written in 1939, the year Alcoholics Anonymous published its self-titled book, *Iceman* depicts a distorted double of A.A.'s recovery pitch that is a method of manipulating vulnerable people into surrendering their only ideals. The play describes an alcoholic, philandering traveling salesman who returns to his lowest drinking haunt sober, preaching a newfound serenity to his former drinking companions. With missionary patience and evangelical fervor, the salesman goes to work unburdening each of these alcoholic characters of their personal illusions. This central plot movement, the cast of characters, their speech, and the details of their setting, all work to produce caricatured rehearsals of each of the major strands of the modern drunkard's conversion: the religious, the politically radical, the literary-philosophical, and the therapeutic. The play reveals each of these languages of redemption to be little more than rationalizations of the alcoholic's low point, an exposure that discredits the conversion form itself as an epistemological conceit whose purpose is to give transcendent authority to temporal, self-interested ideas. But the play reserves its harshest treatment for the strictly self-soothing spirituality that would replace these ideals, imputing to it a more deceptively sinister material power play, one that destroys the moral imagination and renders its converts submissive. The play ultimately links this false rhetoric of selflessness to the recovery politics of the Depression-era state, implicitly wondering what its citizens are being asked to submit to.

The play's deep sense of disillusion is not overly concerned, then, with alcoholism, but with the kinds of citizen-subjects that recovery language produces. It imagines the alcoholic's surrender as the subjective internalization of inhuman external forces. This political register is built into the play's setting, in its space, time, and style. Harry Hope's, the location of all the action, is the kind of flophouse barroom produced by temperance-driven laws, its interior design and its daily rhythms structured by the progressive-era regulation of alcohol sales and consumption. This regulatory framework is not repressive but rather sets the conditions for intemperate drinking, unrealistic dreaming, and evangelical exhortation. The personal reform movement that disrupts this norm collapses the legal structure into its subjects, forcing them to accept that they are the compulsive, amoral consumers the laws assume, rather than the authors and protagonists of moral dramas that may yet end in triumph. This reduction of contending ideals to a single reality offers a grim interpretation of the ways that both A.A. narrative and the New Deal state were asking subjects to accept their own proven limitations. The play does not critique policy nor even political theory, but spins a dark national allegory out of the rhetoric of serenity and security, pessimistically limning an emergent model of therapeutic citizenship and suggesting its worst implications. It anticipates the diagnosis rendered by Thomas Szasz and others on the far side of the New Deal era of an overweening "therapeutic state" that uses the language of self-realization to police human aspiration.[3]

O'Neill spoke of the play in both the personal and societal registers that, taken together, constitute the ideology-producing function of the drunkard's conversion narrative. In defense of his pitiful characters he explained that they represented universal human frailty or, evoking again the intersection of T. S. Eliot's Christian piety and A.A. spirituality, "the weakness found in all men." The second grand frame O'Neill invoked to justify the play's darkness was American national decline. Using a rhetoric common in the 1930s, he said at a publicity event for the first staging of the play in 1946 that the nation had "squandered [its] soul" in material pursuits. This dark language was not a good fit with the optimistic outlook of either national politicians or public intellectuals in the 1940s, a fact which may help explain the poor reception that greeted the first production. O'Neill echoed Roosevelt's New Deal narrative in his diagnosis of American "self-seeking," but his play refused FDR's optimistic prophecy of redemption as surely as it mocked leftist faith in collective salvation. The O'Neill of *The Iceman Cometh* was, as John Patrick Diggins has put it, "frozen in the world of liberalism that can never reach the goal of radicalism." Another way of understanding this liminal position is that *Iceman* discredits the very redemption form necessary for narrating any ideology, even New Deal liberalism, from crisis to fruition.[4]

The Iceman Cometh announces the end of the century-long ideological contest over the meaning of the drunkard's conversion and warns against the bland, reductive surrogates that seem poised to replace it. The play exposes the drunkard's conversion as an ideological mechanism in each of its religious, political, literary, and therapeutic manifestations. In doing so it links an emergent addiction recovery narrative to the changing role of the state through the lens of drinking. This analysis of the play makes sense of a stark division in its critical reception, between naturalistic and expressionistic readings. Both modes are at work in O'Neill's aesthetic, through a stylized evocation of urban naturalism, the form at the heart of the broad era of the saloon and the mission, the period when alcoholic and religious intoxication were symbiotically connected sources of American culture. The play eulogizes the cultures of saloon excess and missionary fervor as flawed and delusional, yet governed by a productive and humane tension, a mutual commitment to the dramatic performance of social ideals. It worries that the ostensibly neutral, therapeutic turn in self-expression as well as in political rhetoric represents a more deceptive and manipulative claim to foundational truth.

False Bottoms

In *The Iceman Cometh* O'Neill took up the raucous tradition of the drunkard's conversion at the historical moment when A.A. was transforming it into a more settled, psychospiritual recovery narrative. The play's intervention recognizes, though, that the genre makes meaning not polemically, but affectively, in its formal turning point at the conviction of sin or hitting-bottom moments that prove a life has been lived by the wrong values. *Iceman* is a drama of "the bottom": the play is very explicitly set at this terminus, either in death or just short of it, of the alcoholic decline. In one of the most frequently quoted passages in the play, Larry Slade explains to the newcomer Don Parritt what "kind of joint" the ironically named Harry Hope's Saloon is: "It's the No Chance Saloon. It's Bedrock Bar, The End of the Line Cafe, The Bottom of the Sea Rathskeller! Don't you notice the beautiful calm in the atmosphere? That's because it's the last harbor. No one here has to worry about where they're going next, because there is no farther they can go."[5] *Iceman* does not dramatize alcoholic decline; all of Hope's "inmates" are at the nadir of descents known only in the various backstories that emerge about them. Their remaining energy goes toward imagining restored glory and grubbing drinks.

Hope's saloon is a physical manifestation of the narrative site shared by the various modern alcoholism narratives that owe their shapes to the drunkard's conversion.[6] O'Neill presents this spiritual floor as a contested and constructed location, rather than the foundational, pre-intentional space it is known as in each instance of the conversion tradition. Just as *Iceman* denies alcohol its role as the bringer of unwelcome truth, so the play denies that such truth dwells at the alcoholic low point. *Iceman*'s nadir, by the standards of these other narratives, is not a true bottom. Hope's is not the place where illusions evaporate, leaving pure truth and self-knowledge distilled. On the contrary, at *Iceman*'s bottom careers, relationships, and agency have been submerged in alcoholic fantasies, and what remains is not self-knowledge but only the delusion that these goods can be recovered. The sole clarifying aspect of life in Hope's saloon is its merciless exposure of this self-deception to others. Larry Slade completes his explanation to Parritt by alluding to what remains of life in this last refuge: "Although even here they keep up the appearances of life with a few harmless pipe dreams about their yesterdays and tomorrows, as you'll see for yourself if you're here long." Though "harmless" in and of themselves—they are plans to recover careers, to get married, to be socially legitimate—the stakes of these pipe dreams, as Slade argues elsewhere, are high. The characters' glorious visions are both impossible to bring to fruition, and yet the only means by which they can understand themselves according to socially approved conventions as subjects in a viable narrative. Such illusions not only "keep up the appearances of life," but are the only thing standing between the characters and the play's conception of psychic death. Hope's sea-floor can sustain a stasis that O'Neill once went so far as to call "deep inner contentment" because it is a place of untroubled lies, not transformational truths.[7] In this, the play suggests, the bottom is not qualitatively different from anywhere else.

The conflict of the play flows from a reformed drunkard's efforts to change the meaning of this site by drafting it and its denizens into a conversion narrative. The play opens with Hope's regulars awaiting the arrival of traveling salesman Theodore "Hickey" Hickman, whose money, charisma, and "periodical" drinking binge will make possible the celebration of Harry's birthday. But when Hickey arrives at the end of the first act he is not drunk as usual and ready to lead a debauch, but sober and preaching some brand of "peace" he has found, one that has cured him of the need for alcohol. Over the course of the next two acts, Hickey shames all of the characters into facing the falsity of their pipe dreams by trying to put them into effect and inevitably failing. Hickey promises that the shock of this disillusion will give way to a state of peace, as the tensions of self-deception are lifted and the shame of failure abates. Like any good evangelist, Hickey puts his own story front and center, describing his decline and crisis as the worst of all, and performing his new, enlightened state as a model for his audience. But it is not until he has forced his subjects to confront their own impotence that he reveals the details of his catalyzing failure and subsequent disillusionment: after years of widely spaced but catastrophic, adulterous drinking binges, he has murdered his wife, Evelyn, in a mercy-killing to relieve her from the endless crushing of her hope, and him from the guilt that her grief brings on.

Even before Hickey reveals this deed, though, the conversion cure fails in *The Iceman Cometh*. Although Hope's saloon is a social bottom, the play's true nadir is the loss of hope and dissolution of self that occur when characters follow Hickey's plan and are forced to give up the delusional, compulsive narrating of their futures. Instead of finding peace, the characters descend into states of waking death, epitomized by the sudden impotence of alcohol—the medium, in the play, for the regime of the pipe dream. Characters in this state, reached most explicitly by Harry Hope in the third act, become not humble but cynical, alternating between anger and dejection, and losing the ability to believe others and themselves. The only way out is to retreat back into self-deception. When Hickey finally admits that he killed Evelyn as a way to free them both from the constant cycle of promise and betrayal by which his alcoholism structured their marriage, the other characters write off his whole project, and build back up their old illusions, reinstating the "tomorrow" narratives of their pipe dreams.

O'Neill's play takes for granted what in conversion narrative is hard-won wisdom: that the romantic ideal of the heroic self is illusory. But the play mocks the various ideologies that insist redemption lies beyond such disillusion. Instead of serving as a central turning-point, disillusion in *Iceman* is the site of the drama, where each of the narratives—religious, literary, and political—that claim the meaning of alcoholic decline appear in one character or another. These different narratives vie to construct the truth that the low point will, retroactively, have revealed. The play's bottom is not a social fact, but an imaginary space where revolutionary politics, ironic detachment, evangelical conversion, and therapeutic recovery, contest subjects who might speak their visions into existence. By satirizing this contest, *Iceman* repudiates the notion central to alcoholic narrative that the drinker's collapse reveals truth that precedes human will, imagination, and agency. The play depicts the ideals discovered at the bottom to be articles of faith whose purpose is to legitimate programmatic narratives. It exposes the conceit of the narrative's foundationalism—the notion that addictive decline strips away the illusions of ego and of social convention to reveal a priori truth—as a generic convention of conversion and its secular doubles. *Iceman* in effect deflates the significance of hitting bottom as a primal scene of modern literature and of all forms of redemption from the various iterations of modernity as a crisis. As a sustained investigation into the meaning of this key formal and conceptual location, the play serves as a meta-text for modern alcoholism narrative.

Hickey arrives bearing a new, post-ideological dispensation. The opening acts establish the characters' various pipe dreams as faith-based self-concepts, preparing the ground for Hickey's entrance as an old-fashioned revivalist intent on converting his former drinking partners and their bar. On the first report that Hickey is nearby, sober and claiming to be a changed man, Hope's inmates believe he is planning to pull an elaborate Salvation Army gag on them, one which they anticipate playing along with: "Tell him we're waitin' to be saved!" It emerges quickly that he is not playing a practical joke, nor has he joined the Salvation Army, but that he has undergone some form of conversion, and is devoted to evangelizing the entire bar to this faith with what the regulars come to call his "bughouse preaching."[8] What he offers is a secular recovery narrative that aims at sober mental serenity rather than divine bliss. But it comes to appear just as dangerous as religion, or anarchism, or alcoholism itself, and all the more so because of its contemporary appeal and its disguising of ideology within a language of pragmatism.

Hickey's message is not religious. Like several self-help movements of the 1930s, it fuses spiritual and psychological language in a newly expert, but still recognizably evangelical, style. He maintains as a point of pride that he "didn't fall for the religious bunk," and yet he is relentlessly styled a revivalist, in his rhetoric and in how other characters perceive it. They describe his "Reform Wave" as a temperance missionary's combat against the saloon world. Hickey's characterization draws on both the comic and the sincere traditions of the sinner turned preacher who returns to his old haunts to save his former companions. He flatters, coaxes, and cajoles the other characters, like a versatile evangelist alternating his style of address for maximum effect. For much of the play, he exudes a religious serenity and kindly concern; occasionally he resorts to fiery exhortation.[9] What does a lowbrow, pseudo-religious mode mean in a play written in 1939 and first staged in 1946? Born-again religion was not a live target in O'Neill's day. In literary culture, evangelical religion had been a punching-bag for going on a half-century.[10] In the 1930s, revivalism was alive and well in popular subcultures, but it was not a movement in which artists perceived an intellectual or even social threat.

Contexts for Hickey's evangelism are scarce in the critical literature on

Iceman. Typically it is associated with vague Americanisms such as sales-manship or blind optimism or capitalism. Joel Pfister offers an exception, arguing that O'Neill used Hickey's language to critique American popular-izations of Freudian psychology, as being snake-oil substitutes for the tragic worldview of drama.[11] In the context of Hickey's conversion pitch, I see a better candidate in the self-improvement culture of the 1930s that married psychology and religion, and which owed more to James, Jung, and media-savvy Protestant ministers than it did to psychoanalysis. This religious component, central to American self-help and middle-class mutual aid, is explicit in the language of and about Hickey. This language is not merely a feature of the play's 1912 setting; it echoes 1930s revivalism and, more impor-tantly, the psychologized forms of it that were infusing middlebrow inspira-tional literature even during the Great Depression.[12]

As a pragmatic, secular adaptation of conversion style and structure, Hickey's message has its closest analogues not in American churches but among the secular redemption narratives that proliferated in the 1930s. And as a program that replaces eternal salvation with relief from compul-sive desire, its nearest counterpart among those recovery narratives is that of Alcoholics Anonymous, the movement that would transform popular understanding of the addictions that pervade O'Neill's late plays. *The Ice-man Cometh* reads in plot, style, and even in its theory of alcoholism as a dramatic critique of A.A. Hickey appears to his former drinking compan-ions sober, carrying the message of a simple, pragmatic plan for achieving peace of mind and sobriety. He calls on these drunks to account honestly for their thoroughgoing inadequacy, on the evidence of the complete failure of their various projects of self-mastery. Hickey acknowledges a debt to evan-gelism through his father's preaching, a grudging admission of influence that echoes the Big Book's muted acknowledgment of A.A.'s Oxford Group origins and its ongoing insistence that it is not a religious program.[13]

Hickey's theory of alcoholism is, like that of the Big Book, one that runs deeper than drinking, to the fundamental orientation of the self to the world. He shares A.A.'s ambivalence about "underlying causes and conditions" of alcoholism, identifying drinking as the proximate cause of the crisis but rec-ognizing that the problem runs deeper than the habit itself. A.A. identifies "selfishness—self-centeredness!" as "the root of our troubles," concluding that "our liquor was but a symptom." Similarly for Hickey, pipe dreams, as he says, "are the things that really poison and ruin a guy's life and keep him from finding any peace" (81). Once he was able to "throw overboard the damned lying pipe dream that'd been making me miserable, and do what I had to do for the happiness of all concerned . . . then all at once I found I was at peace with myself and I didn't need booze any more. That's all there was to it" (79). For Hickey as for A.A., the deep root of alcoholism is a delusional sense of individual mastery.

The most significant similarity between Hickey and early A.A. narrative is the rhetoric of confessional testimony in his speeches. His emphasis on his own failures and his alternatively serene and intense style places him, with A.A., in the tradition of the drunkard's conversion as it had reemerged in the 1930s. Hickey, like the early A.A. members in their spiritual messaging, is adamant that his "program" is based entirely on the truth of personal experience, not on the adoption of dogma. At Harry's birthday party at the end of act 2, when the inmates are unsettled by the anger that Hickey's prodding has brought out in Harry, Hickey takes on his most exhortatory tone in expounding what he calls his "line of salvation." His is the mode of the reformed drunkard, the confessional evangelical, testifying to his own depths of sin and the miracle of his rebirth:

> (*He addresses them now with the simple, convincing sincerity of one making a confession of which he is genuinely ashamed. . . . They stare at him, bitter, uneasy and fascinated. His manner changes to deep earnestness.*)
> But here's the point to get. I swear I'd never act like I have if I wasn't absolutely sure it will be worth it to you in the end, after you're rid of the damned guilt that makes you lie to yourselves you're something you're not, and the remorse that nags at you and makes you hide behind lousy pipe dreams about tomorrow. You'll be in a today where there is no yesterday or tomorrow to worry you. You won't give a damn what you are any more. I wouldn't say this unless I knew, Brothers and Sisters. This peace is real! It's a fact! I know! Because I've got it! Here! Now! Right in front of you! You see the difference in me! You remember how I used to be!

Hickey builds to a preacher's fervor by establishing credibility in the mode of confessional sincerity, the performative logic of the drunkard's conversion and the A.A. narrative. The arch-cynic Slade is drawn in by the narrative even as he dryly mocks its religious tone: "I think it would help us poor pipe-dreaming sinners along the sawdust trail to salvation if you told us now what it was happened to you that converted you to this great peace you've found" (147–48). It is the hallmark of A.A.'s hardboiled filter for confessional sentiments that it can move the irreligious toward religion without directly asking them to give up their skepticism.

Hickey's attestation of personal experience as a way of inviting audience identification is a central convention of the long era of the drunkard's conversion. It recalls Upton Sinclair's communist firebrand who draws Jurgis in by attesting, "I know how much it is to ask of you—I know, for I have been in your place, I have lived your life." It echoes Jerry McAuley's testimony to having been "one of the worst drunkards in the Fourth Ward" and Samuel Hadley's response: "I began to say to myself, 'I wonder if I, too, could be saved?' There was a sincerity about this man's testimony that carried conviction with it." And, finally, Bill Wilson's response to his own Christian evangelist: "He had come to pass his experience along to me—if I cared to have it. I was shocked, but interested. Certainly I was interested. I had to be, for I was hopeless."[14] *The Iceman Cometh* recognizes this personal mode as the rhetorical engine driving the power of the conversion narrative over hardboiled but vulnerable subjects.

Stylistically, Hickey invites identification by using the language of the self-consciously worldly middle-class man, a drinking-oriented style keyed to retaining social status while repudiating gentility and naiveté. Like A.A. narrators, he undergirds his occasional flights of serenity by often flaunting the jocular vulgarity of the saloon, most notably in the performance that finally pushes the inmates out the door of Hope's: "(*Abruptly he becomes sympathetic and earnest.*) Because I know exactly what you're up against, boys. I know how damned yellow a man can be when it comes to making himself face the truth. I've been through the mill, and I had to face a worse bastard in myself than any of you will have to in yourselves" (189). Elsewhere he denounces temperance and Prohibition, and asserts his saloon masculinity in slangy claims to "know all about that game," as "the guy that wrote the book," who "finally had the guts" to give it up (79). His language describes a self-aware, empirically proven personal solution, not a plan of moral hygiene or sentimental apotheosis.

Despite all these similarities, it would be a mistake to describe Hickey as a mouthpiece for A.A., or *The Iceman Cometh* as a play about A.A. As Thomas Gilmore has shown, Hickey deviates in several key ways from A.A.'s tenets. For one thing, he has not sworn off all alcohol, taking a drink to prove to his friends he is not a temperance reformer. In effect he claims to be cured of addiction, whereas the A.A. disease model holds that "the first drink" will always reset the narrative to the moment of crisis. With a miracle cure in hand, Hickey's style is more exhortatory than that of most A.A. narrators, who tend to remain more rigorously confessional. Importantly, too, Hickey attempts to manage the inmates' lives, rather than simply offering them an example to follow. This manipulation becomes most explicit in his stage-direction of Harry's party (135–36), which places him directly at odds with the A.A. allegory of the "actor who wants to run the whole show," its illustration of the "self-will run riot" that is the fundamental maladjustment of the addict.[15] In the end, O'Neill's depiction of a *manipulative* evangelist is not directly about A.A., but a deeper and wider trend in American culture.

The play confronts psychospiritual recovery language, evoking A.A. only in its particular application to the problem of alcoholism. It is much more concerned with the political implications of this worldview and its claim to truth. As the play concludes, the inmates finally and rapidly get drunk, with the exception of the ex-radical Larry Slade, who has successfully encouraged his would-be protégé Parritt to kill himself for betraying his mother and her anarchist movement. The young informer is the only character who dies, and Slade is the only one who, because of the death of his cherished detachment this event forces him to confront, cannot emerge from the state of total deflation that Hickey's narrative has brought on. Hickey's self-knowledge is suicidal, while Slade's boasted objectivity is revealed, by play's end, to be just another illusion, his own particular pipe dream. O'Neill presents the rhetoric of recovery as demanding the surrender of ideals, collectivist and individualist alike, in the conviction that they are impossible, unreasonable delusions. In a post-religious world, this surrender promises not salvation but only subjective contentment, which, in the play, never arrives to soothe the humiliation of defeat. *Iceman* suggests that at the close of the 1930s, drinkers and radicals alike were being urged to "surrender" to a Higher Power that may not countenance their ideals or any others.

The State of Recovery

"Recovery" in the 1930s primarily referred to the federal government's effort to dig the country out of the Great Depression. As I noted in chapter 4, Franklin D. Roosevelt's administration advanced a complex and conflicted set of policies but told a fairly consistent narrative of recovery, a national story of sin, decline, crisis, and renewal. FDR's writings and speeches, and even the language of some New Deal laws, described an economy and a populace that had been in thrall to a regime of compulsive "self-seeking," the deflationary results of which had produced "dark realities" and, most dangerously, a "nameless, unreasoning, unjustified terror which paralyzes needed efforts to convert retreat into advance."[16] The depth of this crisis provided experiential evidence of the insufficiency of unfettered individualism.

This conviction of sin became the basis of a new, pragmatic wisdom that would replace the wild swings of boom and bust with not only a sober, stable economy, but a subjective feeling of security among the citizenry—serenity, to use A.A.'s term—unprecedented in history.

The Iceman Cometh in its treatment of the drunkard's conversion speaks not directly to New Deal policy but to this kind of rhetorical appeal in a time of crisis. Hickey bears his message of recovery to a place in 1912 that is desolate, haunted by the same political and material ideals that seemed to have been lost in the Depression: Hugo's ranting and Larry's musing on anarchistic freedom; Harry, McGloin, and Joe Mott's talk of the glories of Tammany Hall's heyday; and the memories of lawyers, journalists, veterans of colonial adventures, and the son of a disgraced investment con-man. Hickey offers as compensation for these losses a predatory narrative presenting itself as pragmatic, empirically discovered truth, leading his vulnerable auditors to voluntarily concede their idealistic ambitions in favor of submission and passivity. The play paints a grim picture of redemption rhetoric, protesting an emerging popular therapeutic language which suggested that the addictive nature of human striving could be escaped via acts of submission. The play sees this submission as conceding too much to the limited view of human agency; or, if agency is illusory in any case, to the limits of imagination, which if accepted would declare defeat prematurely. In giving up their illusions, the inmates of Hope's saloon are being asked by their ringleader-turned-preacher to cease narrating their own aspirations.

The play connects personal recovery narrative to the state not only in the way Hickey's program usurps political ideals, but in the way the characters' movements are structured by the law. In the introduction to the play O'Neill expends considerable effort explaining the role of the Raines Law as the legal structure that determines its social space. The dense description is concerned with how that space both complies with and yet evades the law:

> Harry Hope's is a Raines-Law hotel of the period, a cheap ginmill of the five-cent whiskey, last-resort variety situated on the downtown West Side of New York. . . . The renting of rooms on the upper floors, under the Raines-Law loopholes, makes the establishment legally a hotel and gives it the privilege of serving liquor in the back room of the bar after closing hours and on Sundays, provided a meal is served with the booze, thus making a back room legally a restaurant. . . . Hope being a former minor Tammanyite and still possessing friends, this food technicality is ignored as irrelevant, except during the fleeting alarms of

reform agitation. Even Hope's back room is not a separate room, but simply the rear of the barroom divided from the bar by drawing a dirty black curtain across the room. (vii–viii)

The 1897 law in question was not merely a municipal ordinance governing liquor sales, but a comprehensive state law governing licensing, sales, consumption, and taxation, in an effort to curb political corruption and the vice of drinking, in response to a reform movement.[17] The law produces the physical division of Hope's, the status of its regulars as tenants—"inmates," as they are called in the play—and their presence downstairs late into each night.

But while the Raines Law structures the setting, it does not, because of Hope's exploitation of its loopholes, directly control the habits and attitudes therein. In *Iceman*'s familiar setting of urban realism, the laws regulating alcohol sales and consumption are conspicuously toothless. They order space, producing a curtained-off back room, flop-rooms above, and, occasionally, a moldy sandwich at the center of each table, but they do not place limits on how much and how often alcohol is consumed, nor do they cause its consumers to change their attitudes toward morality and civics. The limits lie only in the drinkers' wallets and the whims of the proprietor, the owner of the space and the alcohol. The inmates are not reformed by the law. They remain unrepentant, alcoholic radicals, nihilists, reactionaries, pimps, gamblers, and political machine hangers-on.

The play's Progressive Era legal structure, a morally motivated set of external restrictions, leaves untouched the inner workings of the physical and mental spaces it creates, in a way its New Deal analogue did not. The Roosevelt Administration's 1933 Beer-Wine Revenue Act, among its very first responses to the Depression and a political facilitator of Repeal, was a package of regulation and taxation.[18] The Beer-Wine Act was not as intentionally intrusive as the Raines Law, and ostensibly, in its anticipation of Repeal, it had the opposite effect, legally liberating rather than restricting the consumption of alcohol. But in practice, it brought more alcohol consumption under the purview of government control. It commenced the New Deal by eliminating one of the leading signs of unbound behavior in the 1920s: lawless drinking under Prohibition, an icon of irrational exuberance that remains a common metaphor for the speculative mania that preceded the Crash.

Drinking under the Raines Law in *Iceman* is not very different from drinking during Prohibition. Legal boundaries created drinking spaces, inside the law but mostly outside it, where there was room for unlimited excess. By contrast, under the Beer-Wine Act, under the National Recovery Administration, and ultimately under the state regulatory codes it spawned, every drink was in theory measured, for alcohol content and for economic value, by the state. By discouraging the return of the pre-Prohibition saloon (barring brewers from owning or controlling them), and by setting limits on alcoholic content, the law anticipated drinking to be less a social practice than an economic transaction with an individual effect. The new national liquor law essentially changed the state's role in drinking from one of setting boundaries to one of being present in the very acts of consumption, economic and physical.[19]

The Beer-Wine Act was the first salvo in the New Deal's transformative program of economic intervention.[20] Two months after its passage, Congress approved the National Industrial Recovery Act, the law, ultimately overturned as unconstitutional, which laid out in specific terms a national recovery narrative, based on the goal of raising consumption to activate production. (It created, for example, the Federal Alcohol Control Administration.) Though NIRA was short-lived, the New Deal's approach to national governance survived the 1930s, transforming the relationship of citizen to government, not only by taking an active hand in what had been thought of as private affairs but also by elevating the role of consumer to equal importance as that of worker. To overcome distrust of such dramatic change, and to gain the support of a populace for policies that encountered stiff opposition from powerful interests, Roosevelt's recovery narrative was also one of consent, describing citizens as those who are "ready and willing to submit our lives and property to [a common] discipline." In the broader narrative, this submission is the outcome of a conversion experience, in which the nation as a whole as well as each citizen is convicted, through the proof of their own suffering, of the self-destructive nature of pure individualism.[21]

The message of conversion that Hickey brings to Hope's saloon would have the inmates internalize what were previously external limits on their behavior and ambitions. Rather than adjust the forces constricting their behavior, Hickey aims to tear down and rebuild their internal orientations, redirecting them from the world-changing and the life-changing to mere acceptance of their lots. In his plan to deflate self-seeking and impose stability and sobriety, Hickey attempts to transform the space inside Hope's the way the Raines Law could not. He would change the function of the law from setting boundaries on aspiration, to constituting those very aspirations. The scene-setting of act 3—that moment which indicates Hickey has been able to upset the landscape of this world and shift it toward his pragmatic, "honest" alternative—contains language that resonates with New Deal and Depression discourse: there is now a free lunch counter in which a "dealer" serves soup; most of the visible inmates, indolent in the opening acts, are now working, in the first scenes of labor in the play. Hickey's success actually denatures alcohol, deadening its effects as did, to drinkers used to Prohibition spirits, the 3.2 percent beer permitted under the Beer-Wine Act. Hickey's diluting effect suggests his knowing appeal to old drinking chums has succeeded where the zeal of the temperance reformers behind the Raines Law had failed. His recovery narrative has entered this space and, by embracing individual limitation, turned what had been merely legal boundaries into the sum of its imagination.

Hickey's program fails, because his ideal of contentment turns out to be disguising an effort to violently suppress the desires and frustrations that arise in all human relations. His old friends do not experience liberating relief upon the collapse of their pipe dreams, instead falling into deathlike misery and stasis, experiencing alcoholic withdrawal as the physical embodiment of their vulnerability and distress in being dragged from one state of reality to another. This anti-ecstasy turns the emotional logic of conversion on its head, making it the experience of utter defeat rather than transcendent triumph. Further, in attempting to rectify this situation by performing his entire personal testimony in act 4, Hickey's own narrative breaks down at the crucial moment of transformation, when he arrives at the memory of his crime.[22] That Hickey himself is stuck at the moment of conviction is evident when he literally convicts himself by calling the police to come and hear him confess to Evelyn's murder. Hickey's recovery narrative collapses. His failure to account for his own motives suggests that the narrative itself was just another delusion of self-mastery. But because its deception was deeper, its self-destruction is more violent.

The Iceman Cometh is not hostile to liberalism per se, but it deeply distrusts a narrative that in its promises of stability and serenity summons therapeutic rather than tragic subjects, presenting the undeniable truth of experience as one that requires "surrender" rather than "self-seeking." Hickey's substitution of mere quietism for the end goal, and the murder of his wife that is his self-described conversion moment, suggest that the morbid results of his attempted conversions all flow from the corrupted motives behind the message. At the same time, those conversions that send Hope's inmates into deathlike states force them to confront actual truths about themselves. Thus the murder that is the traumatic heart of Hickey's program stands not for false conversion but for the logic of freedom-via-submission that is conversion itself. Hickey's message, and method, cast as death-dealing the recovery narrative that promises passage from egotistical delusion to liberating truth via the destruction of the willful self. The delusional nature of this self is the inescapable fact of the human experience, the play suggests, and any conversion is merely from one form of it to another. To "surrender" this self is simply to place oneself at the mercy of new temporal forces.

After just such a usurpation of the inmates' aspirations has brought on the hell of waking death, the external force of the law reappears in the play's conclusion as a welcome return to the status quo. In the second half of the play, references to legal accreditation and the law become more frequent, as when Willie Oban, the alcoholically disgraced Harvard law graduate and son of a stock fraudster, warns Parritt to "remember, they get you in the end" (180). Ultimately, it is the arrival of the Law that closes down Hickey's recovery shop, arriving as the external arbiter of life and death. The gang at Hope's resent the detectives Lieb and Moran, but accept that they are doing what lawmen should do: stepping in to police the boundaries at the farthest reaches of human transgression, such as murder. Their names suggest "love" and "death" as the perennial counterparts in tragedy to these legal limitations.[23] This version of the law has proven feeble in its ability to control intoxication, but it is no less respected as fulfilling the state's role in a kind of natural law, in which the ultimate limits are unassailable but within them imagination, ideals, and appetites have free reign. In contrast, Hickey's "reform wave" leaves no space, mental or material, untouched by its ideology.[24]

Coda for the Culture of the Saloon and the Mission

The time frame that *The Iceman Cometh* encompasses—from the characters' remembered glory days to the time of the play's action to the year in which O'Neill wrote it—spans roughly the period from the Civil War to World War II. This broad conception of setting is also that of the material examined in this book, or what I have called the era of the saloon and the mission. These two institutions were the social sites of the linguistic performances, both the drunken and the pious, that animated O'Neill's play and alcoholism discourse more generally. In this context, the variety of claims on the meaning of alcoholism that I've examined appear as rounds in a century-long exchange between alcoholic and evangelical performances in American culture. Recognizing this dynamic as the play's ultimate source material helps explain aesthetic qualities that have confused and divided critics. This critical division in turn illuminates the role of the drunkard's conversion as a location of American cultural politics in the modern period and beyond.

O'Neill arrived at his mature style in 1920 by, as one critic has put it, "chart[ing] a difficult course between expressionism and realism."[25] Judging from its critical reception, *The Iceman Cometh* had not resolved the tension twenty years later. *Iceman* appears in critical responses as either the reproduction of a familiar, if disreputable, social reality or an expressionistic allegory of deep human desires and frustrations. Critics disposed to emphasize O'Neill's biography, armed with knowledge of his participation in the Manhattan low life circa 1912, read the play as naturalistic.[26] Encouraged by O'Neill's own references to his sources, these critics see *Iceman* drawing on an alcoholic subculture that O'Neill experienced in early adulthood and ever after gave pride of place in his imagination. The realism of this ethnographic romance then underwrites the play's larger philosophical ambitions.

By contrast, another strand of criticism sees the play's "reverberant symbolic interior" as more important than its "naturalist facade."[27] For such critics, the play's significance lies not in the mimetic exposure of society's dregs but in its emergent postmodernism, O'Neill's drunken derelicts linking the cellar world of Maxim Gorky's *The Lower Depths* to Samuel Beckett's deracinated hobos.[28] Critics in this vein acknowledge both sides of the "realistic-symbolic nature of the play," but prefer the latter half of the combination, attributing the play's deferred reception—it was not until the 1956 staging that it won its reputation as among his best—to its affinity with Existentialist thought.[29] Harold Bloom evokes the surface/depth dynamic when he refers to O'Neill's "phantasmagoric naturalism," but for Bloom it is the naturalist element—its "persuasive imitation of human personality, particularly in its self-destructive weaknesses"—that fails the play's philosophical ambitions and reveals O'Neill's "infinite" inferiority to Beckett.[30] This critical history does not provide a sense that the two perceived modes are mutually productive; rather, it suggests that readers, directors, and audiences will choose one or the other as the primary framework of meaning, depending on their temperament and outlook.

This divide reappears, in even sharper focus, in approaches to the play's depiction of drinking and alcoholism, which read it as either clinically factual or as cartoonishly symbolic of some more abstract pathology.[31] Both sides of this divide miss the way modern alcoholism narrative is, as I have attempted to show throughout this book, almost always both mimetic and expressionistic, both a claim to realism and the rewriting of a perennial religious mythology of the self. *The Iceman Cometh* dwells in this doubled space. What is important is not that O'Neill's characters rail, shake, and hallucinate just as real alcoholics do, but that they do so in ways that provide entry for ideological capture by the competing cultural faiths the play invokes. Rather than reflecting a pre-ideological reality of alcoholism, drinking in the play gives social form to circular patterns of idealism, fear, defeat, and escape. Compulsive drinking is an instance of this experiential pattern that provides rhetorical purchase for the counternarrative of conversion, a transformation that breaks the addictive cycle by appealing to a state of transcendence. As the barflies' jests about Hickey's Salvation Army conversion and temperance preaching suggest, drinking is the social and linguistic location, in this kind of setting, where the carnival and the revival speak to, and need, one another.

This dialogue is key to understanding the play's reception as both historically particular and at the same time otherworldly. The exact time and place laid out in the dense, novelistic introduction seems at odds with what emerges on stage as a space that is isolated from the ordinary passage of time and vista of landscape. Harry Hope's in 1912—beyond being a composite of the bars O'Neill remembered from his youth—is at a geographic and chronological epicenter of saloon culture in the industrial era. Hope's and the strongly typed identities and languages of its inhabitants evoke urban drinking scenes between 1850 and 1950, a milieu whose literary and historical capital was Manhattan. It is the site of low-life tales and drunkard's conversions, in sensational, reformist, and fictional narrative from Jerry McAuley to John Dos Passos, and from T. S. Arthur to Damon Runyon. The need to fully bring to life the "atmosphere" and "warmth" of such a place was the reason O'Neill gave for the astounding length of the play.[32] Hope's is a space of the cultural imagination, rather than documentary history, its setting an era and a style of American representation as much as it is a social reality. It is a dive bar near the waterfront, an iconic space of the era of industrial labor, massive immigration, and machine politics. It sits at the threshold of the American landscape, straddles the American social order, and is a touchstone of popular and literary culture.[33]

In this space, the conversation between drinking culture and spiritual conversion is neither a mimetic recollection nor a symbolic contrivance of O'Neill's play. On an intellectual plane, both romantics and reformers take as fundamental the affinity between intoxication and religious ecstasy.[34] During the era of the temperance movement, the saloon and the mission shared space on city streets, in backwoods clearings, in colloquial speech, and in storytelling style. Not only does the record show missionaries seeking out dens of vice for their greatest victories over sin, but it also reveals drinkers embracing, even if often in a spirit of parody, revival rhetoric and feeling.

The cultural history of drinking in America is replete with parodic imitations of revivalism and with actual individual and mass conversions. In the century from 1850 to 1950 that *The Iceman Cometh* speaks from, these affinities played out in the social rituals of public spaces—the saloon and the mission—both devoted to achieving altered states of mind.[35]

Places like the historic Harry Hill's Concert Saloon and the fictional Harry Hope's "bedrock bar" are as important to the drunkard's conversion narrative as were the missions. Drinking narrative and conversion narrative recognize and speak to one another at such sites because both lay claim to special, detached insights about the world and the self, and both invest enormous amounts of energy into performing the truths they discover there, in ways that flout presumed social conventions. The unreconstructed drinker, like the convert, identifies the alcoholic bottom, typically in a dive bar, a gutter, or a jail cell, as a place where foundational reality can be narrated into existence. This space, when combined with the culture and physical effects of drinking, frees the knower to perform, in parody or in temporary delusional belief, all manner of rhetoric, conventional or fantastic.[36] *The Iceman Cometh* is devoted to such performance, epitomized in the characters' initial expectation that Hickey's reported sobriety is part of a gag in which he'll arrive in Salvation Army gear, pretend to be "saved," and try to reform the whole gang. Such antics are part of the salesman Bill Wilson's story, too: the first night Wilson was exposed to the Oxford Group, he arrived at the midtown Calvary Mission drunk, with a new barroom friend he had picked up along the way, and barged to the front of the service to proclaim his salvation. One of the ultimate results of this performance was his writing five years later in the Big Book, Hickey-like, that "most of us feel we need look no further for Utopia," for "we have it with us right here and now."[37]

This kind of passage from the saloon to the mission conserves the dramatic aspects of social self-performance. In conversion narrative, the massive swing from the despair of the bottom to the ecstasy of eternal life either produces, or is produced by, the performative aspects of revivalism: the postures of submission, the contagion of tears, the swooning, even sometimes mass hysteria. The style is ostentatiously sincere, rather than parodic, but, from an outside perspective, it is no less carnivalesque. In *The Iceman Cometh,* the inmates of Hope's find it hard to express in words what they feel is the profoundly unsettling difference in Hickey's new preaching mode from that of his former, drunken, master-of-ceremonies style. *Iceman's* exploration of the intoxication-conversion dialogue is not merely the dramatization of a philosophical element in alcoholism narrative. It also draws on a historical phenomenon, in the linguistic and spatial permeability between the saloon and the Christian mission. This mutual form of cultural production is often lost to romanticists of literary drinking, whose focus is on the extent to which Prohibition-era writers sought rhetorical and geographic distance from America's religious culture.

The play recreates this historical proximity in its constant repetition of synonyms for drinking and drunkenness mingled with the frequent use of missionary evangelism as the dominant metaphor for the striving toward ideals, or as the comic imitation of such striving. The play uses twenty-nine different synonyms for drinks, drinking, and drunkenness, from an "eye-opener" to a "snootful," and from being "oreyeyed" to getting "paralyzed." Religious language takes on a contrapuntal effect to all this drink-talk. Each of the "movements" in the bar—anarchism, pipe dreaming, and Hickey's reform—are described primarily in religious terms. The Salvation Army is a stock vehicle of jokes or jibes. Blasphemy, mild and intense, is the standard form of profanity. Ed Mosher, the carny con-man, describes the preacher's son Hickey as "that drummer son of a drummer," whose "spiel" is aimed at "corrupt[ing] you to temperance" (183). The play constantly suggests that salesmanship, fraud, and preaching are related dialects of a fundamental American language of idealism crossed with desire.

If there is one shared watchword in *Iceman's* fragmented moral lexicon, one that names each of the claims to the experiential reality of the saloon, the mission, the political cell, and the philosopher's refuge, it is "wise," in the sense of being "wised up" to some secret knowledge or hard reality. In literature, the term dates to the 1890s, in, for example, Stephen Crane's reports from saloons in Manhattan's Tenderloin district, and in fellow newspaper man and urban colorist George Ade's play *Artie* (1896). New York storytellers like Runyon helped make this milieu's "wise guy" a central figure of popular comedy in the decades leading up to World War II. This "Runyonesque" strain of saloon-mission culture leads to the lighthearted stage nostalgia for the low life that culminated in the musical *Guys and Dolls*.[38] But the concept of disillusion and the various hardboiled styles associated with it also stand for the kinds of profound changes in sensibility, philosophy, and politics that define the modern period. This seriousness is evident in comparisons of the setting of *Iceman* to those of plays by Gorky and Beckett, and in the life-or-death terms in which A.A. narrators articulated their achievement of disillusion.

"Wise" and "wised up" appear repeatedly in *The Iceman Cometh*, as synonyms for "informed" with a deeper resonance of worldly knowing.[39] The phrase embodies the play's self-contained economy of language, a key component of the saloon's unique, out-of-this-world, bottom atmosphere. The dialogue's consistency is profoundly constructed, yet produces for many critics a mimetic naturalism. The literary throwback effect of this language is evident in the relationship of these voices to the characters who speak them. Regardless of whether or not the characters are renderings of people O'Neill had known, the cast consists of outrageously broad caricatures, familiar stock types from novel, newspaper, and stage, vaudeville included.[40] These types are limned in their introductory descriptions, but they are carried forward by their stereotypical voices: Noo Yawk Irish and Italian, Harvard-effete, stage Negro. As with many of O'Neill's plays, it may be a function of *Iceman*'s length, and the relentless consistency of its voices, that its dialogue can be taken seriously at all. The play distinguishes its voices clearly from one another, perhaps explaining its artificially broad range of accents. But these conventions serve another purpose.

Iceman can read, and typically performs, as naturalistic because it draws on the conventions of naturalism, but they are the conventions of the time in which the play is set, not those of the times in which it was written and staged. The play returns to the heyday of literary realism—and to the Manhattan saloon as one of its homes—and there deploys the conventions of that place and its style. By drawing on the aesthetic of an earlier era, *Iceman*'s naturalism reads as spatially and chronologically isolated, allowing it to work also as an existentialist space. This stylistic dislocation is the mechanism by which the play constructs the alcoholic bottom as a place where reality's foundations are contested, and produces the wide divergence in its aesthetic reception.

It is in this space that *Iceman* engages, to a degree rare among modern literary texts, with the explicitly salvific side of addiction narrative, in effect putting the religious, literary, and therapeutic narratives into conversation with one another by returning to their source locations in American culture. The play depends on the fact that conversion is a perennial and inevitable counterpart of addictive decline narrative, no matter how hard the decline narrator tries to create distance from conventional evangelical rhetoric— whether in Hickey's disdain for his father's "religious bunk," in modernist expatriate efforts to draw on a morally neutral, European drinking ethos, in A.A.'s partial psychologization of conversion, or in FDR's claim that the New Deal was erasing the difference between the practical and the ideal.[41]

The play suggests that this dialectic between the addictive pattern and the ideal of transcendence is what structures American perceptions of modernity as a crisis that calls for religious redemption as its solution. At the same time it tries to get beneath this discourse in a way most modernist uses of alcoholic narrative do not, using the saloon-speak concept of the "pipe dream" as a baseline dynamic that governs both. In *Iceman,* as Hickey has his way with his supposedly hard-bitten old friends, the hardboiled stance appears no match for therapeutic conversion. The ease with which this surface cynicism melts away recalls the early A.A. narratives, and suggests that the modernist sense of despair is often a self-pitying pose that is not only vulnerable to, but in fact perfectly suited to—may even be a strawman created by—conversion narrative. Indeed, once Hickey's evangelism begins to produce its unintended results, the merciless claim to truth in the conversion narrative deflates the parodic, performative qualities of the saloon's engagement with it. This once-playful exchange loses any vestiges of humor and parody, becoming a bitter conflict over the play's known universe. When the disillusioned inmates accept their powerlessness, the prevailing mood becomes one of deathly gloom, where the very medium of the saloon, alcohol, has "lost its kick."

The implication of this collapse in the play's mood is that in a secular era, in the era of economic recovery rather than ecstatic transformation, by presenting conversion in a pragmatic, nonreligious guise, the evangelists have taken an unfair advantage over their traditional marks in the saloon. Amid the rise of European fascism, with the Roosevelt Administration appearing to lose its philosophical bearings in the face of judicial defeats and recessions, the postwar liberal order that emerged was by no means a budding reality in the late 1930s. It was not clear what collective vision Americans were being asked to internalize in lieu of their idealistic traditions and their messy material interests. The real suffering involved in both alcoholism and economic depression made promises of redemption and serenity especially alluring. In the play's conclusion, though, no sooner has the new salvation won its converts than it self-destructs by its own self-deception, and by the absence of the enduring truth it had called on to replace human agency. So, the play suggests, while conversion almost always wins the battle—saloons are shuttered, reform waves sweep in, evangelical optimism is made politically mandatory—its own contingencies make its claim to finality unsustainable. There will always be another bottom to hit; in recovery terms, human beings are chronic relapsers. Bill Wilson, in A.A.'s Big Book, claimed that the rare alcoholic who cannot stay sober using A.A.'s method is one who is, beneath the addiction, constitutionally incapable of being honest with himself. O'Neill's play suggests that this group includes a large portion of humanity who might be better served by clinging to their pipe dreams rather than giving them up to an ill-defined higher power.

8

Recovery Memoir and the Crack-Up of Liberalism

> There is a crack, a crack in everything
> That's how the light gets in.
>
> —Leonard Cohen, "Anthem" (1992)

> It was two days before she died without regaining consciousness,
> as I say in the memoir they are paying me so handsomely for.
>
> —Charlie Smith, "Heroin" (2000)

IN HIS 1956 MEMOIR *THE Cup of Fury*, Upton Sinclair traces the theme of alcoholism through his life and times, focusing on the dozens of writers, artists, politicians, and workers he knew who were its victims. Beginning with the dizzying instability of his childhood due to his own father's periodical binges, he documents his booze-saturated early environs in both New York City and the South, and the centrality of alcohol to his *Jungle*-era social analysis, before turning to his time amid the "group of brilliant and brave Americans who lived to write and died for wine."[1] He dwells at length on his friends Jack London and Sinclair Lewis, and relates anecdotes about many others, including Sherwood Anderson, Theodore Dreiser, the socialist firebrand Eugene Debs, and the modern dance legend Isadora Duncan, all of whom, he contends, were badly damaged or utterly destroyed by alcohol. He chastises older figures like H. L. Mencken for their reckless encouragement of drinking in young writers, decries the use of London's image to sell whiskey in the 1950s, and condemns the marketing of beer to college students as an insidious poisoning of the next generation's best minds. He concludes with a paean to Alcoholics Anonymous as the historical salvation of the American writer.

Written in his late seventies, near the end of Sinclair's active writing career, *The Cup of Fury* is a singular book, but one whose eccentricities reveal broader trends in the cultural meaning of alcoholism and recovery. It is a memoir of alcoholism by a lifelong teetotaler who was nonetheless opposed to Prohibition. It is the last work by a major American writer that in its call for universal abstinence could still be termed a temperance tract. After a series of largely failed books on Cold War politics and liberal Christianity, *The Cup of Fury* was Sinclair's only success of the 1950s, despite being published by a small religious press.[2] In it, Sinclair makes the first systematic case for the essential role played by pathological drinking in American modernism, and assembles the first of the now-familiar rosters of alcoholic modernists. Hinting occasionally at the ways fellow writers had teased him as a prude and dismissed his work as moralistic, Sinclair's memoir reads on one level as a kind of good boy's I-told-you-so to the wild-child modernists he outlived. But his characteristically earnest style conveys genuine sympathy, and, more interestingly, his polemic reaches beyond alcohol and literature. It is a document that articulates the major elements of postwar liberal culture through the lens of what historians call the Alcoholism Movement.[3]

In both his historical interpretation and his social analysis, Sinclair invokes and endorses the primary institutions responsible for shaping the contemporary concept of alcoholism and image of the alcoholic. He cites new theories and recent data—on what alcoholism is and whom it afflicts, on who drinks and how much, and on what the societal consequences are—from sources including the Yale Center of Alcohol Studies, books by academic experts and recovering alcoholics, and public advocacy agencies. He advances one of the primary goals of these advocates when, in constructing a composite figure of the writer-as-alcoholic, he promotes a frank but deeply sympathetic view. In Sinclair's set of interwoven life-narratives, alcoholics are onetime social drinkers who, through a combination of chemical vulnerability and bad influences, started on the path to chronic disease at a time when they were too young, impressionable, and (as writers) ambitious to know better.

In the trinity of research, advocacy, and recovery institutions, for Sinclair the greatest of these is A.A. In his impassioned endorsement, he retells his personalized history of modern American drinking as the narrative of a fall from grace that necessitates A.A.'s arrival: "Victims fell by the wayside, and there was nobody who could help them, no refuge, no care, no hope. That condition existed all through the early years of my life, when the men of my family were being mowed down like grain before the scythe of the harvester.

It existed all through my mature years, when my literary friends and colleagues were sharing the same ghastly fate. It existed up to the late 1930s. Then . . . Alcoholics Anonymous was born." A.A. would have saved these writers, Sinclair implies, by revealing to them their problem and providing them the spiritual tools to solve it. In fleshing out this religious narrative, Sinclair asserts an intellectual version of a standard postwar language of religious tolerance, in which all are welcome to understand in their own way "the same power many of us call our Heavenly Father."[4]

Sinclair's liberal construction of alcoholism reaches even to Cold War intrigue and ideological warfare. In a surprising interlude in the middle of the book, he tells stories of various diplomats and writers, including Dreiser, whom Soviet and western communists manipulated with alcohol. "I have lost friends to their fold," he intones, hinting at deep anger, "and I have seen how they use liquor in their unceasing war against freedom." It is, he avers, one of their leading tactics: "The Communists use liquor as a sort of Geiger-counter, proving for the weaknesses of men and women. They have used it to gain recruits; they have used it to steal a nation's most guarded secrets." Sinclair, a strident socialist for much of his adult life, essentially apologizes for American writers' dalliances with communism by blaming it on the Reds' exploitation of their chemical vulnerability to alcohol. For Sinclair booze was a barometer, even, of the fall of the revolutionaries' leftist virtue. The Bolsheviks were prohibitionists, he writes, but the "brutal men who came out on top in Russia knew that a drunken people would be easier to hold in subjection than a sober people," and so established a state monopoly on liquor that made it the nation's only free-flowing commodity.[5] The Soviets' tolerance of drinking was thus a cynical perversion of freedom itself, and a telling marker of alcohol's unfitness for American democracy. Among the many denunciations of communism and shadings of prewar fellow traveling by loyal liberals, Sinclair's tale stands out in its unique marriage of the Red Menace and the Demon Rum.[6]

These awkward combinations of temperance anachronism and therapeutic sensibility simply reveal with unusual transparency the liberal framework for the cultural transition around alcoholism represented by the recovery narrative. They articulate the deep structural affinity between the emergent conception of alcoholism and some of the dominant values of postwar culture: institutionalized expertise, consensus morality, a rhetoric of tolerance, and the belief that these values were bringing about a society both more efficient and more democratic than its definitive rival.[7] Returning to Sinclair's accounts of self-destructive writers, we can recognize that in constructing his new literary history, he applied to its leading figures one of the central cultural effects of the Alcoholism Movement. Instead of merely delineating and bemoaning their drinking habits, he attributed to modern writers the shared identity of the alcoholic. Sinclair retells their lives as a collective cautionary tale about how this identity is acquired. In urging young people to learn lessons from this suffering rather than enter into their own downward spiral, he asserts the liberal values that went into creating this new understanding of alcoholism. The writers themselves could have done this redemptive work, he grieves, had they been born in time for the Recovery Movement.

Turning the authorial self to the task of constructing and redeeming an alcoholic identity was not as straightforward as Sinclair suggested. Some of the same currents of reactionary individualism and stylistic revulsion that troubled the modernist relationship to the drunkard's redemption lived on and sometimes intensified in postwar literary culture. Furthermore, not all left-leaning writers, and not all Americans, accommodated themselves to the new liberal order as easily as Sinclair did. Among those who told their stories of recovery, some were not ready or able to imply that they had achieved sobriety on society's terms. Recovery memoir eventually became the literary home of the postwar alcoholic identity, but it remained at the same time a vehicle for envisioning a more just society. This function has been a submerged but definitive point of contention in addiction writing, in modes that variously reflect and diverge from the fate of liberalism as a sociopolitical order.

Confessional first-person memoirs and sympathetic third-person accounts of recovery may owe much of their structure and affect to the story form developed in A.A. meetings and twelve-step print culture, but they proliferated and had their wider influence in the realm of commercial culture. In popular television dramas and Oscar-winning films, and from critically acclaimed novels to celebrity memoirs, since the 1950s alcoholism has appeared as a tragic affliction and either A.A. or a similar mode of surrender, support, and redemption has appeared as the way out.[8] The same formal structure whose religious and political meaning was hotly contested in the drunkard's conversion now supported a neutral paradigm of psychospiritual well-being. This new content was value-laden and symbolically resonant, to be sure, but the experience it described was limited to a small minority of unfortunates, and any explicit argument it made was usually about the nature of addictive compulsion, not the structure of society or the heavens. The Alcoholism Movement's successful depoliticization of the problem turned its representation from a medium of stark controversy into a progressive epistemological discourse composed of a still-familiar nexus of scientific research, public health communications, and wisdom literature. Recovery as a mode of experiential truth-telling continues to inform popular culture, literary form, and social expectations.

As I argued in chapter 4, A.A.'s contribution to this sense of neutrality originated in its members' social rehabilitations, which summoned a model of spiritual conversion through the kind of social ideal envisioned in liberal responses to the Depression. But while A.A.'s mode of self-interested selflessness expressed a model of postwar citizenship, its principled organizational opposition to commercial incorporation, state funding, and, at a deep level, consumer desire, left it independent from the midcentury realignment of state and private power. A.A., and many of the similar recovery subcultures that it influenced, remained insulated to a considerable degree from these external power structures.[9] But the more wholly public institutions of the Alcoholism Movement—the research institutes, treatment clinics, corporate employee assistance programs, and public awareness campaigns—were very much creatures of this postwar state. Their influence, along with broader societal shifts toward what some have termed a "therapeutic culture," helped create a market for recovery narrative.[10] Commercially published recovery narratives tended, then, to refract the grassroots culture of the twelve-step movement through the powerful lenses of expert addiction discourse and media marketing exigencies.

Despite this establishment status, recovery narrative has continued to serve as a site for contesting the foundational assumptions and aspirational promises of American society. Indeed, whatever consensus has existed around recovery was no more secure than the liberal settlement itself, which began visibly fracturing in the 1960s along fault lines that had never healed.[11] Since the middle of the twentieth century, then, the most revealing cultural representations of addiction have been those that problematize recovery, while still operating within the genre's bounds of plausible realism and climactic redemption. Various kinds of authors have refused, revised, or anxiously adopted the recovery story, exposing again the sociopolitical architecture of the genre that is the subject of this book. In the discussion that follows, I range through several examples of these differently inflected stories in order to frame recovery's ongoing construction and contestation of a liberal vision of society, from both within the mainstream and among its discontents.

Recovery, even when it expressly urges the idea that addiction is a value-free, pre-ideological disease state, still conveys sociopolitical meaning in its vision of redemption. Just as in the drunkard's conversion, in the recovery story what the addict witnesses at his or her moment of hope is a picture of an ideal social world. This imagery is inexorably, and often quite explicitly, bound to political discourse. In clear-cut examples, conservative Christian recovery stories seek to restore religion to the therapeutic "public square," rejecting the mode of collective procedural wisdom initiated by A.A., in favor of authoritative religious claims.[12] Left-leaning liberal recoveries assert visions of social tolerance at their moments of hope, often identifying redemption with the mutual support found in a once-proscribed relationship across differences of class or race. And, despite the routine critical association of recovery with reactionary self-help individualism, some storytellers have identified the grassroots culture of recovery, especially as it exists in broken and forgotten places, as a quiet form of communal resistance and reconstruction in the aftermath of the collapse of liberalism (see my discussion of *The Wire* in the conclusion).

Recovery memoir's politics arises at the intersection of the identity categories of authorship and alcoholism. Unlike meeting-group testimony, published variations of recovery narrative invite audience identification through the filters of sales figures and reviews. The hybrid identity of the recovering author is not always a seamless creation. Memoirs that aspire to literary significance, especially, must negotiate with an ideal of the heroic artist that does not submit easily to the "surrender of self" that twelve-step conversion calls for. The tensions that result in turn reveal the political valences of authorship as a model of individualism. To understand the importance of this dynamic, I begin by scrutinizing F. Scott Fitzgerald's essay sequence of the mid-1930s, "The Crack-Up." Although they include only limited references to alcohol, Fitzgerald's meditations unmistakably evoke the collapse of the hard-drinking modernist author, not just in the person of Fitzgerald himself, but in the terms by which this figure embodied the high-literary meaning of drinking discussed in chapter 6. Furthermore, Fitzgerald's self-autopsy offers prescient glimpses into what new vision of author-as-alcoholic would emerge instead in the literary marketplace. His reflections foretell both the emergence of recovery memoir as a literary genre and the fault lines within it that continued to make it a site of contested social meaning and even political prophecy.

For much of this book I've tried to bring to light the continuities between the era of temperance and the era of alcoholism, by focusing on ways that the essential purposive structure of the drunkard's conversion narrative not only survived, but played an important role articulating shifts in modern social, political, and cultural history. My approach here is to bridge another hard break in the cultural history of alcohol, between the heyday of the boozy modernist novel and the era of the confessional memoir. Rather than cover all the ground between, I use this reading of "The Crack-Up" as a lens that brings into focus the tensions among several modes of contemporary recovery memoir: confessional sensation, earnest advocacy, minority survival story, and the progressive rediscovery of religion. In each of these forms and others, recovery mediates the construction of authorial identity on the grounds of what is left of the liberal vision of society's redemption.[13]

The Unwilling Surrender

The narrative ethos of the recovery movement holds that every addict's story is unique in its particulars, but that all exhibit the same structure and reveal the same essential principles. Indeed, the emotional appeal of this similarity is necessary for the process of identification required to bring the isolated addict into mutual-aid recovery. By contrast, the ethos of literary innovation associated with modernism blanches at the collective and the formulaic, in fiction and nonfiction alike. And it especially rejects the sentimental relief associated with recovery and redemption. Ironically, as I argued in chapter 4, the A.A. recovery narrative was first developed by, and for, men who had internalized this attitude. For this reason, writers who emulated both the literary styles and the drinking habits of the modernist legends have often found themselves living out a recovery narrative that they reject on aesthetic grounds. The memoirs that result often have been tormented affairs. In effect, they motion toward the appeals of confession and reformation, but they cannot assimilate the surrender of heroic individualism into their gendered senses of literary authorship. One of the originators of this mode was the journalist-adventurer William Seabrook, who caused a minor stir with his memoir *Asylum* (1935), which chronicled his institutionalization for alcoholism. Though Seabrook ostensibly violated traditional proscriptions on male admissions of failure, he did so with a bluster that, like Hemingway's proud humility, conserved the heroic self intact. Even more revealing than this hybrid form, though, was F. Scott Fitzgerald's late career bout of hand-to-hand combat with recovery narrative.

In this discussion I want to shift debates over the relationship between drinking and the modernist social imagination, or between intoxication, social rebellion, and creativity, toward a consideration of what recovery as a literary structure meant for the authorial identity. For Fitzgerald it seemed to imply its obliteration. Fitzgerald's 1936 essay series "The Crack-Up" speaks with unequaled clarity the contest between the modernist and confessional descendants of drunkard's conversion. "The Crack-Up" consists of three short pieces published in consecutive issues of *Esquire,* describing Fitzgerald's loss of energy and ideals over the previous two years. Biographical readings have surmised the extent to which Fitzgerald's breakdown fits what is known about his drinking habits and the symptoms of alcoholism, a diagnosis that Fitzgerald preemptively denies in the essays by falsely claiming six months of sobriety at the time of writing.[14] More to the point of this study, Fitzgerald's decline narrative is cut from traditional conversion cloth, while his attempt at a defiant, modernist sequel struggles vainly to refuse the religious structure and social logic of recovery. Despite his open hostility toward it, a recovery narrative threatens to take over Fitzgerald's hardboiled performance of self. His defensive crouch embodies the way modernist decline narrative stood temperamentally against the redemptive sentiments but struggled to find alternative structures for relating the lessons of hard experience. Fitzgerald's effort to sustain the tragic note in a confessional form that generates strong pressures toward redemption produces a tone of petulance and self-pity. Modernist conviction narrative, even while it is ostensibly performing social criticism, has no sustainable defense against the expectations of redemptive relief when one of its own deepest values is the construction of a triumphant authorial persona.

Fitzgerald describes his decline not in terms of drinking, but yet in a sequence of experiences, and even in a style, that would not be out of place in an A.A. narrative. Despite its ironic tone and its syntactic polish, it anticipates "Bill's Story," Bill Wilson's autobiographical introduction to *Alcoholics Anonymous.* (Fitzgerald's claim of six months' abstinence would even put his "sobriety date" somewhere close to Robert Smith's—June 10, 1935, which is memorialized as the founding date of A.A.) Like Wilson, Fitzgerald begins by recalling the early promise of a life that seemed fitted to a self-reliant society: "Life was something you dominated if you were any good," he avers. "It seemed a romantic business."[15] He also provides the familiar realization that the pathogen had been present all along, lying deeper than its specific material iteration, in ways prefigured in the puncturing of childhood ideals. Then come the various ways that the crisis, through the complacency of habit William James described, creeps up deceptively, as long-held principles and convictions melt away (A.A.'s "loss of spiritual values"). Once the problem surfaces, escapism—for Fitzgerald not first intoxication, but adolescent fantasies of athletic and military prowess—provides returns that diminish to zero, giving way to the inescapable consciousness of the bottom.

Fitzgerald aligns his decline with the national trajectory of boom and bust more explicitly than do the first A.A. narrators. His earlier experience of ecstatic happiness "was not the natural thing but the unnatural—unnatural as the Boom; and my recent experience parallels the wave of despair that swept the nation when the Boom was over."[16] Echoing FDR's New Deal rhetoric as well as A.A.'s revision of masculinity, this despair demands a transformative confession of failure if reform is to proceed. And indeed, Fitzgerald's bottom brings a conviction of inadequacy as an unprecedented and terrifying self-knowledge, "a measure that no one ever adopts voluntarily." Fitzgerald realizes the extent to which he has relied on others for his intelligence, his personal style, his social relations, his politics, and even his "artistic conscience," bringing him to the melodramatic conclusion that he himself is nothing, "not an 'I' any more—not a basis on which I could organize my self-respect" (78–79). In conversion narrative, this kind of moment is the great surrender of self, opening the door to God's grace and direction. In recovery, this humility also permits asking other people for help.

Fitzgerald is reputed to have refused an offer to try A.A. in 1939, saying it "can only help weak people because their ego is strengthened by the group."[17] These essays three years prior reveal that Fitzgerald's notion of "strength" is bound up with his sense of the personal inner engine that should drive literary narrative, fictional or not. His interpretation of complete failure and what it makes possible rejects recovery narrative on each of the religious and political terms that run through alcoholism narrative since the turn of the century. In a series of religious allusions, Fitzgerald takes on the Christian response to the despair he has described. Explaining the essays' titular metaphor as his feeling of being a still-usable but fundamentally flawed "cracked plate," he aligns his interpretation of the decline narrative with that of "Broken Earthenware," the original English title of Harold Begbie's *Twice-Born Men*. But the difference between shards that can be knit by God, if the broken person will only let them go, and a plate that still looks and behaves like a plate but has an irreparable, shameful flaw, encapsulates the religious optimism of recovery versus the tragic view of modernist conviction. The first essay ends with a gospel quotation that specifically understands this problem as the one salvation is designed to solve, but the next essay begins by averring that nothing, least of all the secularized "all-weather beatitude" of selflessness, can lift "the dark night of the soul" (74–75).

Most of all, Fitzgerald's battle against conversion takes place on the fields of narrative structure and authorial persona. Fitzgerald clings to the character-centric narrative established by decline, even as he tries to resist the redemptive ending it urges. A friend offers him a chance to recenter the narrative beyond the main character, by thinking of his "crack" as a feature of the universe of which he is a part, not of himself in particular—a move analogous to the roles of Original Sin, the disease model of addiction, and the critique of capitalism in separating failure and success from the essential self. But Fitzgerald rejects this invitation to transcendent meaning, on the precise grounds of his allegiance to character-driven narrative. One either exhibits "vitality" or suffers from "discouragement," he insists, "like health or brown eyes or honor or a baritone voice" (73–74). Character is essential, leaving both systems and symptoms as mere epiphenomena.

Redemption as an *ending* offends Fitzgerald's literary taste, and in any case, he suggests, its political and religious sponsors are dead. He denigrates Seabrook's sober "movie ending," and in a mock-apology for the confessional mode, he defies readerly expectations of a happy ending. He describes his own conclusion as dwelling, unregenerate, in the broken state ("that is the real end of this story"), embracing it in a decision to live entirely selfishly, the precise opposite of the calls to service made by Christianity, socialism, and A.A.[18] He repudiates the evangelical solutions to the addict's dilemma, revolution or salvation, as the relics of an imagined past or the poses of an inferior literary stratum. In an abrupt parenthetical conclusion to the second essay, he wonders whether he has lost the ideal reader necessary to writing: "I have the feeling that someone, I'm not sure who, is sound asleep—someone who could have helped me to keep my shop open. It wasn't Lenin, and it wasn't God" (79–80). Fitzgerald suggests that Marxism and Christianity were never available to him, because they already had ceased to inhabit the narrative structures of tragedy to which their conversions would respond. Their claims to supply meaning to human tales of crisis and revelation had expired.

Literary alcoholism trades on analogies among underclass creatures, bourgeois fools, and tortured writers, while at the same time creating formal distance, in highly controlled styles of writing, from characters unable to control their own desires. Fitzgerald writes as a high priest of such distance who has finally been overwhelmed, like Barnes's Matthew O'Connor, by the confessional demands of his characters. In the essays' peak moment of rhetorical revelation, he isolates the core of his problem in literary terms, begging in italicized desperation to know *"why I had become identified with the objects of my horror or compassion,"* a fate he says, contra Sinclair and his Progressive Era urge to identify downward, "spells the death of accomplishment" (81). Fitzgerald's shock at having become one of his own grotesques—his own version of the hitting-bottom epiphany—may be the clearest way of understanding the inception of the alcoholic writer's memoir as literature's concession to the age of self-help.

In writing his own breakdown, Fitzgerald prefigured the way contending strands of decline, conviction, and conversion, once commingled in nineteenth-century reform genres but fragmented by the cultural politics of the early twentieth century, would become entangled once again after World War II, in the rise of recovery memoir as a vehicle for narrating addiction. But if recovery memoir became a relatively coherent genre, nevertheless it is one that has continued to bring together various purposes that are not all moving in the same direction. It troubles the boundaries that divide writing into the categories of literary and generic, fiction and nonfiction, even male and female.

These conceptual binaries are among those that have structured the cultural production of social meaning in decisive ways since World War II. The research, advocacy, and recovery institutions of the Alcoholism Movement helped shape their formulation in addiction narrative. But increasingly, and especially in commercially successful narratives, recovery speaks through the largely private market institutions of the treatment and media industries, the successors to the Alcoholism Movement. Recovery narratives still rely on content supplied by the scientific, public health, and mutual-aid worlds, but their overarching meanings more often articulate the interests of therapeutic and cultural institutions. And both between and within these industries lie further contending interests, in the continual competition for audience and authority that the market demands. In memoir, biography, and reality television, especially, powerful institutions of the neoliberal order vie over a redemption moment whose cultural power owes its origins to the turmoil of modern liberalism's founding.

The most public exposure of these tensions in recent memory revisited the disjunction between authorship and confession at the heart of Fitzgerald's essays, but did so in a way that ranged powerful forces in the culture industry against one another. James Frey's falsified memoir of alcoholism and drug addiction, *A Million Little Pieces* (2003), features ostentatiously fragmented and repetitive prose, an aggressively masculine narrator, and a plot that tells of wild drinking and drug abuse giving way to painful withdrawal and wrenching self-knowledge at a treatment center. Like its precursors in modernist fiction, the story smuggles in the redemptive structure and felt relief of conversion narrative by dressing it in an attitude of self-aggrandizing masculine stoicism. The intensity of Frey's gender-performance—far outstripping Fitzgerald's in both violence and vanity—was matched by that of the culture-industry clash his work called up.

In Frey's case it is the twelve-step spirituality of surrender offered to him in a treatment clinic that actually stands for the feminized submission he refuses. Trysh Travis aptly sums up Frey's physical destruction of twelve-step literature as an act of metaphorical violence designed to establish his modernist aesthetic as a form of masculine mastery.[19] Tellingly, Frey's own ideal of the feminine is as the object of his grandiose condescension, in his fierce sense of loyalty toward a tragic young female addict in treatment with him. In his all-willpower "just hold on" mantra of recovery, he romanticizes her brokenness as occupying a plane far above the dismal clinic, its beaten-down ethos of surrender, and its earnest but unimaginative counselors.[20] Far from accepting addiction's proof of his own limitations, he concludes his story by striding into a bar, ordering a shot, and manfully staring it down without drinking it. *A Million Little Pieces* transparently attempts to deploy simultaneously the recovery memoir's claim to brave self-disclosure and the modernist novel's gendered panic in the face of lost cultural authority.

If proof were needed of this type of refusal narrative's reliance on the felt structures of confession and conversion, it came in Frey's embrace by Oprah Winfrey and her television audience in a program in late 2005. Winfrey's rise to stardom in the late 1980s and early 1990s was based on her elevation and embodiment of the ethos of recovery, which broadened in the 1980s from alcoholism to not only drugs but all manner of compulsion and trauma. Winfrey distinguished her talk show from other daytime fare by eschewing sensational confrontation and mere voyeurism in favor of messages of healing, which she often linked to her own experience of having been sexually abused by a family member. In a program in 1995 on women in recovery, Winfrey revealed her former crack cocaine use, establishing personal sympathy with addicts who, she said in the language of A.A., "believe the disease is stronger than the power of God." When she assured them that, in her experience, "there is nothing greater than the spirit within you to overcome" and that "you and God can conquer it," she epitomized the post-twelve-step equation of the omnipotent God with the individual's indomitable spirit.[21]

Winfrey founded Oprah's Book Club in 1996 as a project to promote reading, but in particular to expose readers normally attuned to self-help and

popular bestsellers to the literary tradition.[22] The club constituted a commercial empire of recovery culture trying to appropriate the edifying benefits of Great Literature, with only uncertain awareness of the extent to which
that literature often strains against the project of edification. A prominently
placed Winfrey quotation at the book club's website used the A.A. phrase for
what both intoxication and spiritual practice provide, and it recalls William
James's addition of literature to the category: "Even as a kid, my memories
are of books *taking me out of myself*" (emphasis added). The club's selections
combined works of the latter-day canon by Toni Morrison and Maya Angelou with new literary successes by Edwidge Danticat, Andre Dubus III, and
Jonathan Franzen, as well as mid-list fiction and memoir by writers including Maeve Binchy and Anna Quindlen. In 2003, the club undertook a foray
into the wider world of Great Literature, with John Steinbeck's *East of Eden*
and then, in 2004, novels by Gabriel García Márquez, Carson McCullers,
Leo Tolstoy, and Pearl Buck. The book club's selections resulted in new editions with Oprah's seal attached, and often bulging new sales figures.

In 2005, *A Million Little Pieces* joined three novels by William Faulkner
as that year's Oprah recommendations. Introducing the memoir as the club's
latest pick, Winfrey hailed the fearless honesty of Frey's confessions. It is a
testament to both the appeal of the truth-claim in confessional memoir and
the conversion ethos built into romantic refusal narratives such as Frey's that
Winfrey seemed, in her adulation, not to notice or mind that Frey had repudiated the recovery culture and the Christianity that are important sources
of her own therapeutic worldview. The club project was willing to accommodate the literary conventions of the ambiguous ending and the moral
provocation. After all, Frey's work had followed *As I Lay Dying, The Sound
and the Fury,* and *Light in August* as selections.

It emerged that Frey had concocted the sensational details of his addiction, and that his own experience was little more than that of a well-to-do
young man who took to alcohol and drugs, was arrested for drunk driving,
and submitted to treatment in a prestigious clinic. Winfrey defended her
endorsement by appealing to the "underlying message of redemption" that
"resonates with millions of people" regardless of the factuality of its details.
When bad press continued to mount, Winfrey changed course, interrogating
and excoriating Frey and his editor, Nan Talese, in person on her program,
for their fraud on her, her audience, and the reading public. The television
critic Troy Patterson aptly described this program as a public cleansing ritual
for Winfrey's brand. And, as Allan Borst has written, the controversy only
reinforced Oprah's connection to recovery culture by becoming a shared

trauma for her, her audience, and Frey that required mutual, redemptive confessions.[23] Soon afterward Winfrey suspended the book club, and then relaunched it in 2006 with a single entry, Elie Wiesel's *Night*. The moral authority of Wiesel's Holocaust memoir was called on to purify not only Oprah's Book Club but, it seemed, the trauma memoir as a genre.

Frey's attempt to recreate modernist masculinity from within the genre of the recovery memoir and Winfrey's attempt to transfer her audience's sentimental expectations to texts with aspirations to literary seriousness together had exposed the conflicts among rival cultural allegiances—to notions of truth, definitions of literature, and professional identities—in which modern alcoholism narrative had been forged a century earlier. Commentary on the affair divided between pundits who castigated Frey and his publisher for their deception and critics who lectured Winfrey and her public on their failure to understand the prerogatives of the literateur. (Some of the tribal division that characterized this debate spilled over from a well-publicized dustup in 2001, when Jonathan Franzen expressed unhappiness at the affixing of the Oprah's Book Club badge to his novel *The Corrections*.)

The story that emerged had Frey originally shopping his manuscript as a novel but receiving nothing but rejection. Finally Talese offered to publish it at Doubleday, but only as a memoir, a genre in which it could make a claim on the public's desire for true sensations. Even if conceived as a novel, Frey's turning his stint in rehab into a tale of dramatic self-destruction and triumphant self-will had been an act of professional self-creation, the textual manifestation of his avowed intention to become the next great American literary man's man. This project involved calling out Dave Eggers and David Foster Wallace as effete intellectuals and naming his own legacy that of Ernest Hemingway, Henry Miller, and Jack Kerouac, who, he pointed out, were not averse to fictionalizing their own real-life bad behavior. It also included, at some point, having the initials for the phrase "Fuck the bullshit, it's time to throw down" tattooed on his arm.[24] This two-fisted authorial image practically predicts his hostility in *A Million Little Pieces* toward the surrender of heroic individualism asked of him in rehab.

Frey's twelve-step foil is not directly A.A., though, but the therapy on offer at Hazelden, the prestigious Minnesota addiction-treatment complex where he went, in real life and in his book, for rehabilitation. Hazelden was founded in 1949 by members of the early A.A. movement in the upper Midwest, as a sanatorium for male "alcoholics of the professional class." Its first program was "simply a translation of Bill W.'s basic insight," and its clinics remain committed to a twelve-step framework.[25] Its nonprofit foundation now operates nine treatment clinics around the country, a research center, a public advocacy lobby, a graduate school in addiction counseling, and an active publishing arm. It is likely the most influential therapeutic institution of the Alcoholism Movement, and one that has entered aggressively into the realms of publishing and media.

Hazelden's director of public advocacy, William Cope Moyers, is a graduate of the center and the author of his own recovery memoir, *Broken: My Story of Addiction and Redemption*. Cowritten with Katherine Ketcham, a prolific recovery writer, *Broken* received some significant public notice because of Moyers's earlier career at CNN and his position at Hazelden, and because he is the son of the well-known progressive journalist Bill Moyers. In *Broken*, the elder Moyers puts together rescue teams to extract his son from crack-houses in Harlem and Atlanta, and his voice becomes prominent through alternately poignant, stern, and desperate letters sent to his son. The son wrestles openly in his book with the advantages and the challenges of having a famous father. Ultimately, the experience brings them closer together. Bill Moyers produced a documentary in 1998 called *Addiction: Close to Home*, and the two appeared together in publicity events for the younger Moyers's book.

Moyers's sobriety salvages this familial relationship and others, but the ultimate trajectory of his redemption is his professional identity as an advocate of recovery culture. Moyers has a classic conversion experience when, in treatment outside Atlanta, he prays for guidance and a voice whispers "St. Paul"—the Minnesota city where he had undergone his first inpatient treatment, at Hazelden. He takes this miracle as a sign to move there and get involved in the addiction treatment world, but not before interpreting it via the classic A.A. appeal to William James. The next chapter begins with the scene of his resignation from CNN, by "divine inspiration." In the concluding movement of the book, he describes making his own identity as a recovering addict the centerpiece of his war on "the stigma" of addiction, and recounts grateful messages from addicts and their families in response to his efforts in this realm. It is remarkable that more than half a century after Marty Mann originated what became the National Council on Alcoholism and Drug Dependence, that stigma can be invoked using the same rhetorical conventions and described as having the same power as it ever did. It is almost a self-referential concept, one that the entire addiction-advocacy project cannot but hinge on, regardless of past successes and cultural changes. It creates an odd shift in the tenor of Moyers's book, as he turns from a genuinely affecting confessional mode and into this institutional language, in closing scenes of policy work and in a fact-filled and activist epilogue.[26]

In their rival claims about the nature of the addict and about the efficacy of Hazelden's twelve-step therapy, *Broken* and *A Million Little Pieces* retrace the modernist-era antagonism between the full spiritual redemption and the troubled literary gesture. But in this latter-day dispute, what is openly at stake is neither the shape of society nor the humanity of the lower orders, but, more narrowly, the manner in which addiction can serve as the basis for a public identity. The construction of such an identity is a defining outcome of the Alcoholism Movement, but here we see its legacies in the treatment and media industries still contesting its nature.

In terms of the social meaning of the drunkard's conversion, Frey's and Moyers's memoirs are in roughly the same category. In their confessional vulnerability and their sympathy for fellow addicts, they each assert a kind of democratic social ethos. Both predicate their dramatic appeal and their revelatory insights on journeys through the social hierarchy from alcohol to crack cocaine, the drug associated most closely with the urban poor. They trade on the authenticity of their inevitably harrowing descents, the social depths justifying what then become individual heights of transcendence in recovery. But these social stories ultimately serve larger projects in their memoirs, those of claiming public identities through powerful institutions.

Moyers's book gives stark accounts of his drug use and offers a testament to family support, treatment professionals, A.A., and the Steps, but like so many memoirs, what it ultimately narrates is the achievement of a public identity, in Moyers's case as a spokesman for the treatment industry and the specific mission of Hazelden. Thus he channels this individual redemption into the mission of the massive private addiction treatment industry itself, an institutional legacy of the Alcoholism Movement and the public-private structures of the liberal state. The trajectory of Frey and *A Million Little Pieces*, by contrast, tells an internal story of the culture industry and the often-arbitrary distinctions it has developed in conversation with the consuming public's desire to know itself via its reading choices.

Broken and *A Million Little Pieces* highlight the different ways that the institutions which facilitate the production of recovery narrative, in the addiction treatment and media industries, can shape the meanings of even the most personal stories, drawing them paradoxically toward models of redemption that are more individualistic in appearance as they express institutional values. It is not that Moyers, and even Frey, do not want to make common cause with other addicts in telling their stories—both explicitly say that they do, and many readers have responded positively. But their modes of inviting this identification serve mediating institutional forces in ways that go beyond the contextual difference between published book and meeting-room testimony. Frey and Moyers activate the same densely entangled set of purposes that has characterized all of the historical forerunners of recovery narrative in the cultural marketplace. But despite their uniqueness they seem particularly limited in their visions. Instead of imagining social ideals, they assert institutional power.

Recognizing the way such forces shape the meaning of these texts need not imply the existence of a pure, unmediated alternative in the realm of grassroots recovery culture, let alone in commercially published recovery narrative. A.A.'s vision of mutual aid itself emerged in intimate confessional communities that, as I argued in chapter 4, embodied an ideal of the liberal reform of individualism in the Depression era. Insofar as Frey's and Moyers's memoirs owe key aspects of their structure and affect to A.A. but tell their recoveries in the service of market-driven and state-backed institutions, they represent a neoliberal turn in recovery narrative. An alternative tradition, no less commercial and mainstream, strives to assert instead a left-liberal vision of reform.

Visions of Renewal

The oil painting *The Man on the Bed* first appeared in the A.A. magazine *Grapevine* in 1955 (under its original title, *Came to Believe*), and it has since become an icon of twelve-step culture (see fig. 7). It depicts two men sitting by the bed of a gaunt drinker, carrying the message of A.A. Recovery's primal scene of human sympathy, it features three middle-class white men. The image of hope dawning in the eyes of the frail alcoholic is haunting, but the difference between him and his two visitors measures the social distance from the alcoholic bottom to restored health and status in a few pounds of weight, a firm grip, and a clean suit. While the twelve-step movement already had expanded beyond this initially limited social sphere, for some writers, simply gaining access to the tools of recovery was not enough. As long as society did not provide a legitimate social identity for the minority addict to return to, then recovery was a much more difficult story to tell, and was inevitably an activist tale.

Depictions of irredeemably compulsive drinking and drug use have survived as methods of illustrating the social injustice that persisted, and in some areas intensified, in the second half of the twentieth century. As Djuna Barnes's *Nightwood* suggests, salvation at the alcoholic bottom necessarily eludes subjects that cannot enter into a social role that would manifest it.

This is the realm of failed conversions and cataclysmic convictions, a drinking pattern in autobiographical novels of women's and minority experience. It is joined by a more buoyant mode that might be termed the radical apotheosis, exemplified by several of the Beat movement writers, for example, in their poetic quests for transcendence outside of mainstream social and psychological structures, rather than in redemptive reconciliation with them. Intoxication and addiction were central tropes in the Beats' critique of American success mythology in the Cold War era.[27]

Gay writers, especially, for decades after the creation of A.A. could not plausibly depict the social redemption that the recovery drama requires as its final act.[28] Gay people have been present in A.A., out to one another and to some of their straight fellow members, since its inception.[29] While in reality many gay and lesbian alcoholics were able to sober up while remaining closeted to the wider world (making special use of A.A.'s tradition of anonymity) or out only in gay-liberation circles, in the public realm this was not an experience that they could easily, if at all, represent. When queer writers took up addiction as a topic, they often drew on the romantic-tragic strands of the tradition, using addiction as another one of those vehicles through which an outsider social position enables both social criticism and formal innovation. Some, like Allen Ginsberg in *Howl* (1956), continued and imaginatively expanded the countertradition in which intoxication and destructive compulsion are tropes of social protest. Examples of conviction narratives in which society offers little or no framework for redemption include John Rechy's *City of Night* (1963) and June Arnold's *Sister Gin* (1975). As homosexuality has become more socially accepted, though, gay writers' stories of addiction have increasingly become recovery memoirs.

To consider such stories to be simply recovery narratives by authors who "happen to be gay" would be to repeat and extend the assumption of cultural insignificance in recovery that I've striven with historical and formal analysis to unseat. When a gay addict finds a vision of social sympathy at the moment of hope for recovery, this vision necessarily responds to a wider world where that sympathy is uncertain or withdrawn. This structure of meaning holds even for authors who have achieved mainstream popularity. For example, in his 2003 memoir, *Dry,* Augusten Burroughs describes his alcoholic descent and eventual recovery in tandem with the experience of a close friend's death from AIDS, weaving them together so closely in the final movement of the book that their meanings become inseparable. In *Dry,* recovery becomes a story of survival and social reproduction at a crucial moment in gay history, toward the end of the AIDS fatality crisis and just before the emergence of gay marriage as the dominant political issue. The book is rigorously confessional, eschewing the editorial voice entirely. But it creates a space from within the realm of cultural marketing (Burroughs was an advertising writer) where recovery can expand the liberal social vision.

The specificity of this vision does not preclude robust participation in the wider formal tradition. Like so many recovery subjects before him, from the "worst bums in the fourth ward" to the blasphemous roustabouts of A.A., Burroughs sets up the drama of recovery by emphasizing his ostensible unsuitability for its fundamental sincerity. Burroughs is able to enter this tradition by foregrounding his sexuality and the irreverence of gay culture. Much of *Dry* describes the life of a young advertising "creative" in Manhattan, in an endless round of manic work, hard liquor, cocaine, and sex. He winds up in a step-based rehab (in Minnesota, naturally) where he learns some lessons, but back in the real world he hates meetings and eventually relapses. Recalling Jerry McAuley's backsliding in the old Fourth Ward, Burroughs's Manhattan is simply not a place that wants him to stay sober.

Instead of using this stark unsuitability to set up a dramatic spiritual surrender, Burroughs's final descent and ultimate survival tell a story of the AIDS epidemic. As his professional and personal life begin to fall apart, a beloved ex-boyfriend, an emotionally stable and wise figure who is now his best friend, enters his final physical decline brought on by HIV. Burroughs nurses this friend, affectionately nicknamed "Pighead," through months of suffering. When he dies, Burroughs's bottom falls out. He becomes physically dependent on alcohol and takes up a crack cocaine habit learned from an unstable boyfriend. His low point arrives in a den of unknown crack smokers, but hope is deferred until the arrival of a posthumous gift from Pighead. A gold pig's head with the inscription "I'm watching you. Now stop drinking," it prompts a fuller expression of love and grief than his alcohol-dulled senses had allowed. Like many such moments of surrender in recovery narratives, though, it does not make for instant healing. Instead, it is the decisive moment of hope that, in the felt structure of the narrative, makes his ultimate sobriety all but inevitable.

After this climactic experience, Burroughs offers only the briefest summary of the substance of his recovery, jumping ahead one year to the "plain, almost monastic process of waking up, taking a shower, going to an AA meeting and then doing this again and again." While A.A. is a lifeline, his recovery continues to flow from the "gift" that Pighead gave him. A meeting is like "a mini-brainwash," a friend tells him, it "kind of fixes you for a while." But, "if I'm really wallowing in self-pity, then I'll tell myself, 'Pighead would give anything to feel this uncomfortable right now.' " The memoir closes with Burroughs's noticing the Manhattan streetlamps flickering over his head, and imagining it is Pighead using the once-addicting city streets themselves to send him messages of love and care.[30]

Burroughs structures his redemptive ideal using a convention that is both consistent with conversion tradition and oriented toward social progress. Pighead's gold charm is an unreciprocable gift given by one who has earned the wisdom of suffering to one undertaking the work of survival. It is a concrete secular counterpart to the "unmerited gift" that in Christian theology and much twelve-step spirituality describes God's grace as the governing principle of recovery and indeed all love. As a gift from a mentor to a now-independent protégé, it even echoes the structuring role recovery played at the 1955 A.A. convention, when the founding "old-timers" handed over the fellowship to its members, giving up hierarchical control in favor of the devolved democracy called for in the Twelve Traditions.[31] But in the substance of Burroughs's tale this convention is inextricable from the context of gay life in the late twentieth century. It is a message of healthy self-care, nurturing community, historical continuity, and, finally, social reproduction in the time of a plague.[32] The enduring bond Pighead establishes with Burroughs enables his own survival of a "social disease" in the form of addiction, which in turn makes possible his public identity as a gay writer who bears universal wisdom.

Recovery writing—at first as a therapeutic practice, based on his experience with twelve-step rehabilitation—was the vehicle through which Burroughs developed this authorial voice and literary career. In 1999 St. Martin's Press acquired but postponed publishing a novel that Burroughs wrote from the depths of his addiction, expressing greater interest in a subsequent proposal he based on the journals he had been keeping during his early recovery. This project became *Dry*, but in their talks Burroughs and the press decided to publish first a memoir of his traumatic childhood, in what became his reputation-making hit, *Running with Scissors*.[33] When *Dry* was subsequently published, then, instead of defining him as a professional recovery author, it fit into his established identity as a memoirist with rich funds of both personal trauma and literary talent.

Alternatively, some memoirists began their careers aiming for literary achievement in other genres, but did not gain public authorial identities until they developed a voice for life writing in their recoveries. Anne Lamott, for example, has become a leading memoirist of recovery culture, even though she has not written a book built exclusively around addiction. Lamott's early career as a novelist foundered in the 1980s as she became addicted to alcohol and drugs. Toward the end of the decade she found religion, got sober, and had a child, experiences that became the basis of a second career in nonfiction. Her books on motherhood and on writing in the early 1990s were well received, but she has earned an especially devoted following for her subsequent books on faith, works that make frequent reference to her recovery. Lamott's recovery theme has been essential to her unique success bridging the often-separated markets for literary memoir and spiritual wisdom writing. In these works, her recovery mediates the reconciliation of literary and religious meanings and sensibilities, as well as a range of identity themes from gender and race to poverty and single motherhood. Although Lamott has been hailed as the voice of a general rediscovery of religion, her writing articulates a particularly left-liberal vision of the perennially social meaning of the addict's religious redemption.[34]

In *Traveling Mercies: Some Thoughts on Faith* (1999), the book that established Lamott's reputation for spiritual storytelling, addiction and recovery structure her relationship to religion, as both an artist and as a social self. In a chapter called "Thirst," she tells the specific story of her recovery. In shape, content, and code words it is unmistakably an A.A. story, though she maintains what A.A. calls "anonymity" by never naming it as such. But it is in the opening section of the book, titled "Overture," in which she tells of her religious conversion, that she establishes the social terms of her addiction and her vision of redemption.[35]

The addiction crisis that Lamott translates into spiritual collapse emerges in distinctly gender-specific terms. As for Burroughs, Lamott's use of the "deepest of sinners" convention draws extra energy from the extent to which her self-destructive behaviors violate not just religious morality but still-powerful social norms. Her drug-fueled sexual relationships with married men fall into the cultural (if not religious) category of the "unforgivable" for women, raising both the intensity of the confessional appeal and the stakes of what grace might ultimately accomplish. But significantly, as saturated as it is with the imagery of sexual sin, Lamott's final conviction does not read as a failure to meet society's moral expectations for women, but as a feminist failure of self-care.[36] High and drunk and still bleeding badly a week after an abortion, she finds that her physical and emotional exhaustion outstrips even her capacity to self-medicate. "Shaky and sad and too wild to have another drink or take a sleeping pill," she simply smokes a cigarette and turns off the light. The loss of blood both materially facilitating and spiritually symbolizing the total evacuation of her will, this is the moment that Jesus appears as a physical presence watching over her "with patience and love."[37] In the manner of drunkards' conversions since the Civil War, grace appears upon the involuntary surrender of the self, but it is a surrender sealed on the terms of the drunkard's social identity. In other words, Jesus does not appear completely unbidden.

The longer trajectory of Lamott's conversion is carried along by vehicles of God's grace that owe their origins to the progressive Christian tradition. After an earlier, drug-induced conviction experience, she had been meeting regularly with "an old Civil Rights priest" to talk about her sense of brokenness and the possibility of a spiritual solution that could somehow overcome her "Elmer Gantry" prejudices against Christianity (42–43). She peppers her story with similar signs of her politically and culturally inbred hostility to religion. Because these feelings are grounded in her progressive identity, it takes progressive Christianity to bring her to God.

The ultimate mediator of such a salvation is a scrappy, soulful black church on the wrong side of the tracks in Marin City, California, near her makeshift Sausalito home. She stumbles upon it because of its proximity to a ghetto flea market she visits after particularly bad weekend binges. She finds herself drawn to the gospel music emanating from the run-down St. Andrew Presbyterian, which vibrates with hearty singing, a lot of hugging, and social justice preaching. The singing, especially, "wore down all the boundaries and distinctions that kept me so isolated," Lamott recalls. "Sometimes so shaky and sick that I felt like I might tip over, I felt bigger than myself, like I was being taken care of, tricked into coming back to life" (48). In the long tradition of the progressive recovery, Lamott's addictions have laid her low but, serendipitously, this social depth is a place where God has a special home.

Lamott's description of her attraction to this church is convincing and evocative, but at the same time it is a recognizable performance of the white liberal romance with the authenticity of black bodies and black soul. She indulges in the flea market's "wonderful ethnic food," and describes the relief from self-consciousness that arises from feeling like just another person in a place where status doesn't seem to matter. Every mother in this ghetto is "powerful," the preacher at St. Andrew looks just like Marvin Gaye, a mother signs lyrics to "a gorgeous stick-thin deaf black girl," and the "radical old women" of the church were famous for having contributed church money to Angela Davis's defense fund. Lamott, by contrast, feels "as frozen and still as Richard Nixon," until the singing "pulled me in and split me wide open" (47). Whatever degrees of condescension and inspiration a reader finds Lamott's conversion at this church, the terms of her transformation measure a major trajectory of liberalism since the 1960s, in the history-redeeming apotheosis of the civil rights movement. The passage from Upton Sinclair's implication that recovery would inoculate American writers from communism to Anne Lamott's multicultural redemption marks the shift in cultural emphasis of mainstream American liberalism between the Cold War and culture war eras.

Lamott's formal baptism in this politically righteous religion fuses literary and religious meaning in a manner that authenticates her new, crossover authorial identity. Her personal moment of surrender establishes this pattern by joining her own vernacular epigram ("Fuck it: I quit") to the formal Christian literary tradition exemplified by the George Herbert couplet she begins to find everywhere. Then, at St. Andrew, the handsome preacher reads Langston Hughes's "Dream Dust" as he pours the water over her head. This literary blessing remakes her by resituating her at the center of her gathered church family, biological family, and family of friends. Her new identity is founded on a spiritual equality that is made possible by this liberal communal vision and its historical ancestors.

The fusion Lamott articulates itself has a long tradition, exemplified by one of her main images for addiction's role as redemptively clear evidence of human insufficiency. In her first passage toward conviction, she describes herself as "cracking up," like a pane of glass or a vase on the verge of shattering. In retrospect, she realizes that these traceries would play the epiphanic role invoked by Leonard Cohen in what she pluralizes to the "cracks in everything" of "Anthem" (39–40). This metaphor of the cracked object appears in every realm of conversion-recovery culture, from *Broken Earthenware*, Harold Begbie's 1909 Tory interpretation of the Salvation Army, to F. Scott Fitzgerald's stubbornly individualistic "cracked plate" to Cohen's "cracks, cracks in everything" and even to Drew "Dr. Drew" Pinsky's fusion of medical authority and self-help wisdom in *Cracked: Putting Broken Lives Together Again*.[38] Each text and the genre it represents turns on the dramatic recognition of these fissures. But each interprets them differently and, accordingly, offers a very different model for how they might be repaired or redeemed. The variety of ideological projects this single, narrow metaphor has been put to in the last century is a microcosm of the pattern this book has been devoted to explicating.

Lamott's conversion is remarkably evocative of the experience of the middle-class drunkard at the Gilded Age rescue mission. Her tiny cabin on a friend's houseboat becomes like Samuel H. Hadley's Harlem holding-pen or Bill Wilson's hospital room, a place of desolation where God enters to touch the sinner directly. Following the religious trail of tears to its wellspring in the slum, she is enveloped and transformed there by a vision of spiritual equality. The ghetto church vouchsafes to her the same unshakeable vision, not only of religious sincerity but also of divine social reality. The spiritual, social, and political union possible in a black church can heal a personal brokenness because it already has redeemed human identity differences on wider, social and historical scales.

The original site of this redemption has its own tales to tell, though: the Civil Rights–era ghetto was not without recovery memoirs, and they too implied various responses to liberalism. In these characteristically tenuous redemptions, subjects achieve sobriety in spite of social oppression and remain in danger of being overwhelmed by it. Claude Brown's 1965 autobiographical novel, *Manchild in the Promised Land,* tells of a brutal childhood in a Harlem where heroin addiction loomed. Brown dedicated his ghetto memoir to Eleanor Roosevelt, because of her role founding the reform school that took him off the streets and set him on the path to higher education. Piri Thomas's 1967 memoir of Spanish Harlem, *Down These Mean Streets,* was more explicitly an addiction recovery memoir, although it is primarily known as another story of ghetto childhood. After getting clean in a prison conversion, Thomas returns to his old neighborhood, the scene where he was victim and victimizer, and finds little opportunity there to grow his sobriety into security. He ends his story as it began, watching at close range as a junkie shoots heroin, with little hope beyond a grim revulsion at the image of what he once was and again could be. These stories go beyond sympathy for the addict as a victim of disease to the direct consideration of social environment as the causative factor. They insist the conditions for recovery are not a secure social reality, but a very local vision of an ideal "world-as-it-should-be" that must be fought for in the wider society if it is to survive.

The point in distinguishing Lamott's late twentieth-century vision of multiculturalism from these earlier minority protest-recoveries is not to mark out degrees of authenticity. Journeys across real social terrain are the authenticating conventions of recovery, from whatever the starting point. They defend the redemption story against the skepticism that long has troubled conversion narrative in an ever-secularizing modernity. This tension surrounding sincerity is perennial in the conversion genre, dating to Jonathan Edwards's concern over the imitative quality of conversion, to the public spectacle of the notorious saloonkeeper John Allen's conversion in 1868, and to William James's implausibly bright distinction between the transfiguring heat of real religious experience versus the cold "cant" of "second-hand" conversion. All along there has existed a fundamental unease with the fact that such intense, life-changing, even supernatural events exist not just as a pattern of human experience but in what is obviously an imitative and performative cultural genre, and a fairly rigid one at that.

Addiction, unquestionably a painful and often fatal condition, exerts great pressure on this question of how genre and reality fit together. The addict's almost definitional loss of agency seems to immunize the story against the skeptical suggestion of ulterior motive built into the notion of cultural imitation. Every iteration of recovery narrative examined in this book answers this problem with a particular resolution of the dynamic at the heart of the drunkard's conversion: what is found to be metaphysically true at the bottom of an addictive breakdown is made socially manifest in the subject's subsequent rehabilitation. As recovery memoirs navigate the sweeping market imperatives and unreliable taste-making intricacies of the contemporary publishing and media industries, they still manage to assert ideal visions of social sympathy, in manners still freighted with the import, first of the eternal fate of souls, then with the fierce ideological contests, that were their earlier stakes.

Lamott and Burroughs create transformational visions within their recovery memoirs that both draw on and insist on liberalism's promise of social equality. Although working safely within the commercial publishing realm, their recovery memoirs make genuine interventions in cultural politics because their transformational visions take place on social terrain that is actively contested in American public life. They do so by achieving the fusion Fitzgerald found he could not, in aligning their authorial identities with the subject position of recovery. Burroughs advances his identity as a memoirist of universal appeal even while exploring some of the most stigmatized elements of gay life, while Lamott's recovery allows her to insist on a faith that is both passionately progressive and passionately Christian. Their visions have traction because they successfully convey the sincerity (unlike Frey) and disinterestedness (unlike Moyers) characteristic of twelve-step culture.[39] In order to do so, they have to invoke widely accepted liberal principles before they can apply them in these contested areas. If, as some believe, the twentieth-century iteration of liberalism is in its death throes in the new millennium, then it may, paradoxically, require a *less* realistic kind of recovery narrative to imagine its redemption.

CONCLUSION

Addiction in a New Era of Recovery

Perhaps no mental illness is more a product of its social setting than
addiction to narcotics. . . . Thus, in part the natural history of drug
addiction is like that of a society; it must be rewritten every few years.

—George E. Vaillant, "The Natural History of
Narcotic Drug Addiction" (1970)

Progressive liberals seem incapable of stating the obvious truth:
that we who are well off should be willing to share more of what
we have with poor people not for the poor people's sake but for our
own; i.e., we should share what we have in order to become less
narrow and frightened and lonely and self-centered people.

—David Foster Wallace, *Consider the Lobster
and Other Essays* (2006)

NEW KINDS OF SOBRIETY STORIES have always emerged during times
of socioeconomic crisis. Because these crises have been those of
urban industrial capitalism, poor city neighborhoods have been the settings
for these stories since the temperance era. The slums and addiction are concrete manifestations of modern society's sociopolitical failures: the first in
the landscape, the second in the person, and together mutually constructive
of a pathological social environment. The most intricate and influential narrative exploration of this historic trope in the early twenty-first century was
The Wire, a series created by David Simon that centered on the drug trade in
poor sections of Baltimore and ran from 2002 to 2008 on the HBO network.
The Wire depicts heroin addiction as an affliction locally influenced by poverty, but also as a manifestation of larger structural conditions. The hidden
forces that flow from these conditions bind all the various players to patterns
of destructive behavior, seeming to make both social reform and individual
regeneration nearly impossible.

Through several of its character arcs, *The Wire* denies viewers the easy pleasures of redemption, hoping instead to hold their gaze on the unjust socioeconomic relations that send its characters into crisis. One way it does this is through Jimmy McNulty, a memorable instance of the crime-drama type of the antiheroic detective, who never comes to terms with his own demons, the traumas of the job, or frustration at systemic corruption. Another is in the witty and hapless street character Reginald "Bubbles" Cousins, a homeless heroin addict. Bubbles's poetically elliptical style of speech acts as the program's prophetic voice, while his status as a far-gone addict allows him to move somewhat freely among the power bases in the show's world. Bubbles survives and scores by using the knowledge and even wisdom he has learned on the streets, knowledge he shares with the police in exchange for money and, at times, friendship. It is in fact the betrayal of this relationship, by a careless young officer, that leads to Bubbles's downfall, when his close friend dies after ingesting a poisoned hit of heroin that Bubbles had been preparing for a tormentor. After this tragedy at the end of the show's fourth season, he hits what appears to be his final bottom, and spends the final season in recovery.

Through Bubbles's sobriety, *The Wire* explores recovery and suggests its potentially wider significance. It sounds, in the end, a familiar note of redemption, but one that is tenuous enough to keep the fundamental and unresolved causes of material suffering in its view. Bubbles gets clean in Narcotics Anonymous (N.A.) by staying in touch with a sponsor, attending meetings, and doing the kind of service work that is the vehicle of twelve-step spiritual regeneration. When a newspaper reporter discovers him at a soup kitchen and seeks to profile him for the public, Bubbles is offered the opportunity to star in a public recovery story. In the past he has enjoyed having an audience for various kinds of performances, but he senses that the journalist will choose a sensational and redemptive story template that is fundamentally untrue to his experience and his ongoing struggles. Discussing the article with his sponsor, Bubbles expresses discomfort with someone telling his recovery narrative in a way that makes him appear more saintly than he thinks he is. "A lot of folks volunteer places," he grumbles. "A lot of folks share at meetings. Plenty of motherfuckers wake up every day and not get high. Man making me sound special for doing what the fuck I need to be doing."[1] Without invoking the twelve-step principle of anonymity, Bubbles memorably identifies the fundamental tension between the surrender of the self and the laudatory public recovery narrative.

Bubbles's objection gestures toward the ethical and even political differences between the purposes of the meeting-room testimony and the published narrative. His sponsor, Waylon, encourages him to go easier on himself, and to take a perspective that allows for some pride in how far he has progressed. Twelve-step spirituality suggests that one recovering addict is no better than another, but all are miracles and should understand themselves as such. But what Bubbles is also making clear, especially in the context of his story being made public, is that he knows the redemptive moment is being constructed for purposes that are not his own, and that may in fact betray his experience by their false, society-affirming optimism. His may be the kind of story that allows readers, as Twain's new judge did with Pap Finn, to believe the problem of addiction begins and ends in the personal vulnerabilities of the addict.

The Wire offers similar resistance to redemptive storytelling in the context of the recovery group. N.A.'s twelve-step meetings and personal sponsorship work for Bubbles, but he refuses to embrace wholly the redemptive moment at the end of the story, suggesting instead that to do so would betray those who, by no fault of their own, did not survive. In the penultimate episode of the series, Bubbles celebrates the one-year anniversary of his sobriety at an N.A. meeting. For recovering addicts, this event is often a moment to articulate the spiritual redemption they have achieved and to recite the evidences of its social manifestations in material comfort and new or repaired relationships. Bubbles, though, addresses the meeting by hesitantly observing that he is not yet reconciled with his family and conceding only that "time" (not anyone's agency) might make things better. All he manages beyond that, by way of a speech, is to refuse what he feels is expected of him at this moment, the "letting go" of his sense of guilt over his friend's death. "Ain't no shame in holding onto grief, as long as you make room for other things, too," he says with finality.[2]

This method of constructing full story arcs that nevertheless trouble narrative expectations of release and closure was central to the sociopolitical ethos of The Wire. In the gestural conversion common to literary recovery narrative, a sign of redemption provides sentimental but realistic relief, while keeping the attention on the heroic individual. In The Wire, individuals can have redemptive experiences, but not the kind that ameliorate or distract from the causes of suffering: institutionalized poverty, destructive drug policy, and political corruption that ensures nothing fundamental will change. The Wire's interrogation of recovery helps build its case against the politics and economics of inequality. At the same time, its depiction of Bubbles, Waylon, and some of their group members is its only vision of uncorrupted social sympathy and the lone kernel of community in this broken place that has developed a viable project of regeneration. It is a devastating critique of conventional liberalism, but also a sign that recovery culture can begin to nurture what might lie beyond it.

The Wire's recovery narrative brings the sociopolitical conversation about addiction back to the world of Jerry McAuley and his Helping Hand rescue mission in uncanny ways. And, like the drunkards' conversions, its message is aimed less at securing identification with the next Bubbles than at changing the lives of would-be liberal reformers in the audience: the kind of lesson that Helen Stuart Campbell learned in Water Street. In her belief that slum conversions should facilitate political awakenings in middle-class would-be "radicals," Campbell did not suffer from the delusion bemoaned by David Foster Wallace, another chronicler of recovery, in the second epigraph to this chapter. Wallace's call for a more honestly self-interested liberalism may not match the message of The Wire, and it may strike some as a narcissistic motive for social reform. But his comment draws attention to the essential ethical outlook at the birthplace of recovery narrative: the liberal witness's confession of an insufficiency equal to or greater than that of the poor convert. It is the democratic ethical stance that A.A. internalized in its own mutual-aid principles.

In a very different medium and with a very different sensibility than The Wire, Wallace's novel Infinite Jest also uses mutual-aid recovery as a forum for developing alternative social relations in an apocalyptic, post-liberal milieu. In the 1996 novel that cemented Wallace's reputation and emerged as one of the most compelling fictions of the contemporary era, recovery is less a plot structure than it is a pervasive undercurrent. The world of sober houses and step meetings appears as the subterranean alternative to a mainstream world gone mad with consumption. Despite its unstable social dynamics and its self-help clichés, recovery culture offers a way of ordering inner life and outer experience that resists this fascistic consumerism. Infinite Jest depicts a society in which every citizen is infected by addictive compulsion, and only those badly damaged, outcast denizens of the underground world of recovery have a language, however apparently hackneyed, for recognizing it.[3]

These works definitively link their characters' personal failings to the collapse of liberalism, each focusing on opposite sides of the drug coin: The Wire on drug policy, Infinite Jest on the desire economy. Their uses of recovery cast A.A.'s radical organizational structure in a new, forward-looking light, recalling Bill Wilson's once-voiced hope that recovery would fulfill a vision of society organized by voluntary, but life-saving, mutual aid. The addiction recovery testimony of the intimate meeting group continues to serve as the basis for publicly disseminated stories in both first- and third-person voices. And as the story form moves from private to public realms, and from nonfictional to fictional genres, and back again, it produces the same kinds of meanings it always has, in visions of the world as it should be that are built from the ashes of the world as it is.

The purpose of the Part I of this book was to show that the precursors to contemporary addiction recovery narrative, the variations on the drunkard's conversion that arose between the Civil War and World War II, developed as vehicles for advocating various philosophical and political beliefs. The discourse surrounding alcoholism in that era was not, as is widely believed, defined mainly by moralistic condemnations of the drinker, nor by the politics of temperance reform. The felt structures of these conversion stories were those we recognize in recovery today—descent, revelation, rebirth, reconciliation—except that they were attached to more explicit wider claims. Nor was the recovery narrative that emerged from this period based on the insight that addiction is a disease whose nature bears no relation to these collective visions. A.A.'s innovation came in its modification of that conversion formula in response to the Depression-era failure of a shared social and political ideology. Recovery narrative, though ostensibly limiting its scope to personal sobriety, was constructed from conventions that had been developed for such reformist purposes. Some of its early narrators felt it to be a vanguard in the redemption of modern society.

In Part II I argued that modern literature was deeply engaged with the redemptive ethos and programmatic purposes of drinking narrative. Critics have associated drinking in modern literature with the defiance of Prohibition, and an attitude toward consumption that was bohemian rather than moralistic, hardboiled rather than sentimental, and philosophical rather than therapeutic. But in fact these binaries break down on close scrutiny. The realists confronted the drunkard's conversion in its role as a competitor for the narrative interpretation of class relations. Interwar modernists sublimated this class politics to interior experience, but still used the social decline of the alcoholic to explore the fine-grained politics of relational ethics. The role of alcohol in modern literature thus was closely related to, indeed helped along, the development of a popular therapeutic culture surrounding addiction. Modernist writers have been imagined as "unapologetic" alcoholics, holdouts against the therapeutic mindset, but the fact is that, in their work at least, they were making the same turn inward as did recovery narrative. Both movements reoriented drinking narrative by adapting the conventions of a political and religious heritage to projects of finding equally broad meanings in personal spiritual welfare.

The nuances of this imaginative literature shed a uniquely penetrating light on how the nonfictional forms made meaning and what purposes they served. These works illuminated the tensions, at different moments, by which depictions of addiction as an individual experience served as venues for talking about political and philosophical crises and their potential resolutions. These tensions emerged in a series of contrasts: between Mark Twain's evisceration of the drunkard's conversion as a reactionary deception and Upton Sinclair's wholehearted application of it to socialism; in the difference between modernist drinking novels that end with redemptive insights and those that descend to calamitous binges; and in the various ways contemporary recovery narratives make space for both literary sophistication and sociopolitical meaning within the redemption paradigm. Each chapter explored the ways addiction narratives have been, and remain, oriented formally around the ideological axes of the long liberal era.

This insight into the modern development of recovery narrative allows us to take a fresh look at what critics are increasingly calling a stale genre.[4] It encourages us to take a category associated almost exclusively with private experience and reconnect it to the broader philosophical and political categories through which it was forged, the debates that animated public discourse in the twentieth century. The established view of addiction's conceptual development makes "privatization" of the genre inevitable. It describes a shift from moralism to medicalization, in which recovery serves as a bellwether for the mainstreaming of a secular, psychological, and now neurochemical worldview. This approach has tended to isolate the significance of addiction recovery in therapeutic culture, cutting it off from moral and political ideas and obscuring its role as a touchstone of modernity.

My purpose has not been to repoliticize addiction, but to rediscover some of its essential ways of making meaning. This project has highlighted the extent to which the mental health concepts assimilated, rather than replaced, the earlier paradigms' expressions of social relations and metaphysical beliefs, in ways that shaped contemporary conceptions of self. I also have presented counter-evidence to the idea that scientific research and medical treatment drove the rise of recovery narrative, in the features of recovery that have not changed since the days of the drunkard's conversion. Broadly speaking, the addict's decline, irrespective of the perennially present, ever-shifting notions of addiction as a physical and psychological illness, has narrated the crisis of the self under modern conditions, whether those of industrial poverty or the fear of epistemic collapse. This built-in high purpose has been fundamental to the concept of addiction since its emergence. It, and not the disease model, is the most significant legacy that contemporary recovery narrative inherits.

But even if we agree on the formal legacy of that historical cultural function in contemporary addiction discourse, we must still ask what significant role it plays today. Recovery narrative involves the discovery and assertion of foundational values. But is that ideological structure in the contemporary genre as *reformist* in purpose as it was in its polemical precursors? Most readers and critics perceive recovery stories as journeys to hard-won personal wisdom, movements from blind self-centeredness to balanced self-awareness. This kind of change does not call for systemic reform, but simply describes the delayed achievement of normal social ethics, with an added bonus of deeper insight into their grounding. And this is indeed the role such stories have played, as long as they have idealized a reigning paradigm of self. But how unanimous and stable is this paradigm? The liberal social shift that was articulated in A.A.'s influential model of self was never fully secured, and it has long been considered in steep decline. Many believe we have entered a period of accelerated change. And as the fundamental role of the state has been called into question in a new era of economic "recovery," narratives of compulsive consumption and its relief have once gain become significant proxies for debate about the revision of societal values.

The postwar political order proceeded on the assumption that institutional structures ought to reflect a consensus ideal of social interdependence. This idea was articulated by the Roosevelt Administration during the 1930s, was cemented in the national war effort, and bore its last great policy fruits in the 1960s, with the Johnson Administration's Great Society. But even as those latter programs were going into effect, the underlying consensus had begun to decay, to the point that today, while still living with some of its institutional legacies, Americans no longer agree on their premises: neither on the nature of social relations, nor on the belief that government ought to reflect and sustain them. While some analysts believe its demise was economic in first causes, the fragmentation of this order has been experienced as a failure of social assumptions and civic culture. For example, the various liberation movements of the Civil Rights era were successful in securing minority rights, but less so in facilitating economic equality. And the hostilities of that era continue to be reflected, and exploited, in deep political division.

If recovery narrative was indeed a cultural product of the mid-twenti-eth-century liberal realignment, then we might expect its fortunes to have changed along with those of the wider society. Tensions within recovery cul-ture in the postwar decades did reflect the challenges posed to its social poli-tics. The most salient alternatives to A.A.-style narrative came from women and from racial and sexual minorities, whose stories demonstrated ways that surrendering autonomy could be redundant, and mainstream social rehabilitation could be impossible. Generally, though, just as civil rights movements sought access to the legal standing and ultimately the promise of security the New Deal had established, minority recovery tales did not reject the twelve-step path to redemption but revised it to account for the challenges of social exclusion. Where such recognition is found or forged, recovery culture has flourished, as some of its most influential voices have been those of African Americans and women. In this model, recovery cul-ture marks and advances progress toward equality.[5]

Tellingly, more thorough rejections of recovery principles have come from opponents of liberalism, who have often applied the same terms to cri-tique mutual aid that they use to attack the New Deal consensus. Those who are hostile to the very aims and premises of procedural liberalism and the welfare state tend to identify recovery narrative and its various performances as their cultural proxies. These critiques often rest on defining recovery institutions as dogmatic belief systems, rather than as the relatively flexible social practices and oral traditions that they are. But despite this inadequacy, political critiques of recovery culture are correct in their instinctive senses that social re-integration through mutual aid is a project entwined with lib-eral visions for society. Most such criticism falls into two camps, which are broadly speaking from the right and the left. Critics from the right complain that recovery enshrines a model of addiction that shirks personal responsi-bility, evacuates the moral hazards of consumption choices, and teaches a substitute form of dependency.[6] The leftist critique of recovery culture sees it relentlessly personalizing social dysfunction that is more properly thought of as having political origins and solutions.[7] Each isolates some aspect of recovery rhetoric that is an irritant to the anti-liberal temperament in ques-tion. The political distance between these critiques reflects the identification of recovery with the ideology of the liberal age.

None of these concerns seem to have dimmed the popularity of recov-ery culture, redemption narratives in various media, and ultimately of the sympathetic social visions they express. Critiques emerged in the 1960s and became most strident in the 1980s, when the sociopolitical order forged by the New Deal was first felt to be truly lost. And yet recovery's role as a mechanism for rehabilitating the self seems never to have receded. During the same 1980s in which majorities of voters twice responded positively to Ronald Reagan's rhetorical attacks on the liberal state, recovery culture not only survived but expanded to explain all manner of behavioral compulsion, from sex and drugs to eating, shopping, and accruing debt. In other words, recovery seemed to flourish just when the liberal social consensus was felt to be cracking up.

This disjunction could imply one of three things. It could mean that twelve-step culture really had no lasting link with modern liberalism, after the coincidence of their simultaneous birth during the Depression. But, as I argued in chapter 8, the range of subgenres in published recovery since World War II do describe efforts to work out problems of liberalism on the grounds of the social self. Alternatively, the popularity of recovery in a conservative age could signal a later break in the formative link with liberalism. Mutual-aid institutions like A.A. are insulated, organizationally, from a high degree of external change. The growth of recovery might even have been compensating, as in the nineteenth century, for the inadequacy of state services. Finally, recovery's popularity may in fact indicate a deeper and wider acceptance of the social ethics underlying liberalism than individual elections and short-term reactions can disprove. It may even indicate that attacks on the ameliorative functions of government lack long-term popular appeal. The next deep crisis of state could be expected to help answer these questions.

Such a crisis arrived, in the recession that began in 2008. Economic stagnation and unemployment became severe enough that, as in the 1930s, the national narrative turned into one of *recovery,* and much domestic policy debate began to center on responding to material scarcity. Once again, while this use of the term "recovery" described the reversal of economic trends, the discourse around it addressed fundamental questions of social relations and the role of the state. Finally, perhaps even more in this era than in the aftermath of the 1929 stock market crash, Americans worried that excessive, even compulsive consumption is a self-destructive national tendency. Politicians and commentators have frequently wielded addiction as a metaphor to encompass all these concerns. Phrases such as "our addiction to oil," "our addiction to cheap consumer goods," "our addiction to processed foods," and "dependency on big government" are ubiquitous.

If addiction is acting as a conceptual category for understanding national crisis, then recovery is once again a platform for rethinking the fundamental relationships of citizen, society, and state. Recovery narrative, as I have worked to show, is a vehicle for describing changes in foundational self-concepts, as understood through social ethics and, simultaneously, as called for in programs of reform. Sobriety stories construct stark images and lofty ideals of the ways Americans relate to one another, of what value they place on their own needs and desires relative to those of others, and to what extent they believe their own fate to depend on what A.A. called "our common welfare." If indeed American society has entered a phase from which a new kind of citizenship and a new conception of state power will emerge, then we can expect in the meantime to see a shifting or even fragmented addiction discourse as a both a symptom and a site of this process.

As political commentators of various stripes have invoked addiction metaphors to describe the crisis, they also have called on recovery to characterize its role as a historical turning point for American society. "Wall Street got drunk," George W. Bush told the audience at a fundraiser in the summer of 2008, when it first became widely known how badly exposed firms like Lehman Brothers were. "And the question is, how long will it sober up?" Others proposed programs of national recovery inspired by the A.A. model. Rich Karlgaard, the publisher of *Forbes*, offered a twelve-step program for economic recovery. The political scientist Thomas Barnett devised a "Twelve-Step Recovery Program for American Grand Strategy," written in close approximation of A.A.'s language and starting with "Step One: Admit that we Americans are powerless over globalization." Finally, leading figures of the far right came out as recovery warriors, from Glenn Beck's call for Republicans to use the Twelve Steps to overcome their destructive addiction to progressive policies to Newt Gingrich's claim that A.A.'s Big Book had brought him to religion even though he was not an alcoholic.[8] With many evangelical churches creating twelve-step-derived recovery ministries, spiritual depth has supplanted helpless victimhood in the right's view of recovery. Its language has been incorporated into the Reagan-esque story of reclaiming national greatness.

Liberal cultural commentators, too, have proposed that compulsive consumption is an epidemic among the citizenry and may be responsible for the crisis threatening the state as a whole. In 2004 the novelist Kurt Andersen wrote a narrative of American financial behavior since World War II for *Time Magazine* titled "The End of Excess: Is This Crisis Good for America?" It is oddly evocative of Bill Wilson's tale of manic drinking and stock speculating and F. Scott Fitzgerald's personal crash that seemed so closely bound to the national calamity. The next year Judith Warner wrote a cover story for the *New York Times Magazine* arguing that "dysregulation" has become the keynote of modern American culture. "For in the anything-goes atmosphere of our recent past, it wasn't just external controls that went awry; inwardly, people lost constraint and common sense, too," Warner wrote. "Now there is a case to be made that problems of self-regulation—of appetite, emotion, impulse and cupidity—may well be the defining social pathology of our time." Warner's notion of self-control is a broader category than addiction, but one that contains it and has historically been informed by it.[9] Myriad other commentators see the American narrative of the future organized around the question of whether the nation can solve the problem of uncontrolled consumption, in light of the global distribution of resources and power and the political struggles expected to ensue. In these political and cultural critiques, recovery's analogical and metaphorical applications are flying apart, deployed on behalf of widely divergent points of view rather than any emerging consensus.[10]

Historically, ideological contention over the symbolic meaning of addiction and recovery has influenced the development of the core concepts themselves. Is the nature of addiction itself entering a period of renegotiation? Evidence would seem to point in opposite directions. On one hand, neuroscientists have converged on a model of addiction that describes it in fairly straightforward terms as a brain disease, the proverbial "hijacking" of the brain's reward circuitry. Such models have gained in complexity, now recognizing the importance of memory processes, rather than mere pleasure receptors, in understanding the long-term threat of relapse and the role of the social environment.[11] The historian David T. Courtwright describes the more comprehensive summary of the "NIDA paradigm," the model developed by researchers at the National Institute on Drug Abuse as "a chronic, relapsing brain disease with a social and genetic component, significant comorbidity with other mental and physical disorders, long-term changes in brain structure and function visible in imaging studies, and a defining loss of control over drug craving, seeking and use despite adverse consequences."[12] Neuroscientists increasingly strive for comprehensive explanations, and media reporting confirms the sense that the problems they attack will one day soon be "solved."

But what constitutes the "social component" and "adverse consequences" are factors that, at certain points in the past, have changed more rapidly and more profoundly than contemporaries anticipated.[13] The socially constructed slipperiness of these categories might not fundamentally change the brain paradigm, but it can dramatically alter its relevance and applicability.

The long view would suggest that even the brain science model must eventually, as Courtwright puts it, "pass into the classics under the pressure of revision."[14] In the two-century history of the addiction concept this kind of change has less often been the product of a "scientific revolution" than of shifts in what constitutes rational and acceptable behavior, in social ethics as well as consumption habits.

If research funding, media reporting, and popular science writing are reliable indicators, the authority of neuroscience seems only to be increasing. But despite not being able to exert similar influence, a number of social scientists, philosophers, psychiatric researchers, and cultural critics share distinct but overlapping senses of skepticism about the disease model and its sociopolitical uses.[15] Some have waged long battles against disease-model government advocacy and recovery culture, and in the process have sometimes been marginalized as eccentric ax-grinders, retrograde moralists who would endanger addicts by returning them to the days of castigation and shame.[16] Recently, though, public challenges to the disease concept have become less controversial. The research psychologist Gene Heyman, for example, found a relatively warm reception for his revisionist case that addiction and its cessation are matters of choice.[17] Heyman points out that the disease model invokes a distinction between voluntary and involuntary behavior that is socially constructed, and applied differently depending on context.

Even when viewed through a framework of pathology, the difference between a problematic habit and the disease of addiction is not always clear, and it often depends on the user's social outcomes rather than physical state. The American Psychiatric Association's fifth edition of its authoritative *Diagnostic and Statistical Manual of Mental Disorders*, scheduled for publication in mid-2013, is on course to discard the distinction between "abuse" and "dependence" on alcohol and other substances, in favor of a single, substance-specific "use disorder" of varying criteria-derived intensity. While some of the criteria, such as "tolerance" and "withdrawal," relate to physical dependence, the overall emphasis is on "impairment or distress" as manifested in undesirable outcomes, rather than in the inference of a brain condition. This distinction is of paramount importance to advocates for those who suffer from chronic pain, for example, who reject the category of "addiction" for physiological dependence on opioid painkillers used for medical purposes.[18]

Addiction research and recovery culture have long enjoyed an arm's-length relationship that is nonetheless mutually beneficial. The two realms grew together, beginning in the 1940s, often with the same public figures promoting both the disease theory of addiction and the spiritual method of recovery.[19] Even though researchers soon dismissed the model of alcoholism as an "allergy" that A.A. first embraced, recovery's functional use of the disease concept could accommodate almost every future iteration of it. A.A. members, in fact, were prominent among the early research subjects used by the creators of the modern disease concept.[20] Step 1, the admission of powerlessness, simply required validation of the premise that addiction is a condition that overrides the faculties of rational choice in regard to the substance. And this has been a premise by which the brain disease and recovery culture have remained on parallel tracks, as both have expanded to cover not only drug consumption but also compulsive behaviors.

A new debate about the fundamental nature of addiction would necessarily be affected by political ideology and cultural narrative. Such a foundational debate, in turn, would facilitate the creation of new metaphorical uses of addiction and exemplary depictions of recovery. After all, in the absence of a dominant paradigm to ground mimetic realism, imaginative models are less easily dismissed as fanciful. As in the nineteenth century, they might, in fact, help shape the narrative conventions used to illustrate the next paradigm. If the nature of addiction is a more open question, then particular depictions of it can come to seem less deceptively polemical and more like efforts to describe its deep truth.[21] In such an era, recovery narrative will not only be more diverse, but each instance will be more openly programmatic, since at the very least it will be presenting a picture of addiction that is not universally shared, that indeed some will see as false. If foundational beliefs about human agency, social identity, and societal organization are to be renegotiated, recovery narratives cannot help but become more openly purposive, since recovery narratives depend on the assertion of such values.

From the standpoint of mainstream recovery culture, this development would be disastrous, threatening a return to the days when alcoholics found not just their legal standing but their very self-concepts bound to religious and political controversies over which they had no control. But from the historical perspective developed in this book, the increased attention to the role of public values in recovery narrative may be an inevitable and, possibly, useful development. Without an easy appeal to an uncontroversial disease concept, recovery might be able to embrace more openly its role of describing the effective social re-integration of alienated people—a function that some researchers have found is the most effective role of mutual aid in the treatment of addiction.[22] The sponsors and narrators of the drunkard's conversion called this function moral reform. Without much difference in actual process, we might be more comfortable calling that role by another name, such as social reconstruction.

Innovative cultural works—the kind that tend to both provide insight into and critique the direction society is heading in—have looked to recovery for just this function, by focusing on the social meaning of addiction and the mutual-aid practices of recovery, rather than on the clinical or consumerist aspects of either. Far from being a tired-out middlebrow genre, recovery is a vernacular language in a flexible formal system that can coexist with both the most exhaustive commitments to realism, and the most daring literary experiments, as *The Wire* and *Infinite Jest* exemplify. Recovery remains the subject of stories that imagine the renewal of basic social relations in an age of their breakdown.

Notes

INTRODUCTION: Addiction Recovery and the World as It Should Be

1. George W. Bush, *A Charge to Keep: My Journey to the White House* (New York: Harper, 2001), 133, 136; Barack Obama, *Dreams from My Father: A Story of Race and Inheritance* (New York: Times Books, 1995), 93–94. For evidence of these generic ancestries, compare Bush's evangelical rebirth to Jerry McAuley's claim that "Jesus came and took the whole thing out of me" (see chapter 1), and Obama's to the "Educated Agnostic" among Alcoholics Anonymous's first one hundred members (see chapter 4).

2. Lisa Miller, "Trying Times for Trinity," *Newsweek,* March 15, 2008.

3. Glenn Hendler, *Public Sentiments: Structures of Feeling in Nineteenth-Century American Literature* (Chapel Hill: University of North Carolina Press, 2001), 50; Elaine Frantz Parsons, *Manhood Lost: Fallen Drunkards and Redeeming Women in the Nineteenth-Century United States* (Baltimore: Johns Hopkins University Press, 2003), 12.

4. Parsons, *Manhood Lost,* 15; Thomas Augst, "A Drunkard's Story: The Market for Suffering in Antebellum America," *Common-Place* 10.3 (April 2010), www.commonplace.org/vol-10/no-03/augst. Beyond drunkards' narratives, scholarship on the broader categories of alcohol use and temperance reform similarly approaches them as constructing and contesting fundamental values of nineteenth-century society. For an early and influential example of such scholarship, see Barbara Epstein, *The Politics of Domesticity: Women, Evangelism, and Temperance in Nineteenth-Century America* (Middletown, CT: Wesleyan University Press, 1981).

5. The term "alcoholism" was coined by Magnus Huss, a Swedish doctor, in 1849, and was only partially taken up by American physicians by the end of the nineteenth century. It did not attain widespread use in America until the 1940s. Alcohol researchers adopted the phrase in the same era but continued to debate its usefulness throughout the twentieth century. William L. White, *Slaying the Dragon: The History of Addiction Treatment and Recovery in America* (Bloomington, IL.: Chestnut Health Systems, 1998), xiv–xv.

6. Trysh Travis attributes this neglect to the way critical assumptions about what constitutes expressive writing remain beholden to the binaries established in the age of literary modernism, between the sentimental and the "honest," the simplistic and the complex, the imitative and the original. Travis, *The Language of the Heart: A Cultural*

History of the Recovery Movement from Alcoholics Anonymous to Oprah Winfrey (Chapel Hill: University of North Carolina Press, 2009), 267–69. In chapter 6 I discuss the way these values have also prevented critics from seeing how much alcoholism narrative in modern literature draws on the form and feelings of the drunkard's conversion.

7. The term "purely clinical" was used by Malcolm Lowry's wife to describe Charles Jackson's 1944 psychoanalytic alcoholism novel, *The Lost Weekend,* whose success had dampened Lowry's hope that his *Under the Volcano* would be received as an unprecedented interpretation of alcoholism as modern spiritual crisis. John W. Crowley, *The White Logic: Alcoholism and Gender in American Modernist Fiction* (Amherst: University of Massachusetts Press, 1994), 136. Lincoln advocated for redeemed drunkards as the best spokesmen for the temperance cause, and urged the compassionate treatment of active drinkers. "Address to the Springfield Washington Temperance Society," February 22, 1842, in *Lincoln: Speeches and Writings, 1832–1858,* ed. Don E. Fehrenbacher (New York: Library of America, 1989), 81–89. Whitman's novel of the same year was an immature expression of his romantic, transformational imagination in the tale of a drunkard's ecstatic redemption. Walt Whitman, *Franklin Evans; or, The Inebriate: A Tale of the Times* (1842; repr., Durham: Duke University Press, 2007). The women's rights advocates of the Women's Christian Temperance Union endorsed "gospel temperance" as the best hope for the drunkard and his innocent victims. Sarah W. Tracy, *Alcoholism in America: From Reconstruction to Prohibition* (Baltimore: Johns Hopkins University Press, 2005), 78–81.

Regarding the neglect of recovery narrative in the humanities, it required a wholly unorthodox approach to American letters for a quasi-authoritative source finally to acknowledge, if only in a six-page essay, the importance of addiction recovery to the literary imagination. Greil Marcus and Werner Sollors included a narrative of A.A.'s founding in their free-spirited, culturally voracious 2009 anthology on American literary history: Michael Tolkin, "1935, June 10: Bill Wilson Meets 'Doctor Bob,'" in *A New Literary History of America,* ed. Greil Marcus and Werner Sollors (Cambridge: Harvard University Press, 2009), 695–700.

8. I draw on the formula "the world as it is versus the world as it should (or ought to) be" because of its provenance in the same patterns of exchange among philosophical, religious, psychological, and political discourses out of which recovery narrative emerged and in which it continues to exert influence. Since the late nineteenth century, this way of expressing the dialectic between the real and the ideal has appeared in temperance tracts, interpretations of Kant and Nietzsche, treatises on political science, arguments for foreign policy realism, and progressive theologies. William Hoyle, *Wealth and Social Progress in Relation to Thrift, Temperance, and Trade* (Manchester: United Kingdom Alliance, 1887), 189; Edward Bellamy, *Equality* (New York: D. Appleton, 1898), 251; Edward Caird, *The Critical Philosophy of Immanuel Kant,* vol. 2 (New York: Macmillan, 1889), 192; Georges Chatterton-Hill, *T he Philosophy of Nietzsche: An Exposition and an Appreciation* (New York: D. Appleton, 1913), 19; Thurman W. Arnold, *The Symbols of Government* (New Haven: Yale University Press, 1935), 90.

9. Sacvan Bercovitch, *The American Jeremiad* (Madison: University of Wisconsin Press, 1978).

10. On the rise of the addiction concept, see Harry Gene Levine, "The Discovery of Addiction: Changing Conceptions of Habitual Drunkenness in America," *Journal of Studies on Alcohol* 39 (1978): 143–74; and White, *Slaying the Dragon*, 1–20.

11. Benjamin Franklin, *Autobiography* (New York: Henry Holt, 1916), 88–91.

12. Ibid., 147, 149.

13. Benjamin Rush, *An Inquiry into the Effects of Ardent Spirits upon the Human Body and Mind* (1804; repr., Boston: James Loring, 1823), 20.

14 Lincoln, "Temperance Address," 84. On this change in the practices, volumes, and morals of alcohol consumption, see W. J. Rorabaugh, *The Alcoholic Republic: An American Tradition* (New York: Oxford University Press, 1979), and Mark Edward Lender and James Kirby Martin, *Drinking in America: A History*, rev. ed. (New York: Macmillan, 1987), 41–86. For discussion of the methods behind consumption estimates, see Greg Austin and Ron Roizen, "How Good Are the Conventional Estimates? Stalking the Origins of Historical U.S. Per Capita Alcohol Consumption Statistics" (1993), www.roizen.com/ron/how-good.htm.

15. Jonathan Edwards, *Treatise on Religious Affections* (1754; Boston: James Loring, 1824), 44.

16. See, e.g., Benjamin Franklin, "A Drinker's Dictionary" (1737), in *A Benjamin Franklin Reader*, ed. Walter Isaacson (New York: Simon & Schuster, 2003), 108–13.

17. On the relationship between temperance ideas about alcohol and sentimental culture, see the essays in David S. Reynolds and Debra J. Rosenthal, eds., *The Serpent in the Cup: Temperance in American Literature* (Amherst: University of Massachusetts Press, 1997); and Hendler, *Public Sentiments*. For a variety of approaches to the rise of sentimental culture, see Shirley Samuels, ed., *The Culture of Sentiment: Race, Gender, and Sentimentality in Nineteenth-Century America* (New York: Oxford University Press, 1992).

18. *Lincoln: Speeches and Writings*, 86. John W. Crowley, *The Drunkard's Progress* (Baltimore: Johns Hopkins University Press, 1999), provides a highly useful historiography of the Washington Society and a representative collection of narratives. For other treatments of the Washingtonian movement as a cultural phenomenon, see Hendler, *Public Sentiments*, 29–52, and Augst, "A Drunkard's Story."

19. Crowley, *Drunkard's Progress*, 6–7, 15. For details on the fate of the Washingtonians amid the rise of the institutional prohibitionist movement, see Ian Tyrrell, *Sobering Up: From Temperance to Prohibition in Antebellum America, 1800–1860* (Westport, CT: Greenwood Press, 1979), 206–18. Sean Wilentz, in his landmark study of early labor politics, interprets the Washington Society as an organized response to the post-1837 economic crisis that played a role in the very formation of the American working class upon the breakdown of the old artisan system of urban labor. He further contends that its establishment of working-class mutual-aid practices had lasting influence beyond its organizational life. Wilentz, *Chants Democratic: New York City and the Rise of the American Working Class, 1788–1850* (New York: Oxford University Press, 1984), 307–14.

20. On the thin strands of direct influence running from the Washingtonians to the rescue missions through Methodist missionary work, see Katherine Chavigny,

"American Confessions: Reformed Drunkards and the Origins of Therapeutic Culture" (PhD diss., University of Chicago, 1999), 152–90.

21. Rush, *Inquiry*, 31–32.

22. Charles G. Finney, *The Memoirs of Charles G. Finney: The Complete Restored Text*, ed. Garth M. Rosell and Richard A. G. Dupuis (Grand Rapids, MI: Academie Books, 1989), 23–24. Although it would be possible to trace the transmission of the modern conversion narrative further back, to figures like George Whitefield and Jonathan Edwards, this revival history starts with Finney because his conversion and his institutional leadership represent (indeed, helped establish) the norms of nineteenth-century evangelism. See Charles E. Hambrick-Stowe, *Charles G. Finney and the Spirit of American Evangelicalism* (Grand Rapids, MI: William B. Eerdmans, 1996).

23. Samuel I. Prime, *The Power of Prayer* (New York: Charles Scribner, 1859), 21; Finney, *Memoirs*, 601n; Arthur Bonner, *Jerry McAuley and His Mission*, rev. ed. (Neptune, NJ: Loizeaun Bros., 1990), 19. Kathryn T. Long describes the 1857–1858 evangelical revival in New York City as a movement of the urban middle class that democratized and laicized American religious practice, essentially establishing interdenominational evangelicalism the national religious consensus. She names McAuley and the rescue missions as among its fruits. Long, *The Revival of 1857–58: Interpreting an American Religious Awakening* (New York: Oxford University Press, 1998), 32, 40–41, 105.

24. R. M. Offord, ed., *Jerry McAuley: An Apostle to the Lost* (New York: American Tract Society, 1907), 18–19, 30–31.

25. Samuel H. Hadley, *Down in Water Street: A Story of Sixteen Years Life and Work in Water Street Mission* (New York: Fleming H. Revell, 1902), 68–80.

26. "Henry H. Hadley 2d, Mission Worker, Dies; Once a 'Roustabout,' He Was Converted by His Father 27 Years Ago on Bowery," *New York Times*, April 10, 1933; Mel B, *New Wine: The Spiritual Roots of the Twelve Step Miracle* (Center City, MN: Hazelden, 1991), 52–54.

27. *"Pass It On": The Story of Bill Wilson and How the A.A. Message Reached the World* (New York: A.A. World Services, 1984), 120–21. Ernest Kurtz has also observed this similarity between Wilson's and Finney's conversions in *Not-God: A History of Alcoholics Anonymous* (Center City, MN.: Hazelden, 1991), 183.

1. The Drunkard's Conversion and the Salvation of the Social Order

1. Helen Stuart Campbell, *The Problem of the Poor: A Record of Quiet Work in Unquiet Places* (New York: Fords, Howard & Hulbert, 1882), 13.

2. R. M. Offord, ed., *Jerry McAuley: An Apostle to the Lost* (New York: American Tract Society, 1907), 140.

3. Quoted in Samuel Hopkins Hadley, *Down in Water Street: A Story of Sixteen Years Life and Work in Water Street Mission* (New York: Fleming H. Revell, 1902), 76.

4. Gerald Peters, *The Mutilating God: Authorship and Authority in the Narrative of Conversion* (Amherst: University of Massachusetts Press, 1993), 9; Glenn Hendler, *Public Sentiments: Structures of Feeling in Nineteenth-Century American Literature* (Chapel Hill: University of North Carolina Press, 2001), 29–52; John Rumbarger, "The 'Story'

of Bill W: Ideology, Culture, and the Discovery of the Modern American Alcoholic," *Contemporary Drug Problems* 20 (1993): 759–82.

5. See, for example, the claim that "the realist vision of the urban underworld involves a disciplinary relation between seeing (seeing and being seen) and the exercising of power. The realist investment in seeing entails a policing of the real." Mark Seltzer, "Statistical Persons," review of Elaine Scarry, *The Body in Pain,* and Michael Fried, *Realism, Writing, Disfiguration, Diacritics* 17.3 (Autumn 1987): 85. This kind of critique is doubly easy to apply to the moralistic uses of realism adopted by reform writers such as those who publicized McAuley's story. For an example of how it has been applied to rescue mission writing, see my discussion of Robert Dowling's analysis of Helen Stuart Campbell in chapter 2.

6. The liberatory interpretation of religious conversion is most convincingly applied to narrators from unambiguously oppressed social groups; there is some danger of misappropriation in applying it to merely disreputable subjects who, despite ethnic and class bias, could through their redemptions claim the privileges of white manhood. (This is Glenn Hendler's interpretation of working-class drunkards' redemption narratives in the Washingtonian movement of the 1840s, for example.) Accordingly, it is important to recognize that the rescue missions were neither revolutionary in their implications nor highly controversial in their reception. The lasting significance of their intervention in the established social discourse was in their appropriations by other writers, and in their laying the foundations for popular therapeutic strategies of self-making, not in any revolutionary effect they had in their own time.

7. Amy Kaplan, *The Social Construction of American Realism* (Chicago: University of Chicago Press, 1988), 7.

8. Virginia L. Brereton, *From Sin to Salvation: Stories of Women's Conversions, 1800 to the Present* (Bloomington: Indiana University Press, 1991), 29.

9. This disciplinary/subversive dialectic has animated criticism of sentimental women's fiction since at least Nina Baym's 1978 study *Woman's Fiction: A Guide to Novels by and about Women in America, 1820–1870* (Ithaca: Cornell University Press). Elaine Frantz Parsons's *Manhood Lost: Fallen Drunkards and Redeeming Women in the Nineteenth-Century United States* (Baltimore: Johns Hopkins University Press, 2003) and Carol Mattingly's *Well-Tempered Women: Nineteenth-Century Temperance Rhetoric* (Carbondale: Southern Illinois University Press, 1998) are examples of temperance studies that recognize the movement's combination of class-inflected moral regulation and social empowerment for women.

10. On rescue missions as being among the responses to real and perceived social fragmentation attending America's period of urbanization, see Paul Boyer, *Urban Masses and Moral Order in America, 1820–1920* (Cambridge: Harvard University Press, 1992), 135. John Higham's seminal *Strangers in the Land: Patterns of American Nativism, 1860–1925* (New Brunswick, NJ: Rutgers University Press, 2002) documents the resurgence of nativism in this era, coinciding with new waves of European immigration. Relevant here are his chapters "Crisis in the Eighties" and "The Nationalist Nineties," which document widening social chasms in an age of economic depression and a concomitant rise in anti-Catholicism, anti-Semitism, and racial nationalism. Notably,

one of the leading nativist polemicists was Rev. Josiah Strong, a Congregational minister who was also an influential Social Gospel theologian. On his widely read *Our Country: Its Possible Future and Its Present Crisis* (1885), see Higham, *Strangers in the Land*, 39, 42, 76. Strong's influential combination of humane evangelical social theology with defensive ethnic supremacy suggests the challenge McAuley and other immigrant converts faced in winning genuine respect rather than condescension.

11. In the introduction to her book *Gender and the American Temperance Movement of the Nineteenth Century* (New York: Routledge, 2008), Holly Berkley Fletcher provides a helpful account of the historiography of the temperance movement, surveying the process by which its importance to culture, politics, and a wide range of social issues has come to be recognized (1–5).

12. The term "gospel temperance" was popularized by J. M. Van Buren in his 1877 book of that title. As such, it referred to the Christian case for lifelong abstinence, not to a method of reform for drunkards. For definitions of gospel temperance as a historical movement centered on the style of conversion testimony discussed here, see Katherine Chavigny, "American Confessions: Reformed Drunkards and the Origins of Therapeutic Culture" (PhD diss., University of Chicago, 1999), 151–53; and Jared C. Lobdell, *This Strange Illness: Alcoholism and Bill W.* (New York: Aldine de Gruyter, 2004), 42.

13. Scholars examining A.A. have often concluded that its practices of mutual emotional support, semi-communal storytelling, social integration, and mentorship are beneficial and often hard for alcoholics to find elsewhere. See, e.g., George Vaillant, *The Natural History of Alcoholism, Revisited* (Cambridge: Harvard University Press, 1995), 254–69.

14. Helen Stuart Campbell's book *The Problem of the Poor* (1882) is a topic of the next chapter; William James's and other psychologists' uses of the Water Street drunkards' conversions as evidence of religion's material effects occurred between 1896 and 1902 and are explored in chapter 3. And the progressive journalist Ray Stannard Baker made the contemporary Water Street mission a leading example of Christian social work in his 1910 book investigating the state of American religion, *The Spiritual Unrest* (New York: Frederick A. Stokes, 1910).

15. The centrality of stepwise decline to temperance narrative can be seen in broadsides, books, and illustrations from throughout the nineteenth century in the Library of Congress's temperance collection. See also Elaine Parsons's definition of the drunkard narrative in *Manhood Lost*, 3–4.

16. Sarah W. Tracy, *Alcoholism in America: From Reconstruction to Prohibition* (Baltimore: Johns Hopkins University Press, 2005), 79. Early proponents of the medical understanding of the symptoms of alcoholism also tended to strongly endorse the religious cure, including Benjamin Rush (see the introduction); F. Baldwin Morris, M.D., in *The Panorama of a Life . . . A Treatise for the Cure of Opium and Alcoholic Inebriacy* (1878); and H. M. Bannister, director of the Eastern Hospital for the Insane in the late nineteenth century. See William White, *Slaying the Dragon: The History of Addiction Treatment and Recovery in America* (Bloomington, IL: Chestnut Health Systems, 1998), 71, 76.

17. Parsons presents the stories of women invading drinking spaces and redeeming the masculinity corrupted there as the primary cultural response to the temperance-era drinker's decline story. Certainly this was a leading trope of the institutional temperance movement. And it is also true that drunkards' conversions sometimes draw on the sentimental redemptive power of a wife's loyalty and love. I argue, though, that the rescue mission narratives of personal religious transformation had a deeper and more lasting impact on the culture of addiction and its treatment than did confrontational temperance politics.

18. Katherine Chavigny traces drunkards' conversion testimony through these various institutions and their links in "American Confessions," 152–90. On the social and cultural dynamics surrounding the conversion of low-status drinkers in the New York City revival, see Kathryn T. Long, *The Revival of 1857–58: Interpreting an American Religious Awakening* (New York: Oxford University Press, 1998), 40–44. On the roots of Practical Christianity in American theology, and its flowering in various cultural forms in the late nineteenth century, see Gregory Jackson, *The Word and Its Witness: The Spiritualization of American Realism* (Chicago: University of Chicago Press, 2009), 56–61, 159–61.

19. George M. Marsden, *Fundamentalism and American Culture,* 2nd ed. (New York: Oxford University Press, 2006), 80–84.

20. Norris Magnuson, *Salvation in the Slums: Evangelical Social Work, 1865–1920* (Metuchen, NJ: Scarecrow Press and the American Theological Library Association, 1977), 12–13, 140, 93.

21. Chavigny's "American Confessions," as well as Arthur Bonner's *Jerry McAuley and His Mission* (Neptune, NJ: Loizeaux Bros., 1990), provide the most sustained historical attention to the gospel rescue missions. The movement also earns brief discussions in works on urban religion in the nineteenth century, such as Aaron I. Abell, *The Urban Impact on American Protestantism* (1943; Hamden, CT: Archon, 1962), 95, 138; Magnuson, *Salvation in the Slums;* and Marsden, *Fundamentalism.* Probably its most influential contemporary treatment has been as a model for Marvin Olasky's polemical theory of pre–welfare state social provision, which itself was an intellectual influence on George Bush's 2000 campaign theme of "compassionate conservatism." See Olasky, *The Tragedy of American Compassion* (Washington, DC: Regnery Gateway, 1992), 94.

22. Olasky, *Tragedy of American Compassion,* 93–94.

23. Baker, *Spiritual Unrest,* 150.

24. The skeptics included religious leaders as well as newspaper cynics. Rev. J. Willet, in *The Drunkard's Diseased Appetite* (1877), claimed conversion was only helping heavy drinkers, not true inebriates, and that lay missionaries in their zeal were confusing the two. Similarly, Rev. Charles Warren scoffed, "It is hard to believe that any man in such a state of voluntarily-induced imbecility, too drunk to hold intelligent converse with men, can be competent enough to transact business with God" (quoted in White, *Slaying the Dragon,* 78).

25. David Reynolds, "Black Cats and Delirium Tremens: Temperance and the American

Renaissance," in *The Serpent in the Cup: Temperance in American Literature,* ed. David S. Reynolds and Debra J. Rosenthal (Amherst: University of Massachusetts Press, 1997), 27, 30. The rescue mission literature strove to gain distance from what Reynolds identifies as the morally ambiguous mode of "dark reform" writing. Reynolds goes so far as to suggest that the disrepute of the Washingtonians helped cast doubt on the efficacy of all moral suasion, contributing to the growing belief in the reform movement that alcohol itself, not its drinkers, was the problem, and that prohibition was the only solution.

26. Bonner, *Jerry McAuley and His Mission,* 26–33.

27. Helen Stuart Campbell, *Darkness and Daylight; or, Lights and Shadows of New York Life: A Woman's Story of Gospel, Temperance, Mission and Rescue Work* (Hartford, CT: A. D. Worthington, 1892), 248–50.

28. Ibid., 59.

29. See, e.g., Bonner, *Jerry McAuley and His Mission,* 28; and Campbell, *Darkness and Daylight,* 236.

30. Campbell, *Darkness and Daylight,* 202.

31. Offord, *Jerry McAuley,* 29, 30; Hadley, *Down in Water Street,* 30. McAuley's "beefsteak" line was a favorite of both evangelical instruction pamphlets and turn-of-the-century domestic guides. See e.g., *Good Housekeeping,* October 1896, 167; and Laura B. Hibbard and Mary Alice Vaughan, *Home Cookery* (Laconia, NH: Laconia Press Association, 1904), 38.

32. In addition to the secular Washingtonian autobiographies of the 1840s, Methodist holiness missions produced at least two published drunkards' conversions in the 1870s: W. T. Cox's *Out of the Depths* (1876), and D. N. Tucker's *A Struggle for Life and Victory through the Lamb* (1879). For the context in which these conversions occurred, see Chavigny, "American Confessions," 190.

33. George Monteiro, *Stephen Crane's Blue Badge of Courage* (Baton Rouge: Louisiana State University Press, 2000), 97–98.

34. See, e.g., *The Outlook* 72.6 (11 October 1902): 374.

35. Offord, *Jerry McAuley,* 300.

36. The geography of Hadley's narrative remains a template for the middle-class addiction story and the way it plays against the American upward mobility narrative. Hadley's drinking takes him from a pious Ohio childhood to a Harlem saloon, a prison cell, and a waterfront rescue mission. Similarly, A.A. founder Bill Wilson's drinking biography involved passage from rural Vermont to New York City, and back and forth from saloons to upper-middle-class family settings, culminating in a fateful journey of vague intent to a downtown rescue mission. As we will see in chapter 8, today's upper- and middle-class drug addiction memoirs do much the same thing, drawing heavily for social drama on the addict's descent to places where he or she "doesn't belong."

37. Baker, *Spiritual Unrest,* 147.

38. Offord, *Jerry McAuley,* 135.

39. Ibid., 10.

40. Hadley, *Down in Water Street*, 76.

41. Ibid., 171–73.

42. These and other examples of temperance visual culture can be found under the Temperance heading at the Library of Congress's online Prints and Photographs Reading Room, www.loc.gov/rr/print/list/picamer/paTemper.html.

43. Baker, *Spiritual Unrest*, 150.

44. For an example of late gospel temperance visual narrative that conserves the more purely allegorical style, see G. E. Bula's 1908 "Gospel Temperance Railroad Map," available at http://hdl.loc.gov/loc.gmd/g9930.ct001880.

45. Campbell, *Problem of the Poor*, 13–14. As a writer who cut her teeth as a sentimental biographer in the mid-nineteenth century, it is not surprising that Campbell used physiognomy to stand for the fatalistic moral science that was so undermined by McAuley's life. But beyond that context, it is not especially useful to discuss the various theories of social determinism that were influential in the era, since the missionaries and converts themselves tended only to invoke them in a general way (in the manner of McAuley's eulogist), and in ways that were bound up with temperance fatalism about drinking, folk genetics, and Christian predestination. This last category was the most important one in which Christianity influenced addiction narrative; the conversions marked a decisive moment when evangelicalism's rejection of predestination helped to establish a universalist-therapeutic spiritual culture in the twentieth century.

46. Ibid., 21.

47. Campbell, *Problem of the Poor*, 64.

48. Charles G. Finney, *The Memoirs of Charles G. Finney: The Complete Restored Text*, ed. Garth M. Rosell and Richard A. G. Dupuis (Grand Rapids, MI: Academie Books, 1989), 26.

49. Hadley, *Down in Water Street*, 108.

50. Emma Whittemore, *Delia, Formerly the Bluebird of Mulberry Bend* (New York: Door of Hope Mission, 1893).

51. Offord, *Jerry McAuley*, 244. This programmatic imagery of social rehabilitation recalls Paul de Man's suggestion that autobiography, far from documenting a life already lived, may "produce and determine the life" and be "governed by the technical demands of self-portraiture and thus determined, in all its aspects, by the resources of his medium." De Man's reversal of the referential formula, where a reality brought into being by signification replaces the ideal of a perfectly referential language, simply evades the complexity of social communication and physical embodiment. But in the case of these before-and-after images, the reconstruction is so simple, and the goal of providing contrast with the "after" photographs so transparent, that the "before" sketches indeed seem constituted only by "the demands of self-portraiture." The fuller written narratives feature a similar structural simplicity, but their greater sociolinguistic density across the sequence of degradation, intervention, and regeneration allows for considerably more variation in social emphasis. See Paul De Man, "Autobiography as De-facement," *MLN* 94.5 (December 1979): 920.

52. Whittemore, *Delia,* frontispiece.

53. Campbell, *Problem of the Poor,* 14; Hadley, *Down in Water Street,* 42.

54. Campbell, *Darkness and Daylight,* 220, 237–45.

55. This dynamic of highly qualified multiculturalism compares to the kind of religious pluralism that emerged out of the Bible-in-schools debates of the nineteenth century, as interpreted by Tracy Fessenden in *Culture and Redemption: Religion, the Secular, and American Literature* (Princeton: Princeton University Press, 2007). Fessenden argues that a key function of the space of religious tolerance that emerged was to define hard boundaries that excluded intolerable religions and races.

56. Arguments for this kind of relationship between conversion and a static social order include Peters, *The Mutilating God,* 9–14; Charlotte Linde, *Life Stories: The Creation of Coherence* (New York: Oxford University Press, 1993), 16; and Peter G. Stromberg, *Language and Self-Transformation: A Study of the Christian Conversion Narrative* (Cambridge: Cambridge University Press, 1993), 15.

57. Samuel H. Hadley, "The Holy Spirit in His Relation to Rescue Work," in *The Holy Spirit in Life and Service,* ed. A. C. Dixon (New York: Fleming H. Revell, 1895), 116–19. The turn away from social work by evangelicals, which corresponded with the rise of fundamentalism as a reaction to "modernist" doctrine and its progressive politics, did not become decisive until the 1920s. See Marsden, *Fundamentalism,* 84. It was at this point that social work in the city became primarily associated with Catholic and mainline Protestant churches. In fact, some mainline churches undertook this work by adopting the rescue mission model itself, after it had been pioneered but to some extent abandoned by evangelicals. As I noted in the introduction, the rescue mission at which A.A. founder Bill Wilson declared himself "saved" in 1934 was operated by a staid Episcopalian church, but had recently been superintended by Samuel H. Hadley's son.

58. Baker, *Spiritual Unrest,* 152–53.

59. Bonner, *Jerry McAuley and His Mission,* 33. For more on "The Allen" and his tolerance for religion, see Luc Sante, *Low Life: Lures and Snares of Old New York* (New York: Macmillan, 2003), 182–83.

60. Offord, *Jerry McAuley,* 114, 116.

2. "What a Radical Found in Water Street"

1. R. M. Offord, ed., *Jerry McAuley: An Apostle to the Lost* (New York: American Tract Society, 1907), 164.

2. Emma Mott Whittemore, *Mother Whittemore's Records of Modern Miracles* (Toronto: Missions of Biblical Education, 1947), 8. The Whittemores' discovery of the missions is also recounted in Offord, *Jerry McAuley,* 242–44; and in Samuel H. Hadley, *Down in Water Street: A Story of Sixteen Years Life and Work in Water Street Mission* (New York: Fleming H. Revell, 1902), 43–44.

3. Offord, *Jerry McAuley,* 173–74.

4. Whittemore, *Mother Whittemore's Records,* 9.

5. John Daniel Walters, *History of the Kansas State Agricultural College* (Manhattan: Kansas State Agricultural College, 1909), 133–35.

6. Ross E. Paulson, "Helen Stuart Campbell," in *Notable American Women, 1607–1950: A Biographical Dictionary,* ed. Edward T. James (Cambridge: Harvard University Press, 1974), 280–81.

7. Ibid.

8. Helen Stuart Campbell, *The Problem of the Poor: A Record of Quiet Work in Unquiet Places* (New York: Fords, Howard & Hulbert, 1882), 7–8. In the following paragraphs page numbers will be cited parenthetically in the text.

9. Offord, *Jerry McAuley,* 140.

10. "Mrs. Herndon's Income," *Critic,* April 3, 1886, 164–65.

11. Helen Stuart Campbell, *Prisoners of Poverty: Women Wage-Workers, Their Trades and Their Lives* (Boston: Little, Brown, 1887), 80–81. *Prisoners of Poverty* was followed by a European study, *Prisoners of Poverty Abroad,* in 1889.

12. Campbell, *Prisoners,* 251, 255.

13. Ibid., 257.

14. Paulson, "Helen Stuart Campbell," 281.

15. For a detailed delineation of the deep historical roots and wide application of homiletic culture, see Gregory Jackson, *The Word and Its Witness: The Spiritualization of American Realism* (Chicago: University of Chicago Press, 2009).

16. Jackson, *The Word and Its Witness,* 157–58.

17. Charles M. Sheldon, *In His Steps: "What Would Jesus Do?"* (Chicago: Advance Publishing, 1897), 9–10.

18. Ibid., 68.

19. Ralph H. Gabriel, quoted in Ronald C. White and Charles H. Hopkins, *The Social Gospel: Religion and Reform in a Changing America* (Philadelphia: Temple University Press, 1976), 146.

20. Though it is widely assumed to be reactionary because of its subtitle's popularity as a catchphrase in contemporary evangelical circles, for four decades scholars who have given *In His Steps* close attention have recognized its decidedly progressive orientation. See, e.g., Charles H. Hopkins, *The Rise of the Social Gospel in American Protestantism, 1865–1915* (New Haven: Yale University Press, 1940), 144; Sydney E. Ahlstrom, *A Religious History of the American People* (New Haven: Yale University Press, 1972), 776–77; James H. Smylie, "Sheldon's *In His Steps:* Conscience and Discipleship," *Theology Today* 32.1 (April 1975): 32–45. Most recently and comprehensively, Gregory Jackson exhaustively contextualizes Sheldon's homiletic style and practical theology, concluding that the novel and its ilk "reenergized" Protestantism in ways that facilitated believers' participation in Progressive Era activism. Jackson, *The Word and Its Witness,* 213–14.

21. This reformist orientation mattered, in terms of the journeys that Social Gospel thinkers and their movements took in this era. For example, some leading figures of the Social Gospel moved quite fluidly from Sheldon's model of obligation into a more radical Christian Socialism. Consider, for example, George D. Herron's passage from his debut speech in 1890, "The Message of Jesus to Men of Wealth," to his 1895 lecture series titled *The Christian State: A Political Vision of Christ,* to his 1900 address to the Social Democratic Party, "Why I Am a Socialist." See Hopkins, *Rise of the Social*

Gospel, 185. Sheldon's novel represented a recognition that America's upper-middle and even mid-middle classes were, relatively speaking, wealthy, and had to confront their obligations accordingly. His was a rhetoric of duty that preceded the burgeoning ideological and stylistic divisions between evangelical and liberal, mainline and radical, Christianity, differences that would only later come to appear as definitive chasms.

22. Ray Stannard Baker, *The Spiritual Unrest* (New York: Frederick A. Stokes, 1910). The idea of "unrest" in Baker's usage refers to a failure of church life to respond to or give conceptual cohesion to the broad base of spiritual need in American society. For a discussion of this crisis as a topic of concern in Baker's era, see Rick Ostrander, *The Life of Prayer in a World of Science: Protestants, Prayer, and American Culture, 1870–1930* (New York: Oxford University Press, 2000), 58–67. More relevant to the larger concerns of this book, the concept of spiritual hunger, philosophical dissatisfaction, thirst for meaning, etc., has been a trope binding addiction recovery discourse to the analysis of western modernity since the rise of the drunkard's conversion in the early nineteenth century. This connection comes to the surface most decisively in William James's and Carl Jung's spiritual interpretations of addictions as modern conditions, for which religion is the only known cure (see chapters 3 and 4).

23. Baker, *Spiritual Unrest*, 93–99. In the following paragraphs page numbers will be cited parenthetically in the text.

24. For more on the Emmanuel Movement and its impact on alcoholism discourse and treatment, see Katherine McCarthy, "Early Alcoholism Treatment: The Emmanuel Movement and Richard Peabody," *Journal of Studies on Alcohol* 45 (1984): 59–73.

25. While Baker mined religious social work for sources of progressive energy, Rauschenbusch firmly located the roots of social religion in scripture and "primitive Christianity." But Rauschenbusch also observed the recent import of the reverse influence, pointing out that modern instances of transformative religion, whether progressive or not, had taken inspiration from secular revolutions of the nineteenth century. He cited as examples the influence of the Italian revolutionary Joseph Garibaldi's biography on revivalist Dwight L. Moody, and the labor movement's influence on social egalitarianism as informing the Welsh revival of 1904. Walter Rauschenbusch, *Christianity and the Social Crisis* (New York: Macmillan, 1907), 337. Baker agreed with his general argument that "there is not less of moral enthusiasm or spiritual activity in America, rather far more of it, but the church somehow has ceased to lead and inspire as it did in former times." Baker, *Spiritual Unrest*, 189.

26. Campbell's male contemporaries seem not to have appreciated her arguments about the close link between subjective self-concept and societal reform. In addition to Baker's and Rauschenbusch's apparent ignorance of her work, her former editor (and leading Social Gospelist) Benjamin Flower wrote that her work "skims over the surface of conditions, and though often very helpfully suggestive, she fails to strike at the root of economic evils" (quoted in Paulson, "Helen Stuart Campbell," 281).

27. Walter Rauschenbusch, *A Theology for the Social Gospel* (New York: Macmillan, 1922), 5.

28. Paul T. Phillips, *A Kingdom on Earth: Anglo-American Social Christianity, 1880–1940* (University Park: Penn State Press, 1996), 54.

29. Citations are to Jane Addams, "The Subjective Necessity for Social Settlements," in *Philanthropy and Social Progress,* ed. Henry C. Adams (New York: Thomas Y. Crowell, 1893), 1–26. See also Addams, *Twenty Years at Hull-House* (New York: Macmillan, 1911), 113–28. It is instructive to contrast the humanist conference in Plymouth, Massachusetts, at which Addams gave "Subjective Necessity" in 1892, and the Brooklyn "Holy Spirit" conference two years later at which Samuel H. Hadley rejected the division of the poor into worthy and unworthy. The two events reflect the early stages of what would become a more thorough division between secular and religious social work in the twentieth century. Social workers sought technocratic, professional legitimacy, while evangelical activists divided among theologically liberal reformers and anti-modern fundamentalists.

30. Addams, "Subjective Necessity," 19.

31. Ann Lane, *To Herland and Beyond: The Life and Works of Charlotte Perkins Gilman* (New York: Pantheon, 1990), 163.

32. See, e.g., "Books and Magazines," *New England Kitchen Magazine: A Domestic Science Monthly* 1.5 (July 1894): 307.

33. Robert W. Dimand, "Nineteenth-Century American Feminist Economics: From Caroline Dall to Charlotte Perkins Gilman," *American Economic Review* 90.2 (May 2000): 480–84.

34. Lane, *To Herland and Beyond,* 184.

35. Charlotte Perkins Gilman, "Human Nature," in *Charlotte Perkins Gilman: A Nonfiction Reader,* ed. Larry Ceplair (New York: Columbia University Press, 1991), 46.

36. Helen Stuart Campbell, *Household Economics: A Course of Lectures in the School of Economics in the University of Wisconsin* (New York: G. P. Putnam's Sons, 1897), 11. Lamarckian models of evolution were popular among Christian progressives, in part because they allowed for human choice in the evolutionary process and a lasting, genetic benefit to social change. Such theories would seem to fit especially well with the conversion model of personal change by confirming the sense that spiritual transformation affected every aspect of the individual's being and could pass down a spiritual legacy in the world. For an overview of various Christian positions on evolution, see Michael Ruse, *The Evolution Wars: A Guide to the Debates* (New Brunswick, NJ: Rutgers University Press, 2001), 105–14.

37. Charlotte Perkins Gilman, *Women and Economics: A Study of the Economic Relation between Men and Women as a Factor in Social Evolution* (Boston: Small, Maynard, 1898), 146, 150, 153, 294.

38. Kabi Hartman, "What Made Me a Suffragette: The New Woman and the New (?) Conversion Narrative," *Women's History Review* 12.1 (March 2003): 45.

39. See Ceplair in *Charlotte Perkins Gilman: A Nonfiction Reader,* 43, 85.

40. The panoptical-punitive interpretation of photographic realism in the slums has been influential since the early 1980s but has more recently been widely contested. For a discussion of this divergence around Riis's work, see Peter Bacon Hales, *Silver*

Cities: Photographing American Urbanization, 1839–1939 (Albuquerque: University of New Mexico Press, 2005), 274. Gregory Jackson's response to this interpretation of Riis and Campbell is especially helpful, drawing on a close study of the roots of Social Gospel narrative. The homiletic tradition of interpreting sensory experience spiritually stood "in explicit opposition to the increasingly secular and skeptical epistemology of modernity," Jackson writes. "Social Gospel audiences would have perceived the sensory encounter as springboards to transcendent knowledge and thus to spiritual enlightenment. . . . Riis's realism thus emerges as an aesthetic site that adjudicates the deeply contested threads of science, religion, psychology, and philosophy, allowing the seemingly sentimental plot to sit alongside the real and the transcendent to coexist with the empirically immanent." Jackson, *The Word and Its Witness,* 220.

41. Robert M. Dowling, *Slumming in New York: From the Waterfront to Mythic Harlem* (Urbana-Champaign: University of Illinois Press, 2008), 22. In Dowling's view Campbell represents a transitional, halfway point between melodramatic moralism and documentary realism in writing about the slums, in a style he terms "moral realism."

42. On the "bullying" interpretation of temperance, see Nicholas O. Warner, *Spirits of America: Intoxication in Nineteenth-Century American Literature* (Norman: University of Oklahoma Press, 1997), 13.

43. Helen Stuart Campbell, *Darkness and Daylight; or, Lights and Shadows of New York Life: A Woman's Story of Gospel, Temperance, Mission and Rescue Work* (Hartford, CT: A. D. Worthington, 1892). My analogy between Campbell's writing and Riis's work is partly inspired by Keith Gandal's reading of Riis's reportage and Stephen Crane's fiction in this era. Gandal argues that their forms of realism were less concerned with monitoring and controlling the poor than with working out a new, psychologically based morality among the middle class. The realists' subtle admiration for street toughs represented a stage in the middle-class embrace of phenomena such as self-esteem and the phasing out of more pious, Victorian notions of humble good character. Notably, this notion of personal confidence seems at odds with the dramatic self-sacrifice that Sheldon, Baker, and Rauschenbusch called for in their Social Gospel. But the model of personal transformation that Campbell and others drew from the missions developed in parallel with Gandal's notion of self-esteem. Keith Gandal, *The Virtues of the Vicious: Jacob Riis, Stephen Crane, and the Spectacle of the Slum* (New York: Oxford University Press, 1997).

44. Emma Mott Whittemore, "The Holy Spirit in His Relation to Rescue Work," in *The Holy Spirit in Life and Service,* ed. A. C. Dixon (New York: Fleming H. Revell, 1895), 119.

45. Anne Lamott, "My Mind Is a Bad Neighborhood I Try Not to Go into Alone," *Salon .com,* March 13, 1997, www.salon.com/1997/03/13/lamott970313/.

3. The Varieties of Conversion Polemic

1. On Wilson's conversion experience, see *"Pass It On": The Story of Bill Wilson and How the A.A. Message Reached the World* (New York: Alcoholics Anonymous World

Services, 1984), 120–21; on Sunday's, see William T. Ellis, *"Billy" Sunday: The Man and His Message* (Swarthmore, PA: L. T. Myers, 1914), 40–41.

2. William James, *The Varieties of Religious Experience: A Study in Human Nature* (New York: Longmans, Green, 1903), 268n. Well into the twentieth century, medicine, research, marketing, and culture were not often distinct categories in the temperance world. Consider this title: *The Alcohol, Tobacco, and Opium Habits: Their Effects on Body and Mind and the Means of Cure, with Temperance Songs and Hymns,* by Walter K. Fobes (1895). The real point of Fobes's combination of medicine and merriment was to pitch a cure-all named Re-Vi-Vo.

3. *"Pass It On,"* 124–25.

4. Gerald E. Meyers, *William James: His Life and Thought* (New Haven: Yale University Press, 2001), 462.

5. James wrote a preface for one such book by a former student: Edwin D. Starbuck, *The Psychology of Religion* (London: W. Scott Ltd., 1900). See also George B. Cutten, *The Psychology of Alcoholism* (New York: Scribner's, 1907), 277–317; and Harriet E. Monroe, *Twice-Born Men in America; or, The Psychology of Conversion as Seen by a Christian Psychologist in Rescue Mission Work* (Philadelphia: Lutheran Publication Society, 1914). For a discussion of these and some contrary opinions from the era, see William L. White, *Slaying the Dragon: The History of Addiction Treatment and Recovery in America* (Bloomington, IL: Chestnut Health Systems, 1998), 76–78.

6. *"Pass It On,"* 114, 381–86.

7. The legitimizing effect that began with this appeal to James still reverberates. Acceptance of the objective neutrality of conversion-based recovery culminated in passage of the Hughes Act in 1970, establishing federal funding for the A.A.-influenced treatment of alcoholism that had spread through private clinics. It was James and Jung and their roles conceptualizing the spiritual method of recovery that Bill Wilson called on in the congressional hearings leading up to the Hughes Act, rather than any aspect of alcoholism research that had taken place in the intervening half-century. See Ernest Kurtz, "Alcoholics Anonymous and the Disease Concept of Alcoholism," *Alcoholism Treatment Quarterly* 20 (2002): 5–39. This state endorsement persisted, in the willingness of courts to order alcohol offenders to attend A.A. meetings, in effect if not in letter.

8. Harold Begbie, *Twice-Born Men: A Clinic in Regeneration: A Footnote in Narrative to Professor William James's "'The Varieties of Religious Experience"* (1909; Cambridge, MD: Messengers of Hope, 1994), 217.

9. For a wider view of the history of "psychoreligious cooperation" in the twentieth century, see Stephanie Muravchik, *American Protestantism in the Age of Psychology* (New York: Cambridge University Press, 2011), 1–24. Muravchik interprets A.A. as among the most harmonious and productive legacies of this process.

10. The simple image of Wilson as grand synthesizer appears in Susan Cheever, *My Name Is Bill: Bill Wilson—His Life and the Creation of Alcoholics Anonymous* (New York: Simon & Schuster, 2005), 238. For a rigorous, scholarly antecedent to this interpretation, see the classic exposition of intellectual and religious synthesis in A.A.

in Ernest Kurtz, *Not-God: A History of Alcoholics Anonymous* (Center City, MN: Hazelden, 1991), 188–89. For a seminal deconstruction of James's role in the Wilson narratives, see Matthew J. Raphael, *Bill W. and Mr. Wilson: The Legend and Life of A.A.'s Cofounder* (Amherst: University of Massachusetts Press, 2000), 81–90.

11. William James, "The Scientific View of Temperance" (1881), in *Essays, Comments, and Reviews* (Cambridge: Harvard University Press, 1987), 19–21; Jared C. Lobdell, *This Strange Illness: Alcoholism and Bill W.* (New York: Aldine de Gruyter, 2004), 44.

12. Howard M. Feinstein, *Becoming William James* (Ithaca: Cornell University Press, 1999), 47, 57, 301, 305, 345.

13. Meyers, *William James*, 31.

14. William James, *The Principles of Psychology*, vol. 2 (New York: Henry Holt, 1905), 541.

15. Quoted in Feinstein, *Becoming William James*, 294n.

16. James, *Principles of Psychology*, 547, 565.

17. Feinstein, *Becoming William James*, 308–12.

18. In his twenties, James was increasingly troubled by knowledge of inherited mental instability in his family, seeing in his every ailment potential evidence of degeneration. Earlier, after Bob had gotten secretly engaged to a first cousin who also suffered from a nervous condition, William vociferously objected, on the grounds of their match bringing children into the world whom, he believed, would be doomed to suffer such a condition. Ibid., 304.

19. Robert D. Richardson, *William James: In the Maelstrom of American Modernism* (New York: Houghton Mifflin Harcourt, 2007), 119.

20. Feinstein, *Becoming William James*, 244; James, *Varieties*, 161.

21. William James to Thomas W. Ward, March 1869, quoted in Feinstein, *Becoming William James*, 306.

22. Feinstein argues that James's narration of his own crisis both echoed and distinguished itself in significant ways from the one that had led to his father's spiritual conversion (and relief from an alcohol habit) a generation earlier. During this time Henry Sr., who had shepherded William into pursuing a scientific career, was indeed urging upon his son the example of transformative spiritual revelation as the only cure for a crisis of self-belief and the related problem of material determinism in philosophy. William's ultimate liberation from his condition was, if not a decisively spiritual experience, shaped by the intellectualized model of religious conversion his father advocated. See Feinstein, *Becoming William James*, 245.

23. James, *Varieties*, 65.

24. William James, *Writings, 1878–1899* (New York: Library of America, 1992), 756–57. This tension between habit-management and conversion in James's thought, and his conscious effort to resolve it, illustrate helpfully a too-rarely observed distinction in the history of the American self, between rational self-improvement and spiritual regeneration. Often taken to have blended inseparably in Protestant individualism, they just as often stand apart or in uneasy tension (no more so than in A.A.). Famous self-improvers from Ben Franklin to Jay Gatsby admitted of no divine inspiration, while the great revivalists held self-directed change to be a dangerous and ultimately

fruitless process, absent the unwilled touch of God's grace as felt in the emotional upheaval of conversion.

25. David A. Hollinger makes a similar but broader point in " 'Damned for God's Glory': William James and the Scientific Vindication of Protestant Culture," in *William James and a Science of Religions: Reexperiencing "The Varieties of Religious Experience,"* ed. Wayne Proudfoot (New York: Columbia University Press, 2004), 9–30.

26. James, *Varieties,* 268.

27. James may not have invented the study of religious psychology, but he seems to have inspired its coalescence into a field. In 1904, James's former students G. Stanley Hall and Edwin D. Starbuck joined Leuba, George A. Coe, and two others in founding *The American Journal of Religious Psychology and Education* from Hall's base at Clark University. It lasted until 1915. At least six different authors produced books with the exact title, "The Psychology of Religion" between 1897 and 1929. The first of them, by Starbuck, was a dissertation produced under James's direction, and a source of evidence in *Varieties.* Another was by Coe (Chicago: University of Chicago Press, 1916), whose earlier work James also had cited in *Varieties* (240–41). Dozens of other psychologists, pastors, theologians, and popular writers also wrote on this topic, many of them more openly performing religious apologetics than did James. See, e.g., Oscar S. Kriebel, *Conversion and Religious Experience* (Pennsburg, PA.: Oscar S. Kriebel, 1907).

28. James H. Leuba, "Studies in the Psychology of Religious Phenomena," *American Journal of Psychology* 7 (1896): 309–85, 372.

29. James, *Varieties,* 157–60, 160–62, 201–3; Feinstein, *Becoming William James,* 242.

30. James, *Varieties,* 268.

31. Martin E. Marty, "The Varieties of Contexts for Reappraising *The Varieties. . . ,"* *Journal of Consciousness Studies* 9 (2002): 142.

32. One mainline reviewer was heartened by James's "powerful defense against materialism," but troubled by his focus on "extreme" and "abnormal" experience. *Lutheran Church Review* 22 (1903): 200–201. A Scottish churchman credited James with "vindicat[ing] the right of Religion to be recognized as an ineradicable constituent element in human nature," but chastised him for "contemptuously" disregarding theology and for failing to differentiate the emotional and intellectual Christian traditions. Robert Forgan, "*The Varieties of Religious Experience,* Professor William James: Some Critical Notes from the Christian Standpoint," *Expository Times* 14 (1903): 566. Even the anonymous reviewer for James's own alumni magazine, while welcoming the book's brilliance as a boon to Harvard's reputation, was troubled by James's cavalier treatment of "beliefs and institutions" in favor of "exaggerations and perversions," and speculated that James's intent may have been to shock. "James's 'Varieties of Religious Experience,' " *Harvard Graduates' Magazine* 11 (1903): 194–98. This critique of James remained conventional among pro-religion writers who advocated more rational forms of "conversion." See, e.g., Frederick Morgan Davenport, *Primitive Traits in Religious Revivals: A Study in Mental and Social Evolution* (New York: Macmillan, 1905), 280.

33. A Quaker writer welcomed James's respect for the life of George Fox and the Society of Friends he founded, basking in the praise of "a careful and cool professor of psychology in Harvard University." *The Friend* 77 (1904): 110. Another anonymous writer interpreted *Varieties* as helping to prove theism, with an authority flowing from the image of James "as the cool philosophical observer . . . noting phenomena as the scientist sees them." "The Art of Prayer," *New Outlook* 83 (1906): 858. Another mainline outlet credited *Varieties* with "clear[ing] by its inductive study and statement in terms of psychology many difficulties of thought." *Congregationalist Christian World* 89 (July 23, 1904): 113. See also Kriebel, *Conversion and Religious Experience*, 4, on the "most helpful and suggestive" role of James and others in advancing the intellectual cause of religion.

34. W. T. Stead, "The Revival in the West and the New National Free Church," *Review of Reviews* 31 (1905): 85–86.

35. Philip Vivian, *The Churches and Modern Thought* (London: Watts, 1906), 266.

36. Stead, "Revival in the West," 86.

37. Begbie, *Twice-Born Men*, 15–18.

38. As in studies of vice and poverty in New York, in studies of London's poor the empirical analysis was rising in epistemological stature over the moral reform polemic, though their styles and purposes were still intertwined.

39. Begbie, *Twice-Born Men*, 28. In the following paragraphs page numbers will be cited parenthetically in the text.

40. The "slum angel" was prominent in the gender typology of Salvation Army literature in Britain and America. See Diane Winston, "Living in the Material World: Salvation Army Lassies and Urban Commercial Culture, 1880–1918," in *Faith in the Market: Religion and the Rise of Urban Commercial Culture*, ed. John M. Giggie and Diane Winston (New Brunswick, NJ: Rutgers University Press, 2002), 13–36. Begbie's angel was identified as Kate Lee and her career memorialized two decades later in Minnie L. Carpenter, *The Angel-Adjutant of Twice-Born Men* (New York: Fleming H. Revell, 1922).

41. Begbie's transparent condescension brings to the surface the class connotation of the word "decent" in James's approving reference to the Salvation Army in *Varieties*: "General Booth . . . considers that the vital step in saving outcasts consists in making them feel that some decent human being cares enough for them to take an interest in the question whether they are to rise or sink." James, *Varieties*, 203n.

42. One reviewer claimed that "Prof. William James has enthusiastically accepted the book as a 'footnote in narrative' to his own work." "Twice-Born Men," *American Review of Reviews* (1910): 384. I have found no independent documentation of any such endorsement by James.

43. The fact that the author badly misspelled Begbie's surname suggests *Twice-Born Men* was established in this role by reputation. F. T. Mayer-Oakes, "The Authority of Jesus and Its Meaning for the Modern Mind: A Study in the Psychology of Jesus," *American Journal of Religious Psychology and Education* 4.3 (July 1911): 209.

44. Harold Begbie, *Life-Changers: Narratives of a Recent Movement in the Spirit of Personal Religion* (London: Mills & Boon, 1923), 114.

45. Daniel Sack, *Moral Re-armament: The Reinventions of an American Religious Movement* (New York: Macmillan, 2009), 89–95.

46. *Alcoholics Anonymous: The Story of How More Than 100 Men Have Recovered from Alcoholism* (New York: Works Publishing, 1939).

47. Bill Pittman, *A.A.: The Way It Began* (Seattle: Glen Abbey Books, 1988), 193.

48. John W. Crowley, *The White Logic: Alcoholism and Gender in American Modernist Fiction* (Amherst: University of Massachusetts Press, 1994), 27–28.

49. The sailor's impressive physique also acts as a counterexample to London's claims throughout *The People of the Abyss* that Britain's urban poor were physiologically stunted as a result of genetic degeneration brought on by the urban environment.

50. Jack London, *People of the Abyss* (New York: Macmillan, 1904), 39. In the following paragraph page numbers will be cited parenthetically in the text.

51. See Jeanne Campbell Reesman, *Jack London's Racial Lives: A Critical Biography* (Athens: University of Georgia Press, 2009), 239–42; and Crowley, *White Logic*, 20.

52. Jack London, *Martin Eden* (New York: Review of Reviews Co., 1909), 47–48. The proper foil for this kind of story is less rescue mission conversion narrative than it is the related genre of the drunkard reformed by a good woman. One example is Owen Kildare, *My Mamie Rose: The Story of My Regeneration* (1903), in which a hard-drinking Bowery rowdy transforms, conversion-style, through the love of a good-hearted young schoolteacher. In *Such a Woman* (1911), Kildare wrote a rescue mission novel that echoed the life of Jerry McAuley's widow, Maria, in which a hard-drinking Irishwoman, once redeemed, wins the heart of the upper-class Protestant missionary.

53. London, *Martin Eden*, 158–59. In this and the following paragraph page numbers will be cited parenthetically in the text.

54. Pete Hamill, "Jack London and John Barleycorn," in Jack London, *John Barleycorn* (New York: Modern Library, 2001), xxv. The quotation at the beginning of the paragraph is from the back cover of this edition.

55. John Sutherland, introduction to *John Barleycorn: Alcoholic Memoirs*, by Jack London (New York: Oxford University Press, 2009), xi.

56. Ibid., xiii.

57. London, *John Barleycorn*, 200; this and all subsequent page references are to the 2001 Modern Library edition. Despite this hostility to redemption narrative, in his endorsement of Upton Sinclair's *The Jungle* London implied a belief in an alternative form of evangelical awakening, when he promised it will "wake thousands of converts to our cause." See chapter 5.

58. Ibid., 208–9.

59. Crowley, *White Logic*, 40.

60. See critiques of James's anglo-Protestant definition of "religious experience" by Charles Taylor, *Varieties of Religion Today: William James Revisited* (Cambridge: Harvard University Press, 2002), 9–15, 22–29, and Hollinger, "'Damned for God's Glory,'" 10–11.

61. James, *Varieties*, 6; Leuba, "Psychology of Religious Phenomena," 371.

62. Leuba, "Psychology of Religious Phenomena," 310. James elsewhere was less dismissive

of the social reproduction of culture, though he was fairly consistent in his view that it was a second-order reflection of singular innovations. He argued that the majority of temperamental and affective tendencies, notably those that distinguished Americans from people of other nations, were the result of "mimicry." Unlike the theorists of "imitative impulse" he invoked, he preserved an important place for originality. "Invention and imitation, taken together, form, one may say, the entire warp and woof of human life, in so far as it is social," he told students. James, *Writings, 1878–1899*, 832.

63. James, *Varieties*, 201, 203.

64. Samuel Hopkins Hadley, *Down in Water Street: A Story of Sixteen Years Life and Work in Water Street Mission* (New York: Fleming H. Revell, 1902), 76.

65. James, *Varieties*, 267.

66. Ibid., 387.

67. Nicholas O. Warner, *The Spirits of America: Intoxication in Nineteenth-Century American Literature* (Norman: University of Oklahoma Press, 1997), 26.

68. This uncertain conceptualization of outer expressions versus inner states in *Varieties* has not gone unnoticed. Wayne Proudfoot argues that James's pragmatism can be seen in germinal form in *Varieties*, growing through his attempt to understand religion, in "Pragmatism and an 'Unseen Order' in *Varieties*," in Proudfoot, *William James and a Science of Religions*, 2–3, 34–35. Richard Rorty, in his stern brand of neo-pragmatism, sees James's attention to subjective, inner experience in *Varieties* as an embarrassing detour from the main line of the pragmatic tradition, which, in Rorty's view, leads inexorably to linguistic habits. Rorty, "Some Inconsistencies in James's *Varieties*," in Proudfoot, *William James and a Science of Religions*, 86–90.

69. Jeremy Carrette, "The Return to James: Psychology, Religion and the Amnesia of Neuroscience," in *The Varieties of Religious Experience*, Centenary Edition (London: Routledge, 2002), xxxix–li. In a similar defense of James's contemporary relevance, the philosopher of religion Charles Taylor argues, in *Varieties of Religion Today*, that despite all the limitations flowing from James's narrow anglo-Protestant view of religion, his attempt to fuse it with science still represents a deeply nuanced and enlightening engagement with the conditions defining modernity.

70. James, *Varieties*, 425.

71. Begbie, *Life Changers*, 114; William T. Stead, *If Christ Came to Chicago!* (London: Review of Reviews Co., 1894), 328–29.

72. James, *Writings, 1878–1899*, 880.

4. New Deal Individualism and the Big Book of Alcoholics Anonymous

1. A.A.'s success in shaping the culture of treatment and mutual aid is one of the factors that make its impact hard to measure. A.A.'s role is difficult to isolate from other causes and effects, including social factors, clinical treatment, and what some researchers point to as addiction's natural tendency to peter out with age. For a concise discussion of these problems, see Keith Humphreys, *Circles of Recovery: Self-Help Organizations for Addictions* (Cambridge: Cambridge University Press,

2004), 109–25. The most recent research suggests that A.A. does offer most alcoholics a better chance at recovery, specifically by providing alternative social outlets. John F. Kelly, Bettina Hoeppner, Robert L. Stout, and Maria Pagano, "Determining the Relative Importance of the Mechanisms of Behavior Change within Alcoholics Anonymous: A Multiple Mediator Analysis," *Addiction* 107.2 (2012), 289–99.

2. On the absence of a post-temperance definition of alcohol's harm, see Mark E. Lender and James K. Martin, *Drinking in America: A History* (New York: Simon & Schuster, 1987), 182–93. On A.A. and the disease model, see Ernest Kurtz, "Alcoholics Anonymous and the Disease Concept of Alcoholism," *Alcoholism Treatment Quarterly* 20 (2002): 5–39. On A.A. and neo-orthodox religion, see Ernest Kurtz, *Not-God: A History of Alcoholics Anonymous* (Center City, MN: Hazelden, 1991), 180–98.

3. Robin Room describes this relationship between A.A. and popular storytelling as a generational narrative in "Alcoholism and Alcoholics Anonymous in U.S. Films, 1945–1962: The Party Ends for the Wet Generations," *Journal of Studies on Alcohol* 50 (1989): 368–83.

4. Will Rogers, "Bacon, Beans, and Limousines" (President's Organization on Unemployment Relief radio broadcast, October 18, 1931), in *Radio Broadcasts of Will Rogers*, ed. Steven K. Gragert (Stillwater: Oklahoma State University Press, 1983), 67.

5. Franklin Delano Roosevelt, "The Forgotten Man" (radio address, Albany, NY, April 7, 1932), in *The Essential Franklin Delano Roosevelt* (New York: Random House, 1995), 13–16.

6. The works of several scholars have informed my conception of A.A. narrative as a transformation of individualism from one form to another. In a study of recovery structures in various types of literature, *Sobering Tales: Narratives of Alcoholism and Recovery* (Amherst: University of Mass Press, 1997), Edmund O'Reilly draws on Gregory Bateson's "ecology of mind" philosophy to argue that A.A.'s "surrender" theology provides a way out of dualistic Western thought and into a "complementary" model of self and world. George H. Jensen describes the performance of A.A. narrative as the ritual transformation of the drinking self into the sober self, in *Storytelling in Alcoholics Anonymous: A Rhetorical Analysis* (Carbondale: Southern Illinois University Press, 2000), 114–15. Mariana Valverde's approach to alcoholism in *Diseases of the Will: Alcohol and the Dilemmas of Freedom* (New York: Cambridge University Press, 1998) is especially useful. Valverde approaches alcoholism as a series of historically constructed relationships between legal and social authorities and conceptions of self. Trysh Travis describes A.A.'s mode of self-surrender as "alcoholic equalitarianism," a stance that collapses competitive individualism in favor of compassionate sympathy for human imperfection. Travis, *The Language of the Heart: A Cultural History of the Recovery Movement from Alcoholics Anonymous to Oprah Winfrey* (Chapel Hill: University of North Carolina Press, 2009), 63–74. Scholars of religion have extended the observations of early clerical supporters of A.A. by interpreting this function theologically. See Ernest Kurtz and Katherine Ketcham, *The Spirituality of Imperfection: Storytelling and the Search for Meaning* (New York: Bantam, 1992); and Linda A. Mercadante, *Victims*

and Sinners: Spiritual Roots of Addiction and Recovery (Louisville: Westminster John Knox Press, 1996).

Assessments of implicit political ideology in A.A. cluster in two nodes: in one, left-oriented critics are confident that from its origins A.A. has expressed reactionary individualism, a service to capitalism that was consummated in the proliferation of twelve-step fellowships during the Reagan era. See John Rumbarger, "The 'Story' of Bill W: Ideology, Culture, and the Discovery of the Modern American Alcoholic," *Contemporary Drug Problems* 20 (1993): 759–82; and Craig Reinarman, "The Twelve-Step Movement and Capitalist Culture," in *Cultural Politics and Social Movements,* ed. Marcy Darnovksy, Barbara Epstein, and Richard Flacks (Philadelphia: Temple University Press, 1995), 90–109. Historians and critics who attend more closely to the Depression context and grassroots mutual-aid aspects of A.A.'s origins tend to identify it as a dramatically democratic development in American civic life, but are less certain about how it informs specific modes of cultural politics. Ernest Kurtz was among the first to align A.A. with the New Deal when he compared it to other "practical unions" that responded to the Depression, in labor organization, the Civilian Conservation Corps, the veterans' bonus march, and the retirement pension movement. Kurtz, *Not-God,* 162. Andrew and Thomas Delbanco's 1995 essay on the origins and prospects of A.A. similarly put it into conversation with New Deal policy, describing its combination of mutual dependence and personal responsibility as analogous to the public provision of labor under the Works Progress Administration. "A.A. at the Crossroads," *New Yorker,* March 20, 1995, 50–63. Stephanie Muravchik has argued more generally that A.A. practices promote social and civic connection as opposed to individual atomization, and democratic equality rather than social hierarchy. Of interest to my argument, she quotes a 1945 letter to Bill Wilson from Jesuit priest Edward Dowling, an intimate spiritual adviser to Wilson and an early theological interpreter of A.A., asserting that "A.A. has proved that democracy is a therapy," whereas "the monarchic and aristocratic principles never cured alcoholism." Muravchik, *American Protestantism in the Age of Psychology* (New York: Cambridge University Press, 2011), 81–82, 110–11. Surveying this variety of interpretations, Matthew J. Raphael concludes that twelve-step recovery has no inherent politics, but as a mode of personal reconstruction can facilitate participation in wider movements. He also points out that descriptions of A.A. as reactionary have often taken aim at spin-off movements that put disease-concept language in the service of "pop-psychological determinism" in a manner unrecognizable to A.A. Raphael, *Bill W. and Mr. Wilson: The Legend and Life of A.A.'s Cofounder* (Amherst: University of Massachusetts Press, 2000), 55–64.

7. Repeal was not only an early source of tax revenue for New Deal programming, but offered a preview of the Roosevelt Administration's focus on promoting consumption as a means to national economic health. Lender and Martin, *Drinking in America,* 172.

8. Martin Rubin provides a helpful overview of this pattern of thought in the 1920s and 1930s, especially as a context for new forms of cultural expression, in "The Crowd, the Collective, and the Chorus: Busby Berkeley and the New Deal," in *Movies and Mass Culture,* ed. John Belton (New Brunswick, NJ: Rutgers University Press, 1996), 65–69, 82–83.

9. John Dewey, *Individualism Old and New* (New York: Minton, Balch, 1930), 20, 109.

10. John Dewey, *Liberalism and Social Action* (New York: G. P. Putnam's Sons, 1935), 58.

11. Alan Brinkley, *The End of Reform: New Deal Liberalism in Recession and War* (New York: Alfred A. Knopf, 1995), 5–6.

12. On the New Deal's ideological inconsistencies versus its emergent model of state, see Alan Brinkley, "The New Deal and the Idea of the State," in *The Rise and Fall of the New Deal Order, 1930–1980*, ed. Steve Fraser and Gary Gerstle (Princeton: Princeton University Press, 1990), 85–86; and Daniel T. Rodgers, *Atlantic Crossings: Social Politics in a Progressive Age* (Cambridge: Harvard University Press, 1998), 409–12. On the subsequent difficulty of linking cultural formations to New Deal liberalism, see the very helpful discussion in Michael Szalay, *New Deal Modernism: American Literature and the Invention of the Welfare State* (Durham: Duke University Press), 2–21.

13. Historians do speak of Roosevelt's "theory of history" as a key intellectual component of the New Deal, in which the nation's freewheeling growth period must give way to one of stable maturity. David M. Kennedy, *Freedom from Fear: The American People in Depression and War, 1929–1945* (New York: Oxford University Press, 1999), 375.

14. Franklin D. Roosevelt, "First Inaugural Address, March 4, 1933," in *The Essential Franklin Delano Roosevelt*, 32; *Alcoholics Anonymous: The Story of How More Than 100 Men Have Recovered from Alcoholism* (New York: Works Publishing, 1939), 74.

15. Thurman Arnold, *The Symbols of Government* (New York: Harcourt, Brace & World, 1962), 123–26.

16. Arthur M. Schlesinger Jr., "The Broad Accomplishments of the New Deal," in *Saving American Capitalism*, ed. Seymour Harris (New York: Alfred A. Knopf, 1948), 78.

17. Kennedy, *Freedom from Fear*, 188, 273.

18. Susan Cheever, *My Name Is Bill: Bill Wilson—His Life and the Creation of Alcoholics Anonymous* (New York: Simon & Schuster, 2005), 110; *Dr. Bob and the Good Oldtimers: A Biography, with Recollections of Early A.A. in the Midwest* (New York: Alcoholics Anonymous World Services), 40.

19. Robert Thomsen, *Bill W.: The Absorbing and Deeply Moving Story of Bill Wilson, Co-Founder of Alcoholics Anonymous* (Center City, MN: Hazelden, 1975), 186. The fact that late in life Wilson testified before Congress as it considered federal funding for research and treatment suggests the extent that, whatever his libertarianism looked like, it came in the context of a broad liberal consensus about the legitimacy of the federal government's involvement in public health. Kurtz, "Alcoholics Anonymous and the Disease Concept," 34–35.

20. *Dr. Bob and the Good Oldtimers*, 127; Ruth M. McKenney, *Industrial Valley* (New York: Harcourt, Brace, 1939), 203.

21. David Lloyd and Paul Thomas, *Culture and the State* (New York: Routledge, 1998), 2–5, 156–60. This is similar to the theoretical approach taken by A.A.'s leftist critics, only I apply it with greater attention to the mode of individualism recovery narrative leaves behind and to the mutual-aid insights required to arrive at the new mode of self.

22. Dewey, *Liberalism and Social Action*, 61–62.

23. The works that more directly influenced the early A.A. are better characterized as

Christian inspiration and New Thought spirituality rather than psychological self-help, though the two categories overlap. A.A. historians have found reading lists on which certain titles reappear frequently, including James's *Varieties of Religious Experience,* James Allen's *As a Man Thinketh* (1902), A. J. Russell's Oxford Group conversion-reportage, *For Sinners Only* (1932), and Emmet Fox's spiritual-not-religious interpretation of the gospels, *The Sermon on the Mount* (1934). Bill Pittman, *The Roots of Alcoholics Anonymous* (Center City, MN: Hazelden, 1988), 192–97.

24. Dewey, *Liberalism and Social Action,* 53, 54.

25. The details of the A.A. story here and below are drawn from the A.A. publication *"Pass It On": The Story of Bill Wilson and How the A.A. Message Reached the World* (New York: A.A. World Services, 1984), and Kurtz, *Not-God.*

26. Garth Lean, *On the Tail of a Comet: The Life of Frank Buchman* (Colorado Springs: Helmers & Howard, 1988), 151.

27. Kurtz, *Not-God,* 44–45, 56–59, 77–81; *"Pass it On,"* 169–74; *Alcoholics Anonymous Comes of Age: A Brief History of A.A.* (New York: Alcoholics Anonymous World Services, 1957), 74–75.

28. Raphael, *Bill W. and Mr. Wilson,* 105.

29. Some interpret this problem of self-interest, as in the "prosperity gospel," as a contradiction that undermines the entire post-Christian self-help project. See, e.g., Micki McGee, *Self-Help, Inc.: Makeover Culture in American Life* (New York: Oxford University Press, 2005). I understand the eternal/earthly reward disjunction more broadly and sympathetically, as a practically inescapable tension in religious belief and as an animating dialectic of American culture.

30. On the history of the Big Book's construction, see Travis, *Language of the Heart,* 118–34; Kurtz, *Not-God,* 68–76; and *"Pass It On,"* 190–206.

31. Christopher Breu, *Hard-Boiled Masculinities* (Minneapolis: University of Minnesota Press, 2005), 2–3, 6–11.

32. Michael Tolkin, "1935, June 10: Bill Wilson Meets 'Doctor Bob,'" in *A New Literary History of America,* ed. Greil Marcus and Werner Sollors (Cambridge: Harvard University Press, 2009), 695–700.

33. *Alcoholics Anonymous,* 352–53. Throughout the remainder of this chapter, *Alcoholics Anonymous* will be cited by page number in the text.

34. In the explanatory chapters, Wilson concentrates his persuasive efforts on scientific objections, drawing heavily on James's argument that the dismissal of religion is a failure of empirical inquiry. Wilson's main arguments in "We Agnostics" for trying out religious belief are analogies to modern technologies that required "leaps of faith" by their inventors. *Alcoholics Anonymous,* 64. The narrator of "An Artist's Perspective" articulates another Jamesian indictment of skepticism, in what would become a standard A.A. rebuke of the alcoholic's attitude toward religion, as the intellectual error of "contempt prior to investigation." *Alcoholics Anonymous,* 380. The Big Book helped spread the twentieth-century misattribution of this phrase to Herbert Spencer, the nineteenth-century social and political theorist. Its true origin appears to be as a paraphrase of William Paley. Michael St. George, "The Survival of a Fitting Quotation," http://silkworth.net/fitquotation.pdf.

35. Thomsen, *Bill W.*, 213–14.

36. This stylistic effect lies just beneath the surface of A.A.'s custom of placing spiritual habit before ideational belief. As Slavoj Žižek has noted, A.A.'s saying "Fake it 'til you make it" echoes Blaise Pascal's dictum "Only kneel and pray, and you will believe." Žižek sees this injunction as an anti-intellectual mechanism of fundamentalist ideology, and he reads into it an extension of the Freudian theory of conversion as the relief of finally submitting obediently to the authority and security of a father. In Žižek's analysis, the mind's ceding of faith to the body relieves the tension of sustaining unverifiable ideas. Žižek's reductive psychoanalytic skepticism, however, forecloses a promising avenue into questions of mind and body. Mariana Valverde, for example, pursues this kind of phenomenon into a rich exploration of the role of "habit" in the thought of James, Dewey, and Eve Sedgwick. Valverde, *Diseases of the Will*, 41, 138–39.

37. A.A.'s historical literature identifies the final Big Book editor as Tom Uzell, a "member of the faculty at New York University," who cut as much as half of the original draft. *"Pass It On,"* 204. Trysh Travis provides more detail on Uzell's professional background in writing and theorizing popular psychological uplift. *Language of the Heart*, 131–35. For an account of the various emendations that were made between the first draft, the manuscript that was sent out, and the published first edition, see Raphael, *Bill W. and Mr. Wilson*, 120–22. Despite initial concerns about a commercial publication undermining meeting-based social identification, the Big Book itself became the heart of a burgeoning A.A. print culture through which the processes of identification and surrender evolved.

38. *"Pass It On,"* 161, 199.

39. Ibid., 226.

40. Sigmund Freud, *The Future of an Illusion*, trans. James Strachey (New York: Norton, 1961), 30.

41. Authenticating strategies were a staple of nineteenth-century conversion narratives, often in the inclusion of unverifiable, supernatural details that guaranteed the originality of the convert's experience, despite being part of an obviously infectious and imitative social movement. This is the problem James (invoking Jonathan Edwards) confronted when he argued in *The Varieties of Religious Experience* for a distinction between genuine spiritual experience and what he called "cant" or "second-hand" religion. See chapter 3.

42. Jack London, *John Barleycorn* (New York: Modern Library, 2001), 208.

43. Lori Rotskoff shows how the temperance depiction of women and children as victims of alcohol-maddened men gave way, in the A.A. era, to alcoholism as a marital problem for which wives were held equally responsible. Rotskoff, *Love on the Rocks: Men, Women, and Alcohol in Post–World War II America* (Chapel Hill: University of North Carolina Press, 2002).

44. *"Pass It On,"* 200.

45. One of the earliest examples of the A.A. tenets of firsthand witness and narrative identification used this very quality as its illustration. In Wilson's second visitation by

the Oxford Group, his old drinking partner Ebby Thacher returned, but with a man named Shep Cornell in tow. Cornell claimed also to have been an alcoholic, but Wilson barely believed him, judging him an effete "pantywaist" who might have had one too many cocktails at college. Wilson rehearses this unkindness as an example of his egotistical, judgmental drinking personality. But at the same time, the foundational role of the Ebby story in A.A.'s evangelical origins is predicated on the idea that Wilson had no doubts as to the manly authenticity of his old friend's drinking exploits, as compared to the educated tenderfoot Cornell's. Thomsen, *Bill W.*, 211–12. Another A.A. narrator turns a similar judgment on himself when he realizes upon hearing the stories of his A.A. evangelists that he had been an "amateur and a sissy" in his drinking compared to them. *Alcoholics Anonymous*, 372.

46. Brooks Atkinson, quoted in Harold Cantor, *Clifford Odets, Playwright-Poet* (Lanham, MD: Scarecrow Press, 2000), 94–95. Joseph Wood Krutch expressed similar bewilderment at Odets's "macabre" Marxist treatment of what should have been an ordinary middle-class home, without offering a suggestion of what drama such a home might in fact produce. "The Apocalypse of St. Clifford," *The Nation*, December 25, 1935, 752. For a summary of critical reaction to *Paradise Lost*, along with evidence of its "undercover popularity," see Harold Clurman, *The Fervent Years: The Group Theatre and the Thirties* (1945; New York: Da Capo, 1983), 166–67.

47. John Patrick Diggins, *Desire under Democracy: Eugene O'Neill's America* (Chicago: University of Chicago Press, 2007), 256.

48. Lewis Corey, *The Crisis of the Middle Class* (New York: Columbia University Press, 1994).

49. *"Pass It On,"* 200.

50. On interwar masculinity and the rise of self-help, see Michael Kimmel, *Manhood in America: A Cultural History* (New York: Oxford University Press, 2006), 127–35.

51. In an influential essay, Warren Susman takes the term "commitment," which had been used to describe artists' left-wing affiliations, and redeploys it as a means of describing a society-wide trend toward group-identification that preceded political ideology. Susman, "The Culture of the Thirties," in *Culture as History: The Transformation of American Society in the Twentieth Century* (New York: Pantheon, 1984), 150–83.

52. John Belton, "Re-Imagining American Communities: Hollywood, Hawks, and Ford in 1939," *MLN* 122.5 (December 2007): 1166–79.

53. For a concise account of the Alcoholism Movement, see William L. White, *Slaying the Dragon: The History of Addiction Treatment and Recovery in America* (Bloomington, IL: Chestnut Health Systems, 1998), 178–98, and "The Rebirth of the Disease Concept in the 20th Century," *Counselor* 1.2 (2000): 62–66. The "politics" of the Alcoholism Movement in the twentieth century have been identified in a number of realms, including professionalization, public policy, and gender. See, respectively, Joseph Gusfield, *Contested Meanings: The Construction of Alcohol Problems* (Madison: University of Wisconsin Press, 1996), 17–30; Ron Roizen, "How Does the Nation's 'Alcohol Problem' Change from Era to Era? Stalking the Social Logic of Problem-Definition Transformations since Repeal," in *Altering American Consciousness: The History of Alcohol and Drug Use in the United States, 1800–2000* (Amherst: University

of Massachusetts Press, 2004), 61–87; and Rotskoff, *Love on the Rocks*, 65–69. For further discussion, see chapter 8.

54. Kurtz, "Alcoholics Anonymous and the Disease Concept," 33–35.

55. Lean, *On the Tail of a Comet*, 154–55.

56. Daniel Sack, *Moral Re-armament: The Reinventions of an American Religious Movement* (New York: Macmillan, 2009), 89–90.

57. Reinhold Niebuhr, "Hitler and Buchman," *Christian Century*, October 7, 1936, 1315–16, reprinted in *Christianity and Power Politics* (New York: Scribner's, 1940), 160–65. The difficulty Buchman and his followers had in shaking off his Hitler comment was probably responsible for the movement's metamorphosis into the aggressively interventionist "Moral Re-armament" movement. In this guise it would become a thorn in the side of the labor movement through the 1950s, in its occasionally successful efforts to recruit and "change" union leaders into other-directed men, which in active disputes meant being sympathetic to the goals of management (see, e.g., "Words and Works," *Time Magazine*, October 5, 1953, 38).

58. The formula Roosevelt used famously in a 1932 speech—that the government must restrain private property, "not to destroy individualism but to protect it"—offers the simplest way of understanding A.A. as an instance of New Deal individualism. In the speech, Roosevelt attributed this insight to Thomas Jefferson, situating it at the nation's founding. Franklin D. Roosevelt, "Address to the Commonwealth Club of San Francisco, Sept. 23, 1932," in *Great Speeches* (Mineola, NY: Dover, 1999), 20. He included a modified version of it in the 1933 book *Looking Forward,* which arranged the new president's reformist writings into a kind of national biography. Roosevelt, *Looking Forward* (New York: John Day, 1933), 6.

59. Franklin D. Roosevelt, "Second Inaugural Address," in *The Essential Franklin Delano Roosevelt* (New York: Random House, 1995), 127; *Alcoholics Anonymous,* 72.

60. Roosevelt, "Second Inaugural," 129.

61. Franklin D. Roosevelt, "Remarks at Poughkeepsie, N.Y.," November 2, 1936, www.presidency.ucsb.edu/ws/index.php?pid=15220.

62. Brinkley, *The End of Reform,* 65–85. Brinkley shows that while key New Dealers seized upon stimulus as a recession-fighting tool in 1937, some economists had been arguing since the peak of industrial growth that a new set of cultural attitudes around desire and happiness would be needed to fuel a consumer economy.

63. See Lizabeth Cohen, *A Consumer's Republic: The Politics of Mass Consumption in Postwar America* (New York: Vintage, 2003).

64. Various movements have arisen both within and outside A.A. to resist this individualistic trend, from back-to-basics "primary purpose" meetings to Christian, feminist, and other of what Trysh Travis calls "post-twelve-step" recoveries. Travis, *Language of the Heart,* 6–7.

65. *Twelve Steps and Twelve Traditions* (New York: Alcoholics Anonymous Publishing, 1953).

66. Kurtz, *Not-God,* 74–75.

67. Ibid., 85–86.

68. *"Pass It On,"* 307–14.

69. Szalay, *New Deal Modernism,* 9, 129.

70. *Alcoholics Anonymous Comes of Age,* 224–25.

71. Cheever, *My Name Is Bill,* 175. Huxley's grandfather Thomas, a Hobbesian, had been one of Kropotkin's chief intellectual rivals (*Mutual Aid* was written in response to a Thomas Huxley essay), but Aldous Huxley's utopian thinking was much more in line with anarchism. Wilson, suffering from depression and hoping to achieve spiritual relief similar to his original breakthrough in 1934, later undertook a series of LSD experiments with scientists he met through Huxley, an influential advocate of hallucinogens in humanistic spiritual practice. Wilson connected LSD to recovery through his belief that acid temporarily suppresses the ego, thereby opening wider the channel for God's grace. *"Pass It On,"* 368–73.

72. Aldous Huxley, *Brave New World and Brave New World Revisited* (New York: Harper Collins, 2005), 7.

73. The pseudonymous anarchist Prolecat argues for Kropotkin's influence on A.A. in an unpublished essay provided to the author. A.A.'s critics also have compared the meeting-group to the radical cell. See, e.g., Charles Bufe, *Alcoholics Anonymous: Cult or Cure?* (Tucson: Sharp Press, 1998), 130.

74. See Trysh Travis's discussion of this culturally dominant ideal, its role in AA's theory of alcoholism, and AA's adaptation of religious "surrender" as the way out of it. Travis, *Language of the Heart,* 62–74.

5. Literary Realism and the Secularization of the Drunkard's Conversion

1. See, e.g., the Women's Christian Temperance Union's combination of sensationalism, medical science, and evangelism. Sarah W. Tracy, *Alcoholism in America: From Reconstruction to Prohibition* (Baltimore: Johns Hopkins University Press, 2005), 79.

2. David Reynolds, *Beneath the American Renaissance: The Subversive Imagination in the Age of Emerson and Melville* (Cambridge: Harvard University Press, 1988), 55–59; Philip Fisher, *Hard Facts: Setting and Form in the American Novel* (New York: Oxford University Press, 1987), 169–72.

3. Johnson Jones Hooper, *Adventures of Captain Simon Suggs, Late of the Tallapoosa Volunteers* (1845; Chapel Hill: University of North Carolina Press, 1969), 115.

4. R. M. Offord, ed., *Jerry McAuley: An Apostle to the Lost* (New York: American Tract Society, 1907), 30–31.

5. Mark Twain, *Adventures of Huckleberry Finn (Tom Sawyer's Comrade)* (New York: Charles L. Webster, 1885), 30–32.

6. The King had several literary precursors in the figure of the hypocritical temperance man. See David S. Reynolds, "Black Cats and Delirium Tremens: Temperance and the American Renaissance," in *The Serpent in the Cup: Temperance in American Literature,* ed. David S. Reynolds and Debra J. Rosenthal (Amherst: University of Massachusetts Press, 1997), 29.

7. Twain, *Adventures of Huckleberry Finn,* 167–69.

8. Stephen Crane, *"Maggie, a Girl of the Streets" and Other New York Writings* (New York: Modern Library, 2001), 14–15, 68–69.

9. Crane, *George's Mother,* ibid., 110–11, 127.

10. For a sustained exploration of temperance themes in Crane's life and works, see George Monteiro, *Stephen Crane's Blue Badge of Courage* (Baton Rouge: Louisiana State University Press, 2000).

11. Harold Frederic, *The Damnation of Theron Ware* (Chicago: Herbert Stone, 1900), 342–51.

12. Offord, *Jerry McAuley,* 140.

13. Vachel Lindsay, *General William Booth Enters into Heaven and Other Poems* (New York: Macmillan, 1913), 47, 55.

14. On Lindsay's religion and religious voice, see Ann Massa, *Vachel Lindsay: Fieldworker for the American Dream* (Bloomington: Indiana University Press, 1970), 49–50. George D. Herron's Kingdom movement of the 1890s was a significant precursor to Sinclair's and Lindsay's styles, insofar as Herron merged a Populist rhetoric of discontent into Social Gospel and then Socialist ideas. See Ronald C. White and Charles W. Hopkins, *The Social Gospel: Religion and Reform in Changing America* (Philadelphia: Temple University Press, 1976), 147–56.

15. Jack London, "What Jack London Says of *The Jungle,*" *Chicago Socialist* 6.351 (November 25, 1905): 2, reprinted in Upton Sinclair, *The Jungle* (Norton Critical Edition), ed. Clare Virginia Eby (New York: Norton, 2003), 483–84.

16. On his socialist conversion and his description of *The Jungle,* see Upton Sinclair, "What Life Means to Me," *Cosmopolitan* 44 (October 1906): 591–95, reprinted in Sinclair, *The Jungle* (Norton Critical Edition), 349–50; Michael Brewster Folsom, "Upton Sinclair's Escape from *The Jungle:* The Narrative Strategy and Suppressed Conclusion of America's First Proletarian Novel," *Prospects* 4 (1979): 244.

17. Edward C. Marsh, "The Jungle," *Bookman* 23 (April 1906): 195–97; and Winston S. Churchill, "The Chicago Scandals: The Novel Which Is Making History," *P.T.O.,* June 23, 1905, 66, in Sinclair, *The Jungle* (Norton Critical Edition), 487, 489.

18. Folsom, "Upton Sinclair's Escape from *The Jungle,*" 256. Walter Rideout provides a midcentury exception to this judgment, in *The Radical Novel in the United States, 1900–1954* (Cambridge: Harvard University Press, 1956), 34–35. On the prevalence of the "failed masterpiece" judgment of realist novels by mid-twentieth-century critics, see Amy Kaplan's introduction to her seminal *The Social Construction of American Realism* (Chicago: University of Chicago Press, 1992), 5.

19. John Graham, ed., *"Yours for the Revolution": "The Appeal to Reason," 1895–1922* (Lincoln: University of Nebraska Press, 1990), 177, 183–86, 196–97, 208–17.

20. Sinclair, *The Jungle* (Norton Critical Edition), 81, 234, 242–51, 267. In the following paragraphs page numbers will be cited parenthetically in the text.

21. Sinclair's depiction of the rescue mission echoes London's critique of the Salvation Army in *People of the Abyss,* which was preceded by a similar scene in Stephen Crane's *Maggie,* and in arguments by Protestant reformers such as Thomas Dixon Jr. in his 1896 best-seller, *The Failure of Protestantism in New York and Its Causes.* See

John M. Giggie and Diane Winston, "Hidden in Plain Sight: Religion and Urban Commercial Culture in Modern North America," in *Faith in the Market: Religion and the Rise of Urban Commercial Culture,* ed. Giggie and Winston (New Brunswick, NJ: Rutgers University Press, 2002), 3.

22. William James, *The Varieties of Religious Experience: A Study in Human Nature* (New York: Longmans, Green, 1903), 196.

23. See, e.g., Folsom, "Upton Sinclair's Escape from *The Jungle,*" 248; and Christopher P. Wilson, *The Labor of Words: Literary Professionalism in the Progressive Era* (Athens: University of Georgia Press, 1985), 134.

24. Sinclair, "What Life Means to Me," 349–50; Upton Sinclair, *The Autobiography of Upton Sinclair* (New York: Harcourt, Brace, 1962), 113.

25. Horace Traubel, "*John Barleycorn,*" *Conservator* 25.1 (March 1914): 11–14.

26. Michael Denning, *The Cultural Front: The Laboring of American Culture in the Twentieth Century* (London: Verso, 1997), 249.

27. According to one source, the editor of the *Appeal* sent Sinclair on his legendary research trip to Chicago armed with a plot outline adapted from *Pilgrim's Progress;* see Gene DeGruson, introduction to *The Lost First Edition of Upton Sinclair's "The Jungle"* (Memphis: St. Lukes–Peachtree, 1988), xv. In his post-publication writings, Sinclair cited *Uncle Tom's Cabin,* another evangelical narrative whose characters became allegorical bywords, as his main influence. Sinclair, "What Life Means to Me," 350.

28. This middle-section drift, and not conversion, is the problem Sinclair acknowledged as he struggled to complete the novel. In September 1905, Sinclair apologized to Macmillan editor George Brett for the quality of the second half of the novel, in which, Sinclair said, "the incidents . . . move too swiftly and [the] characters are insufficiently realized." Quoted in Folsom, "Upton Sinclair's Escape from *The Jungle,*" 249.

29. Reynolds, *Beneath the American Renaissance,* 54–56; Reynolds, "Black Cats," 22.

30. Tracy Fessennden, *Culture and Redemption: Religion, the Secular, and American Literature* (Princeton, NJ: Princeton University Press, 2007), 9–12. See also Gregory S. Jackson, *The Word and Its Witness: The Spiritualization of American Realism* (Chicago: University of Chicago Press, 2009).

31. Keith Gandal, *The Virtues of the Vicious: Jacob Riis, Stephen Crane, and the Spectacle of the Slum* (New York: Oxford University Press, 1997).

32. Lindsay, *General William Booth,* 5.

6. The Drinker's Epiphany in Modernist Literature

1. T. S. Eliot, introduction to *Nightwood,* by Djuna Barnes (New York: New Directions, 1961), xv–xvi.

2. *Alcoholics Anonymous: The Story of How More Than 100 Men Have Recovered from Alcoholism* (New York: Works Publishing, 1939), 63.

3. Ernest Kurtz, *Not-God: A History of Alcoholics Anonymous* (Center City, MN: Hazelden, 1991), 219.

4. John W. Crowley, *The White Logic: Alcoholism and Gender in American Modernist*

Fiction (Amherst: University of Massachusetts Press, 1994), 34, 132. Crowley's phrase alludes to a 1929 essay by Joseph Wood Krutch, *The Modern Temper: A Study and a Confession.* Memoirs that helped launch this social framework for modernism include Malcolm Cowley, *Exile's Return* (1934, 1951), Robert McAlmon, *Being Geniuses Together* (1938), Sylvia Beach, *Shakespeare and Company* (1956), John Glassco, *Memoirs of Montparnasse* (1970), and, of course, Ernest Hemingway, *A Moveable Feast* (1964). Ann Douglas culminates the longstanding romantic equation of modernist drinking with transgressive, anti-sentimental culture in *Terrible Honesty: Mongrel Manhattan in the 1920s* (New York: Noonday Press–Farrar, Straus & Giroux, 1995).

5. The best example of this respectable psychospiritual counseling was the Emmanuel Movement, begun in Boston's Episcopalian Emmanuel Church in 1906 and lasting into the 1920s. It hybridized mainline religious wisdom with lightly psychoanalytical theory, producing a handful of reformed drinkers who became professional counselors and authors, such as Courtenay Baylor (*Remaking a Man*, 1919) and Richard R. Peabody (*The Common Sense of Drinking*, 1930). See Katherine McCarthy, "Early Alcoholism Treatment: The Emmanuel Movement and Richard Peabody," *Journal of Studies on Alcohol* 45.1 (1984): 59–74.

6. For a long view of the intoxication-transformation tradition in literature, see Edmund O'Reilly, *Sobering Tales: Narratives of Alcoholism and Recovery* (Amherst: University of Massachusetts Press, 1997).

7. Malcolm Cowley, " 'Not Men': A Natural History of American Naturalism," in *Documents of American Realism and Naturalism,* ed. Donald Pizer (Carbondale: Southern Illinois University Press, 1998), 235.

8. For descriptions of *Manhattan Transfer* as an aesthetic achievement of modernism that is not yet sure of a relation to politics, see Michael Denning, *The Cultural Front: The Laboring of American Culture in the Twentieth Century* (London: Verso, 1997), 165; for a reading of it as a novel of indignant social criticism that falls short of political insight, see Robert C. Rosen, *John Dos Passos: Politics and the Writer* (Lincoln: University of Nebraska Press, 1981), 47–48. Rosen also points out that within a year of publishing *Manhattan Transfer,* Dos Passos joined the editorial board of the *New Masses* and began his political activism.

9. Christopher Wilson's *Labor of Words* is the source of this argument about Progressive Era realism. Dos Passos himself invites its forward application, referring to his aesthetic experiments as efforts to "declass" himself in his writing (Rosen, *John Dos Passos,* 42).

10. John Dos Passos, *Manhattan Transfer* (Boston: Mariner–Houghton Mifflin, 2000), 325. In the following paragraphs page numbers will be cited parenthetically in the text.

11. Jay McInerney, *Bright Lights, Big City* (New York: Vintage, 1984).

12. Walt Whitman, *Franklin Evans; or, The Inebriate: A Tale of the Times* (Durham: Duke University Press, 2007), 92–97.

13. Nathaniel Hawthorne, *The Celestial Railroad and Other Stories* (New York: Signet Classic-Penguin, 1963), 29–48.

14. Desmond Harding, for example, contrasts *Manhattan Transfer* with *Ulysses* as novels of urban modernity, finding Dos Passos's New York a particularly bleak commentary,

its plot a "dark journey toward a rotten core." Harding, *Writing the City: Urban Visions and Literary Modernism* (New York: Routledge, 2003), 128. Phillip Arrington typifies the ambiguity discourse by giving the novel credit for knowing that Herf "will never be able to go 'far' enough to escape the 'smoking rubbish piles' that are the waste and origins of the American myth"; but he also notes the ending's apparent lack of self-awareness, in the highly individualistic gesture by which it repudiates American individualism, "renewing the American myth upon which its attack is based." Arrington, "The Sense of an Ending in *Manhattan Transfer*," *American Literature* 54.3 (October 1982): 442–43.

15. It would take an adherent to full-fledged conversion narrative to consider the gesture as wholly insufficient. Mike Gold zeroed in on "the spiritual malady of tourism" in *Manhattan Transfer* as the reason for Dos Passos's failure, at that point in his career, to either model in his style or embrace in his plot any collectivist solution to the sin he surveyed. *Manhattan Transfer*, for Gold, fails to fulfill the evangelical requirement of emotional identification, generating "no pity, hatred, or love for these bewildered New Yorkers." Gold, "The Education of John Dos Passos," *English Journal* 22.2 (February 1933): 97, 93.

16. Dos Passos expressed reservations about his cocktail-party theme in *U.S.A.* as giving too much attention to a drinking space in which women had an accepted role. These "drawing room bitches," he wrote to Hemingway, are like "fairies getting into a bar—ruin it in no time." This language encapsulates the worst of what the canonical modernists had invested in drinking as a marker of masculinity. Quoted in Denning, *The Cultural Front*, 185. A bitter exchange in letters between F. Scott Fitzgerald and his wife, Zelda, in 1930 suggest a similar preoccupation with drinking and sexuality. When he wrote, "The nearest I ever came to leaving you was when you told me you thot I was a fairy in the Rue Palatine," Zelda wrote back to remind him, "You were constantly drunk. . . . You made no advances toward me and complained that I was un-responsive. You were literally eternally drunk the whole summer." *Correspondence of F. Scott Fitzgerald*, ed. Matthew J. Bruccoli, Margaret M. Duggan, and Susan Walker (New York: Random House, 1980), 240–41, 248. John W. Crowley provides the definitive take on this theme in *The White Logic*.

17. Crowley describes the therapeutic deflation of modernist attitudes to alcohol in his analysis of Peter Jackson's 1944 novel *The Lost Weekend*. Crowley, *White Logic*, 155–56. F. Scott Fitzgerald himself, meanwhile, articulated the heroic writer's contempt for recovery, calling A.A. something that "can only help weak people." Quoted in Tom Dardis, *The Thirsty Muse: Alcohol and the Modern Writer* (New York: Ticknor & Fields, 1989), 152.

18. See, e.g., Mary Chapman and Glenn Hendler, eds., *Sentimental Men: Masculinity and the Politics of Affect in American Culture* (Berkeley: University of California Press, 1999); and Milette Shamir and Jennifer Travis, eds., *Boys Don't Cry? Rethinking Narratives of Masculinity and Emotion in the U.S.* (New York: Columbia University Press, 2002). Thomas Strychacz argues that both the New Critical and gender-revisionist approaches are products of professional concerns in literary criticism that miss the

extent to which modernist masculinities are nakedly "staged" exposures of gender's conditionality. Strychacz, *Dangerous Masculinities: Conrad, Hemingway, and Lawrence* (Gainesville: University Press of Florida, 2008), 4–5.

19. *Alcoholics Anonymous*, 144.

20. V. S. Naipaul, "Michael X and the Black Power Killings in Trinidad," in *The Writer and the World: Essays* (New York: Vintage, 2002), 143.

21. Even as the canon is expanded or discarded, drinking has remained central to the image of creativity in the modern period. Along with the writers Thurman and Barnes, the dancer Isadora Duncan and the singer Billie Holliday, for example, fulfill expectations of self-destructive drinking habits as well as they enrich the notion of modernism as an artistic movement.

22. Crowley, *White Logic*, 115–34.

23. Many of Barnes's newspaper articles have been collected in Djuna Barnes, *New York*, ed. Alyce Barry (Los Angeles: Sun & Moon Press, 1989).

24. Barnes, *New York*, 119, 237.

25. Barnes, *Nightwood*, 52. In the following paragraphs page numbers will be cited parenthetically in the text.

26. Criticism of *Nightwood* is heavily influenced by attention to Barnes's life, no doubt because she put much of her life, especially family and romantic relationships, into her work. See, e.g., Phillip Herring, *Djuna: The Life and Work of Djuna Barnes* (New York: Viking, 1995), xvii, 203.

27. *Diagnostic and Statistical Manual of Mental Disorders: DSM-IV* (Washington, DC: American Psychiatric Association, 1994), 213.

28. While evading the trap of masculinity, the doctor's theories are not free from other conventions of expatriate drinking mythology. For example, he isolates uncontrolled drinking as a peculiarly Anglo-American quality, by indulging in the familiar bohemian valorization of the French as well-balanced naturals. He calls the compulsive, violent nature of American drinking a desperate effort at the self-awareness Americans deny themselves in their culture of moral and physical hygiene: "The French are disheveled and wise; the American tries to approximate it with drink. It is his only clue to himself. He takes it when his soap has washed him too clean for identification." Barnes, *Nightwood*, 90.

29. Laura J. Veltman identifies the Catholic confessional as the central religious site in the novel, and the history of Protestant rhetoric about its sexualization as the foil for O'Connor's inversions of sex and gender. Veltman frames this reading as a corrective to a critical tradition that has primarily read O'Connor's role as a critique of psychoanalysis. Veltman, "'The Bible Lies One Way, but the Night-Gown the Other'": Dr. Matthew O'Connor, Confession, and Gender in Djuna Barnes's *Nightwood*," *Modern Fiction Studies* 49.2 (2003): 204–27.

30. *The Sun Also Rises* and *Nightwood* appear as a kind of matched pair of expatriate novels that explore alcohol and sexuality. Some have speculated that Hemingway's Jake Barnes was named for Djuna Barnes and the rue Jacob salon that she frequented; e.g., Crowley, *White Logic*, 115. Crowley identifies an essential distinction between

Hemingway's hostile and Barnes's tragic approaches to transgressive female sexuality. Ellen Lansky, on the other hand, links the two novels through the A.A.-influenced notion of codependency, in which she sees protagonists roping both romantic partners and readers into their futile quests for consequence-free intoxication. Lansky, "The Barnes Complex: Ernest Hemingway, Djuna Barnes, *The Sun Also Rises*, and *Nightwood*," in *The Languages of Addiction*, ed. Jane Lilienfeld and Jeffrey Oxford (New York: St. Martin's, 1999), 205–24.

31. A.A.'s "disease" plays the role of original sin in that it must be sincerely confessed via a conviction experience before conversion can occur. Its intellectual influences in James's concept of the "sick soul" and Jung's discourse on alienation in *Modern Man in Search of a Soul* place it in conversation with what midcentury critics, drawing on Nietzsche to interpret modernism, would come to call "modern man's spiritual dilemma." Louis F. Kannenstine invokes a similar notion of "metaphysical pain and disorder" as *Nightwood*'s subject, which he suggestively sees Barnes taking "beyond the scope of diagnosis." But he brackets the novel's use of religious forms to explore this condition as "secularized," moving from the language of the soul to that of the "heart." Kannenstine, *The Art of Djuna Barnes: Duality and Damnation* (New York: NYU Press, 1977), 126. A central premise of my reading is that this secularization does not alter the meaning of such a form very much, especially in light of how heavily secularized the religious forms of the nineteenth century were in their purpose and language.

32. This distinction, between a universal lament for human experience and a critique of gender politics, remains a feature of *Nightwood* criticism. Phillip Herring echoes Eliot in arguing that *Nightwood*'s overarching meaning is the metaphysical insight that "human nature is itself perverted and grotesque." Herring, *Djuna*, 207. At the opposite critical pole are the feminist readings that see the novel "explod[ing] the binary structure underlying Western thought" by "refusing the categories of male and female" and "shifting terms of sexual difference." Carolyn Allen, "Writing toward *Nightwood*: Djuna Barnes's Seduction Stories," in *Silence and Power: A Reevaluation of Djuna Barnes*, ed. Mary Lynn Broe (Carbondale: Southern Illinois University Press, 1991), 55. My reading of the novel sees it moving explicitly from the former idea to the latter by discrediting the universality of conversion, a central trope (and ritual) of transformation in western culture. But the novel's enactment of this critique is less liberating than it is constrictive, condemning those with secure social identities to delusion and false religion, and those without it, like O'Connor, to maddeningly useless insight. As Catharine Stimpson suggests, Barnes's handling of various genres (to which I add the drunkard's conversion) gestures toward a radical critique of stability in language, but her imagination was too religious to be postmodern before her time, "too much in thrall to a cosmology of heaven and hell, of salvation and damnation, in which earth is both testing and killing ground." Stimpson, "Afterword," in Broe, *Silence and Power*, 371.

7. *The Iceman Cometh* and the Drama of Disillusion

1. Arthur Gelb and Barbara Gelb, *O'Neill: Life with Monte Cristo* (New York: Applause Books, 2000), 293–95; Doris Alexander, *Eugene O'Neill's Last Plays: Separating Art from Autobiography* (Athens: University of Georgia Press, 2005), 7–9; Cynthia McCown, "1912," in *Eugene O'Neill and His Early Contemporaries: Bohemians, Radicals, Progressives, and the Avant Garde,* ed. Eileen J. Hermann and Robert M. Dowling (Jefferson, NC: McFarland, 2011), 55–60.

2. Tom Dardis distinguishes O'Neill's personal and professional relationship to alcohol from those of other modern writers by virtue of O'Neill's long-term sobriety, attributing to it a late-career productivity that was rare among modernists. Dardis, *The Thirsty Muse: Alcohol and the Modern Writer* (New York: Ticknor & Fields, 1989), 241.

3. Thomas Szasz, *The Therapeutic State: Psychiatry in the Mirror of Current Events* (Buffalo, NY: Prometheus Books, 1975); see also Dana Cloud, *Control and Consolation in American Culture and Politics: Rhetorics of Therapy* (Thousand Oaks, CA: Sage, 1998); and James L. Nolan Jr., *The Therapeutic State: Justifying Government at Century's End* (New York: New York University Press, 1998).

4. Croswell Bowen, *The Curse of the Misbegotten: A Tale of the House of O'Neill* (New York: McGraw-Hill, 1959), 309; James Agee, "The Ordeal of Eugene O'Neill," *Time,* October 21, 1946, 71–78, reprinted in *Conversations with Eugene O'Neill,* ed. Mark W. Estrin (Oxford: University of Mississippi Press, 1990), 186; John Patrick Diggins, "'The Secret of the Soul': Eugene O'Neill's *The Iceman Cometh,*" *Raritan* 19.1 (June 1999): 70.

5. Eugene O'Neill, *The Iceman Cometh* (New York: Vintage, 1957), 25.

6. *The Iceman Cometh,* with its length, its pages of dense background and stage direction, and its frequent passages of what is essentially narrative by the characters, reads very much like a novel, a function of the fact that O'Neill by the mid-1930s was interested primarily in publishing, not producing, his plays. Alexander, *Last Plays,* 53. Kurt Eisen makes the case that *The Iceman Cometh* is a "novelization" of the dramatic form, simulating fiction's construction of psychological and narrative completeness. Eisen, *The Inner Strength of Opposites: O'Neill's Novelistic Drama and the Melodramatic Imagination* (Athens: University of Georgia Press, 1994), 155–58. Performances of the play, however, made significant waves in American drama, notably a 1956 revival directed by José Quintero and starring Jason Robards as Hickey, a 1960 adaptation for live television directed by Sidney Lumet and featuring Robert Redford as Parritt, and an acclaimed production in London and New York directed by Howard Davies and starring Kevin Spacey in 1998 and 1999. Charles A. Carpenter, "Modern British, Irish, and American Drama: A Descriptive Chronology, 1865–1965," http://bingweb.binghamton.edu/~ccarpen/; Diggins, "The Secret of the Soul," 63.

7. Letter to Kenneth Macgowan, December 30, 1940, in *"The Theatre We Worked For": The Letters of Eugene O'Neill to Kenneth Macgowan,* ed. Jackson R. Breyer (New Haven: Yale University Press, 1982), 257.

8. O'Neill, *Iceman,* 74–75, 110.

9. Ibid., 232, 157, 111, 147–48.

10. In addition to famous anti-evangelical writings of the 1920s by Mencken and Sinclair Lewis, see also the parodies of evangelical culture in late nineteenth-century fiction described in chapter 5. High-cultural distance from evangelical religion is also evident in William James's 1902 apologia for the subject matter of *The Varieties of Religious Experience,* in which he cites a prevailing belief that Dwight L. Moody's death in December 1899 would see American revivalism perish with the nineteenth century.

11. Joel Pfister, *Staging Depth: Eugene O'Neill and the Politics of Psychological Discourse* (Chapel Hill: University of North Carolina Press, 1995), 55–64. Among the few critics who read Hickey as an evangelical figure, Robert C. Lee argues that as "the worst of religion," Hickey's style complements Hugo's anarchism in the violence and hypocrisy of systems that would redeem modern society from dehumanizing forces. Lee sees born-again religion and revolutionary politics as nefarious historical relics, broken down in *Iceman* to their "loveless" cores. Anarchism betrays love while evangelism betrays faith, Lee argues; and "it is thus in irony that the Movement is often spoken of as a faith . . . and Hickey's zeal called a movement." Lee, "Evangelism and Anarchy in *The Iceman Cometh,*" in *Eugene O'Neill,* ed. Harold Bloom (New York: Chelsea House, 1987), 66. I argue that this interchangeability of political and religious faiths does more than comment ironically on the similarities of ostensibly irreconcilable reactions to modernity. It also constructs the play's "pipe dream" metaphysic, the relegation of all philosophies to the status of faiths, arbitrary manifestations of the formless hope at the human core. More recently, Mufeed F. Al-Abdullah has pointed out how ruthlessly the play undermines the ideal of redemption for either individuals or societies. Al-Abdullah, "Morgue of the Misbegotten: O'Neill's Pattern of Salvation in *The Iceman Cometh,*" *European Journal of American Studies* 2007.1, http://ejas. revues.org/1166.

12. See, e.g., Henry Link, *The Return to Religion* (New York: Macmillan, 1936); and Smiley Blanton and Norman Vincent Peale, *Faith Is the Answer: A Psychiatrist and a Pastor Discuss Your Problems* (New York: Abingdon-Cokebury, 1940). The classic study of this genre is Donald B. Meyer, *The Positive Thinkers: Popular Religious Psychology from Mary Baker Eddy to Norman Vincent Peale and Ronald Reagan,* rev. ed. (Middletown, CT: Wesleyan University Press, 1988).

13. O'Neill, *Iceman,* 232. In the following paragraphs page numbers will be cited parenthetically in the text.

14. Upton Sinclair, *The Jungle* (Norton Critical Edition), ed. Clare Virginia Eby (New York: Norton, 2003), 287; Samuel Hopkins Hadley, *Down in Water Street: A Story of Sixteen Years Life and Work in Water Street Mission* (New York: Fleming H. Revell, 1902), 76; *Alcoholics Anonymous: The Story of How More Than 100 Men Have Recovered from Alcoholism* (New York: Works Publishing, 1939), 19.

15. Thomas Gilmore, *Equivocal Spirits: Alcohholism and Drinking in Twentieth-Century Literature* (Chapel Hill: University of North Carolina Press, 1987), 48–61. *Alcoholics Anonymous,* 73–76.

16. Franklin D. Roosevelt, "First Inaugural Address, March 4, 1933," in *The Essential Franklin Delano Roosevelt* (New York: Random House, 1995), 30.

17. Ray Burdick Smith, *History of the State of New York, Political and Governmental* (Syracuse: Syracuse Press, 1922), 415–20.

18. David M. Kennedy, *Freedom from Fear: The American People in Depression and War, 1929–1945* (New York: Oxford University Press, 1999), 138.

19. This interpretation of the state's new conceptualization of drinking is my own. For more on the regulation of alcohol and saloons upon Repeal, see Kenneth J. Meier, *The Politics of Sin: Drugs, Alcohol, and Public Policy* (Armonk, NY: M. E. Sharpe, 1994), 155–56.

20. Mark E. Lender and James K. Martin, *Drinking in America: A History* (New York: Simon & Schuster, 1987), 172–73.

21. Roosevelt, "First Inaugural," 33. For the background to inclusion of this phrase in the speech, see Davis W. Houck, *FDR and Fear Itself: The First Inaugural Address* (College Station: Texas A&M University Press), 112–22. See chapter 4 for further discussion of liberal individualism in the New Deal era.

22. O'Neill, *Iceman*, 157, 241–42.

23. Lee, "Evangelism and Anarchy," 66.

24. The only scholar to have given sustained attention to the New Deal as a context for *The Iceman Cometh* is John Curry, in an article focusing on labor in the play in light of Roosevelt's unemployment policies and New Dealers' efforts to convince the public of the need for government's role managing the economy. Curry sees the play's New Deal meaning through the same framework of revised individualism that I invoke here and in chapter 4, but his historical focus is more fine-grained. Whereas Curry sees Hickey's failure to dislodge the inmates' delusions of self-reliance as analogous to failures in New Deal rhetoric and policy in the late 1930s, I focus on the longer-term liberal successes in establishing a public consensus around limited mutual dependence and moving redemption language to the heart of political discourse. Curry, "The New Deal Cometh: Examining *The Iceman Cometh* and *Hughie* in Relation to the Rhetoric of the Roosevelt Administration," *Eugene O'Neill Review* 33.1 (2012): 91–100.

25. Travis Bogard, *Contour in Time: The Plays of Eugene O'Neill* (New York: Oxford University Press, 1988), 135.

26. Doris Alexander sets the standard in this school, exhaustively researching the appropriate places and figures, and interpreting the play based on the extent to which O'Neill deviated from them. Encouraged by O'Neill's own commentary on his source material, biography has also been a fallback assumption for critics. The *New York Times* critic J. Brooks Atkinson, for example, while acknowledging O'Neill's "romantic" predilection for futility and doom, calls on O'Neill's early life experiences in waterfront dives as the basis of the play's "pungently and vividly" drawn character types, the "weak men in a strong world" of whom O'Neill "knew the bitter truth [but] still had a romantic attachment for." Atkinson, "Iceman Returns," *New York Times*, May 20, 1956, reprinted in *The Critical Response to Eugene O'Neill*, ed. John H. Houchin (Westport, CT: Greenwood Press, 1993), 175–76. Atkinson recapitulated this analysis in his introduction to the 1960 television production of *The Iceman Cometh*

directed by Sydney Lumet, calling it a product of O'Neill's genius for understanding life among the "dregs of society." More recently, the late John Patrick Diggins
marshaled this perception of O'Neill into the anti-leftist claim that because of his
youthful adventurism, "O'Neill knew the working class more intimately than most
communist writers," and that his slumbering alcoholics are more representative of
this class than are Clifford Odets's strikers. Diggins, *Desire under Democracy: Eugene
O'Neill's America* (Chicago: University of Chicago Press, 2007), 253–54.

27. Robert Brustein, "Souls on Ice," *New Republic,* October 28, 1985, 25, reprinted in
Houchin, *The Critical Response to Eugene O'Neill,* 192. Brustein wonders at one point
whether Hope's Saloon doesn't *really,* in the play's universe, exist at the bottom of the
sea, in a literal reading of Larry Slade's description of the bar.

28. Gorky's vernacular philosopher Satine invokes drunkenness to articulate the same
kind of equivalence that O'Neill's play draws, between the various forms of salvation:
"When I'm drunk . . . I like everything. Yes. . . . He—prays? Fine! A man can believe
or not believe . . . that's his affair! A man is free . . . he pays for everything himself! . . .
for belief, for unbelief, for love, for wisdom." Maxim Gorki, *The Lower Depths,* trans.
Laurence Irving (London: T. Fisher Unwin, 1912), 178.

29. Normand Berlin, "The Late Plays," in *The Cambridge Companion to Eugene O'Neill,*
ed. Michael Manheim (New York: Cambridge University Press, 1998), 85–86.

30. Harold Bloom, "Introduction," in Bloom, *Eugene O'Neill,* 3–4.

31. Critics interested in alcoholism in the play tend to fall into the realist camp, and
they have debated the accuracy of its portrayal of alcoholism since its first staging
in 1946. Mary McCarthy, in her review of the 1946 stage production, condemned
the play as a faulty piece of naturalism, based largely on the claim that its characters didn't behave like real drunks. Steven F. Bloom, in a 1985 article, worried that
McCarthy's judgment had been codified in anthologies, and attempted a definitive
rebuttal, not only correcting McCarthy's observations about the play but comparing
the play's characterizations to diagnostic standards of alcoholism from the mid-1940s
on. While Bloom turns to medical manuals, Roger Forseth and Thomas Gilmore
apply A.A.-influenced notions about addiction as mimetic standards for O'Neill's late
plays. Mary McCarthy, "Eugene O'Neill—Dry Ice," in *Twentieth Century Interpretations of "The Iceman Cometh": A Collection of Critical Essays,* ed. John Henry Raleigh
(Englewood Cliffs, NJ: Prentice-Hall, 1968), 50–53; Steven F. Bloom, "Drinking and
Drunkenness in *The Iceman Cometh*: A Response to Mary McCarthy," *Eugene O'Neill
Newsletter* 9.1 (Spring 1985): 3–12; Roger Forseth, "Denial as Tragedy: The Dynamics
of Addiction in O'Neill's *The Iceman Cometh* and *Long Day's Journey into Night,"*
Dionysos: The Literature and Addiction Triquarterly 1.2 (Fall 1989): 3–18; Thomas
Gilmore, *Equivocal Spirits: Alcoholism and Drinking in Twentieth-Century Literature*
(Chapel Hill: University of North Carolina Press, 1987), 48–61. Bloom offers a more
promising resolution of the realism/expressionism divide in his reading of addiction
in *Long Day's Journey into Night.* Bloom identifies alcoholism as the vehicle of "a realistic context" for the aesthetic repetition that aligns O'Neill with the bleaker modernist and postmodernist conceptions of human life (159). In this model addiction serves

as a realistic canvas and a formal pattern with which to paint an existentialist scene. Steven F. Bloom, "Empty Bottles, Empty Dreams: O'Neill's Use of Drinking and Alcoholism in *Long Day's Journey into Night*," in *Critical Essays on Eugene O'Neill*, ed. James J. Martine (Boston: G. K. Hall, 1984), 159–77.

32. Breyer, "*The Theatre We Worked For*," 257.

33. Brenda Murphy notes that *The Iceman Cometh*, with Philip Barry's *Here Come the Clowns* and William Saroyan's *The Time of Your Life*, was one of three American plays written in the late 1930s to feature a disruptive intruder entering a close-knit saloon. "In the light of the seemingly endless Depression that wore on to the end of the decade and the continuous threat of fascism in Europe, it is no surprise that all three plays present a group of characters in the grip of a paralyzing idleness that faces a threat from an outside character who tries to enforce his will and his values on the community." Murphy, "*The Iceman Cometh* in Context: An American Saloon Trilogy," *Eugene O'Neill Review* 26 (2004): 215–25. Murphy reads *Iceman* as a story of scapegoating's community-preserving function, ironically applied by a non-functioning community.

34. The equivalence of intoxication and religious ecstasy has a long intellectual pedigree, discussed in chapters 3 and 4.

35. One of the few studies to approach drinking and temperance cultures as mutually productive, rather than diametrically opposed, is John W. Frick's *Theatre, Culture and Temperance Reform in Nineteenth-Century America* (New York: Cambridge University Press, 2003). In addition to the sources cited in chapter 1, also helpful in constructing the culture of the saloon and the mission are Brooks McNamara, *The New York Concert Saloon: The Devil's Own Nights* (New York: Cambridge University Press, 2007); Luc Sante, *The Low Life: Lures and Snares of Old New York* (New York: Macmillan, 2003); and Paul S. Boyer, *Urban Masses and Moral Order in America, 1820–1920* (Cambridge: Harvard University Press, 1992).

36. The traditions of literary realism and stage comedy intersect in the common scene of the political discussion between drunks at a bar or hobos in a breadline. Examples of this trope appear in Crane's New York sketches, in Finley Peter Dunne's Mr. Dooley columns, in Theodore Dreiser's *Sister Carrie*, and in Jake Barnes and Bill Gorton's parodies of temperance rhetoric on their fishing trip in Hemingway's *The Sun Also Rises*.

37. Ernest Kurtz, *Not-God: A History of Alcoholics Anonymous* (Center City, MN: Hazelden, 1991), 18–19; *Alcoholics Anonymous*, 22. Commenting on his sources for Hickey, O'Neill alludes to a general type that evokes the drinking lives of Bill Wilson, Henry Parkhurst, and other early A.A. members: "I knew many salesman in my time who were periodical drunks, but Hickey is not any of them," he wrote in the same 1940 letter to Kenneth Macgowan in which he described the bottom and defended the play's length. "He is all of them, you might say, and none of them." Breyer, "*The Theatre We Worked For*," 258.

38. The importance of Runyon's style to the shift in Broadway theater from straight drama to the blockbuster musical is a significant context for O'Neill's turning his back

on the stage in the 1930s. Through the lens of *Iceman,* the rift can be seen occurring over the treatment of the low life as either light or dark material. On Runyon's role in helping facilitate the journey of "wisecrack" humor from vaudeville to print culture, Broadway, film, and beyond, see Ethan Mordden, *All That Glittered: The Golden Age of Drama on Broadway, 1919–1959* (New York: Macmillan, 2007), 142.

39. When the truth of Hickey's crime begins to emerge, Rocky laments, "I tried to wise de rest of dem up up to stay clear of him, but dey're all so licked, I don't know if dey got it." O'Neill, *Iceman,* 215. Of these, Larry, "the Old Wise Guy," is the only one unable to shake off his conversion at the hands of Hickey.

40. This flirtation with caricature is consistent with O'Neill's career-long dependence on heavily drawn accents. Admirers of O'Neill's "ear for the vernacular" ignore the sheer staginess of his voices on the printed page, which is less evident under the moderating influence of good acting. The stage-negro dialect of Brutus in *The Emperor Jones* (1920) draws critical attention to this habit, because of the extent to which it violates later social conventions. But even in that play, the equally broad cockney of Smithers appears first; and subsequent plays include the cartoonish working-class speech impediment of Yank in *The Hairy Ape* (1922) and the barely decipherable rural New England-ese of the Cabot family in *Desire under the Elms* (1925).

41. Roosevelt, "Second Inaugural Address," in *The Essential Franklin Delano Roosevelt* (New York: Random House, 1995), 129.

8. Recovery Memoir and the Crack-Up of Liberalism

1. Upton Sinclair, *The Cup of Fury* (Great Neck, NY: Channel Press, 1956), 42.

2. Anthony Arthur, *Radical Innocent: Upton Sinclair* (New York: Random House, 2006), 311. Sinclair had so much difficulty finding a publisher for *The Cup of Fury* that in 1955 he made a public appeal for support to reform-minded foundations and potential readers. Upton Sinclair, "Enemy in the Mouth," *New Republic,* March 21 1955, 21.

3. For a concise summary of the Alcoholism Movement, its institutional relations, and its legacies, see William L. White, *Slaying the Dragon: The History of Addiction Treatment and Recovery in America* (Bloomington, IL.: Chestnut Health Systems, 1998), 193–96.

4. Sinclair, *Cup of Fury,* 178, 184–85.

5. Ibid., 111–12, 123–24.

6. Despite his radicalism on the American scene, Sinclair had a history of tense relations with communists, some of which he recounts in *The Cup of Fury.* After speaking out against Soviet rule in the aftermath of World War II, he was denounced by the party's literary arm, and subsequently lionized in a Voice of America broadcast. By the early 1950s, "the old rebel was now an authorized and approved voice of the government," Arthur Anthony concludes in *Radical Innocent,* 308–9.

7. On the rising public influence of psychological expertise, see Ellen Herman, *The Romance of American Psychology: Political Culture in the Age of Experts* (Berkeley: University of California Press, 1996), 238–41. On consensus morality, see Elaine Tyler May, *Homeward Bound: American Families in the Cold War Era* (New York: Basic

Books, 2008). On religious pluralism in Cold War culture, see Jason W. Stevens, *God-Fearing and Free: A Spiritual History of America's Cold War* (Cambridge: Harvard University Press, 2010).

8. The rise to public consciousness of the disease model and A.A.-style recovery in this period is nicely bracketed by two Oscar-winning films: Billy Wilder's *The Lost Weekend* (1944), based on Charles Jackson's autobiographical novel, depicted alcoholism as a psychiatric illness; *Days of Wine and Roses* (1961), an adaptation of a 1958 television drama, depicted A.A. as its cure. Notable published recovery memoirs in the intervening period include actress Lillian Roth's international bestseller *I'll Cry Tomorrow* (New York: Frederick Fell, 1954), and James H. Richardson's *For the Life of Me: Memoirs of a City Editor* (New York: Putnam, 1954).

9. On recovery subcultures, see Trysh Travis, *The Language of the Heart: A Cultural History of the Recovery Movement from Alcoholics Anonymous to Oprah Winfrey* (Chapel Hill: University of North Carolina Press, 2009).

10. The critique of "therapeutic culture" began with Philip Rieff, *The Triumph of the Therapeutic: Uses of Faith after Freud* (New York: Harper & Row, 1966), and was developed by, among others, Christopher Lasch, *The Culture of Narcissism: American Life in an Age of Diminishing Expectations* (New York: Norton, 1978). It has become a discourse of both the right and the left that often targets recovery culture as among the worst excesses of a self-obsessed age.

11. Daniel T. Rodgers is the latest of many scholars and commentators to use a breaking metaphor to describe the fate of the liberal consensus, in *Age of Fracture* (Cambridge: Harvard University Press, 2012).

12. This exclusionary Christian recovery is the kind of story that George W. Bush told in *A Charge to Keep*, the autobiography I cited in the introduction. A sizeable alternative recovery movement now exists within conservative Christian churches, drawing on twelve-step methods but reframing them as explicitly biblical wisdom that leads to specific religious identity. See, e.g., Rick Warren and John Baker, *Celebrate Recovery: A Program for Implementing a Christ-Centered Recovery Ministry in Your Church* (Grand Rapids, MI: Zondervan, 1998). There also is a movement within A.A. to restore the explicitly Christian claims some made in its early days in Akron. See, e.g., Dick B., *The Good Book–Big Book Guidebook: How to Include the Creator's Impact on Early A.A. in Recovery Programs Today* (Kihei, HI: Good Book Publishing, 2006).

13. Trysh Travis's way of understanding the political indeterminacy of contemporary grassroots recovery culture offers a useful counterpoint to my reading of published recovery memoir. Travis suggests recovery is best understood as a kind of cultural populism, which makes "a pronounced and distinctive critique of the modern world and its dominant institutions" and "offers its adherents strategies for negotiating their ways in that world, and even for effecting change within it," but whose political valences are "indeterminate and labile." Travis, *The Language of the Heart: A Cultural History of the Recovery Movement from Alcoholics Anonymous to Oprah Winfrey* (Chapel Hill: University of North Carolina Press, 2009), 270–71. By contrast, the commercial production of recovery memoir makes it dependent on both the

economic and narrative constrictions imposed in the media marketplace, in publishing, television, and film. In published narratives, these institutional and market purposes often reach all the way down to the genre's core purpose. Subsequently, whether in service to these purposes or in resistance to them, a more distinct cultural politics emerges in recovery memoir, one that I argue takes as its starting point the liberal settlement under which the twelve-step recovery narrative was born.

14. Scott Donaldson, *Fool for Love: F. Scott Fitzgerald* (New York: St. Martin's, 1983), 152.

15. F. Scott Fitzgerald, *The Crack-Up*, ed. Edmund Wilson (New York: New Directions, 1945), 69. A pair of essays published in 2012 represented a revival of interest in the "Crack-Up" essays. Patricia Hempl hailed them as the beginnings of modern autobiographical writing, citing some fascinatingly ambivalent responses by the author's contemporaries regarding his new confessional mode. Hempl, "F. Scott Fitzgerald's Essays from the Edge," *American Scholar* 81.2 (Spring 2012). Thomas Heise described them as built from the Depression paradox of persistent American self-improvement confronting material hopelessness. Heise, "Fitzgerald's Depression," *Berfrois*, September 4, 2012, www.berfrois.com/2012/09/thomas-heise-f-scott-fitzgeralds-depression/. My reading explores both of these themes via comparison to their contemporaneous embodiment in A.A. narrative, as described in chapter 4.

16. Fitzgerald, *The Crack-Up*, 84; in the following paragraphs page numbers will be cited parenthetically in the text. Fitzgerald elsewhere made this same equation between his own binge-and-bust and American society's. Critics and biographers often associate this turn with the 1931 story "Babylon Revisited," in which a hard-drinking Fitzgerald-like figure begins to fade. For example, Richard D. Lehan: "What seemed true in terms of his own experience now seemed true in terms of history. 'Babylon Revisited'—a story where the horror of the past prevails—suggests that the depression was an ultimate consequence of misspent vitality, and reveals the way Fitzgerald connected the personal and the public tragedy." Lehan, *F. Scott Fitzgerald and the Craft of Fiction* (Carbondale: Southern Illinois University Press, 1966), 60.

17. Sheilah Graham, *The Real F. Scott Fitzgerald* (New York: Grosset & Dunlap, 1976), 13, quoted in Tom Dardis, *The Thirsty Muse: Alcohol and the Modern Writer* (New York: Ticknor & Fields, 1989), 152.

18. The scene Fitzgerald conjures to imagine this antisocial life invokes a similar image in Emerson's "Self-Reliance," a seminal articulation of the value conversion narrative seeks, ironically enough, to "transcend." Fitzgerald pictures himself alone at work, but with the sign on his door reading *Cave Canem* (beware of dog) instead of Emerson's *Whim*.

19. Travis, *Language of the Heart*, 266–67.

20. James Frey, *A Million Little Pieces* (New York: Doubleday, 2003), 280, 374.

21. "Oprah Reveals on Her Show She Smoked Crack Cocaine during her 20s," *Jet*, January 30, 1995, 51.

22. For a detailed account of the rise of Oprah's Book Club that is also an impassioned defense of its purposes, see Kathleen Rooney, *Reading with Oprah: The Book Club That Changed America* (Fayetteville: University of Arkansas Press, 2005).

23. Allan Borst, "Managing the Crisis: James Frey's *A Million Little Pieces* and the Addict-Subject Confession," *Cultural Critique* 75 (Spring 2010): 149, 165.

24. Two opposing takes on Frey and his false confessions reveal the way critics continue to take sides around the perceived literary-therapeutic divide. The British journalist Laura Barton, interviewing Frey for the *Guardian*, accentuated his bad-boy persona and offered on his behalf a stern defense of literary license. "The Man Who Rewrote his Life," *Guardian*, September 15, 2006. By contrast, Seth Mnookin, a recovering heroin addict writing for *Slate*, explained soberly a set of relations between Frey's falsification of recovery and the blustering quality of his aesthetic style. Mnookin, "Picking Up the Pieces: How James Frey Flunked Rehab, and Why His Fakery Matters," *Slate*, January 12, 2006, www.slate.com/id/2134203/.

   Frey addressed the controversy in an author's note attached to subsequent editions of his book. In a moping tone that stands in jarring contrast to the bluster of the main text, Frey apologizes repeatedly to readers who were "disappointed" to find out he had invented the most dramatic elements of his story. He also rationalizes his "embellishments" by appealing to the fungibility of memory, the uncertain relationship between memoir, facts, and creativity, the demands of compelling narrative, and his desire to write an inspiring story. Ultimately he directs his appeal for sympathy to the actual damage addiction does to the psyche, and in a confession more startling than anything in the original text, admits to having invented its bad-boy persona. "I made other alterations in my portrayal of myself, most of which portrayed me in ways that made me tougher and more daring and more aggressive in reality than I was, or I am. People cope with adversity in many different ways, ways that are deeply personal. I think one way people cope is by developing a skewed perception of themselves that allows them to overcome and do things they thought they couldn't do before. My mistake, and it is one I deeply regret, is writing about the person I created in my mind to help me cope, and not the person who went through the experience." The full text is available at www.randomhouse.biz/media/pdfs/AMLP020106.pdf.

25. Damien McElrath, *Hazelden: A Spiritual Odyssey* (Center City, MN: Hazelden, 1987), 24-25; "FAQs," Hazelden.org. Hazelden was the leading institution in the development of the influential "Minnesota Model" of addiction treatment, a philosophy combining the concepts of "chemical dependence" and spiritual, A.A.-oriented recovery. White, *Slaying the Dragon*, 199-211.

26. William Cope Moyers, *Broken: My Story of Addiction and Redemption* (New York: Viking, 2006), 299-301, 305, 322-23, 328-29.

27. In addition to Ginsberg's *Howl* (1956), see Jack Kerouac's *On the Road* (1957) and William S. Burroughs's *Naked Lunch* (1959). Hubert Selby Jr., although not properly a Beat, employed addiction in similar ways in *Last Exit to Brooklyn* (1964) and *Requiem for a Dream* (1978).

28. Among the most direct evidences of this limitation is the public suppression of Marty Mann's lesbianism. Mann, among the first women to achieve long-term sobriety in A.A., founded the National Committee for Education on Alcoholism in the 1940s and ran it for almost three decades. Although her lesbianism was an open secret

in A.A. circles, as the public face of the Alcoholism Movement she went by "Mrs. Marty Mann" and sometimes made special efforts to protect her sexual identity. Sally Brown and David Brown, *A Biography of Mrs. Marty Mann, the First Lady of Alcoholics Anonymous* (Center City, MN: Hazelden, 2005), 217–18.

29. Audrey Borden, *The History of Gay People in Alcoholics Anonymous from the Beginning* (New York: Haworth Press, 2007), 76–78. In one of the A.A. narratives that Borden transcribes for this history, a gay man who joined A.A. in New York in 1945 makes a compelling case that A.A.'s third tradition, "The only requirement for membership is a desire to stop drinking," stemmed from a decision by the original Akron group to accept a gay member, and that gay membership remained a central issue around which A.A. developed its commitment to the fundamental equality of all alcoholics (14–26).

30. Augusten Burroughs, *Dry: A Memoir* (New York: Macmillan, 2004), 292–93.

31. *Alcoholics Anonymous Comes of Age: A Brief History of A.A.* (New York: Alcoholics Anonymous World Services, 1955), 48.

32. Scholars contest the influence that the AIDS epidemic had on the fundamental nature of gay community, with some arguing that it was an already achieved "maturity" that allowed gay men to respond in highly organized ways. But few disagree that the trauma experienced by survivors, the challenge to which Burroughs applies his addiction recovery, was pervasive and overwhelming. See, for example, Elizabeth A. Armstrong, *Forging Gay Identities: Organizing Sexuality in San Francisco, 1950–1994* (Chicago: University of Chicago Press, 2002), 168–70.

33. David Bahr, "Augusten Burroughs: Dry, but Flying High," *Publishers Weekly*, October 11, 2004, 52.

34. Wendy A. Weaver describes Lamott's *Traveling Mercies* as representative of a general pattern in which people return to an experiential rather than dogmatic Christianity, typically following youthful disenchantment with religion and then hard experience as an adult. Weaver, "Journeys toward Hope: The Quest of Delbanco's *The Real American Dream* in the Autobiographical Writings of Anne Lamott and Kathleen Norris," *Logos* 5.4 (2002): 124–34.

35. Though sobriety and A.A. are far off at this moment in Lamott's life, a recovery sensibility saturates the whole tale. For example, when she uses the memoirist's convention of scrutinizing an old photograph, the "baffled" look she sees on her former face echoes the Big Book's oft-repeated epithet for "cunning, baffling, and insidious" alcoholism as well as Leonard Cohen's "baffled king composing Hallelujah." Anne Lamott, *Traveling Mercies: Some Thoughts on Faith* (New York: Pantheon, 1999), 40. As a filter for interpreting the past, this allusion knits together recovery, religion, and artistry without announcing any single one.

36. The substance Lamott relates of her life in recovery fulfills the gender consciousness established in her downfall. In the absence of larger social and cultural resources, Lamott lives in close bonds of support among women, sustaining her through pregnancy, early motherhood, and a friend's struggle with cancer and eventual death. *Traveling Mercies*, 52–55.

37. Lamott, *Traveling Mercies,* 49. In the following paragraphs page numbers will be cited parenthetically in the text.

38. Drew Pinsky, *Cracked: Putting Broken Lives Together Again* (New York: Regan Books, 2003).

39. Of course, any model so accessible to readers, however daring its politics, is easily assimilable by the publishing marketplace. Recent memoirs by literary agent Bill Clegg, for example, hybridize the Frey and Burroughs models. Clegg describes living as a gay addict, but does so in a sensational style that seems more like a market-driven literary posture than an effort to explore the meanings of addiction and recovery. Clegg, *Portrait of an Addict as a Young Man: A Memoir* (New York: Little, Brown, 2010) and *Ninety Days* (New York: Little, Brown, 2012).

CONCLUSION: Addiction in a New Era of Recovery

1. "-30-," *The Wire,* season 5, episode 10, HBO, March 9, 2008.

2. "Late Editions," *The Wire,* season 5, episode 9, HBO, March 2, 2008.

3. Since Wallace's suicide in 2008, more information has come out about his own recovery from alcoholism and, especially, the role of recovery culture in his thinking. Among the first fruits of the archive of Wallace's personal papers at the University of Texas Austin was an essay by Maria Bustillos on Wallace's annotated collection of popular therapeutic writings. Bustillos also quotes an anonymous note of gratitude that Wallace apparently submitted to Granada House, a recovery facility where he was a resident in the 1980s and which served as the model for Ennet House in *Infinite Jest.* Bustillos, "Inside David Foster Wallace's Private Self-Help Library," *The Awl,* April 5, 2011, www.theawl.com/2011/04/inside-david-foster-wallaces-private-self-help-library.

4. See, e.g., "And the Hits Keep Coming," *Newsweek,* June 10, 2010, which opens with the question, "Is there a 12-step group for people hooked on addiction literature?"

5. On women's recovery cultures and debates surrounding their relationship to organized feminism, see Trysh Travis, *The Language of the Heart: A Cultural History of the Recovery Movement from Alcoholics Anonymous to Oprah Winfrey* (Chapel Hill: University of North Carolina Press, 2009), 190–228.

6. See Theodore Dalrymple, *Romancing Opiates: Pharmacological Lies and the Addiction Bureaucracy* (New York: Encounter Books, 2006).

7. See Craig Reinarman, "The 12-Step Movement and Advanced Capitalist Culture: Notes on the Politics of Self-Control in Postmodernity," in *Cultural Politics and Social Movements,* ed. Marcy Darnovsky, Barbara Epstein, and Richard Flacks (Philadelphia: Temple University Press, 1995), 90–109.

8. Leonard Doyle, "Bush: 'Wall Street got drunk and now it's got a hangover,'" *The Independent,* July 24, 2008; Rich Karlgaard, "America Needs a 12-Step Recovery Program," *Forbes,* December 13, 2010; Thomas P. M. Barnett, *Great Powers: America and the World after Bush* (New York: Penguin, 2010); Jonathan M. Metzl, "Why Glenn Beck and Rush Limbaugh Should Stop Exploiting Their Addictions for Petty Theatrics,"

Alternet, March 24, 2010, www.alternet.org; Walter Armstrong, "Newt Gingrich: 'A.A. Saved My Life,'" *The Fix,* December 12, 2011, www.thefix.com.

9. Kurt Andersen, "The End of Excess: Is This Crisis Good for America?" *Time,* March 26, 2009; Judith Warner, "Dysregulation Nation," *New York Times Magazine,* June 18, 2010.

10. In the most literal and highly theorized example of these political addiction metaphors, the science fiction author David Brin urged addiction researchers to study "self-righteous indignation" as a brain-based addiction particularly harmful because of its role sustaining social and political divisions. In the groundwork for his argument Brin expands the model of addiction as a brain disease to include all "reinforced" pleasures, in the process exposing the official model's limitations in distinguishing harmful from ordinary and even desirable compulsive behavior. Brin, "Self-Addiction and Self-Righteousness," in *Pathological Altruism,* ed. Barbara Oakley, Ariel Knafo, Guruprasad Madhavan, and David Sloan Wilson (New York: Oxford University Press, 2012), 77–84.

11. Stephen E. Hyman, "Addiction: A Disease of Learning and Memory," *American Journal of Psychiatry* 162.8 (August 2005): 1414–22.

12. David T. Courtwright, "Addiction and the Science of History." *Addiction* 107 (March 2012): 489.

13. Mariana Valverde shows that the variety of often contradictory legal and medical responses to addiction in the West have flowed from, and influenced, ever-shifting debates over the nature of the will. Valverde, *Diseases of the Will: Alcohol and the Dilemmas of Freedom* (New York: Cambridge University Press, 1998).

14. Courtwright, "Addiction and the Science of History," 488.

15. See Richard DeGrandpre, *The Cult of Pharmacology: How America Became the World's Most Troubled Drug Culture* (Durham, NC: Duke University Press, 2006), 188–90.

16. See, for example, the penetrating and perennially combative stance taken by disease-model and A.A. critic Stanton Peele, at peele.net.

17. Gene Heyman, *Addiction: A Disorder of Choice* (Cambridge: Harvard University Press, 2009). Newspaper interviews and reviews of Heyman's book were largely friendly. In one radio interview, his work was challenged by officials from both NIDA and Hazelden, the leading legacy institutions of the Alcoholism Movement. "Gene Heyman," *On Point with Tom Ashbrook,* NPR, August 11, 2009, http://onpoint.wbur.org.

18. "Guest Blogging: Siobhan Reynolds," *Points: The Blog of the Alcohol and Drugs History Society,* April 12, 2011, http://pointsadhsblog.wordpress.com.

19. The career of Marty Mann is the leading example of twelve-step recovery and disease-model advocacy working hand-in-hand. See Sally Brown and David Brown, *A Biography of Mrs. Marty Mann, the First Lady of Alcoholics Anonymous* (Center City, MN: Hazelden, 2005).

20. Lorraine T. Midanik, *Biomedicalization of Alcohol Studies: Ideological Shifts and Institutional Challenges* (New Brunswick, NJ: Transaction, 2006), 57.

21. In a splashy but suggestive book, Damian Thompson argues that addiction, in the real economy of consumer desire as well as the psychological rhetoric of human behavior,

has indeed become so pervasive as to create an open question about its definition. Rather than losing all meaning in the breadth of its application, he suggests, addiction is becoming the master experience of modern life, and finding ways to manage it will be the most pressing political and social problem of the future. Thompson, *The Fix: How Addiction Is Invading Our Lives and Taking Over Your World* (London: HarperCollins UK, 2012).

22. George Vaillant, *The Natural History of Alcoholism Revisited* (Cambridge: Harvard University Press, 1995), 357–69; John F. Kelly, Bettina Hoeppner, Robert L. Stout, and Maria Pagano, "Determining the Relative Importance of the Mechanisms of Behavior Change within Alcoholics Anonymous: A Multiple Mediator Analysis," *Addiction* 107.2 (2012): 289–99.

Index

Abbott, Lyman, 63

Adams, Henry C., 75

Addams, Jane, 44, 53–55, 59, 66, 75–77, 79–80, 275n29

addiction: causes and effects of, 6, 120–26, 138–43, 145–46; class's intersections with, 52–55; communities of, 3; governmental interventions and, 85, 95–96, 144–46, 211–16; historical emergence of, 7–11; intoxication and, 6–9, 37, 86, 112, 162, 168, 184–87, 204, 216–19, 229–40; masculinity and, 102–3, 107–10; medical language and, 5–6, 8–11, 51, 73, 87–88, 90, 92–93, 115, 144–51, 155, 181, 197, 232, 248–61; recovery narratives and, 1–2, 204–11; religious responses to, 28–31; therapeutic systems and, 73, 81, 112–15, 120–26, 177–80, 200–216, 242–47. *See also* Alcoholics Anonymous; drunkard's conversion (trope); religion; therapeutic culture

Addiction (Moyers), 237

Ade, George, 220

Adventures of Captain Simon Suggs (Hooper), 159

Adventures of Huckleberry Finn (Twain), 158–60, 250

affect: recovery narrative's uses of, 5, 9–19, 55–75, 81–82, 155, 166–67, 188–90; religion and, 9–10, 159–62; William James and, 86. *See also* sentimentalism

African Americans, 242–47

AIDS, 240–41, 306n32

alcohol. *See* addiction; Alcoholics Anonymous; drunkard's conversion (trope); recovery narrative; rescue missions; temperance movements

Alcoholics Anonymous: class's intersections with, 25, 127–28, 130, 136–44, 150–51, 184–85, 239–47; founding of, 3, 16, 115, 120, 126–31, 270n36; homosexuality and, 240–42, 305n28; *Iceman Cometh* and, 208–11; individualism and, 124–25; masculinity and, 110, 115, 119–20, 129, 131, 136–38, 140–42, 189–90, 210–11, 222; mutual aid structures and, 142–44, 146–47, 166, 170–72, 177–80, 229–39, 251–52, 268n13, 283n6; political roles of, 144–51, 224–25, 227–29, 239, 252, 257–59, 277n7; race and, 240–47; recovery narratives in, 11, 18, 116, 122–23, 148, 188, 200–204, 220, 226–29; religion in, 12, 16–17, 112–14, 120, 127, 134–35, 149, 174–75, 195, 203, 208–10; therapeutic mission of, 73, 81, 112–14, 116–26, 181, 195, 201–4, 211, 221, 223–24, 234–37, 240–42, 248–61, 296n31; William James and, 16, 85, 87, 91, 93, 100, 113, 131–32, 237

Alcoholics Anonymous: masculinity and, 115, 230; publication of, 101–2, 127, 129–30, 202; recovery narratives in, 131–38, 140–44, 148

Alcoholism Movement, 144, 224–29, 233

Alexander, Doris, 299n26

Allen, John, 33, 35, 246

America: class issues in, 127–30, 139–44;

America (*continued*)
  drunkard's conversion trope in,
    7–11, 200–204; economic crises in, 3;
    individualism in, 116, 120–26, 132–33,
    214–22, 289n58; interwar period of,
    119, 129, 136, 180–81; national recovery
    narratives and, 117–26, 144–51, 211–22,
    254–61, 284n7; religion and, 4–5,
    28–31, 155, 159–62, 216–22, 278n24;
    urbanization of, 32–37, 52–55, 182–90.
    See also Alcoholics Anonymous;
    liberalism; modernism (literary); New
    Deal; religion
The American Magazine, 70
American Psychiatric Association, 259
Andersen, Kurt, 257
Anderson, Sherwood, 222
Angelou, Maya, 235
Angels with Dirty Faces (film), 144
anonymity, 148–51. *See also* Alcoholics
    Anonymous
"Anthem" (Cohen), 222, 245
Appeal to Reason, 167
Arnold, June, 240
Arnold, Thurman, 123
Arthur, T. S., 202, 218
Artie (Ade), 220
As I Lay Dying (Faulkner), 235
Asylum (Seabrook), 229
Autobiography (Franklin), 8
Awake and Sing! (Odets), 139

"The Backslider" (*Alcoholics Anonymous*),
    141
Baker, Ray Stannard, 23, 32, 49, 53–55, 70,
    72–74, 273n22
Baraka, Amiri, 191
Barnes, Djuna, 17–18, 177, 179, 191–99, 232,
    239–40, 295n30, 296n32
Barnett, Thomas, 257
Beats. *See* Kerouac, Jack
Beck, Glenn, 257
Beckett, Samuel, 217, 220
Becoming William James (Feinstein), 88
Beecher, Lyman, 112
Beer-Wine Revenue Act, 213, 215
Begbie, Harold: Alcoholics Anonymous

and, 109–10, 113–14; gender and, 198; Jack
    London and, 103–4; religious outlook of,
    16, 96–102; Upton Sinclair and, 165, 170,
    175; William James and, 83, 85–88
Bellamy, Edward, 66
Beneath the American Renaissance
    (Reynolds), 173
The Bible and Temperance (Currier), 42
Big Book. *See* Alcoholics Anonymous
Bill W. and Mr. Wilson (Raphael), 127–28
Binchy, Maeve, 235
"Black Cats and Delirium Tremens"
    (Reynolds), 173
Bloom, Harold, 217
The Blue Badge of Courage (H. Hadley),
    38–39
Borst, Allan, 235–36
Brave New World (Huxley), 150
Brereton, Virginia, 26
Breu, Christopher, 131, 133–34
Bright Lights, Big City (McInerney), 186
"The Broad Accomplishments of the New
    Deal" (Schlesinger), 123
Broadway Tabernacle, 12
Broken (Moyers), 237–39
Broken Earthenware (Begbie), 96, 245. *See
    also Twice-Born Men* (Begbie)
Brooklyn Daily Eagle (newspaper), 192
Brown, Claude, 246
Buchman, Frank, 101–2, 126–27, 145, 289n57
Buck, Pearl, 235
Bukowski, Charles, 190
Bunyan, John, 93–94, 111, 172
Burns, Kit, 33
Burroughs, Augusten, 240–42, 247
Bush, George W., 1–2, 19, 31, 257, 263n1,
    303n12
"A Business Man's Recovery" (*Alcoholics
    Anonymous*), 140

Came to Believe (Robert M.), *143*, 239
Campbell, Helen Stuart: biography of, 56–
    57; McAuley and, 24, 34–35, 42, 44–45,
    81; progressivism of, 51, 53, 56, 59–62, 64,
    66, 73, 75–80, 162, 174, 179–80, 276n43;
    recovery narratives and, 16, 62–63,
    73–74, 251, 271n45, 275n40

Cane (Toomer), 191
Carrette, Jeremy, 112–13
Catholicism, 23–24, 39–40, 48
The Champ (film), 143
Chapman, J. Wilbur, 38
A Charge to Keep (Bush), 303n12
Chavigny, Katherine, 269n18
The Chicago Socialist (Sinclair), 165
"Chinatown's Old Glories Crumbled to
    Dust" (Barnes), 192
Christianity. *See* religion; rescue missions;
    specific denominations
Christianity and the Social Crisis
    (Rauschenbusch), 52, 73
Christianizing the Social Order
    (Rauschenbusch), 31
Christian Union, 63, 66
Churchill, Winston, 166
citizenship, 18, 118–19, 121, 151, 202, 251,
    255–57. *See also* drunkard's conversion
    (trope); masculinity; political discourse;
    self, the
City of Night (Rechy), 240
civil rights movement, 151, 245–46
Civil War (American), 28, 30, 38, 163
class: Alcoholics Anonymous and, 127–28,
    130, 136–44, 150–51, 184–85, 239;
    drunkard's conversion trope and, 39–40,
    49–55, 79–82, 86, 99, 102–7, 118–20, 135–
    36, 156–58, 163–76, 184–85, 187–88, 195,
    227–29, 232–33; gender and, 62, 103, 138–
    44, 170–71, 280n40; modernism and,
    163–76, 200–204; political discourses
    and, 42, 48–51, 164–75; religion and, 25,
    40–41, 49–51, 75–79, 99, 103, 140–41,
    162; rescue missions and, 25, 28–29,
    32–34, 36–37, 39–41, 55–79. *See also*
    recovery narrative; rescue missions;
    socialism
Cohen, Leonard, 222, 245
Communism, 145, 210, 302n6. *See also*
    socialism
compassionate conservatism, 2, 31
Conroy, Nelli, 48
conviction narratives, 179–99, 211–16,
    218–22, 296n31. *See also* Alcoholics
    Anonymous; drunkard's conversion

(trope); recovery narrative; religion;
    rescue missions
Corey, Lewis, 139
The Corrections (Franzen), 236
Courtwright, David T., 258–59
Cowley, Malcolm, 182–83, 264n7
Cracked (Pinsky), 245
"The Crack-Up" (Fitzgerald), 228–33
Crane, Jonathan Townley, 112
Crane, Stephen, 23, 35, 157–58, 161–62, 174,
    190, 192, 220
The Crisis of the Middle Class (Corey), 139
Crowley, John W., 10, 102–3, 107, 110, 181,
    189, 192
Culture and Redemption (Fessenden), 174,
    272n55
Culture and the State (Lloyd and Thomas),
    124
The Cup of Fury (Sinclair), 166, 169, 222–26,
    302n6
Currier, Nathaniel, 41–42
Curry, John, 299n24
cynicism, 34, 130–35, 172, 190, 194, 200–206,
    222–25

The Damnation of Theron Ware (Frederic),
    158, 162
Darkness and Daylight (Campbell), *58, 65*, 81
Davis, Angela, 244
Death of a Salesman (Miller), 143
"Death of a Traveling Salesman" (Welty),
    143
Debs, Eugene, 169, 222–23
Deems, Charles, 24
*Delia, Formerly the Bluebird of Mulberry
    Bend* (Whittemore), 38
Denning, Michael, 172
de Quincey, Thomas, 134
Dewey, John, 121–22, 124–26, 145, 147
*Diagnostic and Statistical Manual of Mental
    Disorders* (APA), 259
Diggins, John Patrick, 203
Door of Hope Mission, 82
Dos Passos, John, 17, 179, 182–91, 196, 218,
    294n16
Down in Water Street (Hadley), 14, *15*,
    38–39, *45*

Down These Mean Streets (Thomas), 246
downward social mobility, 139–44, 179–99, 204–11, 220–21. *See also* drunkard's conversion (trope)
"Dream Dust" (Hughes), 245
Dreiser, Theodore, 182–83, 222, 225
drunkard's conversion (trope): Alcoholics Anonymous and, 127–44; class's intersections with, 39–41, 49–50, 55–66, 79–82, 86, 99, 102–7, 118–20, 130, 138–44, 156–58, 163–76, 184–85, 187–88, 195, 227–29, 232–33; definitions of, 25; downward mobility and, 139–44, 179–90, 192–99, 204–11, 220–21; drug use and, 248–52; gender and, 99–100, 102–3, 182, 195–96, 210, 280n40, 281n52; historical emergence of, 7–11; *Iceman Cometh* and, 201–22; literary modernism and, 177–216, 222–29; medical discourses and, 5–6, 73, 84–85, 95–102, 115, 144–51, 155, 175, 193, 197, 201; memoir form and, 222–29, 240–47, 305n24; national economic recoveries and, 120–26, 144–51, 211–22, 254–61; performativity and, 6, 10–11, 25, 33–37, 110, 216–22; political invocations of, 2–3, 120–26, 144–51, 164–76, 181, 183, 187–88, 252–61, 298n11, 308n10; psychology and, 110–14; rescue mission literature and, 25–27, 32–41, 75–79, 156, 162; sentimental appeals of, 55–66, 81–82, 155, 166–67, 188–90; skepticism of, 49, 72, 131, 138, 187, 200–204, 269n24; social redemption and, 52–55, 57–61, 66–84, 95–102, 117–20, 136–38, 147, 163, 239–47, 271n51, 274n26; submission to authority and, 25–37, 48–49, 99–100, 116–20, 130, 132–33, 177–80, 202–3, 208–11; William James and, 86–89, 92–93, 97–102, 113, 131, 169
The Drunkard's Diseased Appetite (Willet), 269n24
The Drunkard's Progress (Crowley), 10
The Drunkard's Progress (Currier), 41–42
Dry (Burroughs), 240–42
Duncan, Isadora, 222–23

The Easiest Way in Housekeeping and Cooking (Campbell), 57

East of Eden (Steinbeck), 235
economic conditions, 3, 120–26, 138–44, 211–22, 248, 286n29. *See also* class; Great Depression; New Deal
Edwards, Jonathan, 9, 30, 246
Eggers, Dave, 236
Eliot, T. S., 177–80, 197–98, 203
Ely, Richard T., 56, 66
Emmanuel Movement, 73, 88, 293n5
"The End of Excess" (Andersen), 257
Esquire, 230

Faulkner, William, 235
Federal Alcohol Control Administration, 214
Feinstein, Howard M., 88
feminism, 26, 54, 56, 77–79
Fessenden, Tracy, 174, 272n55
Finney, Charles Grandison, 12, 16, 44–45, 77, 93, 266n22
Fisher, Philip, 157
Fitzgerald, F. Scott, 102, 174, 184, 188–89, 228–33, 245, 247, 257, 294n16
Fleming F. Revell Company, 38
Florence Night Mission, 48
Flower, Benjamin, 66
Following the Color Line (Baker), 70
Forbes, 257
Franklin, Benjamin, 8–9
Franklin Evans (Whitman), 187
Franzen, Jonathan, 236
Frederic, Harold, 158, 162
Freedom and Culture (Dewey), 121
Freud, Sigmund, 135, 168, 208
Frey, James, 134, 233–39, 247, 305n24
Fulton Street Noontime Prayer Meeting, 29, 93

Gandal, Keith, 174, 276n43
Gardiner, James, 93
Gardner, Orville "Awful," 12–13
Gaye, Marvin, 244
gender: addiction's relation to, 2, 102–4, 106–10, 182; Alcoholics Anonymous and, 110, 140–41, 189–90; class concerns and, 54–55, 57–59, 62, 103, 138–44, 170–71, 280n40; modernism and, 135–36, 188–89, 191–99; recovery narrative's

relation to, 38–39, 56–57, 65, 73–82, 99–100, 136–38, 195–96, 210, 242–47, 267n6, 280n40, 281n52; religion's relation to, 13, 102–3, 110–14; sexuality and, 47–48, 50; temperance movement and, 26–27, 86. *See also* masculinity; women
George's Mother (Crane), 161
Gibbud, Henry, 33–36, 48
Gifford Lectures (James), 87–88, 92–93, 114
Gilbert, Bradford, 47
Gilded Age, 158–59
Gilman, Charlotte Perkins, 44, 53–55, 66, 75, 77, 79–80
Gilmore, Thomas, 210
Gingrich, Newt, 257
Ginsberg, Allen, 240
Gold, Mike, 172, 201, 294n15
Gorky, Maxim, 217, 220
gospel rescue missions. *See* rescue missions
Gough, john B., 10
Gough, John B., 93
Grapevine (Alcoholics Anonymous), *143*, 150, 239
Great Depression, 16–19, 116, 120–26, 131, 138–50, 208, 211–16
The Great Gatsby (Fitzgerald), 174, 184
Great Society reforms, 254
"Greenwich Village as It Really Is" (Barnes), 192
Guadalcanal Diary (film), 144
Guys and Dolls (Loesser), 200, 202, 220

Hadley, Henry, 38–39
Hadley, Samuel Hopkins: biography of, 38–39, *45*; class issues and, 49, 55, 275n29; conversion of, 13–14, 53, 94, 110–11, 174, 210, 245–46, 270n36; rescue mission management and, 31, 71, 93
Hallelujah, I'm a Bum (film), 139
Hartman, Kabi, 80
Hatch, A. S., 24
Hawthorne, Nathaniel, 187
Hazelden (clinic), 236–38
Helping Hand Mission. *See* Water Street Mission
Hemingway, Ernest, 102, 189, 191, 194, 201, 229, 236, 295n30

Hemsley, Rollie, 148–49
Hendler, Glenn, 267n6
Herbert, George, 245
heroin, 248–52
"Heroin" (Smith), 222
Herron, George D., 273n21
Heyman, Gene, 259
"A High-Toned Old Christian Woman" (Stevens), 177
Hitler, Adolf, 101, 145
Holiness Movement, 14, 29
home economics, 57. *See also* Campbell, Helen Stuart
homosexuality, 240–42, 255, 267n6, 305n28
Hooper, Johnson Jones, 159
Household Economics (Campbell), 57, 78–79
Howells, William Dean, 77
Howl (Ginsberg), 240
Hughes, Harold, 144, 277n7
Hughes, Langston, 245
Huss, Magnus, 263n5
Huxley, Aldous, 150

The Iceman Cometh (O'Neill), 18, 200–222, 297n6, 299n24
If Christ Came to Chicago! (Stead), 95
The Impress, 77
individualism. *See* self, the
Individualism Old and New (Dewey), 121
Infants of the Spring (Thurman), 191
Infinite Jest (Wallace), 251, 261
In His Steps (Sheldon), 52, 67–69, 74, 273n20
Intercollegiate Socialist Society, 172
intoxication (trope), 6–9, 37, 86, 112, 162, 168, 184–87, 204, 216–19, 229–40

Jackson, Charles, 264n7
Jackson, Gregory, 275n40
Jaeger, John, 40–41, 48
James, Robertson, 88–90
James, William: Alcoholics Anonymous and, 85, 87, 91, 93, 100–102, 131–32, 237; familial alcoholism of, 88–89, 91, 278n18; gender and, 102–4; Jack London and, 83, 86, 102, 104–5, 108–9; receptions of, 83, 230–31, 235; recovery narrative

James, William (*continued*)
  and, 16, 92–94, 110–13, 169; religion
  and, 94–102, 121, 155, 279n27; scientific
  credibility of, 84–85, 87, 95–102, 110–14,
  162, 168–69, 175, 208, 247, 277n7, 296n31
Jerry McAuley: An Apostle to the Lost, 43, 46
Jews without Money (Gold), 172
John Barleycorn (London), 102–3, 106–9,
  172
Johnson, Hugh, 124
Johnson, Lyndon, 254
journalism, 12, 192, 220, 229, 232, 267n6,
  273n22. *See also* Campbell, Helen Stuart;
  Crane, Stephen; *specific journalists and
  publications*
Jung, Carl, 85, 131, 168, 208, 296n31
The Jungle (Sinclair), 105, 157, 165–73,
  182–83, 198, 222

Kaplan, Amy, 26
Karlgaard, Rich, 257
Kerouac, Jack, 190, 236, 240
Ketcham, Katherine, 237
Kildare, Owen, 281n52
Knute Rockne, All American (film), 144
Kropotkin, Petr, 149–50

Lamott, Anne, 82, 242–47
Lane, Ann, 77
Lanphier, Jeremiah, 12, 93
L'Assommoir (Zola), 160
Leuba, James, 94–95, 279n27
Lewis, Sinclair, 134, 189, 222–23
liberalism, 120–26, 147, 151, 198–99, 202,
  222–29, 246, 251, 253–54, 256. *See also*
  America; political discourse; Roosevelt,
  Franklin Delano; self, the
Liberalism and Social Action (Dewey), 121
Life and Work of Jerry McAuley (McAuley),
  38–41
Life-Changers (Begbie), 85, 101
Light in August (Faulkner), 235
Lincoln, Abraham, 5, 9–10
Lindsay, Vachel, 155, 157, 163–64, 175
literature. *See* Alcoholics Anonymous;
  drunkard's conversion (trope);
  modernism (literary); realism (literary);

rescue missions; *specific authors and
  works*
Lloyd, David, 124
Loesser, Frank, 200–202, 220
London, Jack: masculinity and, 102–4, 107–
  9, 136, 142, 189, 191–92, 194, 201, 222–23;
  politics of, 16, 103–5, 107–9, 165, 172, 175,
  194–95; recovery narratives and, 109–10,
  114; William James and, 83, 86–88, 102,
  104–5, 109
Long, Kathryn T., 266n22
Long Depression, 3
The Lost Weekend (Jackson), 264n7
Loughlin, Delia, 38, 46, 47–48
The Lower Depths (Gorky), 217

Maggie, a Girl of the Streets (Crane), 23, 35,
  105, 161
Manchild in the Promised Land (Brown), 246
Manhattan Transfer (Dos Passos), 17, 179,
  182–91, 196, 293n14
Mann, Marty, 144, 237, 305n28
The Man on the Bed (Robert M.), *143, 239*
Marcus, Greil, 264n7
Márquez, Gabriel García, 235
Martin Eden (London), 105–6
masculinity: Alcoholics Anonymous and,
  110, 115, 119–20, 129, 131, 142, 210–11,
  222; class's intersections with, 138–44;
  drinking's homosocial contexts and,
  86, 102, 107–9, 136–38, 189–90, 192,
  229, 252; individualism and, 188–89,
  295n28; literary modernism and, 182,
  188–89; performativity and, 131, 229–39;
  recovery narratives and, 2, 136, 229–39,
  267n6; William James and, 102–3. *See
  also* Alcoholics Anonymous; class;
  gender; modernism (literary)
Mayo, John Henry Fitzhugh, 135
McAuley, Jerry: biography of, 38–41;
  Campbell and, 34–35, 42, 45, 57, 59–62,
  271n45; Catholicism of, 39–40; class
  sensitivities of, 50–51, 55, 81; conversion
  of, 13, 33, 36, 53, *58,* 160, 210, 218, 263n1;
  criminal history of, 23–24; funeral of,
  25, 27; Hadley and, 13–14, 93; images
  of, *43;* physiognomy of, 34–35, 42, 44,

49; recovery narratives' dissemination and, 16, 27, 173, 251; renown of, 31; social redemption of, 48–51, 163, 174; William James and, 84, 268n14

McAuley, Maria, 44, 47, 50, 59, 81, 281n52

McCarthy, Mary, 300n31

McClure, Samuel, 70

McCullers, Carson, 235

McInerney, Jay, 186

Melville, Herman, 174

Melvin Trotter, 31

memoirs, 222–47, 305n24

Mencken, H. L., 223

"The Message of Jesus to Men of Wealth" (Herron), 273n21

Methodism, 9, 29–30, 166

Miller, Arthur, 143

Miller, Henry, 236

A Million Little Pieces (Frey), 233–39

mind-body connection, 66, 84–89, 91–93, 163. *See also* neurochemical worldview; psychology; religion; therapeutic culture

Mission of the Living Waters, 40

missions. *See* rescue missions

modernism (literary): alcohol's connection to, 17, 89–90, 102–9, 165–67, 200–204, 211–39, 294n16; class and, 163–76, 200–204; cynicism and, 34, 130–35, 172, 190, 194, 200–206, 222–25; downward social mobility and, 141–44, 204–11; drunkard's conversion trope and, 131–32, 156–57, 177–204; gender and, 86, 102–10, 119, 135–36, 182, 188–89, 191–99; religion and, 85–86, 109–10, 163–64, 173–76, 182–90, 216–22; sentimentalism and, 9, 119–20, 155–56, 189, 225–26; socialism and, 164–73. *See also specific authors and works*

Morrison, Toni, 235

Moyers, William Cope, 237–39, 247

Mrs. Herndon's Income (Campbell), 63

Mutual Aid (Kropotkin), 149–50

mutual aid tropes: Alcoholics Anonymous and, 131–38, 142–47, 166, 170–72, 177–80, 229–39, 251–52, 268n13, 283n6; masculinity and, 3, 86, 102, 107–9, 136–38, 189–92, 229, 252; utopian political

ideals and, 3, 6–7, 120–26, 166, 170–72, 219–20. *See also* drunkard's conversion (trope); liberalism; political discourse; religion; self, the

"My Kinsman, Major Molineux" (Hawthorne), 187

Naipaul, V. S., 190

Narcotics Anonymous, 248–52

narratives. *See* Alcoholics Anonymous; drunkard's conversion (trope); modernism (literary); recovery narrative

National Committee for Education on Alcoholism, 144

National Council on Alcoholism and Drug Dependence, 237

National Industrial Recovery Act, 120, 124, 214

National Institute on Drug Abuse, 258

National Recovery Administration, 124, 146–47, 214

naturalism (literary), 182–83, 203–4, 221, 300n31

neurasthenia, 90–91

neurochemical worldview, 253–54, 258–59

New Age spirituality, 150

New Deal, 117–26, 143–51, 202–3, 211–15, 221–22, 255–56, 284n7, 289n57

New Literary History of America (Tolkin), 131

New Thought therapy, 84, 125, 181

New York Times Magazine, 258

New York Tribune, 63

Niebuhr, Reinhold, 145

Night (Wiesel), 236

Nightwood (Barnes), 17–18, 177–79, 191–99, 232, 239–40, 295n30, 296n32

Nixon, Richard, 244

Obama, Barack, 1–2, 19

Odets, Clifford, 138–39

Offord, Robert M., 40

O'Hara, John, 189

Olasky, Marvin, 31, 269n21

"The Old Colonel and the New Colonel" (image), *45*

One Hundred Men Corporation, 130
O'Neill, Eugene, 18, 139, 190, 200–204,
    216–22, 297n6
"On His Way" (*Alcoholics Anonymous*), 140
"On the Bowery" (illustration), 15
Oprah Winfrey's Book Club, 234–37
Oprah Winfrey Show, 18
Our Continent (Tourgee), 57
"Our Southern Friend" (*Alcoholics
    Anonymous*), 135
Oxford Group, 101, 126–28, 132–33, 138, 145,
    181, 208, 219, 287n45

Pacific Garden Mission, 31
Paget, Violet, 108
Panic of 1837, 3
Paradise Lost (Odets), 139
Parkhurst, Henry, 134, 137–38
Pascal, Blaise, 287n36
Patterson, Troy, 235
The People of the Abyss (London), 103–5,
    107, 109, 195
performativity: drunkard's conversion
    tropes and, 10, 216–22; gender and, 131,
    229–39; recovery narrative and, 6, 11,
    25, 33–34, 37, 110; religious revivals and,
    29–30. *See also* drunkard's conversion
    (trope); masculinity; religion; self, the
Peters, Gerald, 25
Pfister, Joel, 208
Philanthropy and Social Progress (Adams),
    75
Philosophy of Disenchantment (Saltus), 108
photography, 42
phrenology, 23–24
Pilgrim's Progress (Bunyan), 93, 172
Pinsky, Drew, 245
political discourse: Alcoholics Anonymous
    and, 116, 224–25, 227–29; class issues
    and, 3, 17, 19, 42, 48–51, 116–17;
    liberalism and, 120–26; modernism and,
    102–7, 164–73, 191–99; mutual aid tropes
    and, 3–4, 7, 120–26, 166, 170–72, 219–20;
    recovery narrative in, 2, 6, 16, 18, 52–55,
    63–64, 66–79, 118–20, 164–76, 187–88,
    202–3, 211–22, 252–61, 298n11, 308n10;
    religion and, 96–102, 164; rescue

missions and, 25–31, 55–66, 73–80; the
    self's relation to, 2, 17, 25–26, 52–55;
    society's redemption and, 6, 49–61,
    66–75, 79–84, 95–102, 117–20, 136–38,
    147, 163, 183, 188, 229–47
Principles of Psychology (James), 89
Prisoners of Poverty (Campbell), 57, 63–64,
    79
The Problem of the Poor (Campbell), 42, 57,
    59–61, 63, 75
progressivism, 52–55, 57, 59–64, 66–79,
    121–26, 145, 163, 272n57, 273n20
Prohibition, 4, 120, 166, 175, 181, 213, 215,
    224, 252
prostitution, 7, 47, 50, 82
Protestantism, 39–40, 69, 95–96, 145, 161,
    174, 208, 273n20
Proudfoot, Wayne, 282n68
psychology: Alcoholics Anonymous and,
    144–51, 227; drunkard's conversion trope
    and, 84–91, 93, 95–102, 131, 135, 175, 201,
    207; narratives as data and, 110–14;
    religion's relation to, 10–11, 28, 84–85,
    135, 167–70, 279n27, 296n31; rescue
    mission literature and, 81–82; theory of
    habit and, 89–92, 181
Publican's Prayer, 13–14, 98, 160
"The Puncher" (Begbie), 98–102

Quindlen, Anna, 235

race, 1, 7, 18, 26, 34, 48, 70, 191, 227–29,
    240–47, 255, 267n6
Raines Law, 211–14
Raphael, Mathew J., 127–28, 133
Rauschenbusch, Walter, 31, 52, 73–74,
    274n25
realism (literary): Alcoholics Anonymous
    and, 135, 150–51; recovery narratives and,
    17, 35, 157–64, 221, 300n31; slumming
    accusations and, 25–26, 52–53, 155, 180,
    267n6; visual arts and, 42
Rechy, John, 240
recovery narrative: affect and, 9–19, 55–75,
    81–82, 155, 166–67, 188–90; Alcoholics
    Anonymous and, 11, 18, 116, 122–23,
    131–38, 148, 188, 200–204, 220, 226–29;

class's intersections with, 25–26, 39, 48–55, 79–82, 102–7, 127–28, 130, 138–44, 163–76, 242–47; cynical views of, 34, 130–35, 172, 190, 194, 200–206, 222–25; drugs and, 248–52; economic stressors and, 3, 17, 19, 145–46, 248; gender and, 13, 75–82, 99, 102–3, 182, 233–37, 242–47, 267n6; intoxication and, 6–9, 37, 86, 112, 162, 168, 184–87, 204, 216–19, 229–40; literary disseminations of, 38–41, 66–79, 97–102, 177–99, 264n7; masculinity and, 2, 38–39, 102, 136–38; material needs and, 31–37, 52–66, 71, 83, 122–23, 128–31, 147; medical language and, 5–6, 8–11, 37, 51, 73, 87–90, 92, 115, 144–51, 181, 193, 197, 232, 248–61; memoir form and, 222–47, 305n24; mutual support communities and, 3, 7, 10, 16, 131–38, 188–89, 219–20, 229–39, 251–52; neurochemical worldview and, 253–54, 258–59; performativity and, 6, 11, 18, 33–34, 37, 110, 132–33; political discourse and, 2, 6–7, 16, 18–19, 227–29, 252–61, 298n11, 308n10; presidential uses of, 1–2, 19; psychology and, 4, 6, 84–102, 110–14; religion's relation to, 1, 4–5, 31–37, 39–40, 48–49, 79–82, 94–102, 130, 181; secularization and politicization of, 164–76, 204–11; the self's relation to, 6, 116–17, 200–216; society-wide redemption and, 6–7, 16, 32–37, 55–79, 95–102, 116–26, 136–38, 147, 163–73, 181, 239–47, 259–61, 271n51, 274n26; visual media and, 41–48; *The Wire* and, 248–52. *See also* Alcoholics Anonymous; America; drunkard's conversion (trope); modernism (literary); political discourse

religion: affective dimension of, 9–10, 159–62; Alcoholics Anonymous and, 12, 112–14, 125–32, 134–35, 149, 195, 203, 208–10, 224–25; class's intersections with, 25, 40–41, 49–51, 75–79, 99, 103, 140–41, 162, 286n29; conversion structures and, 1, 3–6, 8–9, 11–19, 25, 37, 39–40, 79–82, 94–102, 112, 177–80, 211–22; gender and, 102–3, 242–47; material needs and,

31–37; medical language's relation to, 10–11, 278n24; modernism and, 85–86, 155–57, 163–99, 231–39; politics' relation to, 18, 80, 164, 203; psychology and, 4, 28, 84–85, 110–14, 135, 167–70, 279n27, 296n31; rescue missions and, 25–27, 31–37, 55–75; Second Great Awakening and, 4, 9–10, 12, 28, 36–37, 77, 93; temperance movement and, 28–31, 36–37, 145, 268n13; William James and, 87–88, 90–102, 121

rescue missions: Alcoholics Anonymous, 119; class issues and, 25, 28–29, 32–37, 50–51, 55–75; contemporary recovery narratives and, 11; drunkard's conversion tropes and, 3, 162; financial support of, 28–29; gender and, 26; genealogy of, 11–19; grassroots nature of, 27, 30, 37, 49–50, 121; literary productions of, 98–102, 156; management of, 26, 30; material dimensions of, 11, 32, 35–36, 66–67, 71, 83; mutual transformation and, 55–75; religious purposes of, 31–37, 67–75, 181; skepticism of, 32–35, 49, 72; Social Gospel movement and, 66–75; social redemption and, 25–31, 55–66; spiritual dimensions of, 11; visual media and, 42

Reynolds, David, 157, 173, 269n25
Richardson, Robert D., 91
Riis, Jacob, 71, 80–81, 174, 275n40, 276n43
Rogers, Will, 117
Roosevelt, Eleanor, 246
Roosevelt, Franklin Delano, 17, 115–17, 119–20, 122, 125–26, 145–46, 212–14, 221–22, 254
Rotskoff, Lori, 287n43
Running with Scissors (Burroughs), 242
Runyon, Damon, 202, 218, 220, 301n38
Rush, Benjamin, 8, 10–11

St. Andrew Presbyterian church, 244
Saltus, Edgar, 108
Salvation Army, 31, 85, 96–99, 105, 175, 207, 219
Santayana, George, 84
Schlesinger, Arthur, Jr., 123

science. *See* addiction; psychology;
   recovery narrative
Scott, Jim, 142
Scott, Walter, 158–59
Seabrook, William, 229, 232
Second Great Awakening, 4, 9–10, 12, 28,
   36–37, 77, 93
self, the: addiction's causes and effects,
   6, 120–26, 138–43, 145–46, 255–61;
   Alcoholics Anonymous and, 116–17, 129–
   31, 144–51, 283n6; Alcoholism Movement
   and, 222–29; consumption and, 147–48;
   conviction narrative and, 180–90, 211–16,
   240–47; drunkard's conversion trope
   and, 3, 162–64; economic downturns and,
   139–44, 211–16; Fitzgerald's individualism
   and, 188–89, 228–39; nation's relation
   to, 120–26; New Deal politics and, 17;
   performativity and, 6, 25, 174, 229–39;
   polity's redemption and, 49–52, 66–82,
   164–73, 177–90, 204–11, 239–47, 252–61,
   271n51, 274n26; religious submissions
   and, 25–26, 29, 31–37, 48–49, 99–100,
   116–17, 119–20, 132–33, 177–80, 208–11;
   sociocultural determinants of, 1–2, 25,
   27–28, 52
sentimentalism: Alcoholics Anonymous
   and, 119–20, 189, 225–26; psychology
   and, 112–13; realism and, 9, 17, 35, 166,
   181; recovery narrative's relation to, 5,
   11–19, 34–35, 39–40, 55–75, 81–83, 155–56,
   271n45; religion and, 41–48, 52–55;
   temperance movement literature and,
   9–10. *See also* drunkard's conversion
   (trope); religion; rescue missions
settlement house movement, 75, 77
sexuality, 47–48, 50, 170–71, 190, 198, 240,
   242, 255, 267n6, 294n16, 305n28
Sheldon, Charles, 52–55, 67–70, 73–74,
   273n21
S. H. Hadley of Water Street (Chapman), 38
Simon, David, 248–52, 261
Sinclair, Upton, 17, 105, 165–74, 179, 182–83,
   195–201, 222–26, 253, 302n6
Sister Carrie (Dreiser), 182–83
Sister Gin (Arnold), 240
slumming, 25, 52–55, 80–81

Smith, Charlie, 222
Smith, Robert, 124, 127, 133, 144–45, 230
Social Gospel movement, 29–31, 51–56, 59,
   63, 66–76, 95, 164, 273n21
socialism, 56, 103–9, 157, 163–73, 183, 198,
   201–3, 210, 225
Social Security, 122
Sollors, Werner, 264n7
The Sound and the Fury (Faulkner), 235
spatiality, 32–37, 201–2, 204–11, 219
The Spiritual Unrest (Baker), 23, 70
Stablemates (film), 143
Stead, W. T., 95, 114
Steffens, Lincoln, 70
Steinbeck, John, 235
Stevens, Wallace, 177
Stowe, Harriett Beecher, 174
"The Subjective Necessity for Social
   Settlements" (Addams), 75
Such a Woman (Kildare), 281n52
The Sun Also Rises (Hemingway), 189–91,
   295n30
Sunday, Billy, 31, 173
The Symbols of Government (Arnold), 123
The System of Dante's Hell (Baraka), 191
Szalay, Michael, 149
Szasz, Thomas, 203

Talese, Nan, 235–36
Talks to Teachers (James), 92, 114
Tarbell, Ida, 70
temperance movements: alcohol's moral
   valence and, 8–9, 155–61; gender and,
   26, 86; phrenology and, 23–24; recovery
   narratives and, 6; religious revival and,
   28–31, 36–37; science community and,
   87–88, 99–102; Washington Temperance
   Society and, 3, 9–11, 25, 28, 32–33, 93,
   265n19. *See also* Prohibition; religion
The Temperance Record, 200
therapeutic culture, 227–47, 252–61, 305n24
Thomas, Paul, 124
Thomas, Piri, 246
Thurman, Wallace, 191
Time Magazine, 257
Tolkin, Michael, 131
Tolstoy, Leo, 235

Toomer, Jean, 191
Tourgee, Albion, 57
Traditions. *See* Alcoholics Anonymous
"Transformed" (Water Street pamphlet), 38
Traubel, Horace, 172
"Traveler, Editor, Scholar" (Scott), 142
Traveling Mercies (Lamott), 242–47
Travis, Trysh, 133, 234, 263n6, 287n37, 303n13
Trotter, Melvin, 31
Twain, Mark, 17, 157–59, 162, 250, 253
Twelve Steps, 128–29, 146, 148, 150, 238, 255, 257. *See also* Alcoholics Anonymous
Twenty Years at Hull House (Addams), 75
Twice-Born Men (Begbie), 85, 96, 99–101, 231

"The Unbeliever" (*Alcoholics Anonymous*), 134
Uncle Tom's Cabin (Stowe), 174
urbanization, 32–37, 52–55, 155, 158, 165–68, 182–90, 212–13
U.S.A. trilogy (Dos Passos), 183, 188, 294n16

The Varieties of Religious Experience (James), 84–85, 91–93, 95–96, 100, 102–3, 108–10, 112–13, 282n68
Veltman, Laura J., 295n29
The Virtues of the Vicious (Gandal), 174
visual arts, 41–48. *See also specific works*

Waiting for Lefty (Odets), 139
Wallace, David Foster, 236, 251, 261, 307n3
Ward, Lester, 77–78
Warner, Judith, 257–58
Warren, Charles, 269n24
Washington Temperance Society, 3, 9–11, 25, 28, 31–33, 93, 265n19
"The Waste Land" (Eliot), 198
Water Street Mission: class dynamics in, 55–57; founding of, 13, 24, 31, 251; literature of, 36, 38, 70–71, 73; material needs' answering and, 32, 64; as model for others, 39–41, 59–62, 71, 202; recovery

narratives of, 16; skeptics of, 49; William James's use of, 84, 87, 94, 268n14. *See also* McAuley, Jerry
Welty, Eudora, 143
The Wet Parade (Sinclair), 166
"What Life Means to Me" (Sinclair), 172
Whitefield, George, 266n22
The White Logic (London), 102, 189, 191–92, 194
Whitman, Walt, 5, 10, 172, 187
Whittemore, Emma, 38, 55–56, 82
"Why I Voted the Socialist Ticket" (Lindsay), 164
Wiesel, Elie, 236
Wilentz, Sean, 265n19
Willard, Frances, 29
The Will to Believe (James), 109
Wilson, Bill: *Alcoholics Anonymous* and, 101, 127, 129–30, 134, 137, 222; Alcoholics Anonymous's structure and, 144–45; conversion of, 14–15, 87, 124, 126, 219, 230, 245–46, 270n36, 287n45; drunkard's conversion narrative and, 84, 132–33, 139–40; politics of, 144, 148–50; religion and, 145, 210
Winchell, Walter, 202
Winfrey, Oprah, 234–37
The Wire (Simon), 248–52, 261
"The Wizard in the Street" (Lindsay), 164
women: Jack London and, 105–6; modernism and, 182, 192–99; religious conversion and, 13, 99, 280n40, 281n52; rescue missions and, 26, 56–59, 65, 73–79; sexuality and, 47–48, 50
Women and Economics (Gilman), 79
Women Wage-Earners (Campbell), 57
World War II, 4, 180, 220
Wright, Chauncey, 88

Yale Center of Alcohol Studies, 144, 224
"The Yellow Wallpaper" (Gilman), 78

Žižek, Slavoj, 287n36
Zola, Emile, 160

EOIN F. CANNON is the assistant director of Studies for the America Field in History and Literature at Harvard University. A graduate of Harvard University (AB, 1995) and Boston University (MA, 2002; PhD, 2010) and a former newspaper reporter, he has published scholarly articles on urban literature, ethnicity, and boxing, and a series of online essays on addiction and culture. He serves as the managing editor of Points, the Blog of the Alcohol and Drugs History Society.